Health Psychology in Practice

This book is due for return on or before the last date shown below.

D1354724

Health
PSYCHOLOGY
in Practice

Edited by Susan Michie and Charles Abraham

Blackwell
Publishing

BLACKWELL PUBLISHING
350 Main Street, Malden, MA 02148-5020, USA
9600 Garsington Road, Oxford, OX4 2DQ, UK
550 Swanston Street, Carlton, Victoria 3053, Australia

First published 2004 by The British Psychological Society and
Blackwell Publishing Ltd

2   2007

Library of Congress Cataloging-in-Publication Data

Health psychology in practice / edited by Susan Michie and Charles Abraham.
p. cm.
Includes bibliographical references and index.
ISBN 978 1–4051–1089–1 (pbk : alk. paper)
1. Clinical health psychology–Great Britain.   2. Clinical health psychology–Study
and teaching–Great Britain.   3. Clinical health psychology–Practice–Great Britain.
I. Michie, Susan.   II. Abraham, Charles.

R726.7.H43363 2004
616.89′00941–dc22   2004003935

A catalogue record for this title is available from the British Library.

Set in 10/12½pt Rotis Serif
by Graphicraft Limited, Hong Kong
Printed and bound in the United Kingdom
by TJ International, Padstow, Cornwall

The publisher's policy is to use permanent paper from mills that operate
a sustainable forestry policy, and which has been manufactured from pulp processed
using acid-free and elementary chlorine-free practices. Furthermore, the publisher ensures
that the text paper and cover board used have met acceptable environmental
accreditation standards.

For further information on
Blackwell Publishing, visit our website:
http://www.blackwellpublishing.com

CONTENTS

Part V Professional Roles and Practice 351

CONTRIBUTORS

Charles Abraham
Professor of Psychology, Department of Psychology, School of Life Sciences, University of Sussex, UK

Julian Bath
Health Psychologist, Health Psychology Department, Gloucestershire Royal Hospital, UK

Paul Bennett
Professor of Clinical Psychology, Department of Psychology, University of Wales, Swansea, UK

Mark Conner
Reader in Applied Social Psychology, School of Psychology, University of Leeds, UK

Denise de Ridder
Professor of Health Psychology, Department of Health Psychology, Utrecht University, the Netherlands

Louise Earll
Head of Health Psychology Department, Gloucestershire Hospitals NHS Trust, UK

Eamonn Ferguson
Professor of Health Psychology, Department of Psychology, University of Nottingham, UK

Susan Folkman
Professor of Medicine, Department of Medicine, University of California at San Francisco, USA

David P. French
Lecturer in Health/Exercise Psychology, School of Sport and Exercise Sciences, University of Birmingham, UK

Simon Gilbody
Senior Lecturer in Mental Health Services Research, Academic Unit of Psychiatry and Behavioural Sciences, University of Leeds, UK

Gaston Godin
Professor and Canada Research Chair on Behaviour and Health, Faculty of Nursing, Laval University, Canada

Claire N. Hallas
Chartered Health Psychologist, Royal Brompton & Harefield NHS Trust, UK

Sandra Horn
Lecturer in Health Psychology, Psychology Department, University of Southampton, UK

Marie Johnston
Professor of Psychology, School of Psychology, University of Aberdeen, UK

Kate Kelley
Research Fellow, Research and Development, Worthing Hospital, UK

Máire Kerrin
Senior Lecturer in Organizational Psychology, Organizational Psychology Group, City University, London, UK

Gerjo Kok
Dean and Professor in Applied Psychology, Faculty of Psychology, Maastricht University, the Netherlands

Hannah McGee
Director, Health Services Research Centre, Department of Psychology, Royal College of Surgeons in Ireland, Ireland

Teresa Mendonça McIntyre
Professor of Health Psychology, Department of Psychology, University of Minho, Portugal

Susan Michie
Reader in Clinical Health Psychology, Department of Psychology, University College London, UK

Stanton Newman
Professor of Health Psychology, Health Psychology Unit, Centre for Behavioural and Social Sciences, University College London, UK

Susan J. Paxton
Professor of Psychology, School of Psychological Science, La Trobe University, Australia

Sheila Payne
Professor in Palliative Care, Palliative and End-of-Life Care Research Group, University of Sheffield, UK

Mark Petticrew
Associate Director, MRC Social and Public Health Sciences Unit, University of Glasgow and University of Leeds, UK

Herman Schaalma
Senior Lecturer, Department of Health Education and Health Promotion, Faculty of Health Sciences, Maastricht University, the Netherlands

Karlein Schreurs
Senior Health Psychologist and Cognitive-Behavioural Therapist, Roessingh Rehabilitation Centre, Enschede, the Netherlands

Stephen Sutton
Professor of Behavioural Science, Institute of Public Health, University of Cambridge, UK

Anne Walker
Deputy Director (retired), Health Services Research Unit, University of Aberdeen, UK

John Weinman
Professor of Psychology as Applied to Medicine, Institute of Psychiatry, University of London, UK

Robert West
Professor of Health Psychology, Health Behaviour Unit, University College London, UK

Helen Winefield
Associate Professor, Department of Psychology, University of Adelaide, Australia

Daniel B. Wright
Reader in Psychology, Psychology Department, University of Sussex, UK

FOREWORD

John Weinman

This book heralds a coming of age for the development of professional health psychology. Over the past 20 or so years, health psychology has made huge strides as a discipline but the emergence of a consensus about the professional roles and training needs of health psychology practitioners has inevitably been a slower process. An important early step in this process was the publication of an influential volume called *Health Psychology: A Discipline and a Profession* (ed. G.C. Stone et al.; Chicago: University of Chicago Press, 1987). This book reported papers from a conference which brought together leading US health psychologists in order to focus on training-related issues, not only to define the knowledge and skills base but also to identify the contexts and populations where these could be applied.

Since that time, health psychology has progressed as a discipline in a rapid and exciting way in many countries. The knowledge base has been established by a tide of research that has generated new journals such as *Health Psychology*, the *Journal of Behavioural Medicine*, the *British Journal of Health Psychology* and *Psychology and Health*. Findings and developments have been consolidated in major textbooks and the research base continues to be refined and developed in journals devoted to the discipline, as well as in other psychological and health-related journals.

Founded on this research base, professional development is now clearly taking shape and the present volume makes an important contribution to this developmental process. The authors have used the tripartite model of professional training, which originated in the UK, with its primary conceptualization of professional practice in terms of research, teaching and training, and consultancy as the core for planning this book. In addition, they have acknowledged that professional practice includes a range of other roles involving interventions at different levels, from delivering primary prevention to providing support and behaviour change initiatives in people with major health problems. Thus, there is something here for all health psychologists concerned with professional training, whether as trainers or trainees. There is a distinct UK flavour in the underlying model of professional training because the book is focused upon the competencies that must be acquired by those wishing to practise in the UK. However, as well as being an invaluable guide to those involved in training in the UK, the book also includes important contributions from authors in Europe, the United States and Australia, as well as commentaries from leading psychologists in a range of countries developing health psychology training. Between them, the authors and the commentators have succeeded in providing overviews of the key professional roles and applications for health psychologists wherever they practise.

As health psychology now gets to grips with the reality of professional training, and as professional roles emerge and consolidate, we will begin to get a greater understanding of what health psychologists across the world can and should be doing to improve health and healthcare. This book will provide us with a very important starting point for this process and I am sure that it will play a key role in facilitating the training process. It is also likely to result in many more editions, which will not only take account of future changes in the knowledge base but also of the development of professional roles and responsibilities of health psychologists in the years ahead.

ACKNOWLEDGEMENTS

The editors and publishers gratefully acknowledge the following for permission to reproduce copyright material.

Forms 1 to 7 in Chapter 2, Table 2.1, Table 2.2, Table 2.3 and Table 2.4 are reproduced with the permission of The British Psychological Society, © The British Psychological Society

Table 3.1 is from *The College of Health Psychologists' Course Approval Guidelines.* Australian Psychological Society 2002

Figure 6.3 is reproduced with the permission from the *British Journal of Health Psychology* © The British Psychological Society

Box 8.2 is reproduced with permission of *HNS CRD Report 4*, 2nd edition 2001. York University

Box 8.3 is from the *British Medical Journal* 320, pp. 50–2. Reproduced with permission from the BMJ Publishing Group

Figure 11.1 is from *Intervention Mapping: developing theory- and evidence-based health promotion programmes.* Mayfield 2001

Case Study 13.2 is from 'Keeping Pub Peaceful', C. Lawrence, D. Beale, P. Leather and R. Dickson from *Work-Related Violence: Assessment and Intervention,* 1999. Routledge

Case Study 13.3 is taken from Effective design of workplace risk communications, HSE Research Report (RR) 093, HSE Books 2001

Box 15.1 is reproduced with permission from the *British Journal of Health Psychology* © The British Psychological Society

Box 15.2 is from Baker, R., Reddis, S., Robertson, N., Hearnshaw, H., Jones, B., *British Journal of General Practice* 2001; 51 737–41. Reproduced with the permission of *British Journal of General Practice*

Box 15.3 is from Can psychological models bridge the gap between clinical guidelines and clinician's behaviour? A randomized controlled trial of an intervention to influence dentists' intention to implement evidence-based practice. *British Dental Journal*

The publishers apologize for any errors or omissions in the above list and would be grateful to be notified of any corrections that should be incorporated in the next edition or reprint of this book.

Chapter 1

HEALTH PSYCHOLOGY IN PRACTICE: INTRODUCTION

Susan Michie and Charles Abraham

The importance of health psychology practice is recognized internationally and many countries have professional health psychology training programmes. The UK training programme developed by the British Psychological Society (BPS) Division of Health Psychology specifies training in core areas of competence that are also included in other national training programmes. Chapter 3 of the book explores the relationship between training in the UK and other countries through commentaries by health psychologists from Europe, Australia and the USA.

This is the first book to describe the health psychology competences (that is, knowledge and skills) required to qualify as a health psychologist in the UK. The book aims to do two things: give a broad overview of the topics and competences involved in professional health psychology training and offer sufficient detail and explanation to help trainees and trainers put theory and knowledge into practice. Chapters provide 'how to do it' guidelines and practical examples and show how their topics relate directly to specific competences specified by the BPS, stage 2 qualification. The book will be useful to those considering or undertaking health psychology training, those organizing and delivering health psychology training and those supervising trainees in practice.

The book is divided into five parts:

1 Training Models
2 Research
3 Consultancy and Interventions
4 Training and Teaching
5 Professional Roles and Practice.

Part 1 describes models of training. Chapter 2 (Michie, Abraham & Johnston) outlines the UK training model in detail, considering the historical development of health psychology, the need for trained health psychologists, the content of the British Psychological Society's training programme and the steps required to become a trained health psychologist. Chapter 3 provides an international context and perspectives. The European 'Common Framework' for education and training in psychology, which will regulate professional training across Europe, is introduced (McIntyre). This forms the basis of the European Diploma in Psychology, which is being developed by the European Federation of Psychologists Associations (EFPA). Commentaries on health psychology training in other countries come from the United States (Folkman), Australia (Paxman), the Netherlands (de Ridder and Schreurs), Portugal (McIntyre) and Ireland (McGee).

The ability to design, undertake, evaluate and apply research is central to the competence of a health psychologist and a high level of research expertise is required by the UK training programme. Trainees must complete and write up a systematic review and a major empirical study to the standards set by peer-reviewed journals relevant to health psychology. This corresponds to minimum standards for the attainment of a doctor of philosophy degree in the UK (BPS, 2000). In Chapter 4, Abraham explains the importance of theory to describing, explaining, predicting and changing people's experience and behaviour. This chapter illustrates the way in which theory development, hypotheses derivation and empirical testing build psychological knowledge and establish effective theory-based behaviour-change techniques. The chapter demonstrates the need for health psychologists to be theoretically knowledgeable and to be involved in continuing professional development to update their knowledge of theory and empirical tests of theory. In Chapter 5, Sutton and French focus on the skills involved in research design. They explain how psychology researchers progress from initial questions that highlight the need for research through the process of research design to selecting measures and samples. These authors illustrate how health psychologists can develop research protocols that explain the nature of proposed research and guide research practice. In Chapter 6, Wright and Kelly discuss the way in which quantitative analysis is used to summarize data and evaluate hypotheses and theory. The chapter explains how researchers should examine and report data, describing and describing popular statistical procedures such as regression, t-tests, ANOVA, cross-tabulation and meta-analysis.

There is a recognition that, while much health psychology research involves the collection of quantitative data, important developments have been taking place in qualitative research and systematic reviewing. In Chapter 7, Payne considers the circumstances in which qualitative methods are appropriate, the importance of a 'good' research question, the nature of qualitative data and how to generate high quality data. Payne discusses the transformation of data for analysis, explores a particular example of analyses and illustrates the results. The important question of criteria by which to judge the quality of qualitative research is also discussed. Petticrew and Gilbody introduce the main stages in carrying out a systematic literature review (Chapter 8), including defining the review question, locating and selecting the studies, appraising and synthesizing them (by means of a meta-analysis if appropriate), and finally writing up the completed review. The next two chapters are very much 'how to do it' chapters, focusing on two key areas of academic life, writing successful grant applications and writing for publication. In Chapter 9, Newman emphasizes the importance of familiarizing oneself with the agendas of potential funders and addressing them convincingly. The task is not only to outline what needs to be done in sufficient detail and rigour, but also to make the case for why the applicants are the people to do it. Michie and West, in Chapter 10, address the common pitfalls in writing journal articles and give tips for avoiding them. They stress the importance of being clear, from the beginning, about what the paper is trying to achieve, who the audience is and which journal is being targeted. A section by section guide to writing a paper is provided.

Part 3 is concerned with health psychology consultancy and the design and evaluation of behaviour-change interventions. In Chapter 11, Kok and Schaalma discuss the application of psychological theory to the development of health promotion programmes (e.g., in smoking cessation). The authors describe and illustrate the 'Intervention Mapping' framework which provides guidelines and tools for the selection and application of theory and the translation of theory into programmes and materials. Earll and Bath (Chapter 12) define and describe the process of health psychology consultancy. They identify key tasks that must be undertaken when providing consultancy and highlight the competences required. The process is illustrated by discussion of a variety of case studies. In Chapter 13, Ferguson and Kerrin consider the roles of health psychologists in organization settings. The authors focus on organizational change and the impact of organizational change on employee health. They discuss how organizational theory, particularly theories dealing with organizational change, stress management and safety at work, can inform the practice of health psychologists in organizations. Bennett, Conner and Godin (Chapter 14) examine a variety of behaviour change theories and techniques that health psychologists can use to change individual behaviour. They explain and illustrate approaches based on learning theory, communication theory, social learning theory, social cognition theories and cognitive models of therapy. This chapter complements that by Kok and Schaalma and provides a useful guide to how health psychologists understand and effect behaviour change. Finally, drawing on issues covered in a number of earlier chapters, Walker (Chapter 15) discusses how health psychologists can study and intervene to change the behaviour of healthcare professions. Walker points out that evidence-based healthcare depends upon the behaviour of healthcare professionals and that providing information on best practice (e.g., in national guidelines) may not be enough to establish evidence-based practice. Walker considers interventions to improve the quality of healthcare that target individual health professionals, groups or teams, organizations (e.g., the National Health Service in the UK) and the wider environment in which organizations operate.

Part 4 of the book focuses on teaching and training. In Chapter 16, Winefield considers principles and models of learning, preparations required for teaching, competences for different kinds of teaching and training (e.g., small and large group teaching, workshops and lectures), and different types of audience. She also addresses the important issue of evaluating the processes and outcomes of teaching and training. In Chapter 17, Horn discusses supervised practice, as an effective way of developing professional competences. Horn discusses practical aspects of setting up supervision, the nature and process of supervision, the supervisory relationship and the rights and responsibilities of supervisors and trainees.

Part 5 considers professional issues and practice. Chapter 18 deals with professional issues faced by health psychologists working in a national health service. Professional roles considered include direct patient care and education, training of healthcare professionals, undertaking research and providing consultancy. Using case examples, Hallas addresses some of the pressures, problems and opportunities faced by health psychologists when developing a health psychology service within secondary care. In Chapter 19, Michie describes the development of professional psychology in different parts of the world and some of the issues faced by health psychologists working to have an impact on society, as well as trying to understand it. Professional roles within public health and areas beyond healthcare are addressed. These include working with others in a position to influence health, whether through policy, legislation or redistribution of wealth. The chapter concludes with a call for the content and form of our professional activity to be shaped by an awareness of inequalities in wealth and health, and by a commitment to work to try to reduce them.

FEEDBACK TO AUTHORS

If there are topics that you would like to see included in a future edition of this book, or improvements you would like to see in its form or content, please send your comments to s.michie@ucl.ac.uk or s.c.s.abraham@sussex.ac.uk

REFERENCE

British Psychological Society (2000). *Guidelines for Assessment of the PhD in Psychology and Related Disciplines.* Leicester, UK: British Psychological Society.

Part I

TRAINING MODELS

Chapter 2

HEALTH PSYCHOLOGY TRAINING: THE UK MODEL

Susan Michie, Charles Abraham and Marie Johnston

The World Health Organization defines health as:

> a state of complete physical, mental and social well-being and not merely the absence of disease or infirmity (World Health Organization, 1948).

This definition, which has not been amended since its adoption in 1948, challenges psychologists to define, assess and identify the determinants of 'mental and social well-being'. In addition we know that physical health is shaped by our psychology and behaviour. For example, the Alameda County study which followed nearly 7,000 people over 10 years revealed that sleep, exercise, drinking alcohol and eating habits have measurable effects on mortality (Belloc & Breslow, 1972). Finally, the delivery of healthcare depends on behaviour, the behaviour of healthcare professionals and their patients. Thus the domain of health psychology is extensive.

Health psychology practice includes research, teaching (e.g., health education and training of healthcare professionals), assessment of individuals, groups and organizations and the design and evaluation of health-related interventions. Much of this work involves the application of research findings in organizational settings and so also depends upon an understanding of organizational development and change.

In recognition of the developing body of research and practice in health psychology, the American Psychological Association (APA) established a division of health psychology in 1978. The British Psychological Society established a Health Psychology section with similar functions in 1986. This developed into a Special Group in Health Psychology (SGHP) and then the Division of Health Psychology (DHP) in 1997. Membership of the BPS DHP is a prerequisite for qualifying as a health psychologist in the UK. This chapter describes the UK training programme set up by the DHP. It discusses the purpose of training, the supervisory context of training and the assessment of professional competence in the UK. Full details of the qualification can be found on www.bps.org.uk/documents/qualshealthstage2.pdf.

2.1 THE NEED FOR TRAINED HEALTH PSYCHOLOGISTS

Health psychologists apply psychological theory and methods and research findings to the prevention and management of disease; the promotion and maintenance of health; the identification of psychological factors in physical illness and disability; the improvement of the healthcare systems; and the formulation of health policy. At the same time, demographic changes over the last century have shifted healthcare priorities. For example, there were 9 million people over 65 in the UK in 1991 but this is expected to rise to 12.4 million by 2021 (Matheson & Pullinger, 1999). People over 65 use health services more than others (Department of Health, 2001). They are hospitalized three times as often as younger people, stay in hospital 50 per cent longer and use twice as many prescription drugs (Haber, 1994). Reducing disability and promoting health among older people is, therefore, a primary target for healthcare services. We know that behaviour change interventions can reduce disability in elderly populations (Fries, 2000) and that behavioural interventions can reduce healthcare demand (Friedman et al., 1995). This is just one area in which a focus on preventative health and health-related behaviour change has important implications for health promotion practice and healthcare policy.

In affluent societies, there has been a shift from a prevalence of acute diseases, with short timelines and outcomes of either cure or death, to diseases such as myocardial infarction, cancer, diabetes and asthma which often result in ongoing chronic conditions (World Health Organisation, 1999). Such diseases, while benefiting from treatment based on biomedical science, are also affected by what people think and how they live their everyday lives. Behaviour and its management are seen as central to preventing and managing chronic conditions (Matarazzo, 1982). Many healthcare advances have been brought about by changing the behaviour of patients and health professionals and behaviour change can be seen as a primary healthcare goal (Kaplan, 1990). Understanding the processes that regulate such behaviour is crucial to effective delivery and optimal health outcome. Moreover, behavioural interventions have the capacity to enhance the cost effectiveness of healthcare delivery (Friedman et al., 1995). For these reasons, a better understanding of behavioural and psychological factors is important to the prevention, management and treatment of illness and to the effective delivery of healthcare.

In order to meet a growing demand for evidence-based behavioural interventions in healthcare services, health psychologists need the expertise and capacity to understand and to intervene to change psychological and behavioural processes in health, illness and healthcare. They need to be able to extend the training of medical and other health professionals and also directly apply psychological principles of change at the individual, group and organizational level, focusing both on patients and on healthcare professionals. These competences are distinct from the one-to-one skills required to assess and treat people who are psychologically disturbed or suffering from mental illness and, consequently, require new professional training and standards. Thus health psychologists will need to be able to:

- *conduct research* to develop theory and methods relevant to health-related behaviour;
- *assess*, that is, understand, describe and explain psychological and behavioural processes at individual, group and organization levels;
- *intervene*, that is, generate changes in psychological and behavioural processes that result in improved healthcare and health outcomes;
- *train* health professionals, that is, impart skills of psychological theorizing, assessment and intervention;
- *consult*, for example, advise healthcare service managers on the implementation of psychological and behaviour interventions.

2.2 THE UK CONTEXT

Despite considerable international agreement about the skills required by health psychologists, different countries are developing somewhat different health psychology training procedures, reflecting their historical, material, demographic and political circumstances (see, for example, the international commentaries on UK training included in Chapter 3). The UK is a relatively wealthy industrialized country and its predominant health problems are chronic illnesses such as cardiovascular disease and cancer (Department of Health, 2002). Healthcare is provided by a state-funded National Health Service and client-purchased, private healthcare accounts for only a small percentage of overall healthcare provision. However, the UK currently spends a relatively small proportion of its GDP on healthcare compared to other OECD countries (OECD, 2003). Patients in the UK normally access health services through community-based primary care general medical practitioners (GP) who then refer them to more specialist secondary services.

In the UK, psychological and behavioural aspects of health are addressed, to some extent, in medical and nurse training and also by a variety of applied psychology professions, for example, health, clinical, counselling, occupational, educational and forensic psychologists working within health and related services. Health psychologists work in academic and healthcare settings, teaching students and healthcare professionals, conducting research, assessing patients, developing and managing clinical interventions, informing health promotion and public health policy, and solving particular organizational problems in a consultancy role.

2.3 DEVELOPING THE UK TRAINING FRAMEWORK

In the UK, the professional activities of psychologists, including health psychologists, are regulated by the BPS, a professional and scientific organization. The BPS has legal responsibilities for the accreditation of chartered psychologists (that is, those qualified to practice) and for the regulation of their professional training.

In the early 1990s, before the establishment of the BPS DHP, the BPS special group in health psychology planned a training programme for health psychologists in the UK. The SGHP began by specifying a core curriculum covering the basic knowledge required for research and practice in health psychology (Rumsey et al., 1994). This core curriculum provided the foundation for the BPS stage 1 (trainee-level) qualification in health psychology.

The SGHP also discussed the best framework for professional training following acquisition of the (stage 1) knowledge base. The group decided that a qualified (i.e., stage 2) health psychologist would require research skills, teaching skills, consultancy skills and a set of generic practitioner skills. This framework led directly to the development of the BPS stage 2 (practitioner-level) qualification in health psychology.

Below we describe the UK health psychology training programme developed by the DHP. The programme was designed to create a profession that would complement the skills of other healthcare and applied psychology professions by addressing psychological and behavioural aspects of healthcare in the context of a predominantly nationalized healthcare system.

2.4 BPS QUALIFICATIONS IN HEALTH PSYCHOLOGY

The UK professional qualification in health psychology, launched by the BPS in 2002, meets the legal requirement for health psychologists in the

UK to achieve chartered status. In order to become a chartered health psychologist (CHP), candidates must first be full members of the DHP. In order to be admitted to the DHP they must have three qualifications:

- BPS graduate basis of registration. This is usually conferred by taking an accredited Bachelor-level degree at a UK university.
- BPS stage 1 qualification in health psychology (e.g., MSc in health psychology or the BPS Diploma in health psychology).
- BPS stage 2 qualification in health psychology, involving assessment of 21 units of professional competence (19 required and 2 options).

Membership of the DHP allows a psychologist to apply to the BPS to become a chartered health psychologist. The BPS maintains a register of chartered psychologists, all of whom have undertaken to abide by the BPS code of conduct.

From 2004, all psychology professions in the UK will become legally registered under the Health Professionals Council. This will give professional qualifications in psychology an equivalent legal standing to healthcare professional such as nurses and doctors. The regulation of training and qualifications will then come under the auspices of the Department of Health – not just the BPS.

This chapter focus on the stage 2 qualification but we have also included the core knowledge base covered by all BPS-accredited stage 1 qualifications in Appendix 2.1. The stage 1 qualification builds on the BPS-specified undergraduate curriculum in psychology and normally involves one-year full-time (or equivalent) postgraduate study on a BPS-accredited MSc health psychology or the BPS Diploma in health psychology course. This provides trainees with the knowledge base necessary to begin their practitioner-level, stage 2 training.

2.5 OUTLINE OF THE STAGE 2 QUALIFICATION IN HEALTH PSYCHOLOGY[1]

2.5.1 Two routes to qualification

A trainee health psychologist can study for their stage 2 qualification either through registration with the BPS Board of Examiners in Health Psychology (BoEHP) or by taking a BPS-accredited stage 2 at a UK university. In the former case, the BoEHP is directly responsible for approval of the candidate's supervision and planned work (the role of the Chief Supervisor) and the examination of the candidate's work (the role of the

Chief Assessor). In the latter case, the course director of the accredited university course is responsible for approval of supervision, planning and examination of the candidate's work. In both cases, the candidate will have an individual supervisor approved by the BoEHP and will be examined by two examiners approved by the BoEHP.

BPS accreditation involves inspection of a course and course team by a group representing the training committee of the DHP. The training committee considers the report of the visiting group and, if appropriate, recommends that a course be accredited (sometimes subject to certain changes) by the BPS Membership and Training Board. Once a course has been accredited by the BPS Membership and Training Board then any candidate who passes that course automatically qualifies for the BPS qualification for which the course is accredited. Courses are accredited by the BPS for specified periods of time (e.g., three or five years) but most courses seek to renew their accreditation before this period elapses.

Whether the stage 2 qualification is taken by means of an accredited course or under supervision directly monitored by the BoEHP, it must involve a minimum of two years' supervised experience in appropriate health-related work environments. Consequently, acquisition of stage 1 and stage 2 qualifications takes a minimum of three years' full-time (or equivalent) postgraduate work. Note, too, that some university courses may gain accreditation for both stages 1 and 2 so that one university qualification could confer the BPS stage 1 and stage 2 qualifications allowing direct entry into the DHP.

2.5.2 Competences to be acquired

Work experience supervised by a CHP who is BoEHP-approved is an integral part of the stage 2 health psychology training. The training requires the development and application of academic knowledge and the demonstration of practical skills.

The stage 2 qualification is competence based, that is, it specifies the competence required for practice. Competence refers to what people can do as well as what they know. By articulating required health psychology competences the BPS has defined a minimum standard of practice which all practitioners must reach before qualification. A competence-based qualification allows flexibility in relation to the acquisition of experience across a variety of work settings and tasks, enabling psychologists to train as part of ongoing employment.

The qualification is divided into *units of competence.* Each unit specifies a group of competences that are likely to be used together in completing work tasks. To be examined for the stage 2 qualification (by either route) evidence of completion of 21 units of competence must be recorded and submitted in a portfolio for assessment by two BoEHP-approved examiners. Nineteen of these units are core, or compulsory. The other two are optional but must be chosen from a list of eight. The core and optional units are listed in Appendix 2.2.

Each unit is divided into *components of competence* so that the 19 core units comprise 73 components of competence which describe the basic competences of a UK-trained health psychologist. These are the competences that a health psychologist must acquire to pass the stage 2 examination. The components of competence for all core and optional units are presented in Appendix 2.3.

For each component of competence, *guidelines* have been prepared. These clarify what skills and activities are involved in acquisition of each component of competence. Guidelines for all components are provided in the BPS Regulations for the Stage 2 Qualification in Health Psychology.[1] In Appendix 2.4 we have illustrated these by listing guidelines for each component of competence specified by one core unit, that is, unit 2.3 'Conduct psychological research'. There are between four and seven guidelines to help candidates understand and acquire each component of competence. Candidates should read these guidelines and should refer to them when they are unsure what is involved in a particular component of competence or whether they have yet achieved an appropriate level of competence in relation to any particular component.

The core competences specified by the BPS stage 2 qualification define skills and abilities in *four areas of work*:

1 professional practice (4 units);
2 research (5 units);
3 consultancy (6 units);
4 teaching and training (4 units).

In relation to professional practice, candidates must demonstrate that they have acquired competence in the management of systems relevant to health psychology practice and that they are able to make professional judgments in accordance with current codes of professional legal and ethical conduct.

In relation to research, candidates must demonstrate competence as an independent researcher in health psychology. Competence will be evidenced in: research design, sampling, data collection, data analysis, the evaluation of methods, the discussion of implications of data and the relationship of data to previously published research.

In relation to consultancy, candidates should have an understanding of a range of theories and their application, including theories relevant to communication, organizational development and the management of change as well as systems theory, and theories of group and organizational functioning. Candidates must demonstrate application of a variety of approaches and skills to facilitate, develop and/or enhance the effectiveness of individuals, groups and/or organizations in the maintenance and improvement of health. They must also show their ability to monitor and review consultancy work, using appropriate theoretical frameworks. Their experience must include consultancy with two distinct groups, one of which should be a healthcare professional or group of healthcare professionals. Candidates should demonstrate application of at least two relevant theoretical frameworks and should, ideally, have experience of providing consultancy relating to two of the following: (1) individuals, (2) groups or teams, and (3) organizational systems.

In relation to teaching and training, candidates must be able to assess the learning needs of client groups, design appropriate courses and curricula and demonstrate teaching and training skills including supervision of students. Candidates should be familiar with a variety of teaching methods including lectures, seminars, workshops and role-play sessions and must have experience of both large and small group teaching. They should be able to use a variety of teaching materials including slides (or Powerpoint), video material, handouts, use of booklets, video and audio-taped information and educational packages aimed at the lay population. They should be able to select methods and materials to ensure effective teaching, taking account of their audience and the learning objectives of the course or session. In addition, candidates must have experience of teaching health psychology to a group of healthcare professionals and one other group (e.g., undergraduate students and nurses).

2.5.3 Organizing supervised practice

A trainee may undertake supervised practice while occupied in paid or voluntary work, or as a postgraduate student. The total period must be equivalent to a five-day working week for 46 weeks a year over two years. Work contexts are likely to be within: (1) health services, e.g., primary or secondary care; (2) the community, e.g., schools, community projects; (3) organizations, e.g., occupational health units; and (4) academic settings, e.g., research and teaching posts. The work should include:

- using psychological theory to develop best practice;
- using ethical awareness to develop best practice;
- handling complex situations and demands;
- exercising an appropriate degree of responsibility.

The work must be planned and organized so that the trainee has adequate opportunity to practise and refine the competences specified by the 19 core units of competence and two chosen optional units. Training and development opportunities are required. These may involve completing and revising work under supervision, attending courses, seminars and conferences, undertaking visits and secondments, shadowing and observation activities and being involved in team-work and networking.

2.6 STAGE 2 SUPERVISION

2.6.1 The approved supervisor

Supervision is crucial to stage 2 professional training. The supervisor and trainee must plan, evaluate and, where necessary, revise training experiences so that they enable the candidate to acquire the competences specified by the regulations. The supervisor is responsible for the training process, including acquisition of new skills, gaining supervised practice and documenting the evidence necessary for assessment. The trainee should provide a progress report and receive feedback from their supervisor each month and have at least six face-to-face meetings a year. Quality of supervision is crucial to the comprehensiveness and depth of training.

In the case of trainees enrolling with the BoEHP (i.e., not on an accredited course) the supervisor must be approved by the Chief Supervisor prior to the beginning of the training period. The trainee should agree a contract of supervision with the supervisor, including payment if appropriate. Potential supervisors may be identified using a list of approved CHPs available from the BoEHP Chief Supervisor. Trainees on accredited courses may have their supervision arrangements organized by their course director.

In addition to the approved supervisor, one or more workplace contacts with responsibility for the trainee may be identified in order to facilitate specific areas of practice. A workplace contact may not be a chartered health psychologist, or even a psychologist, but should be an established and experienced professional. The workplace contact must be fully aware of, and committed, to facilitating the plan of work (or Supervision Plan) developed by the trainee and supervisor.

2.6.2 The Supervision Plan

Before commencing supervised practice, a description of the work to be undertaken should be drawn up with the supervisor and submitted as the 'Supervision Plan' (see Figure 2.1) to the BoEHP chief supervisor or the accredited course director. This must be approved before supervised practice can begin.

The overall plan will consist of a series of discrete pieces of work. The number of pieces of work will depend upon their size and complexity. Some trainees may undertake few large-scale projects while others may undertake many smaller pieces of work. This will depend on available work opportunities. Any one piece of work may allow the trainee to acquire many components of competence from a variety of units of competence (both core and optional). For example, a piece of consultancy might include preparation

Supervision Plan (Section One)

Area of Competence (for example, *Generic Professional Competence* or *Research Competence*) ....

Sheet No.: ......

Units in this area of competence (list all units to be covered)	Area of work in which unit will be covered (NB: Asterisk any units to be covered **outside** your normal work, such as teaching a task arranged by you or your supervisor which is not part of your usual work.)	Supporting evidence to be compiled for this unit of competence	*Record here any changes to the plan by writing* **Change** *and the number of the appropriate Section 2 sheet*

Target date for completion: .... Workplace contact?: Yes/No
If Yes please give name: ....

Figure 2.1 Section 1 of the Supervision Plan

of a systematic review and provision of psychological advice, thereby involving development of competence in units relating to consultancy, research and professional conduct. Indeed it is advisable to plan work that will simultaneously involve the trainee in developing competences in more than one unit – otherwise at least 21 pieces of work would be required. The purpose of the Supervision Plan is to specify which units of competence will be acquired during each piece of work and to ensure that the overall package of work allows the trainee to gain competence in the required 21 units. Each of the four areas of competence (professional, research, consultancy and teaching/training) requires its own form (see Figure 2.1). Thus there will be four parts to the Supervision Plan and the same piece of work may be referred to more than once. Each of the four forms must include:

- the units of competence to be addressed, with target date for completion of each unit;
- the supporting evidence which will demonstrate satisfactory performance for the units of competence.

In addition to the Supervision Plan, the trainee will have to submit a variety of details about themselves and their supervisor and:

- a summary explanation of the proposed plan of work;
- a copy of the contract(s) issued by the employing organization(s) outlining main areas of work activity and responsibilities;
- an estimate of the percentage of total work time to be spent on each piece of work;
- expected date of overall completion.

The overall plan will be assessed by the chief assessor or course director in terms of its comprehensiveness (e.g., will it really allow acquisition of all competences specified by the 21 units?), its depth (e.g., are the experience and supervision adequate to demonstrate competence at the required level – e.g., is the planned research likely to be of a publishable standard?) and feasibility (e.g., are enough time and supervision allocated to ensure that the trainee has adequate opportunity to practise and refine skills?).

Candidates who already hold a postgraduate degree that is not accredited by the BPS can request that they be exempted from particular units of competence. For example, someone with a doctoral degree in health psychology might request that they be exempt from some of the units of research competence. Candidates can request such exemption by using the form shown in Figure 2.2. The BoEHP will then decide whether or not such an exemption can be granted.

Application for Accreditation of Prior Learning

(Holders of postgraduate degrees other than accredited qualifications in health psychology)

Please tick the core competence(s) for which you wish to partially demonstrate on the basis of prior learning

Core competence 1:	Generic professional
Core competence 2:	Research
Core competence 3:	Consultancy
Core competence 4:	Teaching and Training

For each core competence in question you should describe in detail your experience, including where, when and how it was gained, whether it was supervised and by whom.

You should then select and describe in detail an area of work already completed which you believe demonstrates competence in that core competence. Coverage of units should be explained and should be accompanied by supporting evidence of the sort which would normally be contained within a 'Portfolio of Competence' (the exceptions are case studies, dissertations and the like which have already been passed by an awarding body as fulfilling the requirements of a postgraduate degree. These should be described rather than submitted). All supporting evidence should be listed and indexed. Continue on a separate sheet if necessary.

To be completed by the Board of Examiners in Health Psychology:
Accreditation of prior learning agreed for the following units:
....

Date of ratification:..........................

Figure 2.2 Application form for accreditation of prior learning

The supervisor and trainee can also request that work undertaken in the *six months prior* to submission of the plan is included in the plan, providing this work did not contribute to the trainee's stage 1 assessment. Note that the inclusion of such work does not constitute an exemption because the work is included in the portfolio and will be examined. If the chief supervisor or course leader considers that the competence has been demonstrated, then the plan can be approved without work experience referring to that unit or units. However, assessment of whether or not particular competences have been demonstrated lies with the examiners of the qualification, not with the chief supervisor or course leader (who approve the Supervision Plan). Thus, evidence relating to units of competence that the candidate thinks they acquired in the six months prior to the submission of the Supervision Plan must be included in the final portfolio of evidence and will be assessed as part of the overall qualification in the same way as other competences.

The period of supervised practice is set in motion formally once the Supervision Plan is approved. The plan will help the supervisor and trainee timetable and evaluate work experiences and also provide the basis of a supervision contract.

2.6.3 Developing and amending the Supervision Plan

Work not included in the Supervision Plan is not accepted as evidence of competence and will not be examined as part of the stage 2 qualification. However, it is acknowledged that planning supervision is likely to be an iterative process. Conditions and opportunities may change over the period of supervised practice, and work planned at the outset may turn out not to be feasible. Revised plans should be agreed with the supervisor. If substantial changes are made to four or more areas of work, the amended plan should be submitted for re-approval to the chief supervisor or course leader. The original plan must be resubmitted along with the amended plan as well as a record of changes (called 'section 2' of the Supervision Plan – see Figure 2.3).

If, for any reason, there is a proposed change of supervisor, the chief supervisor or course leader must be informed immediately. The original supervisor must send a Supervisor's Report describing the supervised practice that has been completed to the chief supervisor or course leader who will forward a copy to the new supervisor. A revised Supervision Plan must be agreed with the new supervisor and submitted for approval by the chief supervisor or course leader.

Supervision Plan (Section Two)

Supervision Plan (Section Two)
Name .... Signature .... Date .... Membership Number ....

Log of changes

This page should be used to keep a log of any major changes to the Supervision Plan (Section One). These are replacement areas of work, and changes in Supervisor or any workplace contacts.

(To be filled in by trainee) Nature of change/reason	Trainee's signature (with date)	Co-ordinating Supervisor's signature (with date)

Copy this sheet as necessary to record further changes

Approval by the Board of Examiners (or Chief Supervisor)

Prior to the end of the period of supervised practice, there are two circumstances in which this form should be sent, with enclosures (see next page) to the Board of Examiners in Health Psychology for re-ratification of the Supervision Plan. These are:

– When a fourth change in an area of work has been entered above
– If a change in Supervisor is being proposed

Date of submission to the Board of Examiners	(To be filled in by trainee) Reason for submission to the Board of Examiners	(To be filled in by Board of Examiners) Comments and action

Continue on a separate sheet if necessary

Figure 2.3 Section 2 of the Supervision Plan

Supervision Plan (Section Two) continued

New areas of work

Use **Section Two** sheets to record proposed new (replacement) areas of work. Mark appropriate Section One sheet 'Change' and refer to the Section Two sheet number.

Additional coverage of units

At the end of the period of supervised practice please undertake as necessary the following.

Use Section Two sheets to record any additional/fortuitous coverage of units that you would like to be evaluated in preference to that originally outlined.

Missing units

At the end of the period of supervised practice (although this should have been considered before!) please indicate in the spaces below by the key role and unit number (e.g. 3.4, 4.1) any units which:

- have not been covered at all

....

....

- have been covered by one area of work only

....

....

Date ....

Candidates should use this form to detail any changes to the Supervision Plan (Section One). Candidates should use a separate sheet for each amendment to Section. Please photocopy as necessary.

Area of Competence (for example, *Generic Professional Competence* or *Research Competence*) ....

Sheet No.: ....

Units in this area of competence (list all units to be covered)	Area of work in which unit will be covered. (NB: Asterisk any units to be covered **outside** your normal work, such as teaching a task	Supporting evidence to be compiled for this unit of competence	*Reference original Section One sheet here*

Figure 2.3 (*continued*)

	arranged by you or your supervisor which is not part of your usual work.)		

Target date for completion: .... Workplace contact?: Yes/No
If Yes please give name: ....

Figure 2.3 (*continued*)

2.6.4 Fees

In addition to payment for supervision, trainees are required to pay fees to the BPS or the university at which they are taking an accredited course. These cover enrolment and assessment. Individual courses will have different fee structures and rates. At present the BPS fees are as follows:

- An initial fee when the approval of supervisor by the chief supervisor is sought.
- An enrolment fee when the Supervision Plan is submitted for approval to the chief supervisor.
- An annual maintenance fee which must be paid on the quarter date following the anniversary of the trainee's enrolment.
- An assessment fee each time the portfolio of evidence is presented for examination, which must be submitted with the registration form.

The Schedule of Fees is available from the DHP website (www.health-psychology.org.uk).

2.6.5 Exceptional circumstances

Most eventualities can be resolved by good supervision, but some may require involvement of the chief supervisor or course leader, who may suggest or approve changes, including a change in supervisor. All such changes must be recorded and countersigned in section 2 of the Supervision Plan (Figure 2.3).

Trainees should normally gather and submit their evidence within five years of enrolment. Trainees who have an illness or encounter other circumstances which might affect their preparation for, or performance during, their examinations should inform the chief supervisor or course leader at the earliest opportunity. Supporting documents will normally be sought and medical certificates will be requested where appropriate. An extension may be granted.

In cases of serious malpractice or unprofessional conduct, action may need to be taken under BPS disciplinary procedures.

2.7 STAGE 2: DOCUMENTING THE EVIDENCE

2.7.1 The portfolio of evidence

At the end of the training period, the trainee will submit a portfolio of evidence designed to demonstrate the required competences and to show the range and extent of relevant work experience. The portfolio should include:

- a list of the 21 units of competence to be examined and brief description of where the evidence of each component of competence specified by these units can be found in the portfolio;
- the approved Supervision Plan, including a plan for each discrete piece of work undertaken (see above);
- the Practice and Supervision Log;
- the Record of Completion of Supervised Practice;
- supporting evidence;
- the Supervisor's Report. This will include a brief outline of the supervised practice undertaken and the professional conduct of the trainee, as well as any difficulties encountered and how these were overcome or may have affected supervised practice. It should also highlight the strengths and weaknesses of the trainee in relation to the units of competence to be examined;
- any appropriate additional clarification and explanation.

This collection of documents forms the trainee's portfolio of evidence. At the end of the period of supervised practice, the entire portfolio should be sent to the chief assessor or course director.

2.7.2 The Practice and Supervision Log

Part 1 of the Practice and Supervision Log (see Figure 2.4) is a diary of the work experience that has allowed the trainee to acquire the competences specified by the 21 units of competence on which they will be examined. The following information is requested in the columns found on the form:

- date of entry (e.g., date of completion of a relevant task or piece of work);
- the unit or units of competence relevant to the work, referenced in brackets (e.g., 1.1 or 2.3);
- the trainee's role: 'primary' if the work is primarily the trainee's own, 'team' if the work in shared with others and 'observer' if the candidate is sitting in for training or development purposes.

Practice and Supervision Log (Page 1)

This log should be completed as a permanent record. Please photocopy as necessary.
Name of Trainee   Sheet No.:

Date	Relevant core competence units	Your role	Name of task or intentions	Outcome

Practice and Supervision Log (Page 2)

This log should be completed as a permanent record. Please photocopy as necessary.
Name of Trainee   Sheet No.:

Date	Supervisor	Contact method	Duration	Area(s) of work discussed	Units/Specific competences addressed

Figure 2.4 Practice and Supervision Log

- the nature of the task or instruction (including proposed action taken, additional procedural details and client or target);
- outcome (including what was achieved);
- future actions to be taken (next steps and implications including any learning points);
- any training or development activities.

Part 2 of the Practice and Supervision Log is a record of supervision. The form asks the trainee to record:

- the date of each supervision session, the duration of the session and nature of supervision (e.g., face-to-face, email or telephone);
- the piece of work or work tasks that were discussed;
- the units of competence and, importantly, the particular components of competence addressed during the supervision. (e.g. 1.1a, 1.1b, 2.3a, 2.3b, etc.).

A copy of this log is sent to the supervisor each month for confirmation.

2.7.3 The Record of Completion

As each area of work indicated in the Supervision Plan is accomplished, a Record of Completion is drawn up (see Figure 2.5). The number of Records of Completion will be determined by the number of pieces of work specified in the overall Supervision Plan. Each planned piece of work should have a corresponding Record of Completion in the portfolio. Each Record of Completion documents:

- completed areas of work and units, indexed to where the evidence for each competence can be found;
- omitted areas of work which were mentioned in either original or amended Supervision Plans;
- the Supervisor's Report;
- report(s) from workplace contact(s), if applicable;
- an outline of the relevant supporting evidence.

2.7.4 Supporting evidence

Each Record of Completion must be accompanied by supporting evidence and any relevant additional material. Supporting evidence may include:

Record of Completion form

Record of Completion

Name .... Date ....
Membership Number ....

Note: A record of completion form should be filled in at the conclusion of each area of work that proceeds from the supervision plan (sections 1 & 2). It is to be submitted at the end of the period of supervised practice as part of the Portfolio of Competence and should be accompanied by the supporting evidence indicated.

All sections should be completed by the health psychologist in training, with the exception of the supervisors' and Board of Examiners' reports.

1. *Area of work* (describe, indicating client/target group, setting and any other relevant details)

Date completed ....

2. *Areas of Competence/units* covered and discussed (reference by number)

3. This area relates to (please circle which)

    (a) The Supervision Plan (Section One)
    (b) The Supervision Plan (Section Two)
    (c) An Extension of Supervision Plan

4. Main *learning points* arising from this area of work

5. Additional *comments* (including reasons for any deviations from the supervision plan)

6. Additional *training and development activities* related to this area of work (with dates)

Figure 2.5 Record of Completion form

7. *Supervisor's report:* Has the health psychologist in training demonstrated competence in this area of work?

YES/NO

Comments

Signature .... Date ....

---

8. *Workplace contacts report* (if applicable)

Comments

Signature .... Date ....

9. *Supporting evidence* accompanying Record of Completion.

Please label each piece of work submitted A, B, C etc. List each area of competence and where in the portfolio it is to be found, using your label. Note that it is unlikely that each piece will reflect all units to the same degree. Each piece of evidence should be countersigned by the Supervisor.

[Example: Unit 2.1 *Conduct systematic reviews*
A. *Dissertation: ch 1 (components 2.1a, 2.1b, 2.1c)*
Unit 3.1 *Assessment of requests for consultancy*
B. *Supervision log, date: (components 3.1a, 3.1c)*
C. *Consultancy report, section 2 (component 3.1b)]*

10. At the end of the period of supervised practice, please send the completed Portfolio of Competence, including this form and the accompanying evidence, to the Board of Examiners in Health Psychology.

Board of Examiners' Assessor's report

I have examined all submissions in relation to this area of work.
Comments

Recommendation: On the basis of the information contained in this portfolio, has the health psychologist in training demonstrated competence in this area of work?

Yes/No.
Any further comments:

Signed .... Date ....

Figure 2.5 (*continued*)

- reports, e.g., assessment/treatment reports, training materials, consultancy/discussion papers;
- notes of meetings;
- research papers, including dissertations and published work;
- video/audio tapes, e.g., of lectures or training sessions delivered.

For all submissions, appropriate measures must be taken to maintain confidentiality and security, for example, deleting or disguising names of clients. Each piece of evidence should be countersigned by the supervisor.

The submitted evidence must be sufficient to demonstrate attainment of the components of competence specified by the 19 core units of competence and the two chosen optional units. The stage 2 qualification defines a minimum body of evidence required to demonstrate competence in each unit or set of units. We discuss this in detail below.

Professional competence

Two forms of supporting evidence are required for units 1.1–1.4. First, the trainee is required to complete the logbook describing experiences that enabled him or her to gain competence in each unit. Second, candidates are required to include four 400-word reports detailing how their supervised experience established the professional competences specified in units 1.1, 1.2, 1.3 and 1.4 (i.e., one report per unit). These reports should illustrate how candidates have learnt from their experience and have changed or developed their professional practice. Ideally the experiences in the logbook should map onto the components of competence of each unit and the reflective reports should clarify how each component of competence was acquired. Thus, for example, the report for unit 1.4 could highlight an occasion or occasions on which the trainee presented feedback to a client. The report could then reflect on the importance of evaluating the feedback needs of a client (component 1a) and illustrate how the trainee achieved this. In addition, the report could explain the importance of preparing and structuring feedback (component 1b) and selecting appropriate methods of communicating feedback (component 1c) as well as illustrating how the trainee has managed these aspects of giving feedback in the past.

Research competence

In addition to describing relevant experiences in the logbook, the minimum supporting evidence required for units 2.1–2.5 consists of (1) a systematic review and (2) a major empirical study. Candidates must submit a report of a systematic review of literature relevant to health psychology of no more than 6,000 words. This must address the three components of competence specified by unit 2.1, that is, it must show that the candidate can conduct a systematic review. It must be clear how and why the search topic was defined and how this was reflected in the search parameters (component 2.1a). The search must employ appropriate databases and sources (component 2.1b) and the report must appropriately summarize findings from the review (component 2.1c). These competences must be demonstrated at the level expected by reviewers of peer-reviewed academic journals.

The systematic review may address some of the components of competence specified by the other four units of research competence but these will also be addressed by the report of the major empirical study which will be a rigorous study of a topic relevant to health psychology. This will be a more ambitious study than would normally be undertaken for completion of an MSc thesis but less ambitious than a doctoral thesis. The report will be no longer than 15,000 words. Collectively the review and systematic review must demonstrate the components of competence specified by units 2.2–2.5. Thus these two reports will demonstrate that the candidate can design psychological research (unit 2.2), conduct psychological research (unit 2.3), analyse and evaluate psychological research data (unit 2.4) and initiate and develop psychological research (unit 2.5).

The candidate should ensure that the supporting evidence, in this case the systematic review and empirical study report, demonstrates each component of competence (see Appendix 2.3) specified by the corresponding units. For example, in the case of unit 2.2 (design psychological research), the reports should make it clear that theoretical models and research findings relevant to the research question were identified (component 2.2.a), and that testable research questions or hypotheses, linked to existing models or research, were generated (component 2.2b). Methods appropriate to testing the hypotheses or answering the research questions should have been designed (component 2.2d), including use of validated psychometric tests and assessment of the psychometric properties of any new measures (component 2.2e). The design of the study should be clearly presented and any special features or revisions noted (2.2.f). Required resources should have been obtained and any constraints relevant to the conduct of the research should have been acknowledged and steps taken to minimize their impact on the research (2.2c). Candidates should ensure that each component of competence is met in this way.

Consultancy competence

In order to demonstrate competence in units 3.1–3.6, candidates must, as well as completing the practice logbook, submit two other types of evidence:

(1) at least one case study and (2) *either* (2a) a demonstration proposal requesting funding for a piece of health psychology consultancy work or (2b) a discussion of the development, negotiation, review and evaluation of a consultancy contract using relevant theoretical frameworks. The case study should include a logbook of the consultancy, a consultancy contract covering in detail how the work was negotiated and any revisions, a timetable of work, a budget, minutes of meetings, correspondence, consent procedures where appropriate, clients' assessment of the consultancy process and evidence of formal evaluation where appropriate.

Collectively, these two pieces of work must demonstrate the candidate's experience of providing consultancy to at least two types of client (e.g., a hospital or ward management group, a headteacher or a manager of a small firm) and one of these must be a health professional or group of health professionals. Ideally they should represent two of the following: (1) individuals, (2) groups or teams, and (3) organizational systems. The evidence in this area must also demonstrate the candidate's application of at least two different theoretical frameworks relevant to consultancy practice.

The candidate must ensure that the submitted evidence demonstrates that they have acquired the components of competence specified by all the units that the evidence refers to. There are six consultancy units comprising 19 components of competence that should be demonstrated by the submitted evidence. For example, considering unit 3.6 (evaluate the impact of consultancy) the candidate should ensure that the consultancy evidence shows that he or she is able to identify and prioritize the client's needs in relation to evaluation and then design an evaluation of consultancy that meets these needs (component 3.6a). The evidence should also demonstrate that the candidate successfully implemented a planned evaluation of consultancy work (component 3.6b) and that the candidate assessed and considered the outcome of the implemented evaluation (component 3.6c).

Teaching and training competence

In addition to entries in the practice logbook, the portfolio must include a minimum of five other pieces of evidence demonstrating teaching competence:

- a log of all teaching experience and teaching supervision;
- a case study based on observed and supervised teaching sessions, to be submitted together with the observer's report (of no more than 1,500 words);

- a 10-minute video recording of the candidate's teaching together with a 500-word written, reflective commentary of what is happening during the recording and how it demonstrates the relevant competences;
- *either* (a) a plan of a teaching session developed by the candidate for a particular professional or educational group, including information on assessment; written material designed to educate the broader lay population *or* (b) a critique of existing educational materials;
- a report of no more than 2,000 words reporting, *either* (a) a small-scale evaluation of a face-to-face teaching programme or course, *or* (b) a small-scale evaluation of an educational package, or written material designed for use with the public.

The evidence submitted to demonstrate teaching competence should clarify that the candidate has used a variety of different teaching methods (e.g., face-to-face teaching such as lectures and seminars, use of educational packages video and audio-taped information) and that the candidate is able to select materials to suit learners' needs and the learning context. In addition, the candidate must have had experience of teaching two different groups (e.g., undergraduate students, nurses or GPs), one of whom must be healthcare professionals.

The candidate must ensure that the submitted evidence demonstrates that they have acquired the 16 components of competence specified by the five teaching and training units. For example, considering unit 4.1 (plan and design training programmes that enable students to learn about psychological knowledge, skills, and practices), the evidence should show that the candidate is able to assess learning needs (component 4.1a), and plan the content and structure of a learning programme (component 4.1b) to meet learners' needs. The submitted evidence should also show that the candidate was able to select training methods and approaches appropriate to the learners and to the learning context (component 4.1c) and to produce appropriate training materials (component 4.1d). Finally, for unit 4.1, the evidence should show that the candidate used appropriate media (e.g., paper handouts, video materials, Powerpoint slides, etc.) to deliver training materials (component 4.1e).

The Supervision Plan, the Practice and Supervision Log, the Records of Completion and all the supporting evidence should be included together in a well-organized file with a clear list of contents and a clear description of where particular units of competence are covered in the portfolio. At the end of the period of supervised practice, this 'portfolio of evidence' should be sent to the chief assessor at the BoEHP or to the accredited course director for assessment.

2.8 STAGE 2 ASSESSMENT: EVALUATING THE EVIDENCE

Two assessors approved by the BoEHP will examine candidates' portfolios of evidence independently and agree a recommendation to the chief assessor or the course director of an accredited course. All trainees will have an oral examination (viva voce) to confirm that the trainee has achieved all the requisite competences in the course of supervised practice. A viva will only be arranged once the chief assessor or course director is satisfied that the portfolio indicates that the candidate could potentially satisfy the stage 2 requirements.

At the viva, the trainee will be asked to present a brief oral account of their supervised practice to the assessors. The assessors can question the candidate about any aspect of the portfolio or the supervised practice relevant to demonstrating stage 2 competences. Trainees may be required to answer questions about any ambiguities in the portfolio, omissions in planned work, deficiencies in the quality of work, or errors (factual, typographical or substantive). They may also be questioned about more general areas of health psychology and asked about specific components of competence.

Candidates who are not taking an accredited course will receive an examination timetable, listing the exact dates for registration, submission of materials and oral examination from the chief assessor. This will clarify when the BoEHP vivas are to be held in the coming academic year and notify candidates that they must normally register for the examination three months in advance (registration forms are available from the chief assessor).

After the examination, successful candidates are issued a Certificate for the Qualification in Health Psychology (Stage 2).

2.8.1 Failure to achieve requirements

If the BoEHP or the examination board of an accredited course is not satisfied that all the stage 2 requirements have been met, the trainee may be required to provide additional supporting evidence or to repeat work or to undertake new areas of work. In this case, the trainee will be informed in writing within three months of submission of the appropriate action. This might involve one or more of the following:

- Where there are serious inadequacies in recording in the Practice and Supervision Log (e.g., lack of detail or explicitness), or insufficient presentation of supporting evidence, the trainee will be required to supply additional material to demonstrate achievement of competence of the relevant units.

- Where there are omissions from the work agreed in the plan, the discretion of the BoEHP or the examination board of the accredited course can be exercised. Additional work and evidence may be required to cover the relevant units.
- Where shortcomings have been identified in the quality or quantity of the trainee's practice, the trainee will be required to repeat, or find new, areas of work to cover the relevant units or components of competence.

Repeated or new areas of work should be specified in an Extension of Supervision Plan (Figure 2.6) which must be approved by the BoEHP or the examination board of the accredited course. Changes in this plan should be kept to a minimum, and any deviations should be reported when the revised portfolio is submitted. The revised portfolio should contain evidence of only the new or repeated areas of work. A maximum of two re-submissions of the portfolio are allowed within five years of enrolment.

2.8.2 Exceptional circumstances

Mitigating circumstances may be taken into account by the BoEHP or the examination board of the accredited course on production of appropriate evidence before they meet to agree examination results.

If candidates consider that the examination was improperly conducted or that mitigating circumstances were not taken into account, they may appeal against the decision of the examiners (Figure 2.7). Appeals should be made in writing within two months of candidates' receiving their results.

2.9 CONCLUDING COMMENTS

This chapter has outlined the need for training in health psychology within the UK and described how this has been addressed by the BPS stage 1 and stage 2 qualifications. It has explained the procedures by which trainees can undertake the stage 2 qualification and how it will be examined. As a competence-based qualification, considerable emphasis is placed on providing evidence to demonstrate the competences and in having procedures to assess them. It is also a new qualification (introduced in 2002) and its operation will need to be evaluated in terms of the

Extension of Supervision Plan

This form is to be completed in the event of proposed changes (from the original plan) in the area of work, or proposed changes to the time to completion of a piece of work, or the resubmission of a failed piece of work.

Please photocopy additional sheets from the Supervision Plan (Section One) for each new or repeated area of work and attach to this front sheet.

Extension of Supervision Plan

Name .... Signature .... Date ....
Membership Number: ....

Your address for correspondence:

....

.... Postcode ....

Telephone Number (work).......................................

Please give a brief description of your current employing organisation and your job description.

....

Name of Supervisor:................................ Membership Number: ....

Position held:..

Address..

Signature...Date.................

Workplace Contact(s) (if applicable)

Name(s): .... Position held: ....

To be completed by the Board of Examiners in Health Psychology
Comments

Any exemptions?

Date of ratification ....Expected date of completion ....

Figure 2.6 Extension of Supervision Plan

Appeals against the Decision of the Examiners

A Grounds for Appeal

Candidates may appeal against the decisions of the examiners *only* on the following grounds:

1 That the examination has been improperly conducted.
2 That the examiners did not take extenuating circumstances into account when reaching their decision. If the candidate believes that there are circumstances or events which occur close to or on the day of the examination which may have affected his or her performance, then it is the candidate's responsibility to make these known to the examiners on or before the examination date.

There is no right of appeal against what the candidate believes is an incorrect result.

B Lodging an Appeal

All appeals must be made in writing to the Registrar of the Board of Examiners in Health Psychology (at the Office of the Society) within two calendar months of the declaration of the examination results.

All appeals must be accompanied by a full written description of the grounds for the appeal.

Any request for a consideration of extenuating circumstances must be accompanied by appropriate external corroboration (e.g., a medical certificate).

C The Appeals Process

All appeals will be considered by an Appeals Sub-Committee of the Membership and Qualifications Board. This Sub-Committee will consist of three members (appointed by the Chair of the Board) who have not been directly involved with the examination process of the candidate making the appeal.

The Chair of the Membership and Qualifications Board may request that additional information be provided by other persons. Those persons may be requested to appear before the Appeals Sub-Committee if this is considered necessary for the proper consideration of the appeal.

The Appeals Sub-Committee will have the power to reject the appeal or to request the Board of Examiners to reconsider its decision in the light of the Sub-Committee's report.

In every case the result of the consideration of the appeal shall be reported to the Membership and Qualifications Board. The Registrar shall inform the candidate of the result of the appeal.

The Society reserves the right to charge a fee to cover the cost of an appeal.

Figure 2.7 Appeals against the Decision of the Examiners

uptake of the training, the effectiveness of training, supervision and assessment procedures, the employment of the trained CHPs and the contribution of these trained CHPs to improving health and healthcare in the UK. It is likely, therefore, that the stage 2 qualification will evolve over time as evidence from cohorts of candidates is considered and career opportunities for health psychologists develop.

NOTE

1 Detailed regulations applying to the stage 2 qualification are available from the BPS (at British Psychology Society, St Andrews House, 48 Princess Road East, Leicester LE1 7DR) and on the DHP website (www.health-psychology.org.uk).

REFERENCES

Belloc, N.B. & Breslow, L. (1972). Relationship of physical health status and health practices. *Preventive Medicine* 1, 409–21.

Department of Health (2001). *National Service Framework for Older People.* London: HMSO.

Department of Health (2002). *Saving Lives: Our Healthier Nation.* London: HMSO.

Friedman, R., Sobel, D., Myers, P., Caudill, M. & Benson, H. (1995). Behavioral medicine, clinical health psychology and cost offset. *Health Psychology* 14, 509–18.

Fries, J.F. (2000). Physical activity, the compression of morbidity and the health of the elderly. *The Royal Society of Medicine* 89, 64–68.

Haber, D. (1994). *Health Promotion and Aging.* New York: Springer.

Haber, D., Looney, C., Babola, K., Hinman, N. & Utsey, C.J. (2000). Impact of a health promotion program course on inactive, overweight or physically limited older adults. *Family and Community Health* 22, 48–56.

Kaplan, R.M. (1990). Behavior as the central outcome in health care. *American Psychologist* 45, 1211–20.

Matarazzo, J.D. (1982). Behavioral health's challenge to academic, scientific, and professional psychology. *American Psychologist* 35, 807–17.

Matheson, J. & Pullinger, J. (eds) (1999). *Social Trends 29.* London: Office for National Statistics.

OECD (2003). *OECD Health Data 2003: A Comparative Analysis of 30 Countries.* Paris: OECD.

Rumsey, N., McGuire, B., Marks, D.F., Watts, M., Weinman, J. & Wright, S. (1994). Towards a core curriculum. *The Psychologist* 7, 129–31.

World Health Organization (1948). Preamble to the Constitution of the World Health Organization as adopted by the International Health Conference, New York, 19–22 June, 1946; signed on 22 July 1946 by the representatives of

61 States (*Official Records of the World Health Organization* 2, 100) and entered into force on 7 April 1948.

World Health Organization (1999) *World Health Report.* http://who.org

APPENDIX 2.1 THE CORE CONTENT OF THE KNOWLEDGE BASE COVERED IN THE BPS STAGE 1 QUALIFICATION IN HEALTH PSYCHOLOGY

1 Context and perspectives in health psychology
  * Historical overview and current theories and approaches in health psychology
  * Awareness of related disciplines (medical sociology; medical ethics; medicine; behaviour medicine; health policy; health economics; medical anthropology)
  * The impact of social and cultural factors
2 Epidemiology of health and illness
  * Causes of mortality/morbidity
  * Behavioural epidemiology
  * Bio-statistics
  * Inequalities in health
3 Biological mechanisms of health and disease
4 Health-related behaviour
  * Theoretical models
  * Protective/promotional behaviour
  * Behavioural risk factors
  * Socio-cultural factors
5 Health-related cognitions
  * Efficacy and control beliefs
  * Attributions
  * Social and individual representations
  * Health beliefs
  * Symptom perception; the perception of pain
  * Perceptions of risk
  * Decision-making by healthcare psychologists; by patients/clients etc.
  * Mood and cognition
6 Individual differences, health and illness
  * Personality factors in health and illness
  * Dispositional optimism/pessimism
  * Locus of control
  * Self-efficacy
  * Negative affectivity
  * Emotional expression and health
7 Stress, health and illness
  * Causes/consequences of stress
  * Models of stress
  * Stress management
  * Stress moderators

- Social support
- Models of coping

8 Chronic illness/disability
  - Coping with chronic illness/disability
  - Pain: theories of pain, management of pain
  - Interventions in chronic illness/disability
  - Issues in caring for the chronically ill

9 Lifespan, gender and cross-cultural perspectives in health psychology
  - Cross-cultural perspectives
  - Gender and health
  - Children's perceptions of illness
  - The role of the family in health and illness
  - Lifespan changes in health and illness
  - Death, dying and bereavement

10 Healthcare contexts
  - Communication in healthcare settings
  - The impact of screening
  - The impact of hospitalization on adults and children
  - Preparation for stressful medical procedures
  - Giving bad news
  - Adherence
  - Communication and patient satisfaction
  - Placebos

11 Applications of health psychology
  - Designing interventions and evaluating outcomes
  - Health education/promotion: i) worksite intervention, ii) community based interventions, iii) public health/media campaigns
  - Specific applications/interventions e.g. in the management of cardiovascular disease, cancer, HIV etc.

12 Research methods
  - Experimental design; cross-sectional and longitudinal designs; single case study designs
  - Advanced qualitative and quantitative data analysis
  - The development of theories, models and hypotheses
  - Health services research
  - Common pitfalls in research

13 Empirical research project

14 Measurement issues
  - Measurement of process
  - Measurement of outcome
  - Individual differences
  - Health-related quality of life

15 Professional issues
  - Ethical codes of conduct
  - Legal and statutory obligations and restrictions

- Inter-professional relations
- European and international perspectives on health psychology

APPENDIX 2.2 STAGE 2 UNITS OF PROFESSIONAL COMPETENCE

1 Generic Professional Competence
   1.1 Implement and maintain systems for legal, ethical and professional standards in applied psychology
   1.2 Contribute to the continuing development of self as a professional applied psychologist
   1.3 Provide psychological advice and guidance to others
   1.4 Provide feedback to clients

2 Research
   2.1 Conduct systematic reviews
   2.2 Design psychological research
   2.3 Conduct psychological research
   2.4 Analyse and evaluate psychological research data
   2.5 Initiate and develop psychological research

3 Consultancy
   3.1 Assessment of requests for consultancy
   3.2 Plan consultancy
   3.3 Establish, develop and maintain working relationships with clients
   3.4 Conduct consultancy
   3.5 Monitor the implementation of consultancy
   3.6 Evaluate the impact of consultancy

4 Teaching and Training
   4.1 Plan and design training programmes that enable students to learn about psychological knowledge, skills and practices
   4.2 Deliver such training programmes (see 4.1).
   4.3 Plan and implement assessment procedures for such training programmes
   4.4 Evaluate such training programmes

5 Optional Units
   5.1 Implement interventions to change health-related behaviour
   5.2 Direct the implementation of interventions
   5.3 Communicate the processes and outcomes of psychological interventions and consultancies
   5.4 Provide psychological advice to aid policy decision making for the implementation of psychological services
   5.5 Promote psychological principles, practices, services and benefits

5.6 Provide expert opinion and advice, including the preparation and presentation of evidence in formal settings

5.7 Contribute to the evolution of legal, ethical and professional standards in health and applied psychology

5.8 Disseminate psychological knowledge to address current issues in society

APPENDIX 2.3 THE SPECIFIC COMPONENTS OF THE UNITS OF COMPETENCE

Unit 1.1 Implement and maintain systems for legal, ethical and professional standards in applied psychology

1.1a Establish, maintain and review systems for the security and control of information

1.1b Ensure compliance with legal, ethical and professional practices for self and others

1.1c Establish, implement and evaluate procedures to ensure competence in psychological practice and research

Unit 1.2 Contribute to the continuing development of self as a professional applied psychologist

1.2a Establish, evaluate and implement processes to develop oneself professionally

1.2b Elicit, monitor and evaluate knowledge and feedback to inform practice

1.2c Organise, clarify and utilise access to competent consultation and advice

1.2d Develop and enhance oneself as a professional applied psychologist

1.2e Incorporate best practice into one's own work

Unit 1.3 Provide psychological advice and guidance to others

1.3a Assess the opportunities, need and context for giving psychological advice

1.3b Provide psychological advice

1.3c Evaluate advice given

Unit 1.4 Provide feedback to clients

1.4a Evaluate feedback needs of clients

1.4b Prepare and structure feedback

1.4c Select methods of communicating feedback

1.4d Present feedback to clients

Unit 2.1 Conduct systematic reviews

2.1a Define topic and search parameters

2.1b Conduct a search using appropriate databases and sources

2.1c Summarise findings from the review.

Unit 2.2 Design psychological research

2.2a Identify theoretical models and research findings relevant to proposed research questions

2.2b Generate testable research questions or hypotheses

2.2c Define the resources and constraints relevant to the conduct of the research

2.2d Identify and describe methods appropriate to proposed psychological research

2.2e Consider use of validated psychometric tests and ensure that new measures are adequately assessed in relation to their psychometric properties

2.2f Prepare, present and revise research designs

Unit 2.3 Conduct psychological research

2.3a Negotiate procurement of resources needed to conduct research and access to specified data and/or participants

2.3b Prepare to implement research protocols

2.3c Conduct preliminary investigations of existing models and methods

2.3d Collect data as specified by research prootcols

Unit 2.4 Analyse and evaluate psychological research data

2.4a Analyse data as specified by research protocols

2.4b Interpret the results of data analysis

2.4c Evaluate research findings and make recommendations based on research findings

2.4d Write up and report research methods and findings

2.4e Review the research process

2.4f Review and evaluate relationships between current issues in psychological theory and practice

Unit 2.5 Initiate and develop psychological research

2.5a Conduct research that will advance existing, models, theories, instruments and methods in health psychology

2.5b Monitor and evaluate studies in relation to agreed protocols

2.5c Clarify and evaluate the implications of research outcomes for practice

2.5d Evaluate the potential impact of new developments on organizational functioning and healthcare practices

Unit 3.1 Assessment of requests for consultancy

3.1a Identify, prioritize and agree expectations, needs and requirements of clients

3.1b Review psychological literature and other information sources for relevant advice, research findings, research methods and interventions

3.1c Assess feasibility of proposed consultancy

Unit 3.2 Plan consultancy

3.2a Determine aims, objectives, criteria, theoretical frameworks and scope of interventions

3.2b Produce implementation plans for the consultancy

Unit 3.3 Establish, develop and maintain working relationships with clients

3.3a Establish contact with clients

3.3b Develop and maintain consultancy contracts with clients

3.3c Develop and maintain working relationships with clients
3.3d Monitor and evaluate working relationships and practices with clients

Unit 3.4 Conduct consultancy
3.4a Establish systems or processes to deliver the planned advice, research, interventions or activities
3.4b Implement the planned advice, research, interventions or activities
3.4c Close the consultancy

Unit 3.5 Monitor the implementation of consultancy
3.5a Review the consultancy
3.5b Implement changes identified by the monitoring process
3.5c Review client expectations, needs and requirements within the consultancy
3.5d Implement quality assurance and control mechanisms

Unit 3.6 Evaluate the impact of consultancy
3.6a Identify evaluation needs and design evaluation
3.6b Implement planned evaluation
3.6c Assess the outcomes of the evaluation

Unit 4.1 Plan and design training programmes that enable students to learn about psychological knowledge, skills and practices
4.1a Assess training needs
4.1b Identify training programme structures and content
4.1c Select training methods and approaches
4.1d Produce training materials
4.1e Use appropriate media to deliver training materials

Unit 4.2 Deliver such training programmes (see 4.1)
4.2a Implement training methods
4.2b Facilitate learning

Unit 4.3 Plan and implement assessment procedures for such training programmes
4.3a Identify assessment methods
4.3b Select assessment regimes
4.3c Establish the availability of resources for assessment procedures
4.3d Produce assessment materials
4.3e Ensure fair appreciation of assessment methods
4.3f Produce relevant records of progress and outcomes

Unit 4.4 Evaluate such training programmes
4.4a Evaluate training programme outcomes
4.4b Identify factors contributing to training programme outcomes
4.4c Identify improvements for the design and delivery of training for implementation in future programmes

Unit 5.1 Implement interventions to change health-related behaviour

5.1a Assess the suitability of client/s for health-related behaviour intervention

5.1b Identify and negotiate the behaviour change goals of the client/s

5.1c Assess the cognitive, behavioural and situational determinants of relevant current behaviour

5.1d Develop a behaviour change plan based on cognitive-behavioural principles

5.1e Ensure monitoring and support for behaviour change plan

5.1f Evaluate outcome

5.1g Negotiate completion, follow-up or referral as appropriate

Unit 5.2 Direct the implementation of interventions

5.2a Establish needs and implement strategies for the procurement of intervention resources

5.2b Assess the capabilities of the people required to conduct and monitor a planned intervention

5.2c Advise and guide the activities of designated others

5.2d Ensure technical support for a planned intervention

5.2e Oversee and direct the conduct of a planned intervention

Unit 5.3 Communicate the processes and outcomes of psychological interventions and consultancies

5.3a Prepare information for dissemination

5.3b Present information to individuals, groups and organisations on the processes and outcomes of psychological interventions, consultancies

5.3c Evaluate the impact of disseminated information

Unit 5.4 Provide psychological advice to aid policy decision making for the implementation of psychological services

5.4a Provide advice on the assessment of policy documents from a psychological perspective

5.4b Monitor, evaluate and feedback on the implementation of policy in relation to psychological services

5.4c Make recommendations to change policy

Unit 5.5 Promote psychological principles, practices, services and benefits

5.5a Seek opportunities for the promotion of health psychology

5.5b Evaluate needs and requirements and benefits relevant to promoting health psychology principles, practices and services

5.5c Evaluate methods and resources for use in the promotion of psychological principles, practices and services

5.5d Select promotional resources and services to demonstrate the value of health psychology principles, practices and services

Unit 5.6 Provide expert opinion and advice, including the preparation and presentation of evidence in formal settings

5.6a Consider the nature of information requests in relation to one's own expertise and evaluate the implications of responses

5.6b Where appropriate provide accurate responses to information requests

5.6c Prepare psychological evidence and produce reports

5.6d Present testimony in formal situations

Unit 5.7 Contribute to the evolution of legal, ethical and professional standards in health and applied psychology

5.7a Monitor and evaluate developments in legal, ethical and professional standards in health and applied psychology

5.7b Implement developments in legal, ethical and professional standards in applied psychology

Unit 5.8 Disseminate psychological knowledge to address current issues in Society

5.8a Identify and analyse psychological components of current social issues

5.8b Present psychological analysis of current social issues

APPENDIX 2.4 COMPONENTS OF COMPETENCE UNIT 2.3 AND GUIDELINES ON THEIR ACQUISITION

Unit 2.3 Conduct psychological research

2.3a Negotiate procurement of resources needed to conduct research and access to specified data and/or participants

2.3b Prepare to implement research protocols

2.3c Conduct preliminary investigations of existing models and methods

2.3d Collect data as specified by research protocols

Component 2.3a: In order to negotiate procurement of resources needed to conduct research and access to specified data and/or participants the competent health psychologist will be able to:

1 Identify resources and timescales required for research preparation and execution.

2 State and agree procedures, structures, strategies and mechanisms for acquiring necessary resources (including, for example, applications to funding bodies).

3 Discuss and agree access to participants and resources with relevant others.

4 Define how research will be conducted within appropriate security, confidentiality and ethical frameworks.

Component 2.3b: In order to prepare to implement research protocols the competent health psychologist will be able to:

1 Seek and acquire any necessary approvals from individuals, groups and departments prior to implementing research designs.

2 Communicate the roles and responsibilities of the individuals involved in research programmes (including the rights and obligations of researchers and their managers/supervisors) and provide training where necessary.

3 Develop and agree measurement instruments to be used with relevant others.

4 Plan pilot investigations using relevant and accurate methods and appropriate sampling techniques.
5 Complete documentation necessary for the implementation of research designs (e.g., ethical approval, letters of permission, participant information sheets, questionnaires etc.) in good time for the start of research.

Component 2.3c: In order to conduct preliminary investigations of existing models and methods the competent health psychologist will be able to:
1 Review and evaluate relevant research literature.
2 Discuss and review the suitability and effectiveness of available psychological models and measures.
3 Undertake pilot studies capable of assessing the appropriateness and effectiveness of existing models, measures and techniques.
4 Review and evaluate the outcomes of the preliminary investigations (in discussion with relevant others, where appropriate).
5 Revise and finalize research questions and methods on the basis of pilot data.
6 Check ethical and confidentiality requirements with relevant others and plan the implementation of ethical data collection procedures.
7 Attribute sources in any communication relating to the evaluation or adoption of methods.

Component 2.3d: In order to collect data specified by research protocols the competent health psychologist will be able to:
1 Implement data collection methods outlined in research protocols working within appropriate security and ethical constraints.
2 Initiate monitoring systems (e.g., procedures for monitoring the quality of data collection) as specified within research protocols.
3 Maintain data recording systems according to agreed formats and procedures specified in research protocols.
4 Review research protocols in light of the interim outcomes of studies and, if appropriate, agree and implement modifications to data collection procedures.
5 Identify and implement procedures to ensure the accuracy of recorded data.
6 Categorise and store data in a manner which would allow other researchers to undertake appropriate analyses, e.g., by explicitly documenting coding frames, categorisation procedures and descriptive statistics.
7 Demonstrate expertise in a number of data collection approaches regularly employed in health psychology, e.g., questionnaire design and administration and the conduct of semi-structured interviews.

Chapter 3

INTERNATIONAL COMMENTARIES

3.1 THE UK PROFESSIONAL QUALIFICATION IN HEALTH PSYCHOLOGY IN THE EUROPEAN CONTEXT

Teresa Mendonça McIntyre

The UK professional qualification in Health Psychology gains particular importance in view of the ongoing efforts to create a European Diploma in Psychology (EDP), which is being developed by the European Federation of Psychologists Associations (EFPA). The EDP, if approved by the European Commission, would be a permit to work as a psychologist in all EU states (Tikkanen, 2002). Therefore, it is relevant to examine the current UK qualification in light of the requirements for the EDP.

The EuroPsych Project, followed by the EuroPsyT project, has been developing a proposed 'Common Framework' for education and training in psychology, which qualifies psychologists for independent practice and forms the base for the EDP (Bartram et al., 2002; Lunt, 2000). The framework addresses three main aspects of training (Lunt, 2000): (1) the time period of education and training to practice independently; (2) the common curriculum and/or internship requirements; and (3) the output or competences required for independent practice.

The duration of education and training needed for independent practice by the Common Framework is a minimum of six years including three phases (Bartram et al., 2002): (1) three years leading to a Bachelor's degree or equivalent; (2) two years leading to a Master's degree or equivalent; and (3) one year supervised practice. The Common Framework seems to correspond to a generic training model with late specialization. There is considerable overlap between the UK three qualifications required to be a chartered health psychologist and the Common Framework. Both models consider 'input' (curriculum) and 'output' or competence dimensions as well as a generic knowledge base in the first stage and a specialized and applied emphasis in the second stage. However, the UK model seems to place a stronger emphasis on competence-based training with a two-year requirement of supervised practice. It is also interesting to notice that the second stage of the Common Framework contemplates two possible routes for professional psychologists: an undifferentiated curriculum leading to further academic training (PhD) or practice as a generalist, and a differentiated curriculum leading to specialized practice in psychology, such as health psychology, the second option being in line with the UK model.

In terms of the contents of the curriculum and required skills, there is overlap in terms of the general knowledge base in psychology. Although the specialized knowledge base is not defined for health psychology, the core content areas proposed fit well within the components of the second stage of the Common Framework: explanatory theories in the specialized domain (e.g., areas 4–7), technological theories (e.g., area 10), methodology (e.g., area 12), academic and general professional skills (area 15), non-psychology theory (e.g., area 1), and a research project or thesis (area 13). The European model places more emphasis on the separation of knowledge and skills requirements. The core content areas proposed by the UK model are also in agreement with those proposed by the European Federation of Professional Psychologists Association (Marks et al., 1998) and the core domains for postgraduate education in this speciality in the US (Belar et al., 2003). An aspect that is clearly defined in the Common Framework and could be made more explicit in the UK model is the theory and skills coverage of individuals, groups and systems.

It is in terms of 'output' or competences required for independent practice in a speciality in psychology, that the UK qualification model may be considered a reference for the European Diploma (Lunt, 2000). Most of the work done by the EuroPsyT project has focused on the 'input' and only recently on the 'output'. By providing a detailed competence-based qualification, with well-defined units of competence, supervision requirements, evidence of competences achieved and assessment of competence, the UK model may serve as an important tool for the European efforts. One big obstacle to the European-wide implementation of the model is the fact that the profession is regulated in only 13 of the member states (Tikkanen, 2002). The implementation of the UK model depends on legislation that regulates the profession and, especially, on the British Psychological Society, a well-organized professional and scientific body with legal responsibilities in terms of training and its accreditation.

The UK qualification in health psychology does propose additional important guidelines to be considered in future European developments: (1) it is very flexible in terms of the settings of practice, allowing the individual to use previously acquired competence (as long as proof may be submitted) and to work while in training; (2) coverage is also ensured by the requirement of four areas of competence (professional, research, consultancy, teaching/training) and at least two target populations; and (3) there is a clear model of supervision, which ensures proper support for the training (e.g., choice of supervisor, frequency of meetings, records of supervision). Again, some difficulties may arise in terms of the implementation of these guidelines across EU countries. The coverage of training may be limited by the fact that there is great asymmetry in the development of health psychology across EU countries and thus not all four areas of competence may be viable. Furthermore, the supervision model is demanding in that the 'culture' of supervised practice as a training requirement is not present in some EU countries and the availability of supervisors in this domain across different settings may be problematic. Finally, the costs involved in all the qualification process may seem excessive in some countries in which education and training are considered a responsibility of the state or government. The different documents on the European Diploma in Psychology stress the concern with balancing out the common platform and the respect for national constraints. In any case, the UK qualification model in health psychology is an important contribution to the advancement of competence-based professional accreditation.

3.2 HEALTH PSYCHOLOGY TRAINING: THE US PERSPECTIVE

Susan Folkman

The training requirements for becoming a chartered health psychologist are impressive, combining academic rigour with practicality. The 15 categories of the knowledge base for health psychology are clearly outlined. The trainee who becomes knowledgeable in each of these areas will have achieved a comprehensive education in health psychology. At the same time, there is latitude as to where and how the trainee can satisfy many of the programme's requirements. For example, the trainee can obtain clinical training as part of his or her regular work, assuming the work is in an appropriate health-related setting with an appropriate supervisor.

There are striking similarities in the UK and US approaches to training health psychologists. The two countries both recognize that health and illness are the product of a combination of factors including biological characteristics, behavioural factors and social conditions. The two countries have both observed a shift in prevalence from acute to chronic illness, and with it, an increasing awareness that people need assistance in learning to manage chronic illness over many years. The two countries also share the same view about the kinds of competences that define a good health psychologist, including familiarity with theoretical models of health and illness, the epidemiology of behavioural issues in health and illness, research methodology, and issues and techniques related to practice.

There are, however, striking differences in the training of health psychologists between the two countries, largely having to do with how psychology is organized. In the UK, the training process, accreditation and practice are regulated centrally, through the British Psychological Society and the National Health Service, and the requirements for becoming a health psychologist have been operationalized at this central level. Further, the specialty of 'health psychology' always includes research, teaching and consultancy skills. By contrast, in the US, the process is decentralized. Training programmes can differ in their goals and their requirements. One programme, for example, might emphasize applied or clinical health psychology while another might emphasize academic health psychology.

The chartering process in the UK is uniform. In the US, it is not. First, there is an important distinction between certification and licensing. Certification refers to a process whereby a clinical training programme is reviewed according to criteria set by a professional organization. The American Psychological Association (APA), for example, confers certification (i.e., 'accreditation', in the UK) on training programmes in clinical and counselling psychology. The standards for such certification are high, and programmes with APA accreditation are generally considered to be more desirable than those without such accreditation. An individual can also receive certification, indicating that certain requirements have been fulfilled. For health psychologists, certification has recently become available through the American Board of Professional Psychology.

Certification, however, does not confer the legal right to practise clinical or counselling psychology. This right is obtained through licensure. Licensure is handled by state governments, which vary considerably in their requirements for practice. At present, health psychology is not an officially designated sub-specialty of clinical psychology in most (if not all) states. To be licensed to practise health psychology, the practitioner must become licensed as a clinical or counselling psychologist. The individual can refer to himself or herself as a health psychologist, but this generally does not carry official recognition. Finally, a substantial minority of individuals who identify themselves as health psychologists function in non-clinical academic roles, primarily involving teaching and research.

In short, health psychologists in the UK and the US are responding to common changes in the patterns of health and illness in their respective countries and share a common knowledge base. The definition of a health psychologist is much more uniform in the UK than it is in the US, and with respect to training and chartering, the UK is much more centralized and the US is much more decentralized.

3.3 HEALTH PSYCHOLOGY TRAINING: THE AUSTRALIAN PERSPECTIVE

Susan J. Paxton

3.3.1 Historical background

The relevance of the application of psychological principles to understanding and managing changing patterns of health and illness became increasingly manifest in the Australian context in the mid-1980s. Clinically trained psychologists were finding roles in health psychology fields, e.g., pain management and treating depression following heart surgery. There also existed a strong health promotion movement that was enhanced by the advent of tobacco taxation revenue being used to fund health promotion research, initially in Victoria in 1987 (Cancer Council Victoria, 2003) and later in other states, that drew strongly on the research skills of psychologists. In addition, by this time influential theoretical models, including the Health Belief Model (Rosenstock et al., 1988) and Theory of Reasoned Action (Ajzen & Fishbein, 1980), and were being applied widely in the understanding of health behaviours in Australia.

While there was a convergence of interest from different fields of psychology applied to health and illness in Australia, neither training in psychology nor public health provided the depth of knowledge and skills that could be readily applied to these issues. More specifically within psychology in Australia, postgraduate clinical psychology programmes provided little training relevant to these important issues. The lack of opportunities for professional development and continuing education in health psychology provided the main impetus for the establishment of the Health Psychology Interest Group of the Australian Psychological Society (APS) early in the 1990s. It became increasingly clear that the interest group provided a focus for activities of an otherwise underrepresented group of psychologists who desired more formal representation within the APS. Consequently, the APS College of Health Psychologists was established in 1996.

Health psychology was conceptualized as falling on a continuum from the application of psychological principles to the promotion and maintenance of health and wellbeing to the application of psychological principles to the reduction of the physical impact of illness. The College identified a set of core competences it believed should be demonstrated by its members that addressed this continuum, while allowing students (and courses) to specialize at one or other end of the continuum, and set out guidelines for postgraduate programmes that would qualify graduates for membership of the College. In addition, College membership may be gained by demonstrating that, through experience, these skills and knowledge have been obtained. The lack of relevant university-based training and strong market demand prompted university psychology departments to step into the breach. There are now 10 Australian universities that deliver College-approved health psychology programmes.

3.3.2 Postgraduate health psychology programmes

Australia has a longstanding structure for university-based specialist training in psychology. The minimum requirement for membership of an APS specialist College is a four-year Honours programme, followed by a two-year, full-time Master's programme, and two years of supervised work in the area. Three-year Doctoral programmes are also an option. Both Master's and Doctoral programmes typically contain three components of approximately equal weighting: course work, practical experience and research. When they were established, postgraduate training programmes in health psychology followed the same model.

The College of Health Psychologists' Course Approval Guidelines (Australian Psychological Society, 2002) specify that coursework will include general advanced level psychological knowledge and competences required for professional practice such as research, counselling, assessment and clinical diagnostic skills, and knowledge of ethical and professional responsibilities. In addition, coursework should address specialist health psychology competences that include an understanding of theoretical models of health behaviours, physiology relevant to understanding major health problems, health promotion, coping with illness and health service systems. Box 3.1 provides the list of core areas of knowledge and skills to be addressed in postgraduate health psychology training.

BOX 3.1 Core content in health psychology to be included in postgraduate health psychology training programmes (Australian Psychological Society, 2002)

Core specialist content
- Biological, psychological and social determinants of health and illness
- Epidemiology of Australian population groups
- Basic physical systems
- Models of health behaviours and behaviour change
- Psychology of health risk factors
- Health beliefs and attitudes
- Systems approaches relevant to health
- Stress, stress management, coping and social support in health and illness.

Health promotion content
- Behavioural epidemiology
- Health promotion strategies and methods (e.g., applied to exercise, lifestyle and nutrition)
- Public health marketing and communication
- Disease prevention (e.g., coronary heart disease, cancer, sexually transmitted diseases, smoking-related diseases and dietary-related problems)
- Consumer behaviour
- Systems and organizations for health promotion in Australia
- Community needs analysis
- Community development, intervention and empowerment strategies.

Clinical health psychology content
- Models of healthcare
- Processes of acute and chronic illness, and seeking medical care
- Developmental issues in acute and chronic illness
- Communication in health settings
- The patient–practitioner relationship

- Psychosomatic, psychophysiological and behavioural medicine principles
- Psychological treatment relevant to health and illness (e.g., pain, addiction, sleep and eating problems)
- Adjustment (e.g., grief, bereavement, death and dying)
- Trauma, disability and rehabilitation.

The Guidelines (Australian Psychological Society, 2002) also specify that, in a two-year programme, students should complete a minimum of 125 days of practical placement. Normally, this experience will be divided into three sections and will include one practical placement in a health promotion setting, one in a clinical health setting and one other in any health psychology setting. Ideally, supervision will be by a member of the College. The third section of training programmes is a research thesis that must report on a piece of independent and original research in any health psychology field. Following completion of an approved health psychology Master's programme, graduates must also complete a further two years of supervised work in a health psychology setting before being eligible for full College membership.

The impetus for the establishment of the APS College of Health Psychologists and professional training programmes in health psychology in Australia was very similar to that behind the establishment of the Division of Health Psychology and requirements for becoming a chartered health psychologist in the UK. However, there are two noteworthy differences in training that derive from differences in the pre-existing models of training for specialist professional psychologists and differences in emphasis in the roles of health psychologists. First, delivery of training programmes is exclusively the province of university departments. The College accredits programmes that meet its guidelines but, unlike the BPS, does not examine students itself. A person who completes an accredited programme and appropriate supervised experience is eligible for College membership. College membership conveys professional advantages associated with recognition of an area of expertise. However, the legal right to practise as a psychologist is not controlled by the College or APS. Similar to licensure in the US, this is regulated by state government Registration Boards.

For example, in Victoria, registration requires a minimum four years of training (usually a three-year undergraduate degree and an honours year) plus two years of supervised experience. A psychologist can also be registered with four years plus a professional Master's qualification. Registration is granted by the Registration Board, which operates in accordance with state legislation.

Another difference between Australian and UK training is that Australian programmes have a foundation in general clinical skills and so build on clinical health psychology. The UK model does not address clinical skills to the same extent. On the other hand, UK training, unlike the Australian model, does prepare health psychologists for consultancy and teaching roles.

Graduates from postgraduate health psychology programmes in Australia readily find employment in either clinical health or health promotion settings. However, there is still a great need for employers and the public generally to be made more aware of the specialist skills of health psychologists. Many job advertisements still specify a requirement for clinical psychology training even when the content of the work is better suited to those trained in health psychology. This situation is changing, however, and there is increasing recognition of the wide and valuable application of the skills of health psychologists.

3.4 EDUCATION AND TRAINING IN HEALTH PSYCHOLOGY IN PORTUGAL AND THE UK: A MEETING OF CONTRASTS

Teresa Mendonça McIntyre

3.4.1 Education and training in health psychology in Portugal

In the mid-1990s, research and clinical interests in the Psychology of Disease guided the development of the first Master's programmes in health psychology in Portugal (McIntyre, 2000; Teixeira, 1999). These programmes are two-year degree courses with one year of coursework and one year for the thesis. They follow the basic education and training in psychology in Portugal, which is a four to five year degree (Licentiate), corresponding to three years of coursework in general psychology and one to two years of preparation in a pre-speciality area, including a one-year supervised internship. The Licentiate gives access to a work permit automatically given by the Psychologists' Union that allows full professional practice in any speciality area.

There is no regulating body for the practice of psychology in Portugal and there are no boards that certify the quality of the training provided at public or private universities. This results in wide variations in the curricula of Master's programmes in this speciality and subsequent asymmetries in the quality of education and practice. Despite this handicap, these programmes have been crucial to the expansion of research and practice in the field of health psychology.

The developments at the education and training levels have been in sharp contrast to the development of the profession. The integration of health psychologists in the healthcare system has been slow. In 1994, the Ministry of Health passed a law creating the profession of clinical psychologist in public hospitals and health centres. However, the few positions opened so far have been for traditional clinical roles, such as in psychiatry departments, rather than in the practice of health psychology. These difficulties forced the expansion of health psychology into other sectors, such as schools, companies and community associations, with an increased focus on prevention.

3.4.2 The UK professional qualification: A Portuguese perspective

In terms of regulation of the profession and of education in health psychology, the UK is perhaps the most regulated country in Europe. In contrast, Portugal is among the least regulated, similar to other countries in southern Europe, such as Italy and Greece, and most Eastern European countries (McIntyre et al., 2000). The UK Professional Qualification Model follows this tradition, being characterized by the following tenets: (1) clear minimum academic and practice requirements for qualification as a health psychologist; (2) a competence-based training model; (3) an evidence-based assessment of competence; (4) a regulating body that defines the units of competence, accredited supervisors and evaluates the proofs of professional competence.

This model can be successful in terms of creating a very homogeneous body of professionals with minimum standards of practice, ensuring a high degree of control of outputs, and ultimately good quality of practice. The model is consistent with a considerable degree of scientific and applied development of the speciality and a high degree of specialization in terms of the practice of psychology. Positive aspects of this model are the following: (1) professional candidates know exactly what they need to accomplish in terms of academic and professional requirements, being able to define a clear vocational and career path; (2) domains of knowledge are clearly defined and competences operationalized;

(3) this results in a professional qualification with guaranteed recognition in terms of the job market and the potential clients. This kind of regulation contributes to an increased definition of the identity of health psychology both within and outside psychology.

For countries such as Portugal, this highly controlled regulation of the profession appears as a distant, if not impossible or undesirable, goal. The lack of affirmation of psychology as a science and a profession in the job market renders high specialization very difficult. Instead, the 'generalist' model seems to permeate education and training as well as practice. Therefore, graduating psychologists must be highly flexible and have broad rather than specialized training in a variety of domains in order to be able to 'survive' in the field. Without a regulating body, some universities have taken on the role of ensuring minimal standards of quality in education and training. For instance, accredited supervised practice is almost exclusively conducted within university programmes. This model of training and practice has costs in terms of lack of a scientifically based practice, lack of mechanisms to evaluate professional quality and malpractice, and a mixed image before the public and other professions.

The inclusion of Portugal and the other countries above mentioned in the EU, has increased the need for convergence of minimum professional standards, dictated by the EU directive on the free mobility of professionals (Lunt & Poortinga, 1996). These efforts constitute a challenge for countries in which health psychology is not as developed, in terms of bringing education and training programmes in line with the EU framework. While universities could continue to take on some responsibility for regulating education and training, there is a need for national, independent bodies that will regulate the profession. National scientific societies could assume this function, similarly to the BPS, although there is a need for legislation that will support these initiatives. The big challenge for countries such as Portugal is going to be the transition from a 'generalist' to a more 'specialized' model of practice in psychology. The UK model is based on early specialization (after three years' undergraduate study) and does not offer a good framework for this transition. However, some principles of the model could be useful in meeting the European framework, namely the clearly defined knowledge base in health psychology, the accredited supervision model, and the competence-based training across a variety of areas of practice. The EuroPsych team seems to be sensitive to this issue as it proposes a common framework based on generic training with late specialization (Lunt, 2000), taking into account the existing asymmetries in the development of psychology across Europe.

3.5 HEALTH PSYCHOLOGY TRAINING: THE IRISH PERSPECTIVE

Hannah McGee

Health psychology research has been conducted in Ireland since the establishment of the Special Interest Group in Health Psychology as a sub-group of the national society – the Psychological Society of Ireland (PSI) in 1986. The Group has been active in organizing symposia at the annual conference; in assisting with the organization of the 10th conference of the European Health Psychology Society in Dublin in 1996; and more recently in contributing to government policy documents and commentary. In November 2003, the PSI acquired divisional status (Division of Health Psychology) and held its inaugural conference in April 2004. The other divisions in the PSI are Clinical, Counselling, and Work and Organisational Psychology. This development signals the consolidation of the status of health psychology as one of the core specialisms of the discipline in Ireland.

As with the UK, training, accreditation and practice in psychology are regulated centrally by the PSI, which currently has approximately 1,700 members. The profession is not statutorily registered. For over a decade, there has been a voluntary system of registration, similar to the UK Chartered Psychologist system, where professionals with four years' relevant and supervised experience in a specialist area following a primary degree in psychology can enlist to indicate their capacity to work independently as psychologists. The title given is 'registered psychologist' (Reg.Psychol.PsSI). An annual listing of registered psychologists is available publicly and the system, although voluntary, has worked very well. However, in association with government, plans are now well advanced to have psychology, alongside a number of other disciplines, included in statutory regulation in the coming year. This will mean that the title 'psychologist' will be legally protected. At present this is a generic registration system and there are no plans to protect specific titles such as 'health psychologist' or 'clinical psychologist', which is somewhat different to the UK system.

Irish training in psychology has always closely mirrored the UK and there has been a tradition of joint accreditation of undergraduate and postgraduate courses and overlap in membership of the two professional societies (many Northern Irish psychologists are members of the Irish PSI as well as the British Professional Society and many psychologists in the Republic of Ireland similarly are members of the British Psychological Society). Thus Irish developments in health psychology as outlined here have been influenced by and are similar to those in the UK, with some time lag given the smaller size of the professional society and the possibilities available for training and employment in Ireland. The UK model is seen by Irish health psychologists as an attractive way of developing independent practitioner status. However, the Irish system may need to be more flexible in its training schedules and timeframes for targets in order to achieve competence because of the smaller pool of possible training opportunities and funds for health psychologists.

An accreditation document for Master's courses in health psychology was approved by PSI in 2001. It specified that such courses must be at least two academic years in duration. Academic input must constitute a minimum 30 per cent of the course time with 40 per cent for practical training and the remainder for an independent research project. Acknowledging challenges in finding practical placements, the Society has stipulated a current absolute minimum of 30 per cent with requirements on courses seeking accreditation to outline what plans they have in place to increase the time allowed if below 40 per cent at the time of review. Fifteen topic areas have been specified in the academic content (document available from info@psihq.ie). Students must complete three placements. Two are obligatory – a clinical health psychology placement (working with individuals or small groups using evaluations and interventions) and a public health psychology placement (working with activities concerning the wellbeing of larger groups). The focus of the third placement depends on the student's interests and can be in either clinical or public health domains.

Since 1992 an EU Directive requires that EU Member States facilitate movement of professionals across national boundaries by providing rapid and flexible evaluation of their training. By flexible is meant that qualifications in other EU countries, for example in health psychology, must be seen to be substantially different in course content and/or duration of training before they can be deemed to be inadequate or not recognized for employment purposes by other Member States. This challenge is one that will face the professional body (PSI) should any health psychologist with qualifications other than those obtained in Irish universities apply for government-funded employment here. It is likely that, as with recognition of undergraduate qualifications from other countries, a list of health psychology courses/qualifications from other EU countries will be seen as being of equivalent standard to the PSI. Linking with the experience of other EU countries engaging in the same process, a European level benchmark course in health psychology may emerge over time.

Membership of the proposed Division of Health Psychology at PSI will be open to those with accredited postgraduate professional qualifications in health psychology or, since such training only became available in 1994, to those with doctoral degrees who registered as postgraduates before 1994 and whose area of research is deemed to be health psychology. Those applying must demonstrate competence in three of four specified areas: professional work, research, consultancy and teaching/training. A grandparent arrangement will operate for two years following the formation of the Division. While following the broad outline of the BPS stage 2 qualification in health psychology, it is not currently envisaged that the schedule of tasks to be completed in the BPS system (19 core units and two optional units) will be required in the same level of detail in the PSI system. BPS requirements would not be easily achieved in a two-year period in most employment situations for Irish psychologists. As the work role is likely to be more constrained by narrower employer requirements, for example a work role as a researcher with no brief from the organization to do teaching, the broad range of experience required is likely to require out-of-hours activities initiated and negotiated separately from employment by the psychologist. At present, the BPS system is thus seen as an attractive but probably unobtainable benchmark for most in Ireland. Two options are possible in the future; the first is that PSI gradually moves toward the BPS model of a specified training period with requirements as described in the stage 2 documents. The other option is that a developing system of continuing professional education (CPE) overtakes this process. As psychologists in PSI will soon be required to report regularly on their ongoing training activities in a CPE system, completing units of competence such as those outlined in the BPS stage 2 documentation may become a focus of CPE activities. This would enable psychologists to register earlier as specialists in health psychology but with a requirement to continually update their skills in their specialism in order to remain on a Society register.

There is currently one taught Master's course in health psychology in Ireland – the Master in Psychological Science (MPsychSc) in the National University of Ireland at Galway (NUIG). The NUIG course was established in 1994. It is a two-year course with academic and practical input and a minor research thesis. The course enrolment is approximately twelve students every second year. To date there are 47 graduates. Most graduates have found employment in Departments of Public Health in health boards across the country or have used the course as a base for completing a PhD in a health-related area. The most notable area of employment has been in cardiovascular-related research. In parallel, a number of academic health psychologists have been employed in university settings to develop training in the health sciences, particularly the teaching of medical students. This has, in a small country, led to a rapid increase in awareness of the role of psychologists in settings other than mental health. It has provided many opportunities for collaboration and created many research posts.

Some challenges face the nature of health psychology training in Ireland. One concerns moving to doctoral status. This step has recently been taken by the clinical psychology courses but not by counselling psychology which, like health psychology, also operates a Master's-level training. This move is seen as both inevitable and welcome. The main problem will be securing funding. Clinical psychology training to doctoral level is funded by the government and health authorities. It is thus very attractive to graduates who can have an apprenticeship salary while training over three years. Convincing authorities to extend this funding to health psychology is a current challenge. One solution, which may work in the Irish setting, is to combine the needs of the health services research community with health psychology training. One possibility is a five-year training scheme funded at apprenticeship level which combines academic input and work which is of direct relevance to an employing organization, such as a health authority. This would allow the graduate time to train but also commit time to an employer's direct service needs. It would also facilitate the development of teaching and consultancy skills.

A second challenge for those considering health psychology as a career is the current nature of available employment. Apart from a few academic positions, most employment opportunities are as researchers in public health settings. This work is often short-term contract work. In Ireland, unlike in the UK, health psychologists join a miscellaneous group of non-medically qualified public health professionals who have no agreed salary scales or career trajectories.

In sum, health psychology in Ireland is developing rapidly and has achieved a high profile both within and without the discipline of psychology in the last decade. A training and accreditation system is in place to ensure that high standards can be achieved. The challenges facing the specialty are, like in most other systems, about funding and security of employment.

3.6 Training in Health Psychology: The UK Model Compared with the Dutch Approach

Denise de Ridder and Karlein Schreurs

Comparing the UK model for training in health psychology with the Dutch model, we especially liked the UK model's multi-component approach covering not only professional competence and consultancy but also research, teaching and training. In the Netherlands, students with a Bachelor's degree in health psychology are required to choose between a one-year professional Master's in health psychology, focusing on what is called in the UK model 'generic professional competence' (and, to a lesser extent, consultancy), or a two-year research Master's, focusing on research and preparing for a PhD. For those who want to further specialize their professional competences in client contacts, there is limited access to the postgraduate training of 'healthcare psychologist' providing on-the-job training of counselling in both mental healthcare and medical care settings. Obviously, both approaches have advantages and disadvantages. Whereas the Dutch system offers a more specialized training in either research or professional competences at the cost of neglecting the other relevant aspect of practising health psychology, the UK system offers the opportunity for a more generic training which may be necessarily somewhat more superficial.

Another distinctive feature of the UK system is that students need to monitor the required competences (and actually have to do a lot of paperwork). We appreciate the active role students are assumed to play in fulfilling the requirements for the training. However, although the listing of activities that need to be undertaken is quite extensive, we wondered why a description of the required level of these competences is lacking. The Dutch system provides a greater role for university supervision in fulfilling the requirements for a professional career in health psychology, as those who want to practise health psychology spend one day a week of their two-year postgraduate training for 'healthcare psychologist' on education in university-based centres.

Again, both the Dutch and the UK system have advantages and disadvantages. What we like about the UK model is the apprentice status of the health psychologist in training who receives immediate feedback from his or her supervisor, even though this arrangement may be somewhat vulnerable to the specific interests of the supervisor. That is, insofar as the supervisor is a 'reflective practitioner', students may benefit from the experience of the supervisor. However, in case he or she is somewhat less reflective, the format of on-the-job training runs the risk of focusing on specific details of the competences required for qualifying. In the Dutch system, supervisors are more distant from everyday practice, inviting the trainee to reflect on his or her professional activities, but we acknowledge that this may result in less detailed knowledge of what is going on 'on the job'.

It is clear that both the UK model and the Dutch model strive for an upgrading of professional health psychology, although both approaches emphasize different aspects. Whereas the UK system highlights training of versatile health psychologists, the Dutch system seeks to educate specialized health psychologists who have distinct competences in either counselling, research or health promotion. We believe that the Dutch approach bears the risk that health psychology may be less easily recognized as a discipline by other professions and by the general public. However, in the Dutch healthcare system it would be difficult to find a setting where psychologists can equally practise all competences required for qualifying as a health psychologist in the UK. We hope that British health psychologists have better chances for practising professional activities and also have an opportunity to combine it with research and teaching.

REFERENCES

Ajzen, I. & Fishbein, M. (1980). *Understanding Attitudes and Predicting Social Behaviour.* Englewood Cliffs, NJ: Prentice Hall.

Australian Psychological Society Ltd. (2002). APS Accreditation Guidelines. Melbourne, Australia: Australian Psychological Society, (www.aps.psychsociety. com.au).

Bartram, D., Dopping, J., Georgas, J., Jern, S., Job, R., Lecuyer, R., et al. (2002). *A European Framework for Psychologists' Training.* Retrieved 30 January 2002 from http://www.europsych.org/framework.htm

Belar, C., McIntyre, T., & Matarazzo, J. (2003). History of health psychology. In I.B. Weiner (ed.), *Comprehensive Handbook of Psychology.* I. *History of Psychology,* 451–64. New York: Wiley & Sons.

Cancer Council Victoria. (2003). About Us – Achievements. www.accv.org.au

Lunt, I. (2000). EuroPsych project funded by the European Union (EU) under Leonardo da Vinci program. *European Psychologist* 5(2), 162–4.

Lunt, I., & Poortinga, Y. (1996). Internationalizing psychology: the case of Europe. *American Psychologist* 51(5), 504–8.

Marks, D., Brucher-Albers, C., Donker, F., Jepsen, Z., Rodriguez-Marin, J., Sidot, S. & Backman, B. (1998). Health Psychology 2000: The development of professional health psychology: European Federation of Professional Psychologists' Associations (EFPPA) Task Force on Health Psychology final report. *Journal of Health Psychology* 3(1), 149–60.

McIntyre, T. (2000). Health psychology in Portugal. *EHPS Newsletter,* April 2000.

McIntyre, T., Maes, S., Weinman, J., Wrzesniewski, K. & Marks, D. (2000). *Postgraduate Programs in Health Psychology in Europe: A Reference Guide.* Leiden, The Netherlands: The European Health Psychology Society.

Rosenstock, I.M., Strecher, V.J. & Becker, M.H. (1988). Social learning theory and the health belief model. *Health Education Quarterly* 15, 175–83.

Teixeira, J. (1999). Psicologia da Saúde em Portugal: Panorâmica Breve [Health Psychology in Portugal: a Brief Review]. *Boletim Informativo* 41, 28–9.

Tikkanen, T. (2002). European Diploma in Psychology: Will it be strong or weak? *European Psychologist* 7(4), 312–13.

RESEARCH

Chapter 4

USING THEORY IN RESEARCH

Charles Abraham

Theories are descriptions of how things, or people, are constructed and how they behave. Theories help us to understand events and to predict what is likely to happen next. Science is the process of generating theories and testing their capacity to account for observations of events. This chapter discusses the nature and application of theory in health psychology.

4.1 THE FUNCTION OF THEORY

Psychologists seek to *describe, explain, predict* and *change* cognition, emotion and behaviour. Theory includes descriptions and categorizations that allow us to distinguish between types of people, for example in relation to cognition or personality, and between types of social situation, for example in terms of work demands or role relations. Theories also articulate causal explanations describing sequences of interconnected mechanisms underlying psychological responses and behavioural patterns. Such theories explain *why* people behave differently and thereby facilitate prediction of the behaviour of particular types of people or people in particular roles and/or situations. This abstraction of processes and principles underlying experience and behaviour is a key function of psychological theory. It provides the basis for generalization and subsequent prediction. For example, Gollwitzer (e.g., Gollwitzer & Brandstätter, 1997) theorized that intentions differ in terms of whether or not they are cognitively elaborated so that they specify when and where the intention will be enacted. Gollwitzer theorized that elaborated or 'implementation' intentions are more likely to be enacted than intentions that are not elaborated in this way. This theory allows us to make predictions that can be tested experimentally (e.g., those induced to form implementation intentions will be more likely to act on their intentions) and, because a body of evidence supports the theory (Gollwitzer & Oettingen, 2000; Sheeran, 2002) it has implications for intervention design (i.e., prompting implementation intention formation may help promote behaviour change). The understanding that follows from empirically supported theoretical explanations enables psychologists to develop and test theory- and data-based interventions, thereby providing an evidence base for professional practice.

Theory development may begin with the observation of patterns or associations. For example, in the 1950s the cardiologists Friedman and Rosenman noticed that many patients with heart disease tended to speak more quickly and behave in a more agitated manner than usual. These patients also sat on the edge of their chairs to such an extent that waiting room chairs were noticeably worn on their front edges (Friedman & Rosenman, 1974). These *associations* between a set of behaviours and disease prevalence led to a theoretical account of individual differences in susceptibility to coronary heart disease (CHD). It was proposed that 'type A behaviour pattern' (TABP) was an important risk factor for CHD. Developing a basic theory (such as 'people who behave in manner X get disease Y') after repeated observation of the same association is called induction. Identification of such associations does not *explain* them. A theoretical account of the causal processes that link events is required before we understand why associations are observed. Without an understanding of the mechanisms generating associations we cannot be certain that associations are reliable. Bertrand Russell (1912) considered the case of an inductivist turkey that was always fed at 9.00 am (see Chalmers, 1978). Many observations in different weathers and seasons confirmed an association between time and feeding. Nonetheless, the rule or theory that 'I am always fed at 9.00 in the morning' was broken on Christmas Eve, when the turkey was not fed!

To *explain* observed associations, psychological theory must transcend correlations and describe causal mechanisms. In the case of TABP and CHD, the origins of the behaviour pattern were explained in terms of psychological processes such as characteristic responses to threat perception, the experience of stress and competitive and hostile responses to perceived threats. 'Type A's were characterized as people who perceive only limited time and resources to meet multiple self-imposed goals and also perceive other people as threats to their wellbeing. The resultant stress was thought to create above-average wear and tear on the cardiovascular system and so create a risk factor for CHD. Thus, observed associations invite explanation and so prompt theory development. However, the same association may be explained by different theories so the explanatory power of any particular theory must be tested. As testing proceeds, theories may be revised and modified and become more detailed in relation to underlying causal processes. Theories at an early stage of development may offer only general frameworks or taxonomies while more developed theories specify particular causal processes that facilitate intervention design.

Theory identifies characteristics that can be measured, and measures enable us to distinguish between types of people in terms of psychological and physiological process. For example, measures of TABP were developed to identify type A people. In the structured interview (SI; Rosenman, 1978), the interviewer elicits impatience and hostility and also monitors the interviewee's non-verbal behaviour. This allows scoring on exhibited type A behaviour. By contrast, the Jenkins Activity Survey (JAS; Jenkins et al., 1971) is a self-report measure assessing TABP on the basis of respondents' reports. The predictive validity of these measures has been tested by examining how effectively they predict heart disease. For example, in a meta-analytic study, Matthews (1988) found that the SI significantly predicted heart disease across 11 prospective studies while, across five available prospective studies, JAS did not. This suggests that the SI detects CHD risk factors that the JAS does not. Thus the SI may be a more reliable measure of the health-damaging aspect of type A behaviour than the JAS. Developing theory specifies new and more detailed characteristics and, thereby, prompts the creation and refinement of new measures.

Once the predictive utility of a theory has been established, deductive reasoning becomes possible. Deduction involves drawing conclusions from premises assumed to be true. For example, if we accept the following premises: (1) those who score highly on the SI are more likely to suffer from heart disease; and (2) Mike scored highly on the SI, then we can draw the conclusion that Mike is more likely to suffer from heart disease than other people. Such conclusions provide foundations for developing interventions. For example, theory-based interventions to reduce for TABP have been designed and evaluated. Novaco (1975) developed a variety of anger management techniques and found that stress inoculation therapy in which participants practised muscle relaxation while rehearsing self-efficacy-enhancing statements about how to deal with potentially threatening situations resulted in effective anger management as measured by self-report and reduced blood pressure elevation in response to provocation in laboratory tests (Novaco, 1978). Similarly, the Recurrent Coronary Prevention Project (Friedman et al., 1986) tested an intervention designed for those who had suffered a heart attack. The intervention included counselling about risk factors and appropriate behaviour change as well as progressive muscle relaxation and cognitive restructuring focusing on bolstering self-esteem and coping with stress. Thirteen per cent of this intervention group suffered further heart attacks compared to 22 per cent of controls. Such findings support the utility of theory by demonstrating that a particular theory can generate interventions capable of changing valued outcomes (e.g., myocardial infarction (MI) incidence). Such results do not, however, in themselves, test the proposed causal processes specified by the theory used to design the intervention.

Applying the health belief model (HBM; Rosenstock, 1974; Sheeran & Abraham, 1996), Jones et al. (1988) conducted a randomized controlled trial (RCT) of an intervention designed to persuade patients using hospital emergency services to make and keep follow-up appointments with their own doctor. The intervention involved assessment of patients' HBM-specified beliefs and delivery of protocol-based, illness-specific educational messages to target beliefs that were not accepted by recipients. The intervention was designed to increase the patients' perceptions of susceptibility to illness complications, seriousness of the complications, and benefits of a follow-up referral appointment in relation to avoidance of complications. It was delivered by a nurse during treatment in the emergency room. Only 33 per cent of routine care patients (i.e., no intervention controls) scheduled a follow-up appointment but 76 per cent of the intervention group made an appointment. Twenty four per cent of the control group kept their follow-up appointment compared to 59 per cent of the intervention group. These are impressive results. They indicate that HBM-inspired interventions can effectively prompt medical consultations. Unfortunately, like many intervention evaluation studies in health psychology, the study did not clarify the extent to which changes in theoretically specified health beliefs accounted for observed changes in behaviour. Thus, while the intervention was found to be effective, the study fails to test the utility of the theory used to develop it (HBM). Knowing that an intervention was inspired by a particular theory and that the intervention was effective in changing health behaviour or health does not mean that we know *how* it had its effect. For example, it is possible that a cognition (e.g., belief) focused intervention which successfully promotes behaviour change has its effect on behaviour through social reinforcement or a reconsideration of goal priorities, rather than the cognition changes specified by the theory (see Kelley and Abraham, in press, for an illustration of mediational analyses). RCTs that do not include mediational analysis limit their contribution to theory development and the development of similar interventions for other populations or for other situations (Michie & Abraham, 2004).

As empirical investigation proceeds, theory and interventions become more sophisticated. For example, in the case of TABP, research indicated that the tendency towards hostility, and particularly interpersonal hostility, is critical to heart disease risk (Matthews, 1988; Miller et al., 1996). Thus, to the extent that interventions can reduce hostility, they are more likely to be effective in preventing subsequent heart disease. Further work demonstrated that negative family interactions generate hostility (Matthews et al., 1996), suggesting the possibility of effective familial rather then individual interventions. Such interventions would allow primary, rather than secondary, prevention, that is, they would inhibit the development of hostility rather than reducing its intensity in adulthood.

4.2 THEORY AND EVIDENCE

So far I have assumed a *rationalist* view of psychological science. I am taking for granted the existence of an underlying reality that can be better understood by selecting theories on the basis of observation and experimentation. This position implies that empirical theory selection distinguishes scientific understanding from non-science and personal opinion. It implies that the truth of scientific theories and knowledge depends upon a specified evidence base and not upon cultural or personal values (even when the theories refer to cross-cultural differences).

Not all psychologists share this perspective. One alternative is a *relativist* perspective in which the value of theories and knowledge is determined, not by objective data, but by historical and cultural factors that change over time. Science and its practices can be seen as only one form of valued knowledge in any particular culture. The value or 'truth' of scientific theory can be construed as dependent upon the position of 'science' within a particular culture or community, rather than any universal or ahistorical body of evidence. In this view, cultural values, rather than experimental data, determine the importance and impact of descriptions of reality on society (see Chalmers, 1978, for a more precise discussion of rationalist and relativist positions and Feyerabend, 1975, for a radical relativist thesis).

Within a rationalist perspective there has been considerable debate about the relationship between theory and evidence. Logical positivists, including Ayer (1936), proposed that the meaning of a proposition or a theory was inherently based in its method of verification. Scientific knowledge was distinguished from other statements by its capacity to describe empirical, or observational, methods that would verify its proposals (e.g., experimental hypotheses). Limitations in this perspective led Popper (1968) to develop the falsification principle, which states that a theory attains scientific status when it specifies empirical observations that could potentially falsify it. Theories are retained when empirical tests fail to falsify them and rejected when data fails to confirm their prediction. Acceptance of this principle involves acknowledgement that future data may falsify theories that are supported by current evidence. Consequently, many scientists tend not to describe data as 'proving' or 'verifying' hypotheses derived from theory but 'supporting' or being 'consistent with' them. However, in practice, falsification opportunities may be limited, because moral or resource constraints prevent key experiments from being undertaken or because it takes time for theory development to generate reliable measures that allow theory testing.

Popper's position was elaborated by Lakatos (1974) who proposed that theories should be viewed as mapping out research programmes with core propositions and more peripheral descriptions of the distinguishing features of types and processes. In this view, data may falsify a peripheral proposition without rejecting the core theory. Thus theories that are broadly supported by evidence become refined over time as empirical evidence clarifies which peripheral propositions are sustainable. For example, research into TABP could be seen as a research programme in which certain propositions have been falsified (e.g., the assumption that a commitment to work and setting of ambitious goals make heart disease more likely) while others continue to be supported by empirical evidence (e.g., that feelings of hostility towards others creates physiological arousal that, over time, damages the cardiovascular system). Such theoretical development redirects intervention design as the detail of causal pathways becomes refined.

Thus, in a rationalist view, theories include descriptions of types (of cognition, emotion, behaviour, people, events and situations) and identify associations between types. More importantly, theory describes causal processes accounting for observed associations. Description of types and processes specify the design-parameters of measures capable of distinguishing between evidence supporting and falsifying theoretical predictions. Once reliable theory-relevant measures are available, psychologists can generate tightly specified hypotheses predicting how events will unfold if they (the psychologists) change an aspect of a theorized type or process. This allows experimental evaluations of theory-based interventions (e.g., RCTs), which not only enable the identification of techniques that can enhance wellbeing, health and longevity, but also provide the most powerful tests of theoretical utility – providing they are designed to assess causal (i.e., mediating) factors. From this perspective, the degree of sophistication of a theory can be judged by the extent to which it details causal processes (and implies concomitant measures) accounting for the types and processes it specifies.

Health psychology research, unlike, for example, research in physics, can be chronicled in decades. Consequently, theories in health psychology vary widely in their descriptive capacity of both types and causal process and, therefore, in their potential to generate new measures and to test (and potentially falsify) their claims using theory-based intervention evaluations. The challenge to health psychologists (who accept a rationalist view of science) is to develop detailed theories (or descriptions) of causal processes that imply experimental tests of their accuracy and, at the same time, clarify the extent to which we can realistically intervene to shape health-relevant behaviours and/or health-relevant social policies and legislative changes that will effectively promote health.

4.3 LEVELS OF THEORIZING IN HEALTH PSYCHOLOGY

Theories describe processes operating at different levels. For example, the theorized psychological processes involved in threat perception and stress experience are, conceptually, different in kind from the theorized physiological processes involved in the narrowing of peripheral blood vessels, increased heart rate and release of cortisol. Both types of theoretical explanation are necessary to generate an explanation of *how* TABP is associated with a greater incidence of heart disease. Describing psychological and physiological processes and mapping the links between them helps to explain how psychological events (e.g., the experience of stress) can induce bodily changes that constitute ill health (such as atherosclerosis).

Some psychologists strive to explain action in terms of unconscious mechanism. This ambition is congruent with the scientific enterprise of identifying causal processes that regulate behaviour (and consciousness). Moreover, much of everyday behaviour relies on unconscious regulation of learned responses. Whether we are playing the piano, playing tennis or driving a car we do not have time to contemplate every action. We rely on the brain's capacity to deploy skilled sequences of action without conscious decision-making.

Behaviourism, one of the most influential theoretical movements in psychology, attempted to shape psychological theorizing in the mould of the natural sciences by focusing on mechanistic explanations of behaviour. Watson (1913) and others advocated abandonment of research into consciousness and focused on behaviour and its associations with environmental stimuli, for example reinforcers. Watson proposed that whatever people experienced, whatever 'inner aspect' existed, could be ignored by psychologists who should limit themselves to objective measurement of environments and behaviour. This approach was successful in developing theories that were supported by experimental data and provided the basis of an impressive array of successful interventions. For example, one implication of operant conditioning (Skinner, 1938) is that when undesirable behaviour is followed by rewarding consequences then withdrawal of that reinforcement and simultaneous reinforcement of alternative behaviours will reduce the frequency, duration and/or intensity of the undesirable behaviour and thereby lead to behaviour change. This has widespread application in health psychology, including an understanding of the maintenance and modification of pain behaviour (e.g., moaning, wincing and avoiding action; Fordyce, 1976).

Despite the success of behaviourist theory in establishing psychology as an applied science, many psychologists have argued that Watson's (1913) approach provides an inadequate basis for psychological theorizing. McDougall (1912) endorsed the study of behaviour but argued that psychologists needed both mechanistic (including stimulus–response) and teleological or purposive theories that explain goal-seeking behaviour (Boden, 1972). McDougall noted that we use various behaviours to reach the same goal. For example, people go running, go to the gym or play team sports in order to get fit. Moreover, we change behaviours as we pursue goals over time and the same behaviour may serve different goals. For example, going to the gym may be a health behaviour for some but, for others, may be centrally linked to improving attractiveness (rather than health). This indicates that, for many action sequences, simple links between environmental cues and behaviour will not adequately describe action regulation. The goals that behaviours serve may determine the priority and persistence invested in particular intentions over time (Abraham & Sheeran, in press). Consequently, knowing that someone is exercising to improve fitness, versus looking attractive, may be useful in predicting their future behaviour (e.g., Bagozzi & Edwards, 2000). Behaviourist theory has demonstrated its adequacy in providing an explanation of, and guide to the modification of, a range of behaviours. However, behaviours involving longer-term action sequence patterns (e.g., consistent condom use; Sheeran et al., 1999) goal theories are likely to be important to understanding observed behaviour patterns. Health psychologists can draw upon a variety of theories including behaviourist theory and goal theory (e.g., Carver & Scheier, 1982; Locke & Latham, 2002; Locke et al., 1981) in testing, intervention effectiveness and mediation processes.

Limitations of the 'black box' behaviourist approach led to the establishment of cognitive behaviourism. For example, in Wolpe's (1978) work on systematic desensitization, we see a focus on people's thoughts as well as associations between events and behaviour. Bandura (1986) contributed to the development of this tradition which involves building theories about people's thoughts and goals as well as associations between their behaviour and environmental events. For example, high self-efficacy renders a proposed action more feasible so that we are more likely to undertake that action. High self-efficacy also supports persistence and exertion so that, controlling for ability, those with high, versus low, self-efficacy are more likely to succeed in tasks they embark on (Bandura 1997). Social cognition theories (including the Bandura's social cognitive theory, the HBM and the theory of planned behaviour; TPB, Ajzen, 1991; 2001) seek to describe and explain thoughts, perceptions and motivation in terms of internal processes, many of which will be unconscious.

The plausibility of cognitive theorizing has been bolstered by use of the computer metaphor. Computers are capable of complex, goal-oriented, sequences of decisions and actions, albeit in strictly circumscribed domains (see, for example, their success in playing chess). We understand the causal processes that generate this decision-making behaviour in terms of the rules embedded in sophisticated programmes and in terms of complex electronic processes. Thus cognitive psychology can be viewed as the construction of 'programmes' that could direct our actions and neuropsychology can be seen as mapping structures and processes that could sustain such 'programmes'. Applying the computer metaphor highlights the importance of different theoretical levels. Examination of electronic processes is unlikely to reveal much about the programs a computer is executing. In order to understand computers we need multi-level explanations embracing electronic processes, machine code operation and program structure. Of course the computer metaphor has its limitations. People are not only goal oriented but conscious (and, as yet, we have few theories explaining the generation of consciousness). Moreover, people interact with the environment to develop their own 'programmes' or cognitive architecture.

Cognition is fundamentally social. The cultures into which we are socialized affect our view of others and ourselves. One of the tenets of cross-cultural psychology (e.g., Smith & Bond, 1993) is that cognitive theories describing thoughts and processes underpinning thoughts need, at least to some extent, to be culture specific (Markus & Kitayama, 1991). Within any culture, people's thoughts and goals are social in that they involve other people. Self-esteem and goal priority are strongly affected by our relationships with other people. Thus, to understand cognition and relationships between people, health psychologists need to employ theories that describe interpersonal processes. This is the domain of social psychology that focuses on theories concerned with persuasion, social identity, social influence, leadership, group dynamics, interpersonal attraction and social support. These theories are important to health psychologists in many areas of practice, from the development of health promotion materials to the development of stress reduction programmes for healthcare professionals.

Health psychologists also need to consider social aspects of psychological functioning at a wider societal level. Evidence suggests that socio-economic status (SES) is a major determinant of life expectancy (e.g., Alder et al., 1994; Marmot et al., 1991; Marmot & Wilkinson, 1999) and may be a more powerful determinant of health outcomes than individual health behaviour. For example, Hein et al. (1992) demonstrated the importance of social class in relation to smoking and heart disease. In a 17-year follow-up study of more than 5,000 men, they found that 20 per cent of CHD events (e.g., heart attacks) could be attributed to smoking in lower social classes while between 50 per cent and 75 per cent of CHD events could be attributed to smoking in higher social classes. These findings imply that it is more beneficial for someone with a higher SES to give up smoking than someone with lower SES because, for those with lower SES, smoking is only one of many risk factors. Thus while understanding the regulation of health behaviour through individual cognition and the processes of persuasion which underpin effective health education are important aspects of health psychology practice, health psychologists must also be aware of societal influences on cognition and behaviour (Carroll et al., 1993). Wilkinson (1996) has argued that societies are more or less unhealthy, depending on the degree of economic inequality generated by economic regulation. If the economic context of society is a determinant of individual health, then theorizing these relationships is important work for health psychologists. Moreover, societal-level theories of health imply that interventions need to be implemented at a political level so that health psychologists must also be political scientists aware of the relationships between the national and global economic policy and individual wellbeing (Bandura, 2000).

It has been said that health psychology is founded on a biopsychosocial model of individual functioning (Schwartz, 1980). We have seen that health psychologists need to be familiar with a broad range of theories that operate at different levels. These range from physiological processes responsible for disease and illness, through to theories characterizing personality (e.g., type A and the five factor model, McCrae & Costa, 1997), theories describing cognitive and affective tendencies (e.g., need for cognition, Cacioppo et al., 1983, and approaches to coping with stress, see Carver, 1997 and Folkman et al., 1986), behaviourist theories, goal theories, theories of behaviour-specific cognition (e.g., the HBM and the TPB), theories that model interpersonal communication and persuasion (e.g., the elaboration likelihood model, Petty & Cacioppo, 1986), theories focusing on interpersonal relationships (e.g., social support, see Cohen & Wills,

1985) theories concerned with the effects of social roles (e.g., employment/unemployment, see Oatley & Bolton, 1985; Karasek, 1979) and theories that articulate the impact of socio-economic structures on behaviour and health (e.g., Wilkinson, 1996).

At this stage in the development of psychological theory we cannot always specify the links between different theoretical levels. This should not concern us. Physicists continue to work on theories that might unify theories of quantum mechanics and gravitation. The Division of Health Psychology of the American Psychological Association was established in 1978. Much has been achieved since but there is much more to be done in theorizing the complex psychological and social processes that impact on our health. Individual health psychologists may specialize in a particular theoretical area and focus on just one or two theoretical levels. This facilitates detailed elaboration of particular theories. However, health psychologists should not lose sight of the wider tapestry of theory that may illuminate patterns in, and connections between, experience, behaviour and health. The development of overarching theories that connect theories operating at different levels is a long-term goal for health psychologists.

4.4 CONCLUSIONS

In 1950 Skinner asked provocatively, 'Are theories of learning necessary?' Skinner's own account of operant condition is a theoretical construction. So, 'yes' we do need theories. However, theory should be tied to empirical tests. Theory that does not help predict future behaviour or health status or facilitate the modification of behaviour or health status is unlikely to have much applied value. Moreover, theorizing should be disciplined. Bandura (2000) has criticized 'cafeteria-style theorizing', which generates many similar theories that share common elements (and see Fishbein et al., 2001, for an example of theory rationalization in relation to behaviour-specific cognition). Empirical work should be directed by existing theory, if only to show that it can be falsified and discarded. In particular, health psychology needs to develop a set of theory- and evidence-based behaviour change techniques that can be used to intervene to reduce health risk behaviours and promote health protective behaviours (Michie & Abraham, 2004).

Any taxonomy of the uses of theory in research is a simplification. Nonetheless, common uses can be identified. Health psychologists may use theory to (1) review what is known about a behaviour and its modification; (2) describe or categorize people and behaviour; (3) test the predictive utility of a theory or model; (4) test the causal processes specified by a theory; and (5) apply theory to develop effective (and cost effective) behaviour-change interventions. These research aims may, in turn, translate into different research designs. For example, testing a theory might involve (a) applying established theory to predict a behaviour to which it has not been applied previously; (b) testing an extension of a theory; (c) conducting an experimental test of the capacity of a theory to describe mediating processes underlying the effectiveness of a behaviour-change intervention. While each of these approaches may generate important data, the third is the most powerful test of a theory's capacity to accurately describe the causal processes that shape health behaviour. Consequently, such tests are most likely to contribute to the establishment of a theory- and evidence-based technology of behaviour change.

Psychological theory can also be assimilated by those we study, thereby prompting consciousness raising. This is an important difference between psychology and the natural sciences. We know that people can change how they think and behave through gaining insights into the processes regulating their own behaviour. Many forms of therapeutic intervention are based on teaching people about psychological principles of change. For example, by understanding the relationship between self-esteem, self-efficacy, perceived threat, hostility, physiological arousal and the functioning and deterioration of the cardiovascular system, people can set themselves new goals and develop new ways of dealing with potentially stressful situations that, through practice, become habitual and automatic. In this way, sharing psychological theory can facilitate the development of people's self-regulatory capacities. Consequently, psychological theory has the capacity to shape people's representations of themselves and so alter the subject of its investigations.

4.5 Core Competences

This chapter should help readers understand and work towards the following seven core components of the British Psychological Society stage 2 qualification:

2.2a Identify theoretical models and research findings relevant to proposed research questions
2.3c Conduct preliminary investigations of existing models and methods.
2.4b Interpret the results of data analysis
2.4c Evaluate research findings and make recommendations based on research findings

2.4f Review and evaluate relationships between current issues in psychological theory and practice

2.5a Conduct research that will advance existing, models, theories, instruments and methods in health psychology

2.5c Clarify and evaluate the implications of research outcomes for practice.

A good knowledge of theory is essential to health psychology practice and all chartered health psychologists in the UK are expected to be familiar with the knowledge base specified by the BPS stage 1 qualification in health psychology. Health psychologists also need to be familiar with theories not studied at stage 1 and, through continuing professional development, to keep up to date with ongoing theoretical developments in their areas of work.

Before embarking on research, it is essential to understand the theoretical context in which one is working. Which theories have been supported and which not? What evidence supports the predictive validity of the theories under consideration? Have theories developed beyond descriptions and loose frameworks into precise specifications of underlying causal processes? Is there adequate experimental evidence to support proposed causal pathways? What populations have the theories been applied to? Answering these questions is a prerequisite to research design competence (see core unit 2.2, especially component 2.2a). Hence the importance of knowing how to conduct systematic reviews (see core unit 2.1). When moving into a new area it may be useful to begin with recent reviews. In addition to health psychology journals (e.g., *Health Psychology*, the *British Journal of Health Psychology* and *Psychology & Health*), journals such as *American Psychologist*, *Annual Review of Psychology*, *Psychological Bulletin* and *Psychological Review* publish informative reviews that may provide initial updates prior to a systematic review.

Theory must be applied accurately. When particular distinctions are made in the literature, e.g., in the TPB, attitudes and perceived behavioural control have specific operational definitions (Ajzen, 1991) and it is vital that these distinctions are applied precisely and that standard measures of the constructs are employed. Otherwise, it may be difficult to link results to previous research and reviewers may rightly criticize the research for failing to apply established psychological theory. An important element of the stage 2 component of competence 2.2.a is the ability to 'identify, describe and evaluate the links between existing theoretical models and findings and the proposed research' (see guideline 2). Similarly, in interpreting the results of research (unit 2.4), it is important that health psychologists 'follow accepted interpretative techniques and interpret data within relevant theoretical frameworks' (component 2.4b, guideline 1). These skills require an updated knowledge of relevant research combined with a commitment to applying theoretical definitions and available measures in a precise manner. They are foundational to research competence (see, e.g., unit 2.5).

A knowledge of theory enables health psychologists to relate issues that arise in everyday practice (for example, in a hospital ward or organizational setting) to theoretical debates in the literature. This is an important research competence (see component 2.4f). Health psychologists should 'monitor research developments' (competence 2.4f, guideline 1) and relate these to theory they use in everyday practice. This enables health psychologists to 'discuss the potential impact of current research and developments with relevant others, including healthcare professionals and policy makers' and, in doing so 'inform relevant others when new research or developments may or will affect current psychological practices' (component 2.4f, guidelines 2 and 3). Staying abreast of research which explores the validity and utility of theory relevant to one's area of practice is an indispensable aspect of the health psychologist research competence.

Health psychologists 'initiate and develop psychological research' (unit 2.5). In order to 'conduct research that will advance existing theories' (component 2.5a) health psychologists must be able to design and conduct research that tests the utility of a theory. This involves being able to 'plan research implied by unanswered questions in the research literature' (component 2.5a, guideline 3) and to 'conduct systematic investigations and experiments that will ensure the collection of valid, reliable and objective data relevant to specified questions' (component 2.5a, guideline 5). Then, once the results are available, health psychologists need to link these to previous data and cautiously evaluate their contribution to the evaluation of theory – both as an explanation of experience and behaviour (basic science) and as a basis for intervention design (applied research). This involves 'assessing the extent to which research findings question or extend existing psychological models' (component 2.5c, guideline 1), 'evaluating the outcomes from existing research to assess their relevance for future research and practice in health psychology' (component 2.5a, guideline 2) and 'assessing the applicability of new findings to particular areas of health psychology practice' (component 2.5c, guideline 3). In addition health psychologists need to be able to evaluate the theoretical implications of new data. Does data support a theory, suggest limitations of application or contradict theoretical propositions? Again, answering these questions depends on a good knowledge of theory and the appropriate operationalization of theoretical constructs – if measures are poor then this may account for observed discrepancies with theoretical predictions.

Thus a good theoretical basis is critical to 'evaluating research findings and making recommendations' (component 2.4c) for future research or intervention design.

Writing up research, that is, 'documenting and recording investigations and experiments accurately to facilitate replication' (component 2.5a, guideline 7) allows other researchers to consider the methods used and the analysis and interpretation of results. This, in turn, facilitates debate and discussion of theory and enables health psychologists to 'discuss methods and findings from research activities with relevant others' (component 2.5a, guideline 8).

REFERENCES

Abraham, C. & Sheeran, P. (in press). Implications of goal theories for the theories of reasoned action and planned behaviour. *Current Psychology*, 22.

Ajzen, I. (1991). The theory of planned behaviour. *Organisational Behaviour and Human Decision Processes* 50, 179–211.

Ajzen, I. (2001). Nature and operation of attitudes. *Annual Review of Psychology* 52, 27–58.

Alder, N.E., Boyce, T., Chesney, M.A., Cohen, S., Folkman, S., Kahn, R.L. & Syme, S.L. (1994). Socio-economic status and health: The challenge of the gradient, *American Psychologist* 49, 15–24.

Ayer, A.J. (1936). *Language, Truth and Logic*. London: Gollancz.

Bagozzi, R.P. & Edwards, E.A. (2000). Goal setting and goal pursuit in the regulation of body weight. In P. Norman, C. Abraham & M. Conner (eds), *Understanding and Changing Health-Related Behaviour*, Amsterdam: Harwood Academic Publishers, 229–60.

Bandura, A. (1986). *Social Foundations of Thought and Action: A Cognitive Social Theory*. Englewood Cliffs, NJ: Prentice-Hall.

Bandura, A. (1997). *Self-efficacy: The Exercise of Control*. New York: Freeman.

Bandura, A. (2000). Health promotion from the perspective of social cognitive theory. In P. Norman, C. Abraham & M. Conner (eds), *Understanding and Changing Health Behaviour: From Health Beliefs to Self-regulation*. Amsterdam: Harwood Academic.

Baron, R.M. & Kenny, D.A. (1986). The moderator–mediator variable distinction in social psychological research: Conceptual, strategic, and statistical considerations. *Journal of Personality and Social Psychology* 51, 1173–82.

Boden, M. (1972). *Purposive Explanation in Psychology*. Cambridge: Harvard University Press.

Cacioppo, J.T., Petty, R.E. & Morris, K.J. (1983). Effects of need for cognition on message evaluation, recall and persuasion. *Personality and Social Psychology* 45, 805–18.

Carroll, D., Bennett, P. & Davey Smith, G. (1993). Socio-economic health inequalities: Their origins and implications. *Psychology and Health* 8, 295–316.

Carver, C.S. (1997). You want to measure coping but your protocol's too long: Consider the brief COPE. *International Journal of Behavioral Medicine* 4, 91–100.

Carver, C.S., & Scheier, M.F. (1982). Control theory: A useful conceptual framework for personality-social, clinical, and health psychology. *Psychological Bulletin* 92, 111–35.

Chalmers, A.F. (1978). *What Is this Thing Called Science?* Milton Keynes: Open University Press.

Cohen, S. & Wills, T.A. (1985). Stress, social support and the buffering hypothesis, *Psychological Bulletin* 98, 310–57.

Feyerabend, P.K. (1975). *Against Method: Outline of an Anarchistic Theory of Knowledge.* London: New Left Books.

Fishbein, M., Triandis, H.C., Kanfer, F.H., Becker, M., Middlestadt, S.E. & Eichler, A. (2001). Factors influencing behaviour and behaviour change. In A. Baum, T.A. Revenson & and J.E. Singer (eds), *Handbook of Health Psychology.* Mahwah, NJ: Lawerence Erlbaum Associates, 3–17.

Folkman, S., Lazarus, R.S., Dunkel-Schetter, C., DeLongis, A., & Gruen, R.J. (1986). Dynamics of a stressful encounter: Cognitive appraisal, coping, and encounter outcomes. *Journal of Personality and Social Psychology* 50, 992–1003.

Fordyce, W.E. (1976). *Behavioural Methods for Chronic Pain and Illness.* St Louis: Mosby.

Friedman, M. & Rosenman, R.H. (1974). *Type A and Your Heart.* New York: Knopf.

Friedman, M., Thoresen, C.E., Gill, J.J., et al. (1986). Alteration of type A behavior and reduction in cardiac recurrences in post-myocardial infarction patients. *American Heart Journal* 112, 653–65.

Gollwitzer, P.M. & Brandstätter, V. (1997). Implementation intentions and effective goal pursuit. *Journal of Personality and Social Psychology* 73, 186–99.

Gollwitzer, P.M. & Oettingen, G. (2000). The emergence and implementation of health goals. In P. Norman, C. Abraham & M. Conner (eds), *Understanding and Changing Health-Related Behaviour*, Amsterdam: Harwood Academic Publishers, 229–60.

Hein, H.O., Suadicani, P. & Gyntelberg, F. (1992). Ischaemic heart disease incidence by social class and form of smoking: The Copenhagen Male Study – 17 years follow-up. *Journal of Internal Medicine* 231, 477–83.

Jenkins, C.D., Zyzanski, S.J., & Rosenman, R.H. (1971). *Jenkins Activity Survey.* Cleveland: Psychological Corporation.

Jones, S.L., Jones, P.K. & Katz, J. (1988). Health belief model intervention to increase compliance with emergency department patients. *Medical Care* 26, 1172–84.

Karasek, R.A. (1979). Job demands, job decision latitude and mental strain: implications for job design. *Administrative Science Quarterly* 24, 285–308.

Kelley, K. & Abraham, C. (in press). RCT of a theory-based intervention promoting healthy eating and physical activity amongst out-patients older than 65 years. *Social Science and Medicine.*

Lakatos, I. (1974). Falsification and the methodology of scientific research programmes. In I. Latatos & A. Musgrave (eds), *Criticism and the Growth of
Knowledge*. Cambridge: Cambridge University Press.

Locke, E.A. & Latham, G.P. (2002). Building a practically useful theory of goal
setting and task motivation: A 35-year odyssey. *American Psychologist* 57,
705–17.

Locke, E.A., Shaw, K.N., Saari, L. & Latham, G.P. (1981). Goal setting and task
performance: 1969–1980. *Psychological Bulletin* 90, 125–52.

Markus, H. & Kitayama, S. (1991). Culture and the self: Implications for cognition,
emotion and motivation. *Psychological Review* 98, 224–53.

Marmot, M.G., Davey Smith, G., Stansfield et al. (1991). Health inequalities among
British civil servants: The Whitehall II study, *Lancet* 337, 1387–93.

Marmot, M. & Wilkinson, R.G. (eds) (1999). *Social Determinants of Health*. Oxford:
Oxford University Press.

Matthews, K.A. (1988). Coronary heart disease and type A behaviours: update on
and alternative to the Booth-Kewley and Friedman (1987) Quantitative Review.
Psychological Bulletin 104, 373–80.

Matthews, K.A., Woodall, K.L., Kenyon, K., & Jacob, T. (1996). Negative family
environment as a predictor of boys' future status on measures of hostile attitudes,
interview behaviour and anger expression, *Health Psychology* 14, 30–37.

McCrae, R.R. & Costa, P.T., Jr (1997). Personality trait structure as a human
universal. *American Psychologist* 52, 509–16.

McDougall, W. (1912). *Introduction to Social Psychology* (5th edn). London: Methuen.

Michie, S. & Abraham, C. (2004). Interventions to change health behaviours:
Evidence-based or evidence inspired? *Psychology and Health* 19, 29–49.

Miller, T.Q., Smith, T.W., Turner, C.W., Guijarro, M.L., & Hallet, A.J. (1996). A
meta-analytic review of research on hostility and physical health. *Psychological
Bulletin* 119, 322–48.

Novaco, R.W. (1975). *Anger Control: The Development and Evaluation of an
Experimental Treatment*. Lexington, MA: Heath.

Novaco, R.W. (1978). Anger and coping with stress: Cognitive behavior interventions. In J.P. Foreyt & D.P. Rathjen (eds.), *Cognitive behavior therapy: Research
and application*. New York: Plenum.

Oatley, K. & Bolton, W. (1985). A social-cognitive theory of depression in reaction
to life events. *Psychological Review* 92, 372–88.

Petty, R.E. & Cacioppo, J.T. (1986). The elaboration likelihood model of persuasion.
In L. Berkowitz (ed.), *Advances in Experimental Social Psychology* 19, 123–205,
New York: Academic Press.

Popper, K. (1968). *The Logic of Scientific Discovery*. London: Hutchinson.

Rosenman, R.H. (1978). The interview method of assessment of the coronary-
prone behavior pattern. In T.M. Dembroski, S. Weiss, J. Shields, S.G. Haynes &
M. Feinleib (eds), *Coronary-prone behavior*. New York: Springer-Verlag, 55–69.

Rosenstock, I.M. (1974). Historical origins of the health belief model, *Health
Education Monographs* 2, 1–8.

Russell, B. (1912). *Problems of Philosophy*. Oxford: Oxford University Press.

Schwartz, G.E. (1980). Testing the biopsychosocial model: The ultimate challenge facing behavioural medicine? *Journal of Consulting and Clinical Psychology* 50, 1040–53.

Sheeran, P. (2002). Intentions–behaviour relations: A conceptual and empirical review. In W. Stroebe & M. Hewstone (eds), *European Review of Social Psychology* 12, 1–36.

Sheeran, P. & Abraham, C. (1996). The health belief model. In M. Conner & P. Norman (eds), *Predicting Health Behaviour: Research and Practice with Social Cognition Models*. Buckingham: Open University Press, 23–61.

Sheeran, P., Abraham, C. & Orbell, S. (1999). Psychosocial correlates of condom use: A meta-analysis. *Psychological Bulletin* 125, 90–132.

Skinner, B.F. (1938). *The Behavior of Organisms: An Experimental Analysis*. New York: Appleton Century.

Skinner, B.F. (1950). Are theories of learning really necessary? *Psychological Review* 57, 193–216.

Smith, P.B. & Bond, M.H. (1993). *Social psychology across cultures*. Hemel Hempstead: Harvester Wheatsheaf.

Watson, J.B. (1913). Psychology as the Behaviorist Views it. *Psychological Review* 20, 158–77.

Wilkinson, R.G. (1996). *Unhealthy Societies: The Afflictions of Inequality*. London: Routledge.

Wolpe, J. (1978). Cognition and causation in human behavior and therapy. *American Psychologist* 33, 437–46.

Chapter 5

PLANNING RESEARCH: DESIGN, SAMPLE, MEASURES

Stephen Sutton and David P. French

Every piece of research starts with a question. For example: How do people respond to the diagnosis of a serious illness? Are 'fear-arousing' communications effective in changing health behaviours? Do attitudes influence health-related behaviour? To move from formulating a general research question of this kind to being ready to conduct a relevant research study requires careful planning. This chapter considers three key aspects of a research study that need to be specified: the research design, the sample and the measures. These will be discussed in turn. Then, a detailed case study will be described to illustrate some of the main points.

5.1 DESIGN

An important aim of quantitative research in health psychology is to draw causal inferences. Health psychologists wish to identify, or test hypotheses about, the *causes* of, for example, stress, smoking and heart disease or the *effects* of, for example, being diagnosed with asthma or watching a cinema advertisement promoting condom use. Research designs differ with regard to the strength of the causal inferences they allow, known as *internal validity* (Shadish et al., 2002).

The main designs used in quantitative health psychology research are cross-sectional, prospective longitudinal and experimental (including randomized controlled trials). These will be briefly discussed in turn.

5.1.1 Cross-sectional designs

Cross-sectional studies are generally the easiest to do and the least expensive. Participants are interviewed, asked to complete questionnaires, or are measured in other ways, on one occasion. The data are typically analysed in terms of group comparisons (e.g., comparing men and women) or in terms of associations or correlations. Cross-sectional designs allow only weak, conditional causal inferences; that is, in order to draw causal inferences from cross-sectional data, it is necessary to make a number of strong assumptions, some of which are not testable (Sutton, 2002). Consider, for example, the relationship between attitudes and behaviour. A researcher may hypothesize that adolescents who develop positive attitudes towards smoking will, as a consequence, be more likely to take up smoking. This hypothesis could be investigated in a cross-sectional study in which a sample of 16-year-olds completes questionnaires about their smoking attitudes and behaviour. Suppose the results show that smokers have more positive attitudes than non-smokers. This association is consistent with the hypothesis that attitudes towards smoking influence the likelihood of taking up smoking. However, there are other possible explanations of the observed association between attitudes and behaviour that cannot be ruled out by the research design. Behaviour may cause attitudes, that is, adolescents who take up smoking may, as a consequence, develop positive attitudes towards smoking, perhaps partly as a way of justifying their behaviour. Or, the observed association between attitudes and behaviour may be due to other variables. For example, adolescents whose parents smoke may, as a consequence, develop positive attitudes towards smoking *and* be more likely to take up smoking. It is difficult to rule out explanations that invoke a third variable, particularly when the variable has not been measured.

Cross-sectional designs can be more informative when one of the variables of interest has fixed values. Suppose the researcher is interested in gender differences in smoking among adolescents. Gender is a fixed variable: it cannot change. An observed association between gender and smoking behaviour cannot be explained by smoking influencing gender, so one of the rival explanations is ruled out.

5.1.2 Prospective longitudinal designs

Stronger causal inferences may be possible if a prospective longitudinal or cohort design is used. For instance, if attitudes towards smoking are measured in a sample of 12-year-old adolescents who have never smoked and they are followed up at age 16, it is possible to examine the extent to which smoking attitudes at age 12 predict smoking behaviour at age 16. In this case, an observed association between attitudes and behaviour provides stronger evidence in support of the hypothesis that attitudes cause behaviour, in particular because the plausible alternative hypothesis that behaviour causes attitudes is ruled out by the design: it is not possible for behaviour at age 16 to influence attitudes at age 12; and past behaviour is controlled by stratification, by selecting only never-smokers at baseline. However, explanations in terms of omitted variables cannot be ruled out so easily.

A second important use of prospective longitudinal designs is to measure change over time in a given variable. For example, do attitudes towards smoking become more positive between the ages of 12 and 16? Change can occur in overall level: the mean attitude score may increase between time 1 and time 2. Individuals may also change relative to other individuals. This second kind of change can be assessed by the correlation between attitude at time 1 and attitude at time 2. A large correlation indicates high stability, that is, little relative change: individuals are maintaining their position relative to other individuals over time. Even in the absence of true change, stability will be less than perfect because the variable of interest will not be measured with total reliability.

5.1.3 Experimental designs

Experimental designs allow the strongest causal inferences to be made. Here the hypothesized causal variable (the independent variable) is manipulated by the investigator, by randomly assigning participants to different levels of this variable, and the dependent variable is measured after an appropriate time interval. Consider a study designed to test the hypothesis that presenting personal risk information in frequency format produces better understanding than when the information is presented in percentage format. Examples of the two formats, based on the materials used in French et al. (in press), are as follows: 'Imagine 100 people with the same test results as you. Your risk is such that 15 of these people would have a cardiac event in the next 10 years' (frequency), and 'Your risk of having a cardiac event in the next 10 years is 15%' (percentage). In such a study, participants would be randomly assigned to two conditions that are designed to be identical except for the key manipulation (frequencies versus percentages).

Many experiments in psychology use non-random methods for assigning participants to conditions, for example alternate assignment or arbitrary distribution of different versions of a questionnaire. Strict random assignment using random number tables or a computer randomization program is preferable. Randomization guarantees that there will be no *systematic* differences between groups at baseline on measured and unmeasured variables that may influence the dependent variable. Any differences between groups must be due to chance alone.

Thus, in an experiment, everything that is under the control of the experimenter is held constant, apart from the experimental manipulation (in the example above, the wording of the instructions and the risk information would be identical apart from the frequency-percentage manipulation), and all other variables are 'held constant' (in the probabilistic sense described above) by randomization. This and the time precedence of the independent variable over the dependent variable allow strong causal inferences to be drawn.

It is desirable to include a *manipulation check*, that is, a measure to check that the manipulation influenced the variable that it was intended to influence, as well as other measures to check that the manipulation did not influence variables that it was not intended to influence. Consider, for example, an experiment to test whether a 'high fear' communication has greater effects on attitudes and behaviour than a 'low fear' version of the same communication. In such a study, it would be important to include a measure of fear arousal to check that the two communications did produce a difference in fear as intended. Measures of other emotions such as empathy could be included to check the specificity of the manipulation.

Experiments are not always possible. For example, in a study of the impact of personal risk information, it would not be possible, or ethical, to randomly assign some participants to being told that their risk is high and others to be told that their risk is low. An alternative in such situations is to use an *analogue* experiment in which participants are presented with hypothetical scenarios and asked to imagine that they are told that their risk is high or low. A key issue here is the extent to which the findings from such studies are generalizable to real settings. A different approach is to conduct a *quasi-experiment* (Shadish et al., 2002). For example, groups of individuals who are given either high or low risk results in a real setting could be compared on relevant variables before and after the consultation. Unlike a true experiment, the investigator has no control over who is given the high risk and low risk results and random assignment is impossible. Although quasi-experiments have lower internal validity than true experiments, they may be the strongest designs that can be used in many circumstances.

The health psychology researcher should select a design that is appropriate to the research question and that maximizes internal validity. However, other considerations are also important. Shadish et al. (2002) define three other types of validity, all of which have implications for study design. *Statistical conclusion validity* refers to the validity of inferences about covariation between two variables. *Construct validity* is the degree to which inferences are warranted from the observed persons, settings, and cause-and-effect operations sampled within a study to the constructs that these samples represent. And *external validity* refers to the extent to which the presumed causal relationship holds over variation in persons, settings, treatment variables and measurement variables. We touch on important aspects of these validity types in the next two sections.

5.2 SAMPLE

Researchers should specify key characteristics of the target sample. For example, should the sample include both men and women, what age range should be included, and, in the case of a patient sample, should the study focus on recently diagnosed cases or also include people with longstanding disease? The required characteristics of the target sample can be formalized as a list of inclusion and exclusion criteria.

As well as defining the target sample, it is also necessary to consider from where and how the sample is to be recruited. It is nearly always the case that the researcher wishes to generalize the findings beyond the sample. Formal generalization of findings requires creating or identifying a suitable *sampling frame*, that is, a complete list of members of the target population, and then using some form of random or probability sampling to draw a sample from that list. This procedure produces a target sample that is representative of the target population. Assuming that the achieved sample (those who provide data for the study) does not differ systematically from the target sample, this procedure allows the findings to be formally generalized from the sample to the target population. For example, a correlation observed in the sample can be used to estimate the correlation in the population with a particular degree of precision indicated by the standard error or confidence interval.

However, most studies conducted by health psychologists use samples of convenience. For example, a study of attitudes to exercise may involve giving questionnaires to students attending a particular lecture course at a single university, because the researcher has easy access to this group. Or a study of how relatives of cancer patients cope with illness in the family may involve recruiting the sample via a single hospital oncology clinic. In such cases, there is no formal basis for generalizing the findings beyond the sample. Nevertheless, if similar findings are obtained in a number of independent convenience samples, this may increase our confidence that the results are generalizable. If sufficient resources are available, it may be possible to build replication into a research study, for example by drawing participants from more than one university or more than one cancer clinic.

The researcher always needs to consider the possibility of selection bias. Those who agree or volunteer to take part in research studies may differ in important ways from those who refuse or do not volunteer. For example, if a researcher is interested in smokers' perceptions of risk, placing an advertisement in a local newspaper may not be the best method of recruitment because it is likely to attract smokers who are highly motivated to quit; smokers who are not interested in quitting – who may have different risk perceptions – are likely to be under-represented. In general, proactive recruitment methods are likely to be better than reactive ones. Two recent reviews give recommendations for maximizing response rates to postal questionnaires (Edwards et al., 2002; McColl et al., 2001). Methods shown to enhance response rates include the following: use of monetary incentives; using short questionnaires; personalizing questionnaires and letters; using coloured ink; contacting participants before sending questionnaires; and sending reminders with another copy of the questionnaire included. Questionnaires on topics that are relevant to participants and that originate from universities rather than other sources are more likely to be returned.

How many participants are required for a given study? This will vary widely depending on the research design, the hypothesis being tested, and the measures being used. Although it is often difficult to estimate precisely, it is advisable to conduct a sample size or statistical power calculation as part of the process of designing a research study (Cohen, 1992). A power calculation addresses the question of how many participants are necessary to give reasonable confidence of being able to detect a true difference or association of a given size. In other words, assuming that a difference or association of a given size exists in the population, how many participants are necessary to be confident of finding a statistically significant difference or association in the sample? A power calculation is important in order to avoid conducting a study that is not powerful enough to detect an effect or association, or 'using a sledgehammer to crack a nut' by including too many participants and thus making the study unnecessarily costly.

As an example, suppose a researcher is planning to compare the effectiveness of an individually tailored booklet for smoking cessation with a standardized booklet giving generic advice. For the power calculation, it is necessary to have plausible estimates of the likely success rate produced by a standardized booklet (perhaps 5 per cent?) and of the improvement in success rate produced by using an individually tailored booklet (say five additional percentage points). It is also necessary to specify the alpha or significance level, or type I error rate (conventionally 0.05), whether the test is one- or two-sided (usually two-sided) and the desired degree of statistical power (commonly 80 per cent). The simplest way of calculating the required sample size is to use one of several power analysis programs that can be downloaded from the internet (e.g., GPOWER, Erdfelder et al., 1996, www.psycho.uni-duesseldorf.de/aap/projects/gpower/; nQuery Advisor 4.0, demonstration version available at www.statsol.ie/nquery/nquery.htm/). In this example, a sample size of 435 per condition (i.e., 870 in total) would be required to achieve the desired level of power.

5.3 Measures

It is currently widely accepted that the fundamental characteristics of good psychological measurement are reliability and validity (see Kline, 2000). The essential feature of reliable measurement is that it is relatively free from *unsystematic* error: there is little 'noise' involved in reliable measurement. Hence, with reliable measurement, whatever is being measured is producing similar measurements across time and across items. Reliable measurement is necessary but not sufficient for measurement to also be valid. Valid measurement also requires that measurements are relatively free from *systematic* error: measurements should be mainly due to the construct that is supposedly being measured, and little else. To the extent that there is a large amount of systematic error present in a measure, due to sources such as response acquiescence or social desirability of responding (see Meier, 1994), it cannot be a valid measure of the construct of interest.

Many different types of measurement validity have been distinguished (see, e.g., Kline, 2000), but the most important are probably construct validity, content validity, and criterion-related validity. When a measure is assessing what it is intended to assess, it is said to have *construct validity*. Construct validity in a measure is ensured to the extent that it has both content and criterion-related validity. To say that a measure has *content validity* is to say that the individual items that make up that measure assess the whole of the construct of interest, and nothing else. *Criterion-related validity* is established to the extent that a measure correlates or does not correlate with measures of other constructs, consonant with theory, both concurrently and prospectively.

It is important to appreciate that reliability and validity are not established once and for all: measures are not intrinsically 'valid'. Instead, measures are reliable and valid with particular populations and for particular purposes. A measure may be reliable and valid in one context or with one sample, but neither reliable nor valid in another. For instance, a measure that has good psychometric properties when used with a student sample may be less valid with a particular clinical sample, due to the demands placed on respondents in terms of the concentration required, or even reading ability. As a precondition for validity is reliability, at the very least the internal reliability (usually Cronbach's alpha, see Cortina, 1993) of all multi-item scales should be calculated and reported on each occasion that a scale is used. An alpha of greater than 0.7 is usually considered acceptable (Kline, 2000).

Although it is not generally expected that the validity of a measure should be determined for each specific research study in which it is used, researchers should be cautious about assuming that a measure has validity when appropriate validation studies have not already been conducted. The greater the differences between the sample and context in the validation study and the sample and context in which the measure is to be employed, the greater the need for validity to be demonstrated. If a validation study is required for a new population of respondents, a sample drawn from this population should complete the measure, as well as other measures with which theory predicts it should be associated. A recent example of this is the validation of the Positive And Negative Affect Scale (PANAS; Watson et al., 1988) in a UK general population sample; previously, the PANAS had been validated only with student and clinical samples (Crawford & Henry, in press). Where an appropriate validation study has not been conducted, doubts should be entertained about the validity of that measure for that specific purpose.

It is often the case that measures will already exist that have demonstrated validity in a similar situation, and these should be used wherever possible. A useful collection of measures for use in health psychology research and practice is available (Johnston et al., 1995), as are reviews of measures in current use (e.g., Johnston et al., in press). A useful feature of many validated measures is the availability of normative data, usually on students, the general public and clinical samples. The use of measures for which normative data are available allows direct comparisons to be made with previous studies; for example, does a new screening procedure result in different levels of distress from those produced by an existing screening procedure? Such comparisons allow research findings to be cumulative.

There are occasions when there will be a need for new measures to be developed. Developing a new measure is a major undertaking. Development of a new scale involves a number of stages, once a literature review has been conducted to ensure that there are no existing measures that can be used, or at least adapted. A useful description of these stages is given by DeVellis (1991). The starting point for this process is to be clear about what it is that the measure should be assessing. Where available, appropriate theory is helpful in determining what should be assessed. Preliminary qualitative pilot work, such as interviews or focus groups, can also be important here, to determine the nature or scope of a construct. On the basis of theory and qualitative work, an initially large pool of items should be created. Care should be taken to ensure that the item construction process is tightly grounded in theory and pilot work, without which content validity is suspect. Quantitative analysis of this initially large number of items is also required, to find out how they perform in terms of distributions and dimensionality, and thereby to filter out problematic items and reduce the pool of items. Finally, a full quantitative validation study is required, where the final measure is decided upon, and its relationship with other constructs is determined, as predicted by theory. A good recent example of this process is described by Gibbons and Buunk (1999).

Even when validated measures are being used, it is often useful to conduct a pilot study in which people drawn from the overall study population are asked to complete a draft version of the questionnaire and to feed back their views to the researchers. This should be done first to check for problems of comprehension, second to check that the questionnaire is acceptable to the study population, and third to check that there are no important issues with regard to the study question that are still not included. A more intensive technique is cognitive interviewing, where respondents are asked to 'think aloud' while completing the questionnaire. If transcripts of these 'think aloud' interviews are examined in a formal protocol analysis, the problems just mentioned may be uncovered, along with any systematic misinterpretations of the questionnaire (Ericcson & Simon, 1993; Willis et al., 1991). To reduce the likelihood of problems of comprehension occurring in the first place, it is generally helpful to check the written materials as a whole for ease of comprehension in the population whose beliefs are being elicited (Valabi & Ferris, 1995). The spelling/grammar features of many word processing packages now calculate indices such as the Flesch Reading Ease score, which yields a score based on a 100-point scale, with higher scores indicating that the text is easier to read. The process just described should be considered particularly when unvalidated measures are used. For example, when the theory of planned behaviour (Ajzen, 1991) is to be used to investigate the predictors of a new behaviour in a different population, it is recommended that the researcher first conducts an elicitation study to identify salient beliefs with respect to the target behaviour in the target population (Ajzen, 2002).

Questionnaire measures are used in nearly all health psychology studies, but other kinds of measures are often appropriate. The method of measurement will depend on the specific research question, but will almost always consist of one of the following: interviews, questionnaires, observation of behaviour, psychophysiological measures, clinical indices, pathophysiological indices, information from healthcare records (see Johnston et al., in press). In all cases, the choice of measures should be based on the theoretical framework in which the research is being conducted. The construct validity of a measure is determined by the extent to which its content reflects theory, and by the extent to which the relationships between this measure and measures of other constructs are congruent with those specified by theory. Without theory, it is difficult, if not impossible, to determine the validity of a measure.

5.4 CASE STUDY: PSYCHOLOGICAL IMPACT OF SCREENING FOR DIABETES

Some of the points made in the preceding sections will be illustrated by describing a study designed to assess the psychological impact of screening for type 2 diabetes in a primary care population. This is a real study, funded by the Wellcome Trust and being conducted at the University of Cambridge, but for present purposes we have modified and simplified the protocol.

5.4.1 Background to study

Type 2 diabetes fulfils many of the criteria for screening, and evaluations of the effectiveness of diabetes screening programmes are in progress (Wareham & Griffin, 2001). In evaluating the cost-effectiveness of a new screening programme, it is important to include an assessment of the psychological consequences. For example, does participating in a screening programme for diabetes make people worry more about getting the disease? Does receiving a negative result make people less likely to make favourable changes to their lifestyle? Currently, there is little direct evidence of the psychological impact of screening people for type 2 diabetes (Marteau, 2002). Research on other conditions suggests that anxiety is unlikely to be raised by being invited to participate in a screening programme (Wardle et al., 1999), or by receiving a negative result (Shaw et al., 1999). However, anxiety is often found to be raised, at least in the short term, when a positive result is received (Shaw et al., 1999). False reassurance is a further possible consequence of screening, especially when screenees are not given information about the meaning of a negative result (General Medical Council, 1999).

The most relevant data on the psychological impact of screening for type 2 diabetes come from a recent study by Park (2001). A total of

355 people aged 40–69, without known diabetes but at high risk of diabetes as assessed by a simple risk score, were randomized to being invited or not invited for screening. In this study, screening was a multi-stage procedure, with those who tested positive on random blood glucose (RBG) being invited for fasting blood glucose and, if positive again, going on to a more definitive oral glucose tolerance test. State anxiety was assessed by questionnaire about seven weeks after the last contact (either test or invitation) between the participants and the screening programme. There was a clear relationship between anxiety and progress through the screening procedure. Those who were invited for screening were significantly more anxious than those not invited. Those who were RBG-positive were more anxious than those who were RBG-negative, with those who were eventually diagnosed with diabetes reporting clinical levels of anxiety. There are therefore grounds for believing that such a multi-stage screening procedure may result in more anxiety than has been reported for other conditions that employ a single-stage procedure (Shaw et al., 1999).

The sample size in this pilot study was relatively small (there were only six people with newly diagnosed diabetes), and only one measure of emotional distress was included. The study outlined here will attempt to replicate this study on a larger scale, including additional measures and extending the length of follow-up. The main aim of this study is to estimate and compare changes in emotional distress in the short and longer term among the main groups generated by the screening process (including those diagnosed with diabetes, and those found not to have diabetes at the first, second or third stage of the screening process).

5.4.2 Design

The psychological impact study will be 'piggybacked' onto an ongoing trial of the effectiveness of screening for diabetes in which patients recruited from a number of general practices are individually randomized to being invited for screening or to control (no invitation). This will allow a comparison of patients invited for screening with those not invited. Thus, like the main effectiveness trial, the psychological impact study is a randomized controlled trial. The advantage of creating the two groups by random assignment is that there should be no *systematic* differences between the two groups at baseline on measured and unmeasured variables that may influence the outcome measures.

However, the study will also involve comparisons between different sub-groups generated by the screening process: those who are invited but do not attend; those who test negative at each stage of the screening process; and those who are diagnosed with diabetes. These groups will not be created by random assignment, of course. Whether or not an individual attends for screening will depend on many factors including their attitudes towards screening and their interest in health issues. Similarly, whether or not an individual receives a positive diagnosis will depend on many factors, including ethnicity and lifestyle behaviours such as diet and physical activity. Thus, although these groups will receive different 'treatments' in terms of exposure to screening procedures, they are also likely to differ in other ways. These comparisons therefore form a quasi-experiment, or more specifically a *non-equivalent group design* (see Shadish et al., 2002). Thus, this study includes both a randomized comparison between those invited for screening and those not invited and a non-experimental comparison of groups generated by the screening process. Inferences about the impact of screening will therefore be stronger for the first comparison than for the second.

The other important feature of the design of this study is that it is a longitudinal study: participants will be followed over time, to assess the short and longer-term impact of screening. Thus, those invited for screening will be asked to complete questionnaires assessing the psychological impact of screening at three time points: after they have attended for their first (RBG) test ($t1$), three months after $t1$ ($t2$), and 12 months after $t1$ ($t3$). Non-attenders and control participants will be sent questionnaires at corresponding time points. This will enable within-subjects analyses of change over time, which provides greater power than cross-sectional comparisons between groups, for the same sample size.

Sample attrition may be a problem in longitudinal studies. At each follow-up point, there will be a proportion of participants who do not return the questionnaire. If non-responders differ systematically from responders, this will reduce the external validity of the study. Differential attrition (where different kinds of people drop out from different groups) is potentially more serious because it also threatens internal validity. For example, if people who are more worried about diabetes drop out to a greater extent from the invited for screening group compared with the controls, this is likely to bias comparisons between these groups at follow-up and may lead to underestimation of the adverse psychological effects of screening.

5.4.3 Sample (including power calculation)

The target population for the psychological impact study will be the same as that for the main trial of the effectiveness of screening. The inclusion criteria for the effectiveness trial are: (1) patients registered at a participating general practice, (2) aged 40–69 years, and (3) in the top 30 per cent in terms of diabetes risk score, calculated on the basis of data routinely collected in primary care. These criteria are designed to yield a sample of people who have an above average risk of having undiagnosed diabetes.

For those participants who attend screening, consent for participation in the psychological impact study will be sought when they attend for their first (RBG) screening test. For non-attenders and those not invited for screening, a consent form and information sheet will be sent through the post with the first questionnaire.

Not all participants in the main trial will be required for the study of the psychological impact of screening. Based on the pilot work by Park (2001), and assuming (1) that 90 per cent of those invited attend for screening and (2) that questionnaire response rates vary between 60 and 80 per cent depending on group and wave of measurement, it is estimated that an initial sample of 2,500 individuals invited for screening and 500 controls will be needed to ensure adequate power for the main analyses (see below for power calculation). These will be drawn from 10 practices. Again based on Park (2001), we estimate that the numbers in the different sub-groups generated by the screening process who will return questionnaires at $t1$ are as follows: 150 with newly diagnosed diabetes, 1,650 people who attend for screening but are not diagnosed with diabetes, 150 non-attenders, and 350 non-invited controls.

The data analysis will involve comparisons between groups. We will use the comparison between the two smallest groups of responders at $t3$ to illustrate the power calculation: those who test negative for diabetes at the third test (estimated $N = 64$ at $t3$) and those with newly diagnosed diabetes (i.e., those who test positive at the third test; estimated $N = 96$ at $t3$). The main outcome measures are continuous or can be treated as such. The simplest way of testing for a difference in means between two groups is to use an independent samples t-test. For t-tests, the appropriate estimate of effect size is Cohen's d, which is defined as the difference between the two group means divided by the standard deviation of the combined groups. According to convention, $d = 0.8$ is considered a 'large' effect, $d = 0.5$ a 'medium' effect, and $d = 0.2$ a 'small' effect (Cohen, 1992). Assuming the standard values of power = 80 per cent and type I error = 0.05, the size of the effect in the population (expressed as Cohen's d) that can be detected in a sample of given size is calculated using the following formula (taken from Howell, 1997):

$$d = 2.8/\sqrt{(N/2)}$$

As we have unequal sample sizes, we first need to calculate the *effective sample size*, which for power calculations like this one is the harmonic mean:

$$\text{Effective sample size} = 2N_1{*}N_2/(N_1 + N_2)$$

Substituting 64 and 96 for N_1 and N_2 respectively in the above formula gives us an effective sample size of 76.8. Inserting this figure in the first formula gives $d = 0.45$. That is, given these sample sizes and assuming a 5 per cent type I error rate, we can be 80 per cent confident of detecting a true difference of size $d = 0.45$. This would be considered a medium effect in Cohen's terms.

The short form (Marteau & Bekker, 1992) of the state scale of the Spielberger State-Trait Anxiety Inventory (STAI, Spielberger, 1983) can be used to illustrate the size of this effect. The short form consists of six items taken from the original STAI, each scored on a four-point rating scale. An individual's total anxiety score is the sum of the item scores. The total score is multiplied by 3.33 to produce a final score within the range 20–80 which is comparable with scores based on the original 20-item scale. In Park's (2001) study, the standard deviation of scores on the STAI short-form was 12. Assuming that the distribution of scores is comparable, the present study has 80 per cent power to detect a difference in means of 5.4 (= 0.45*12) scale units between the two groups. To illustrate the size of this effect, consider two people who give identical responses on the questionnaire except that for the 'worried' item one person indicates that they feel 'somewhat' worried and the second that they feel 'moderately' worried. Their total scores would differ by 3.33 scale units.

In terms of statistical power, comparing the two smallest groups is the 'worst case'. Other comparisons will have greater power. Although, when calculating power, it is convenient to assume the use of a simple test (here using a t-test to compare two groups at one time point), more powerful statistical techniques will be used in the actual data analysis, exploiting the repeated measures design.

The present study will involve sampling from 10 practices. Strictly speaking, the estimate of the required sample size should be inflated to take account of a possible clustering effect. In most cases, this adjustment will be small and can be ignored. However, if a cluster randomized design were to be used, in which *practices*, rather than individuals within practices, were randomly assigned to screening or control, it would be essential to take account of clustering in the sample size calculation (Murray, 1998).

5.4.4 Measures

Given the large samples that will be necessary in this study, to use any other method of assessment than self-completion questionnaires would be prohibitively expensive because of the staff costs involved. The main outcome in this study is emotional distress, and two different measures will be used: the short form of the STAI and the Worry about Diabetes Scale, based on the Cancer Worry Scale (Lerman et al., 1991). The first is a measure of general state anxiety, the second a measure of disease-specific worry. Both are brief instruments, each consisting of six items.

Both the original STAI (Spielberger, 1983) and the short form (Marteau & Bekker, 1992) have been used in many studies, including several screening studies, and have demonstrated good reliability and validity in these contexts. A further desirable feature of the STAI is that, as it has been used in a variety of screening and other studies, there are good normative data available, so that levels and changes in anxiety that are observed in this study can be compared with those obtained in other studies of screening programmes.

On the other hand, general measures of distress are unlikely to be as sensitive to information about health as are measures of more disease-specific distress, such as the Worry about Diabetes Scale. There is even evidence that effects of screening results on general measures of distress are mediated by more disease-specific worries (e.g., Michie et al., 2002). Thus, to the extent that screening for diabetes has any effects on distress, a more specific measure is probably more likely to detect them. By contrast with the STAI, however, the Worry about Diabetes Scale has been less extensively used and evaluated, so there is less reason to be confident about its reliability and validity.

5.5 Conclusion

Planning a research project involves making decisions about research design, sample and measures. To facilitate this process, we recommend that health psychology researchers who are planning a research project write a detailed *research protocol*. This is a document of about six A4 sides that includes at least the following information: background to the study, including a focused literature review; aims and hypotheses; and a description of methods, including design, procedure, sample, measures and a power calculation justifying the sample size. A protocol may also include a timetable and estimated costs. A research protocol is necessary for applications for funding and for ethical approval for a study. It is also invaluable as a guide to conducting the study and to writing up the results.

5.6 CORE COMPETENCES

This chapter should help readers understand and work towards the following core components of the British Psychological Society stage 2 qualification:

2.2b Generate testable research questions or hypotheses
2.2c Define the resources and constraints relevant to the conduct of the research
2.2d Identify and describe methods appropriate to proposed psychological research
2.2e Consider use of validated psychometric tests and ensure that new measures are adequately assessed in relation to their psychometric properties
2.2f Prepare, present and revise research designs
2.3c Conduct preliminary investigations of existing models and methods.

5.6.1 Unit 2.2b: Generate testable research questions or hypotheses

We introduced the chapter by saying that every piece of research starts with a research question. Such questions are often too vague and general and will need to be further specified to turn them into testable hypotheses. For example, an initial research question could be: Do different ways of presenting information about personal health risks have different effects? A testable hypothesis derived from this initial formulation could be: Supplementing textual presentation of personal health risk information with an icon diagram (e.g., 100 small squares, where the probability of harm is indicated by the number of filled squares) improves understanding of the information. This hypothesis goes some way towards meeting the stipulations of 2.2b guideline 5, that is, the researcher should 'clarify how research questions will be operationalized, that is, translated into practical measures and analyses'. The development of such hypotheses should be guided by relevant theory and findings from previous research, that is, as 2.2b guideline 3 notes, the researcher should 'state the purpose, aims and objectives of the research in relation to existing research findings'.

In addition, the formulation of the research question and the development of measures must be 'appropriate to the proposed sampling and analysis procedures' (2.2b guideline 4).

5.6.2 Unit 2.2c: Define the resources and constraints relevant to the conduct of the research

Every research project requires resources, for example, the investigator's time, cost of necessary equipment, office space, travel expenses for research participants, availability of expert collaborators and statistical consultancy. The feasibility of a research project may be constrained by inadequate funding, lack of local expertise, or the time it takes to recruit a sufficient number of participants. Including a timetable and estimated costs in the research protocol helps to identify relevant resources and constraints. The availability of resources affects sampling and statistical power (2.2c guideline 1), the implementation of the research design (2.2c guideline 3) and, where constraints have been placed on the research, the interpretation of data (2.3b guideline 8). It is important that problems are anticipated (2.3b guideline 5) and that the management and research roles of those involved are clear (2.3b guideline 4). When planning a research project, practical considerations are important as well as scientific ones.

5.6.3 Unit 2.2d: Identify and describe methods appropriate to proposed psychological research

'Research methods' is a broad term that includes, among other things, the general approach taken (qualitative versus quantitative), the research design, the methods of sampling and data collection, the choice of measures, and the statistical procedures used to analyse the data. For any particular research project, the health psychology researcher should try to select the most appropriate methods from those available, that is, 'select and justify the methods which will produce objective, valid and reliable data relevant to the research question or hypotheses' (2.2d guideline 2). This requires knowing what options are available (e.g., what are the different research designs that could be used to study the effect of stress on eating?; what are the different methods used to measure stress?) and their respective advantages and disadvantages, so that an informed decision can be made.

Consequently, researchers need to 'review and evaluate research methods applied in similar investigations' (2.2d guideline 1). Of course, choosing methods has implications for data analysis such that researchers should anticipate data analysis during the design phase, that is, 'select and justify analytical and interpretative techniques suitable for the data that will be collected' (2.2d guideline 3).

5.6.4 Unit 2.2e: Consider use of validated psychometric tests and ensure that new measures are adequately assessed in relation to their psychometric properties

In Section 5.3, we recommend that researchers developing a new research project should first find out whether there exist any standardized scales with evidence of reliability and validity that may be suitable for the purpose as recommended by 2.2e guideline 1. Using standardized measures allows the findings from the new study to be compared with those from previous studies, and helps to make research findings cumulative. If there is no suitable measure available, the investigator will need to develop a new measure, but this is a major undertaking. It is important that health psychologists know how to go about developing new measures and assessing their reliability and validity (see 2.2e guideline 2) and that new measures are appropriately piloted (see 2.2e guideline 3).

5.6.5 Unit 2.2f: Prepare, present and revise research designs

Selection of a suitable research design is a key decision in any piece of research. It is likely to involve discussions with relevant others and may need to be amended in response to critical feedback (2.2f guideline 3). Researchers need to be able to 'describe the relationships between research questions, theoretical models and measures specified by research designs' (2.2f guideline 5) and to 'evaluate the extent to which a design constitutes a comprehensive test of relevant theoretical models' (2.2f guideline 5). In Section 5.1, we discuss the research designs that are most widely used in health psychology, namely cross-sectional, prospective longitudinal and experimental (including randomized controlled trials). Research designs also need to take account of any confidentiality, legal and ethical requirements

(2.2f guideline 4). Thus the choice of design for a particular study depends on many factors including cost, feasibility and validity.

5.6.6 Unit 2.3c: Conduct preliminary investigations of existing models and methods

One possible model for conducting research would be to address a number of different research questions by designing and implementing a series of 'definitive' studies, each of which answered one or more of the questions. A model that is more realistic for health psychology research is to address a particular research question by conducting several studies, starting with one or more pilot study, perhaps with a qualitative component, and then moving on to larger-scale quantitative studies. For example, in developing and evaluating a behaviour change intervention, a researcher might review the relevant research literature, undertaking systematic reviews or meta-analysis of previous studies where necessary (2.3 guideline 1) and consider 'the suitability and effectiveness of available psychological models and measures' (2.3 guideline 2). The researcher may need to 'undertake pilot studies to assess the appropriateness and effectiveness of existing models, measures and techniques' (2.3 guideline 3). For example, this might involve consultation with experts from relevant disciplines and interviews and/or focus groups with members of the target population and/or a relatively small-scale and short-term feasibility trial to pilot the recruitment method and other procedural aspects, before mounting a large-scale trial with longer-term follow-up. Evaluation and discussion of the data from these preliminary investigations (2.3 guideline 4) may lead to revisions or reconsideration of initial design proposals (2.3 guideline 5).

REFERENCES

Ajzen, I. (1991). The theory of planned behavior. *Organizational Behavior and Human Decision Processes* 50, 179–211.

Ajzen, I. (2002). Constructing a TPB questionnaire: Conceptual and methodological considerations. September. http://www-unix.oit.umass.edu/~aizen.

Cohen, J. (1992). A power primer. *Psychological Bulletin* 112, 155–9.

Cortina J.A. (1993). What is coefficient alpha? An examination of theory and applications. *Journal of Applied Psychology* 78, 98–104.

Crawford, J.R. & Henry J.D. (in press). The Positive and Negative Affect Schedule (PANAS): Construct validity, measurement properties and normative data in a large non-clinical sample. *British Journal of Clinical Psychology.*

DeVellis, R.F. (1991). *Scale Development: Theory and Applications.* Newbury Park, CA: Sage.

Edwards, P., Roberts, I., Clarke, M., DiGuiseppi, C., Pratap, S., Reinhard, W. & Kwan, I. (2002). Increasing response rates to postal questionnaires: Systematic review. *British Medical Journal* 324, 1183–91.

Erdfelder, E., Faul, F. & Buchner, A. (1996). GPOWER: A general power analysis program. *Behavior Research Methods, Instruments & Computers* 28, 1–11.

Ericsson, K.A. & Simon, H.A. (1993). *Protocol Analysis: Verbal Reports as Data* (revised edition). Cambridge, MA: MIT Press.

French, D.P., Sutton, S., Marteau, T.M. & Kinmonth, A.L.K. (in press). The impact of personal and social comparison information about health risk. *British Journal of Health Psychology.*

General Medical Council (1999). *Seeking Patients' Consent: The Ethical Considerations.* London: GMC.

Gibbons, F.X. & Buunk, B.P. (1999). Individual differences in social comparison: Development of a scale of social comparison orientation. *Journal of Personality and Social Psychology* 76, 129–42.

Howell, D.C. (1997). *Statistical Methods for Psychology* (4th edition). Belmont, CA: Duxbury Press.

Johnston, M., French, D.P., Bonetti, D. & Johnston, D.W. (in press). Assessment and measurement in health psychology. In S. Sutton, A. Baum & M. Johnston (eds), *The Sage Handbook of Health Psychology.* London: Sage.

Johnston, M., Wright, S. & Weinman, J. (1995). *Measures in Health Psychology: A User's Portfolio.* Windsor: NFER-Nelson.

Kline, P. (2000). *The Handbook of Psychological Testing* (2nd edition). London: Routledge.

Lerman, C., Trock, B., Rimer, B.K., Jepson, C., Brody, D. & Boyce, A. (1991). Psychological side-effects of breast cancer screening. *Health Psychology* 10, 259–67.

Marteau, T.M. (2002). Understanding and avoiding the adverse psychological effects of screening: A commentary. In R. Williams, W. Herman, A.L. Kinmonth & N.J. Wareham (eds), *The Evidence Base for Diabetes Care,* pp. 235–41. New York: John Wiley.

Marteau, T.M. & Bekker, H. (1992). The development of the six-item short-form of the state scale of the Spielberger State-Trait Anxiety Inventory (STAI). *British Journal of Clinical Psychology* 31, 301–6.

McColl, E., Jacoby, A., Thomas, L. et al. (2001). Design and use of questionnaires: A review of best practice applicable to surveys of health service staff and patients. *Health Technology Assessment* 5 (31). (http://www.hta.nhsweb.nhs.uk/execsumm/summ531.htm)

Michie, S., French, D.P. & Marteau, T.M. (2002). Predictive genetic testing: Mediators and moderators of anxiety. *International Journal of Behavioral Medicine* 9, 309–21.

Meier, S.T. (1994). *The Chronic Crisis in Psychological Measurement and Assessment.* San Diego, CA: Academic Press.

Murray, D.M. (1998). *Design and Analysis of Group-randomized Trials.* New York: Oxford University Press.

Park, P. (2001). Informing decision-making about screening for type 2 diabetes. Unpublished PhD thesis, University of Cambridge.

Shadish, W.R., Cook, T.D. & Campbell, D.T. (2002). *Experimental and Quasi-experimental Designs for Generalized Causal Inference.* Boston, MA: Houghton Mifflin.

Shaw, C., Abrams, K. & Marteau, T.M. (1999). Psychological impact of predicting individuals' risks of illness: A systematic review. *Social Science and Medicine* 49, 1571–98.

Spielberger, C.D. (1983). *Manual for the State-trait Anxiety Inventory STAI – Form Y.* Palo Alto, CA: Consulting Psychologists Press.

Sutton S. (2002). Testing attitude-behaviour theories using non-experimental data: An examination of some hidden assumptions. *European Review of Social Psychology* 13, 293–323.

Valabi, M. & Ferris, L. (1995). Improving written patient education materials: A review of the evidence. *Health Education Journal* 54, 99–106.

Wardle, J., Taylor, T., Sutton, S. & Atkin, W. (1999). Does publicity about cancer screening raise fear of cancer? Randomised trial of the psychological effect of information about cancer screening. *British Medical Journal* 319, 1037–38.

Wareham, N.J. & Griffin, S.J. (2001). Should we screen for type 2 diabetes? Evaluation against National Screening Committee criteria. *British Medical Journal* 322, 986–88.

Watson, D., Clark, L.A. & Tellegen, A. (1988). Development and validation of brief measures of Positive and Negative Affect: The PANAS scales. *Journal of Personality and Social Psychology* 47, 1063–70.

Willis, G.B., Royston, P. & Bercini, D. (1991). The use of verbal report methods in the development and testing of survey questionnaires. *Applied Cognitive Psychology* 5, 251–67.

Chapter 6

ANALYSING AND REPORTING DATA IN HEALTH RESEARCH

Daniel B. Wright and Kate Kelley

The purpose of all analyses is to summarize data so that they can be easily understood and so that they help the analyst to evaluate whichever hypotheses are of particular interest. In order to do this researchers must carefully examine their data; they should become friends with their data (Wright, 2002, 2003). The purpose of a results section is to report data accurately and to communicate clearly their importance for particular theories to the readers. The normal guidelines for good communication and writing (see Strunk & White, 1979) apply to results sections as well as to the rest of the paper.

In this chapter we describe how researchers should examine their data and describe some of the most popular statistical procedures: regression, *t*-tests, ANOVA, cross-tabulation and meta-analysis. We try to impart some philosophy of how data analysis and reporting should be conducted.

6.1 Exploratory Data Analysis

Researchers spend weeks, months and even years designing studies and collecting data. Decades ago researchers would also spend weeks calculating and recalculating their results. Modern computers mean that these calculations can be done instantly and sometimes researchers appear to spend only seconds on their analyses. This is unfortunate as important aspects of the data are often missed and sometimes the wrong analyses are conducted. Exploratory data analysis (EDA) is an important part of all analyses. EDA refers to a collection of methods which urge the researcher to think about how to summarize the data. EDA methods may also be appropriate for presenting the findings for the reader.

Hoaglin et al. (1983) discuss the four themes, or four Rs, of EDA: resistance, residuals, re-expression and revelation. *Resistance* means statistical tests should not be greatly affected by a few points. Means, ANOVAs, and other traditional statistics can be greatly influenced by single points. EDA encourages researchers to consider alternatives to traditional tests. Wilcox (1998, 2001) describes many of these alternatives and we mention some of these alongside the more traditional tests. *Residuals* refer to how far away individual points are from the model. Large residuals, points that do not fit the pattern of the rest of the data, are called outliers. Often these are the most interesting data points, but often they are data entry errors. Therefore it is necessary to look at these points and investigate whether an outlying data point is one that can falsify an entire theory or one that shows data entry errors occur. *Re-expression* means that sometimes the original variables are not in the ideal form to address the research questions. Sometimes this means transforming a variable so that it is more Normally distributed. Examples include taking the square root of a variable for positively skewed data and squaring the variable for negatively skewed data.

EDA techniques can be used when looking at one variable or looking at the relationships among several variables. Examples for univariate procedures include boxplots (see Figure 6.2 below) and stem-and-leaf diagrams. One of the most useful bivariate methods is a scatterplot (see Figure 6.1 below). Most of the popular statistical packages include these procedures. Where available, exploratory graphical procedures should be used to make sure that important aspects of your data are revealed. These techniques will also guide the researcher in deciding which inferential statistical procedures to use. For those interested in further discussion of how to create good graphs see Tufte (2001); and for making bad graphs see Wainer (1984) and Wright and Williams (2004).

6.1.1 Which test?

When you design your research, you should have some idea about the types of statistical analyses that you will run. However, often considerations of the data that arise during EDA and further thoughts that you have about your research dictate alternative analyses. In this chapter we describe what you should think about when deciding 'which test?', what some of the most common tests are, and how you should report the resulting statistics. All statistical test have the same basic form: Data = Model + Residuals. Residuals refer to the difference between the observed and the predicted values. This is sometimes called the 'error term' because it refers to how much the model fails to predict the data. The fit of the model is determined by how small the residuals are. If the residuals are all very small then we would say that the data fits the model.

In the next section we describe the simple linear regression. Usually regressions are used when you are interested in relationships among continuous variables. Next, we discuss *t*-tests and ANOVAs. These are used when comparing means either among several groups or among several variables for the same group. We then discuss some common statistical procedures for categorical variables. Finally, we discuss meta-analysis. This is a technique used to combine results from several studies and has become increasingly popular in the literature. Throughout this chapter we use examples to illustrate the different techniques and how to report them.

6.2 The Regression: Examining Associations

Regression is one of the most common statistical procedures. Most statistical techniques can be described as some form of regression. Here we consider the *simple linear regression*. This is appropriate when you are interested in the relationship between two continuous variables. The first step is to plot your data using a scatterplot. Figure 6.1 shows a scatterplot between reported levels of activity and reported perceived behavioural control.

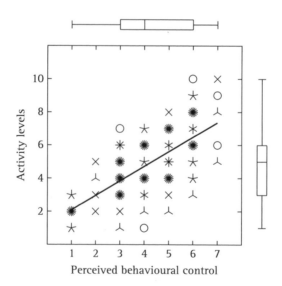

Figure 6.1 Scatterplot comparing reported levels of activity with reported perceived behavioural control

There are several aspects of this scatterplot that are worth explaining. First, we have included boxplots for each of the variables. These boxplots show the reader that neither variable has any obvious outliers and that both are, roughly, symmetrical around their midpoints. Second, there are several points on the plot with several people. This is because the data are discrete; people can respond '6' on the scale, not '6.21'. When data are discrete it is likely that several people will give the same response. To show where several people have given the same response, we have used an option that is available in many packages: 'sunflowers'. If there is a circle, that means there is only one point. For the others each petal represents a person. We have also included a regression line. This shows that high levels of perceived behavioural control are associated with high levels of activity levels. There are several other options that could be included, but it is important not to get carried away. The worst graphs use too many options (Tufte, 2001; Wainer, 1984; Wright & Williams, 2004).

Regressions can be reported in several ways. While the scatterplot is the most informative method, the regression line can be reported. Here it is:

$$Activity_i = 1.22 + 0.88 \ Control_i + e_i$$

This describes the line in Figure 6.1. The value 0.88 means that each unit increase in 'control' is associated with a predicted increase of 0.88 units of 'activity'. It is often called the slope. The value 1.22 is the intercept. This gives the predicted value for someone with a score of 0 on $Control_i$. The e_i stands for the residuals, what is left over.

6.2.1 Pearson's product moment correlation coefficient

The regression line in Figure 6.1 shows that perceived behavioural control and activity are positively associated. The scatterplot shows graphically how close the data are to this regression line. It is often useful to be able to quantify how well the data fit this regression line. Phrased another way, it would be good to have a single number to quantify the strength of the linear relationship between two variables. Pearson's product moment correlation coefficient, usually just called correlation, does this. It is denoted with the letter r. The correlation will lie between -1 and $+1$. A coefficient of $+1$ tells us there is a perfect positive relationship and -1 a perfect negative relationship (see Wright, 2002, ch. 8). Once you have calculated a correlation you should consider how strong the relationship is. This is a subjective notion. For some people and in some situations a correlation of

0.20 may be large, but for others it may be small. A rough guide, based on Cohen (1988), is that correlations near $r = 0.10$ are small, near $r = 0.30$ are of moderate size, and near or above $r = 0.50$ are large.

It is worth knowing how precise the estimate of the correlation is. In general, it is advisable always to report confidence intervals (Wilkinson et al., 1999). This has been done in the tables below. This provides a range where we are confident that the true value lies. Sometimes there is a particular interest in whether the correlation value in the population is equal to zero. This can be tested by seeing whether the 95 per cent confidence interval overlaps with zero. If it does not, then the correlation is significant at the 5 per cent level. The significance of a correlation will be affected by the size of the sample: the larger the sample the smaller the coefficient needs to be to reach statistical significance. Many computer packages report the p value associated with each r value. This is an alternative way to test whether the observed data are likely to have arisen if the true correlation were zero. Most methodologists argue that it is better to report the confidence interval than the p value.

There are several assumptions made when calculating a regression and correlation and also when assessing whether they are statistically significant. Most of these have to do with the residuals appearing randomly scattered about the regression line. The scatterplot will be helpful for checking this. For more complex regressions it is often necessary to use diagnostic tools to help identify patterns in the residuals (see Field, 2000, for details).

Finally, an important aspect of correlation is that a large correlation does not imply causation (Simon, 1954).

6.2.2 Correlations in practice

The correlation coefficient is a useful measure of association. However, it is important to realize its limitations and assumptions. It is a measure of how well a straight line fits the data. There may be a very clear relationship between two variables, but if the relationship is not linear then the correlation coefficient is not appropriate. Also, the correlation can be greatly influenced by extreme data points; it is not resistant. This is why it is vital to examine scatterplots.

Two examples of how correlations are commonly used are now described. Whenever you report a correlation you should have carefully looked at the scatterplot between the two variables. Anscombe (1973) shows how data sets with identical correlations, and even identical regressions lines, means, and standard deviations, can arise from very different scatterplots.

Table 6.1 Correlations between MHLC (locus of control) and NSSQ (social support) with dietary intake

Dietary intake	MHLC score ($n = 68$)	NSSQ score ($n = 68$)
Fat (g)	0.03 (−0.21 to 0.27)	0.02 (−0.22 to 0.26)
Fat (% of calories)	0.02 (−0.22 to 0.26)	−0.10 (−0.33 to 0.14)
Fibre (g/1000 kcal)	0.23 (−0.01 to 0.45)	**0.27 (0.03 to 0.48)**
Fruit/Vegetable servings	0.18 (−0.06 to 0.41)	**0.32 (0.09 to 0.52)**

MHLC = Multidimensional Health Locus of Control; NSSQ = Norbeck Social Support Questionnaire. 95% confidence intervals are shown in parentheses. Correlations in bold are statistically different from 0 at the 5% level.

So, assume for all these examples that the authors began with careful examination of the data.

Murphy et al. (2001) calculated the correlations of locus of control and social support with four measures of dietary intake. Table 6.1 shows the correlations and their 95 per cent confidence intervals for these (calculated using http://glass.ed.asu.edu/stats/analysis/ accessed November 2002). Two of the confidence intervals, those between the NSSQ (Norbeck Social Support Questionnaire) score and the amount of fibre intake and between the NSSQ score and fruit and vegetable servings, do not overlap with zero. Therefore they are statistically significant at the 5 per cent level. Social support is positively correlated with change in dietary intake of fibre and servings of fruit and vegetables. However, the confidence intervals show that these correlations may be small (at the low end of their intervals), and that other correlations may be moderate (at the high end of their intervals). The width of the confidence intervals suggests that the correlation estimates are not very precise. If there had been more participants the confidence intervals would be smaller, and therefore the estimates would be more precise.

Correlations are also used to investigate interrelationships among several variables. For example, Abraham et al. (1999) measured the adherence to malaria medication on return from travelling in The Gambia. Correlations were conducted to examine the interrelationships among the different variables thought to influence adherence. This is commonly reported in a correlation matrix (Table 6.2). The numbers given are the correlation coefficients with their 95 per cent confidence intervals in parentheses. Bold values are significant at the 5 per cent level. One important aspect of a correlation matrix is that several correlations are tested. When you conduct multiple tests it is important to realize that some may reach

Table 6.2 Correlation matrix for Mefloquine users ($n = 106$)

Variable	Adherence on return	Length of adherence	Adherence in region	Perceived side effects
Length of adherence	**0.63** (0.50 to 0.74)			
Adherence in region	**0.31** (0.13 to 0.47)	**0.23** (0.04 to 0.40)		
Perceived side effects	**−0.37** (−0.52 to −0.19)	−0.07 (−0.26 to 0.12)	−0.06 (−0.25 to 0.13)	
Perceived severity	**0.25** (0.06 to −0.42)	0.13 (−0.06 to 0.31)	**0.22** (0.03 to 0.3)	−0.12 (−0.30 to 0.07)

Bold correlations are significant at the 5% level. 95% confidence intervals in parentheses.

statistical significance by chance. Similarly, when conducting multiple tests you should be aware that you are more likely to falsely reject a true null hypothesis *and* more likely to fail to reject a false null hypothesis than if you were conducting only a single test. Some packages, like SYSTAT, make adjustments to the probability levels for correlations. Others, like SPSS, do not.

6.2.3 Multiple regression in practice

Once a relationship has been established among variables health researchers are often interested in predicting the contribution of a variable (predictor variable) to a particular outcome (criterion variable). Regression enables us to do this. Simple linear regression will predict the outcome of a single predictor and multiple regression will determine the unique contributions of several predictor variables in a model. Regression allows researchers to determine how much variance in the criterion variable is accounted for by each specific predictor variable. Abraham et al. (1999) examined how much variance was accounted for using specific cognitive variables in explaining adherence behaviour to malaria medication. This is commonly reported in a table (Table 6.3, based on their Table 4). Often researchers begin with a simple linear regression, and then introduce additional predictor variables at each subsequent step in the regression. Abraham and colleagues began by examining the predictive value of 'intention'. Rather

Table 6.3 Example of reporting a multiple regression[a]

Step	Independent variable	R^2 change	Cumulative R^2
1	Intention	0.341	0.341
2	Perceived behavioural control	0.002	0.343
3	Attitude/Injunctive	0.003	0.346
4	Perceived side effects	0.042	0.388
5	Perceived susceptibility	0.007	0.395
6	Adherence in a malarious region	0	0.395

[a] Regression of cognitive variables and adherence in the region on malaria medication adherence.
Source: Adapted from Abraham et al. (1999, Table 4).

than reporting r, they reported R^2. This is simply the square of r. It is often easier to interpret because R^2 is a measure of shared variance. Therefore, on its own, intention accounts for 34.1 per cent of the variance. In the next step the variable for perceived behavioural control was added. This only increased the amount of variance accounted for to 34.3 per cent. In fact, it was only in the fourth step when perceived side effects was included in the model that the model was improved substantially. Adding this variable increased the fit of the model by 4.2 per cent. With all the variables included 39.5 per cent of the variance was accounted for. This leaves 60 per cent of the variance unexplained.

6.2.4 Alternatives

Regressions and correlations make certain assumptions about the variables. These techniques are greatly influenced by extreme points and are therefore not resistant. There are several robust alternatives to simple linear regression that make fewer assumptions. These include trimmed regression and M-estimator regression (Wilcox, 2001). These techniques are more resistant statistics, meaning that they are not as influenced by extreme points as the simple linear regression is. In most circumstances they are more likely to yield significant results. They are available in some statistical packages (e.g., S-Plus) and are becoming more common. Each of these has alternative correlation measures. However, the most common alternative to Pearson's correlation is Spearman's rank correlation. This involves ranking the data and then conducting a normal correlation.

6.2.5 Extensions

Regression is the most basic of all statistical procedures and it is easily extended to more complex procedures. You can use multiple regression to develop path diagrams for how you feel different variables may influence each other. People often use *structural equation modelling* for this. Another useful extension is when the variable you are trying to predict is binary, where it only takes one of two values. In these circumstances *logistic regression* is often used. These are described in most psychology postgraduate books on multivariate statistics (for example, Munro & Page, 1993).

6.3 COMPARING MEANS

Often health research projects are designed to test for differences among several groups or among several variables. We will begin with the case where you are interested in the difference between two groups or between two variables. The questions are: how different are the two groups?; and, is the difference greater than would be expected to be found by chance alone? When you are interested in difference in the mean, the *t*-test is usually used (see Wright, 2002, for details). There are two types of *t*-test. One *t*-test is when comparing the means of two groups for the same variable. This is called the between, independent, or group *t*-test. The other *t*-test is when you are comparing the means of two variables for one group of participants. This is called a within, dependent, or repeated measures *t*-test.

6.3.1 Boxplots

Before conducting *t*-tests the data should be explored. One of the most useful techniques is a boxplot (Wright, 2002). Figure 6.2 shows boxplots for a study on healthy lifestyles for people over 65 years old (Kelley & Abraham, 2002). Boxplots are useful for identifying outliers and also for showing where the bulk of the data lie. The dots in the boxplot are outliers. These boxplots show that there are a few outliers for both groups. These correspond with people who feel they have unhealthy lifestyles. The bulk of the data, approximately 50 per cent, lies within the box. The box is higher for the intervention group, suggesting that the intervention has a positive impact. Statistical tests are used to see if a difference this size is likely to occur by chance. In most cases the *t*-test is the appropriate test in this circumstance.

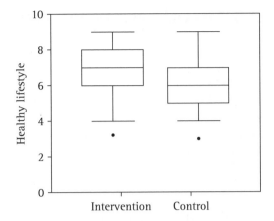

Figure 6.2 Boxplots for people's self-reports of how healthy their lifestyle is. The intervention group is higher than the control group

6.3.2 *t*-tests in practice

The most common statistical test for seeing if the means of two groups differ is the between subjects, or independent, *t*-test. For the data shown in Figure 6.2, the mean for the intervention group is 6.71 and for the control group is 6.15. The difference is 0.56, with a confidence interval from 0.16 to 0.96. As this does not overlap with zero the null hypothesis that the intervention had no effect can be rejected. Traditionally researchers conduct a *t*-test and get the following: $t(187) = 2.77$, $p = 0.01$. From these we are able to reject the null hypothesis and claim that the intervention improves the reported healthy lifestyle. It is best to report $p =$ the value the computer prints rather than $p <$ than some arbitrary convention (Wright, 2003). The exception is where the computer reports that p is 0.000. In these cases you should write $p < 0.001$.

Concentrating just on the intervention group, Kelley and Abraham (2002) were interested in changes over time. They measured ratings of healthy lifestyle before and after the intervention had been implemented. Because this is the same group measured at two points in time the dependent *t*-test was used. The *t* value calculated was 2.34 with 95 df and a *p* value of 0.02, reported as $t(95) = 2.34$, $p = 0.02$. This is a statistically significant difference. As predicted, there was an increase in healthy lifestyle.

6.3.3 **Alternatives to the *t*-tests**

Both *t*-tests make assumptions about the distributions of the variables, namely that they are normally distributed. They are also heavily influenced by extreme points. More resistant alternatives exist. The Mann-Whitney U and Wilcoxon tests are alternatives to the between (independent) and within (dependent) subject *t*-tests, respectively. Both are more resistant to the effects of extreme points and are included in most mainstream statistical packages. More modern alternatives include those based on trimmed means and M-estimators (see Wilcox, 2001).

6.3.4 **ANOVA**

The *t*-tests are appropriate when there are two groups or two variables. When you have more than two groups or two variables the most common procedure is analysis of variance (ANOVA).

In its simplest form, ANOVA has one independent variable and one dependent variable. It tells us whether the group means differ from each other and if the differences are large enough to be unlikely to occur by chance. ANOVA compares whether the variation *between* the groups is greater than *within* the groups. The procedure produces an *F* ratio. The larger the *F* value the larger the differences among groups. If there is a large difference in the total variation among the groups compared to the variation within the groups, there will be a statistically significant difference in the means. The mechanics of conducting ANOVAs can be found in most introductory statistics books.

ANOVA does not tell us where the differences lie. Post hoc analyses, sometimes called contrasts, are needed for this. As with the correlations, when multiple comparisons are made it is important to realize that you increase the likelihood of errantly either rejecting or failing to reject hypotheses. Most statistical packages allow appropriate adjustments to be made. These techniques should be used to complement exploring the data graphically, through boxplots and also graphing confidence intervals. For more details on contrasts see Rosenthal and Rosnow (1985).

ANOVA in practice

Lee (1999) investigated the health habits and psychological wellbeing among young, middle-aged, and older Australian women. For one of the measures (GHQ-12) the *F* ratio calculated was 31.68 with df (2, 494) and a p value of $p < 0.001$, reported as $(F(2, 494) = 31.68, p < 0.001)$. There was a significant difference between the groups on the GHQ-12 scores. Figure 6.3 shows the means and 95 per cent confidence intervals. Most statistical packages can produce graphs like this one. This graph shows that the youngest group has the highest ratings, followed by the middle-aged group, and then the oldest group. The next step is comparing the means among each of the three pairs of conditions (young versus middle, young versus older, middle versus older). A common method that takes into account the three tests being conducted is Student Newman-Keuls post hoc analysis. Lee did this analysis and it showed that the younger women had significantly higher scores than the middle-aged women who in turn had significantly higher scores than the older women.

Alternatives

ANOVAs are greatly influenced by extreme data points. There are two general classes of alternatives. The first class is based on ranking the variables and is traditionally the more common. This includes Friedman's and Jonkheere's tests. The second class, covered in Wilcox (2001), either focuses on the bulk of the data, ignoring extreme points (trimming the data), or uses complex functions that lessen the impact of extreme points (for example, M-estimators). The traditional procedures are available in packages like SPSS. The modern alternatives are becoming increasingly used, but are not yet widely available.

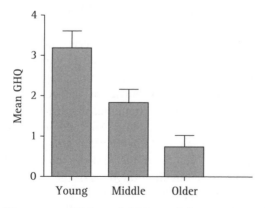

Figure 6.3 The mean GHQ and 95% confidence intervals for young participants (18–22 years old), middle-aged participants (45–49 years old) and older participants (70–74 years old). The data are from Lee (1999, Table 3)

Extensions

The basic ANOVA framework can be extended to more complex designs. It can be used when you have several between-subjects and within-subject variables. This is called a MANOVA, multivariate analysis of variance (see Field, 2000, for an introduction). The basic ANOVA can also be used when you want to statistically remove variation of one variable from the analysis. For example, this occurs when people say there was a difference between the groups even after controlling for social class. This is called an ANCOVA, which is short for analysis of covariance. Making causal inference from these designs can be difficult (Rutherford, 2000).

6.4 Associations for Categorical Data

The tests described so far assume that the individual variables vary along a continuum. However, often the data are categorical: a person gets ill or does not get ill, they smoke or do not smoke, etc. In this section we describe some of the most common statistics for these situations. We focus on measures of effect size. Greenlaugh (1997) suggests odds ratio, relative risk reduction, absolute risk reduction, and the number needed to treat, as ways for measuring the association. The two most frequently used are odds ratio and relative risk. These will be described here in more detail.

6.4.1 Odds ratio

Table 6.4 shows data from a hypothetical intervention study. People were either in an intervention condition or a control condition. The outcome measure was whether the person attended their appointment at an outpatient clinic. The odds ratio is based on the odds. The odds is the frequency of one outcome, here attending, divided by the frequency of all other outcomes, here not attending. The odds of turning up to the appointment if you are in the intervention group is $125/32 = 3.91$. The odds of turning up if you are in the control group is $98/62 = 1.58$. The odds ratio is calculated by dividing the odds of the intervention group by those in the control group, $3.91/1.58 = 2.47$. So the odds of turning up for an out-patient appointment are 2.47 higher if you are in the intervention group.

Consider another example. Bosma et al. (1997) investigated the association of psycho-social characteristics at work and coronary heart disease

Table 6.4 Attendance at an out-patient clinic

	Condition		Total
	Control	Intervention	
Did not attend	62	32	94
Did attend	98	125	223
Total	170	157	317

Table 6.5 The proportion and odds of having a coronary event, broken down by gender and job control

Job control	Respondents' gender					
	Men			Women		
	Data	Proportion (%)	Odds	Data	Proportion (%)	Odds
High	100 of 1000	10.0	0.111	20 of 200	10.0	0.111
Low	100 of 600	16.7	0.2	250 of 1500	16.7	0.2
Total	200 of 1600	12.5	0.143	270 of 1700	15.9	0.189

Data based on Bosma et al. (1977) showing that the lower the job control, the greater the risk of having a coronary event. The data have been created to provide a general gist of Bosma et al.'s findings, but also so that they are round numbers and to show that a gender difference appears unless job control is taken into account.

among civil servants. Table 6.5 gives data that we have created based on their findings (their Tables 2 and 3, rounding numbers to ease the arithmetic, etc.). This gives the number of men and women on two levels of 'job control' and whether they had a coronary event.

The first thing to note from the table is that having a coronary event (for example, a heart attack) is fairly common, around 10–15 per cent. Next, there is a gender difference: 12.5 per cent of men had a coronary event and 15.9 per cent of women did. Translated into odds, the odds of a man having a coronary event is $200/1400 = 0.143$ and the odds of a woman having a coronary event is $270/1430 = 0.189$. The odds ratio is: $0.189/0.143 = 1.32$. You should also report the confidence interval for the odds ratio. It is reported in many statistical packages. So you should say that the odds of having a coronary event are 1.32 times higher for women than for men with a 95 per cent confidence interval from 1.09 to 1.61.

The null hypothesis is that the odds of a coronary event are the same for men and women, which mean the odds ratio should be 1. Because the confidence interval does not overlap with 1 the null hypothesis can be rejected. A closer examination of the table shows that controlling for job control, the proportions and odds of having a coronary event are the same for men and women.

Looking at the impact of job control on having a coronary event, it is clear that low job control is associated with having coronary events. The odds for people with low job control are about twice as large as for people with high job control. The odds ratio is 0.200/0.111 = 1.80 which has a 95 per cent confidence interval of 1.44 to 2.25. As this does not overlap with 1, the null hypothesis can be rejected.[1]

Sometimes researchers calculate the natural logarithm ('ln' button on many calculators) of the odds ratio. While the odds ratio can range from 0 to infinity, the log of the odds ratio can range from −1 to 1, with zero being the point of no association, like the correlation. For these data, the log odds ratio was 0.28 with a 95 per cent confidence interval from 0.09 to 0.48 for gender and was 0.59 with a 95 per cent confidence interval from 0.36 to 0.81 for job control. While the confidence intervals are not symmetrical around the odds ratio, they are for the log odds ratio. Consequently, you can report confidence intervals for the odds ratios as follows: 0.28±0.20 and 0.59±0.22.

6.4.2 Relative risk

While the odds ratio is based on the odds for different groups, relative risk (RR) is based on the proportions for different groups. Using the data in Table 6.4, relative risk is calculated by initially working out the proportion of people attending their appointment in the control group. This is the frequency of those attending divided by the total: for the control group: 98/170 = 0.58, for the intervention group: 125/157 = 0.80. The relative risk is the ratio of these: 0.80/0.58 = 1.38. Thus, people in the intervention are 1.38 times more likely to attend. RR can be calculated for the data in Table 6.5 also. The ratio of coronary events for people in low compared with high control jobs is 16.7 per cent/10.0 per cent which is 1.67.

The main advantage that relative risk has is that it is based on proportions, and people tend to think in proportions, not odds. The main advantage of the odds ratio is that it has better statistical properties. Relative risk, and other related statistics, can sometimes lead to misleading results. We recommend using odds ratios.[2]

6.4.3 The χ^2 test

Normally the odds ratio is used for calculating confidence intervals. The formula for 95 per cent confidence intervals for the odds ratio is complex, but it is printed by many statistical packages (see Agresti, 2002, for computational details). If the confidence interval for the odds ratio does not overlap with 1, then the null hypothesis can be rejected.

Often researchers test the hypothesis that there is no association using the χ^2 test. This is closely related to the odds ratio. The calculations for the χ^2 test are covered in introductory statistics texts (e.g., Wright, 2002).

6.4.4 Extensions

We have only described associations when there are two variables and each variable can take only one of two values. This is called a 2×2 contingency table. The procedures outlined above can be extended to situations where the variables can take on several values. Also, they can be extended to where there are several variables. These are called *log-linear models*. Sometimes there is one particular variable that you are trying to predict. *Logistic regression* can be used in these cases. In these procedures it is necessary to use odds, odds ratios, and log odds ratios, which is another reason to get used to using them with less complex procedures. Agresti's (2002) textbook provides excellent coverage of all these topics.

6.5 META-ANALYSIS

In recent years the number of meta-analyses published in health-related and psychology journals has increased. Meta-analyses are used to determine the effect of treatments, interventions or the influences of a factor. They have been described as a key component of evidence-based healthcare (Moher & Olkin, 1995). The continuing move towards evidence-based healthcare establishes the importance of meta-analysis in health research. But what is meta-analysis?

Simply put, meta-analysis is a technique that allows researchers to combine data sets from different studies and to calculate an overall effect size. The method of calculation depends on the statistics used in the original studies. Frequently used methods include odds ratios and relative risks for categorical data, and standardized differences in means and correlations for continuous data (Khan et al., 2001). Once an effect size is calculated for each study they are combined and meta-analysis methods are used to estimate the overall effect size.

There are many factors to consider when deciding whether to do a meta-analysis, and if you decide to do one, how to. We highlight some of the issues, but for more details on how to carry out a meta-analysis see Rosenthal (1991). First, you have to decide which studies to include in your meta-analysis. The studies must be similar. If the studies use different populations, designs, measurement instruments, etc., the studies cannot be sensibly combined. Similarly, the outcome measure has to be the same in all the studies. For example, it is inappropriate to look at the effect of an intervention on both exercise and healthy eating. The intervention may have had a positive effect on exercise and a negative effect on healthy eating. You should then search for studies. Be aware that many relevant studies may have been conducted which you will not be able to find. For example, non-significant results are often unpublished. This is called the *file drawer problem*. Also, it is often difficult to find papers written in languages other than English.

Once you have decided which studies to include you have to decide which effect size to use. Researchers will often use different statistical procedures and report different effect size measures. Usually these can be combined. Most measures of association for categorical variables can be turned into odds ratios; most continuous measures can be turned into correlations. We recommend using one of these measures. You also have to decide whether to conduct a fixed or random effect meta-analysis. Most published meta-analyses assume a fixed effect size, however, most methodologists argue that the random effect model is more often appropriate (see Field, 2003, for details).

6.5.1 Meta-analysis in practice

Petrosino et al. (2002) reviewed the efficacy of an intervention aimed at preventing crime in juveniles. The intervention, where juveniles see prison first hand, was supposed to scare the juveniles into going straight. The 'Scared Straight' programme had been hailed as a great success in television shows. However, research using proper scientific methods had mixed findings. Petrosino et al. used a random-effects meta-analysis to find out how effective 'Scared Straight' was.

They calculated the odds ratio of offending in the intervention and control groups for seven studies. The results of meta-analyses are typically reported in tables that describe the individual studies and specify the respective effect sizes (see Table 6.6). In this meta-analysis the overall

Table 6.6 A summary of seven studies on the effectiveness of 'Scared Straight'

	Treatment	Control	Odds ratio	95% CI
Finckenhauer (1982)	19 of 48	4 of 35	5.45	(1.65, 18.02)
GERP & DC (1979)	16 of 94	8 of 67	1.51	(0.61, 3.77)
Lewis (1983)	43 of 53	37 of 55	2.09	(0.86, 5.09)
Michigan DOC (1987)	12 of 28	5 of 30	3.75	(1.11, 12.67)
Orchowsky (1981)	16 of 39	16 of 41	1.09	(0.44, 2.66)
Vreeland (1981)	14 of 39	11 of 40	1.48	(0.57, 3.83)
Yarborough (1979)	27 of 137	17 of 90	1.05	(0.54, 2.07)
Total	147 of 436	98 of 358	1.72	(1.13, 2.62)

The data refer to the number of juveniles who offended during the time period looked at in the individual study. The total has been calculated using random effects meta-analysis. *Source*: Data are from Petrosino et al. (2002).

odds of reoffending are 1.72 higher for the people 'Scared Straight' than for the control groups. This finding is important because it shows that a popular programme, used in several countries (including the UK) could be creating, rather than reducing, crime!

6.6 CORE COMPETENCES

The British Psychological Society stage two qualification in health psychology specifies that: 'health psychologists must be independent, competent researchers capable of designing, undertaking, and interpreting psychological research' and notes that 'this may involve applying and/or developing and modifying existing models or theories, methods, and assessment instruments'. This chapter has addressed four of the core components of competence included in Unit 2.4 of the BPS stage 2 qualification in health psychology:

Unit 2.4 Analyse and evaluate psychological research data
2.4a Analyse data as specified by research protocols
2.4b Interpret the results of the data analysis
2.4c Evaluate research findings and make recommendations based on research findings
2.4d Write up and report research methods and findings.

Section 6.1 examined the application of statistical analysis to data and its appropriateness while Sections 6.2–6.5 described some of the popular statistical procedures that are regularly employed in health psychology and how they are reported and written up. You should now be comfortable in deciding which statistical test is appropriate for your data and be confident in analysing and reporting the results. You should be able to identify if a meaningful statistical test has been applied in published studies and understand the results and their implication to healthcare practice. You should also feel more comfortable consulting statistical textbooks to answer detailed questions about analysis.

'Every student of the art of data analysis . . .' begins the classic textbook by Mosteller and Tukey (1977, p. 1). This quote emphasizes that data analysis is not about following some algorithm like a mindless automaton (though it may sometimes seems that way during lectures!). Data analysis is an art. It is the art of communicating your results in a compact, comprehensible, and persuasive way. Like other arts, there are important rules to follow and techniques to help you. Here we have described some of these. We encourage readers to use these techniques, to learn others, but most important, we encourage readers to conduct meaningful and thoughtful data analysis.

Meticulous planning is the key to the success of any research project. The initial stages of developing a research project require careful consideration of appropriate experimental design and potential methods of analysis. At this point it may be necessary to consult other researchers and statisticians for guidance and feedback (see component 2.4a, guideline 1, 'Seek comment from relevant others on the appropriateness of planned analysis').

When the project has been undertaken and the data have been collected, it is essential that time is taken to conduct the analysis. Often the aim of health psychology research is to improve the healthcare of people by changing clinical practice. This aim places considerable responsibility on the researcher to ensure that the data analyses are thorough and accurately conducted with any limitations acknowledged (component 2.4a, guideline 2, 'Accurately use the analytical methods specified in research designs' and guideline 3 'Identify and use techniques to check the accuracy of the output of the analysis'). In addition, in order to understand any applied implications the researcher must 'consider the generalisability of conclusions drawn from research in relation to the limits of sampling, measurement, data collection and analysis' (component 2.4c, guideline 1).

When the researcher is satisfied with their analyses, verification of the analyses and feedback on the results should be sought from statisticians and colleagues working in the field and revisions and reanalysis should be conducted in the light of any feedback (component 2.4a, guideline 5, 'Make necessary revisions in the analysis in response to feedback').

When the researcher is satisfied with the accuracy of the analyses, the next step is to interpret the results in relation to the research aims and the theoretical frameworks applied (component 2.4b, guideline 1, 'follow accepted interpretative techniques and interpret data within relevant theoretical frameworks'). Health psychologists work alongside different professionals whose understanding of research methodology vary and it is important for researchers to pitch the interpretation of their results at a level that their target audience will understand (component 2.4b, guideline 2, 'link interpretations to data analysis techniques in a comprehensible manner appropriate to the recipient audience').

Two issues are central to the translation of research findings into health-care practice. First, the appropriateness of the findings to specific populations and settings. However, even convincing results may not affect practice if the implementation is too costly or impractical (component 2.4c, guideline 2, 'consider the relevance of particular findings to specified populations or settings for which they could potentially have relevance' and guideline 3, 'consider the effects of resource limitations and established practices on the implementation of research-based recommendations in healthcare practice and organisations, generally'). Second dissemination of research findings must be timely, clear and appropriate to ensure the target audience is reached (component 2.4c, guideline 4 'inform relevant others of the results of the research and its implications within an appropriate time frame' and guideline 5, 'develop and justify recommendations for practice and future research based on present results and their interpretations' as well as component 2.f, guideline 3, 'Inform relevant others when new research or developments may or will affect current psychological practices').

NOTES

1 The size of the effect in the real data is smaller than this. The odds ratios for different measures were about 1.50 with people with low job control more likely to have a coronary event.

2 There is a simple relationship between the odds ratio and relative risk, so it is easy to change one into the other. Let $pr1$ be the proportion for one group and $pr2$ be the proportion for the other group. Then $OR = RR((1 - pr2)/(1 - pr1))$ and $RR = OR((1 - pr1)/(1 - pr2))$.

REFERENCES

Abraham, S.C.S., Clift, S. & Grabowski, P. (1999). Cognitive predictors of adherence to malaria prophylaxis regimens on return from a malarious region: a prospective study. *Social Science and Medicine* 48, 1641–54.

Agresti, A. (2002). *Categorical Data Analysis* (2nd edn). Hoboken, NJ: John Wiley & Sons.

Anscombe, F.J. (1973). Graphs in statistical analysis, *The American Statistician* 27, 17–21.

Bosma, H., Marmot, M., Hemingway, H., Nicholson, A.C., Brunner, E. & Stansfeld, S. (1997). Low job control and risk of coronary heart disease in Whitehall II (prospective cohort study). *British Medical Journal* 314, 558–65.

Cohen, J. (1988). *Statistical Power Analysis for the Behavioral Sciences* (2nd edn). Hillsdale, NJ: Erlbaum.

Field, A.P. (2000). *Discovering Statistics Using SPSS for Windows: Advanced Techniques for the Beginner.* London: Sage Publications.

Field, A.P. (2003). The problems in using fixed-effects models of meta-analysis on real-world data. *Understanding Statistics* 2, 77–96.

Greenlaugh, T. (1997). How to read a paper: Statistics for the non-statistician. I: Different types of data need different statistical tests. *British Medical Journal* 315, 364–66.

Hoaglin, D.C., Mosteller, F., & Tukey, J.W. (1983). *Understanding Robust and Exploratory Data Analysis.* New York: John Wiley & Sons.

Kelley, K., & Abraham, S.C.S. (2002). Unpublished data.

Khan, K.S., ter Riet, G., Glanville, J., Sowden, A.J. & Kleijnen, J. (2001). Conducting the review. In *Undertaking Systematic Reviews of Research on Effectiveness. CRD's Guidance for those Carrying Out or Commissioning Reviews.* CRD Report No. 4 (2nd edn).

Lee, C. (1999). Health habits and psychological well-being among young, middle-aged and older Australian women. *British Journal of Health Psychology* 4, 301–14.

Moher, D. & Olkin, I. (1995). Meta-analysis in randomised controlled trials: A concern for standards. *Journal of the American Medical Association* 274, 1962–4.

Mosteller, F. & Tukey, J.W. (1977). *Data Analysis and Regression: A Second Course in Statistics.* London: Addison-Wesley Publishing Company.

Munro, B.H. & Page, E.P. (1993). *Statistical Methods for Health Care Research* (2nd edn). Philadelphia: J.B. Lippencott Company.

Murphy, P., Prewitt, E., Boté, E., West, B. & Iber, F. (2001) Internal locus of control and social support associated with some dietary changes by elderly participants in a diet intervention trial. *Journal of American Dietetic Association* 101, 203–8.

Petrosino, A., Turpin-Petrosino, C., & Buehler, J. (2002). 'Scared Straight' and other juvenile awareness programs for preventing juvenile delinquency (Cochrane Review). *The Cochrane Library*, 4. Oxford: Update Library. See http://www.update_software.com/abstracts/ab002796.htm.

Rosenthal, R. (1991). *Meta-analytic Procedures for Social Scientists* (revised). Newbury Park, CA: Sage Publications.

Rosenthal, R. & Rosnow, R.L. (1985). *Contrast Analysis: Focused Comparisons in the Analysis of Variance.* Cambridge, MA: Cambridge University Press.

Rutherford, A. (2000). *Introducing ANOVA and ANCOVA: A GLM Approach.* London: Sage Publications.

Simon, H.A. (1954). Spurious correlation: A causal interpretation. *Journal of American Statistical Association* 49, 467–79.

Strunk, W. Jr & White, E.B. (1979). *The Elements of Style* (4th edn). Needham Heights, MA: Allyn & Bacon.

Tufte, E.R. (2001). *The Visual Display of Quantitative Information* (2nd edn). Cheshire, CT: Graphics Press.

Wainer, H. (1984). How to display data badly. *American Statistician* 38, 137–47.

Wilcox, R.R. (1998). How many discoveries have been lost by ignoring modern statistical methods? *American Psychologist* 53, 300–14.

Wilcox, R.R. (2001). *Fundamentals of Modern Statistical Methods: Substantially Improving Power and Accuracy.* New York: Springer-Verlag.

Wilkinson, L. and the Task Force on Statistical Inference, APA Board of Scientific Affairs (1999). Statistical methods in psychology journals: Guidelines and explanations. *American Psychologist* 54, 594–604.

Wright, D.B. (2002). *First Steps in Statistics.* London: Sage Publications.

Wright, D.B. (2003). Making friends with your data: Improving how statistical results are reported. *British Journal of Educational Psychology* 73, 123–36.

Wright, D.B. & Williams, S. (2004). How to produce a bad results section. *The Psychologist* 16, 646–48.

Chapter 7

DESIGNING AND CONDUCTING QUALITATIVE STUDIES

Sheila Payne

7.1 INTRODUCTION

This chapter is about designing and conducting qualitative studies. In a major international textbook, qualitative research has been defined by Denzin and Lincoln (2000, p. 3) as:

> a situated activity that locates the observer in the world. It consists of a set of interpretive, material practices that make the world visible. These practices transform the world. They turn the world into a series of representations, including field notes, interviews, conversations, photographs, and recordings, and memos to the self.

Qualitative research methods draw on a range of epistemologies (theories of knowledge) which has implications for how data are collected, how data are regarded during analysis, what claims are made for the findings and even how the different methods should be evaluated. For example, Reicher (2000) considers that there are two major types of qualitative research – experiential (which focuses on how people understand their world) and discursive (which focuses on how language is used to construct the world).

A major challenge for health psychologists is how to use methods of research which are rigorous and credible and allow access to the processes and understandings that they seek to explore. Qualitative methods can be regarded as a toolkit of methods or more fundamentally as a range of approaches which are based on different philosophical positions (epistemologies). What they are *not* is a single method which is set in opposition to a quantitative research method.

7.1.1 Purpose of the chapter

The purpose of this chapter is to enable readers to make informed choices about designing their research and selecting appropriate methods of data collection and analysis. Although the chapter is not a 'how to do it' text in relation to specific qualitative methods, an example of the procedures for one type of grounded theory analysis will be given. Readers will need to seek guidance from specialist texts and, of course, their supervisors, when undertaking qualitative studies (see also the recommended reading at the end of the chapter). This chapter will start by considering how to design a qualitative study and the methods used to generate qualitative data. It will discuss the following questions:

- How are qualitative data to be regarded?
- How are these data to be analysed?
- How is qualitative analysis presented?
- How is qualitative analysis judged?

The chapter will end by reflecting on the impact of qualitative approaches upon participants and researchers. It will conclude by indicating how the chapter contributes to the achievement of the competences required for stage 2 training in health psychology. These are listed near the end of the chapter.

My research is predominantly concerned with understanding loss (see Payne et al., 1999; Payne and Haines, 2002), and my empirical research involves people nearing the end of life and their families, and those experiencing irrevocable losses, such as those who have been bereaved. Such research raises important ethical, practical and methodological challenges and I will draw upon my own and others' research to illustrate some of the dilemmas and issues confronting qualitative researchers.

7.2 'GETTING STARTED' – DESIGNING A QUALITATIVE STUDY

Undertaking research is fun and an adventure according to Willig (2001), but all adventures should start out with careful planning to ensure survival and a successful outcome. In the following section, I will discuss the importance of planning the research by starting with a clear focus and a precise research question. I will then discuss the types of research designs that can be described as qualitative and when it is appropriate to use qualitative methods of data collection and data analysis.

7.2.1 The importance of a 'good' research question

In my view, all good research needs to be focused on a specific topic. This is for the pragmatic reason that by focusing on specific objectives, it is more likely to be achievable in the constraints of finite resources such as time, money and energy. If the research is funded by an external body, such as a Research Council, a charity or government department, the commissioners of the research may constrain the topic by specifying what they wish to have investigated and how much money they wish to spend. If the research is part of professional and/or academic development, the constraints are more likely to relate to the time available and the requirements of the programme of study. One way in which focus is achieved is by defining an explicit research question. Focusing on a specific research question is scientifically important because the more focused the question, the more likely the answer is to be valid and useful. The wording of the research question should make it clear 'what, who and how' will be researched (see Box 7.1). Typically, research questions that seek to explore processes and/or meanings lend themselves to qualitative designs. If you are predominantly concerned with 'what, how many, or how often' questions, these lead to quantitative methods. If instead you want to ask 'why' questions, then qualitative designs may be the methods of choice.

In some methods of analysis, such as grounded theory, the research question may become more focused during the course of the study. Typically in this method, the research question may be rather broad at the outset of data collection but become more refined and specific during the process of data analysis as the researcher gains a greater understanding of the saliency of different issues in the research context. Revising the research question may also lead to more specific focus in data collection. 'Action research' was first developed by Kurt Lewin in the 1940s and refers to an approach to research based on democratic and naturalistic experimentation (Greenwood & Levin, 1998; Hart & Bond, 1995). Action research approaches tend to have three sequential stages; first, an analysis of the context leading to research questions, followed by implementation of a 'change' and finally evaluation of the change. There tends to be a cyclical process of conducting the research in which questions are addressed, changes instituted and evaluated, and further questions identified.

BOX 7.1 Examples of research questions and the types of methods that may be used to answer them

1 What evidence is there that patient involvement in planning healthcare services improves quality of life and satisfaction?
   This question could be answered by doing a systematic review of the literature.

2 How many older people from different ethnic minority groups access complementary medicine?
   This question could be answered by conducting a questionnaire or structured interview survey.

3 How many cancer patients use health information leaflets?
   This question could be answered by conducting a questionnaire or structured interview survey.

4 Is written or electronic information best for helping cancer patients making treatment choices?
   This question could be answered by conducting an experimental study such as a randomized control trial.

5 What are informal carers' experiences of respite care services in one specialist palliative care unit?
   This question could be answered by conducting qualitative interviews to elicit carers' understanding and experience using a grounded theory analysis.

6 How do counsellors conceptualize emotional support?
   This question could be answered by interpretative phenomenological analysis of interview data.

7 How do counsellors' interactions with clients invoke emotional support?
   This question could use transcripts of counselling sessions in a discourse analytic study.

8 Why is serious illness more disruptive to self-concept in some people than others?
   This question could be answered by asking participants for biographical accounts and using narrative analysis to explore relationships between illness and self-concept.

Hypotheses are typically used within a hypothetico-deductive paradigm rather than in most qualitative methods. Silverman (1993) has argued that there is no reason why hypotheses should not be used to guide qualitative research. He suggests that as knowledge accumulates within specific areas of qualitative research, it is appropriate to derive hypotheses about relationships between the phenomena of interest and explore these relationships in subsequent research.

7.2.2 What is 'qualitative' about qualitative research?

Some research methods textbooks present qualitative research as fundamentally different from quantitative research; others suggest that methodologies can be regarded as on a continuum. Kidder and Fine (1987) proposed a dichotomy between the use of qualitative research as referring to open-ended, inductive approaches, described as 'big Q' and the use of qualitative techniques such as asking open questions within the framework of a predominantly structured quantitatively designed study, described as 'small q'. The same method – for example, an interview may be regarded as collecting data which will be transformed through analytic procedures, such as content analysis, into numerical codes, or alternatively through a process of inductive categorization such as in grounded theory – will be labelled as textual conceptual categories. The origins of these data, in this case talk elicited in an interview context, will be the same, although the approaches of the researcher (see Section 7.3 on generating data) might be rather different in structured, semi-structured or unstructured interviews.

This chapter is concerned with 'big Q' qualitative research. This means that it will be about the collection of non-numerical data and those analytic procedures that do not start by transforming phenomena into numbers. These methods are based on a variety of epistemologies. Once again, in my view, it is not always helpful to present this debate in stereotypical terms of a dichotomy between positivism and social constructionism, for example. As Willig (2001) suggests, the term positivism tends to be regarded as a form of abuse. Instead, it is perhaps more helpful to think of realist researchers espousing a continuum of epistemological positions from those who seek an ultimate 'truth' out there in the world to those who reject notions of 'truth' and 'knowledge' altogether. The important point argued in this chapter is that there is not a single epistemological position taken by qualitative researchers, but that the research question should be compatible with the epistemological assumptions of the selected method of analysis. For example, some types of discourse analysis make the assumption that it is possible to identify ways of talking about phenomena and concepts which are available to a number of people within a social group or culture, and those discourses may be potentially available to be drawn upon by some groups but not others. In a study exploring the views of patients nearing the end of life and their health professionals about how a 'good death' was construed, patients and professionals drew on similar (being pain free) and different notions of a 'good' death, for example, suddenly (patients), in one's sleep (patients) and surrounded by family members (professionals) (Payne et al., 1996).

Research designs using mixed methods have been growing in popularity in health services research. Typically, they might involve randomized clinical trials in which standardized outcome measures such as quality of life might be used in combination with a sub-sample of participants being invited to focus group discussions or in-depth interviews. This may be a good way to determine the efficacy of a new intervention and simultaneously collect data on the perspectives of those who use or fail to use the new service or treatment. Mixed methods designs are claimed to encompass the best of both worlds by following the rigorous methods of quantitative research and still enabling the views of service users to be represented. However, qualitative methods should also be rigorous, as is argued in this chapter, and quantitative methods such as 'satisfaction' surveys may also be used to elicit the views of service users. Most mixed methods research uses qualitative research in a 'small q' way, in that the qualitative data supplements the quantitative data collected, rather than *vice versa*.

7.2.3 When to use qualitative methods

There are a number of ways in which research designs may incorporate qualitative methods. These include:

- *Before* using quantitative methods. For example, a qualitative study may be used to explore an area and identify issues that may be included in a questionnaire survey. This approach may benefit the quantitative element of the research but tends to be seen as merely preliminary work before the 'real' research begins.
- *Concurrently* with quantitative methods (mixed methods designs). For example, in a randomized control trial of different cardiac rehabilitation interventions, qualitative interviews were conducted to explore patients' understandings of their heart disease. The findings served to explain why there was no statistically significant difference between the interventions because patients understood their heart disease in different ways

(Bradley et al., 1999). The advantage of including a concurrent qualitative study is that the investigators were able to examine why interventions work or not. They help to account for process issues which may be difficult to understand when measurement of outcomes is the major focus.

- *After* using quantitative methods. Qualitative research may follow a survey or experiment to investigate how and why participants responded in the way they did. For example, Birtwistle et al. (2002) conducted a survey of community nurses to determine the extent of their involvement in delivering bereavement support. He followed this up with semi-structured interviews to explore the reasons for the diversity of practice and what influenced this. Qualitative research has the advantage of capturing diversity and inconsistency which is difficult to achieve when categories (in content analysis) have to be mutually exclusive and are predetermined.
- *Alone.* This chapter is predominantly concerned with qualitative research as a stand-alone design. The advantage is that the methods of data collection and analysis are congruent with the epistemological position of the researcher.

7.3 Generating Qualitative Data

Having decided on a qualitative research design, the next requirement is to think about generating appropriate data. In the following section, I will cover three related issues: first, what is the nature of qualitative data; second, how may these data be accessed; and third, how will the data become transformed in the process of collecting them and preparing them for analysis? Some, but not all, qualitative researchers tend to regard themselves as participants in the generation of data. So there is no assumption made that data are neutral 'objects' waiting to be collected; instead researchers are aware of their role in the shaping and interpretation of phenomena and they usually make this explicit through reflexivity (see later in the chapter).

7.3.1 What is the nature of 'qualitative' data?

The most common types of qualitative data are:

- written text and spoken words;
- observations of behaviour including talk;
- images – recorded as dynamic events (film and video), photographs, drawings, paintings.

Qualitative researchers tend not to work with numerical data but some will use counts in their analysis, for example as evidence of the frequency of a phenomenon or code.

7.3.2 Accessing these data

Elicited talk

The most common way to access data for analysis is to elicit talk via interviews, focus groups and group discussions. Interviews vary in the extent to which they are controlled by the researcher's agenda. In structured interviews, the researcher asks closed questions requiring yes/no answers, or provides predetermined answers which respondents are invited to endorse or reject. The interview schedule is prepared much like a questionnaire and interviewers are often carefully trained to ensure consistency in their style of asking and responding to questions. This approach to interviewing is unsuitable for qualitative analysis. Semi-structured interview formats predefine to some extent the research agenda but enable respondents some freedom to present a range of views and offer new insights. Interview schedules may be loosely specified, for example as a list of topics to be covered. Unstructured interviews are open-ended and typically invite participants to talk about a topic or tell a story with minimal prompts. Interviewers will need training in skills which encourage respondents to feel comfortable, relaxed and able to talk freely. They need to learn how to explore topics using probes to elicit full accounts (specific advice on interview techniques for qualitative research may be obtained from Kvale, 1996; Payne, 1999). Research interviews may be conducted in person or via the telephone and are usually dyadic interactions. While telephone interviews may be more cost effective, they are likely to be most suitable for short structured interviews, which are likely to yield less extensive or 'rich' data and because it is more difficult to establish a rapport with the respondent they may not be suitable for some sensitive topics. They may exclude certain people such as those with hearing problems or those without access to private telephones.

It is also possible to elicit talk from groups of people using focus groups and group interviews. In my view, they are not the same thing. Group interviews are rather like other types of interviews in that the researcher directs the questioning and responses are made to the interviewer. In focus groups, the purpose is to encourage interaction between the participants so that a range of views may be elicited and discussion is generated. Decisions must be made at the outset whether focus group participants should be homogeneous or heterogeneous. This is likely to relate to the research question and topic area. For example, in some cultures women may feel uncomfortable discussing sexual health in mixed gender groups. Asking nursing home care assistants to discuss working practices in the presence of their managers may result in little data because of pre-existing power relationships. Focus groups are generally run by a facilitator, whose role is to introduce topics, encourage participation and address respondent comfort and safety issues, while an observer has the role of recording the nature and type of participation by group members. The number of participants varies from 5–12 depending upon the topic and group. It is a balance between the desire to have a range of views represented and the difficulties of managing a large group, and making sense of the resultant audio-recording. More detailed information about conducting focus groups is available from Hennink and Diamond (1999).

Naturally occurring (spontaneous) talk

Spontaneous talk is widely available in society and some qualitative research (e.g., conversation analysis) is concerned with public talk such as from broadcast media like television or political speeches (see Potter, 1997). Interactions that occur when people occupy specific institutional roles (e.g., doctors and patients) have been recorded, and so have private conversations, but this raises ethical concerns.

Written text

It is possible to collect public documents (e.g., patient information leaflets, government reports), public media (e.g., newspapers, magazines), or private documents (e.g., diaries, essays, biographies), which may be elicited or spontaneous.

Field notes of observations

Researchers may observe social interaction and their written records are described as field notes. Ethnography is an approach to data collection rarely used in health psychology but much more common in other social science disciplines, in which observation forms a key part of data gathering (e.g., Hammersley, 1992). Ethnography has been defined as 'that form of inquiry and writing that produces descriptions and accounts about the ways of life of the writer and those written about'. (Denzin, 1997, p. xi). Like other methods, ethnography has evolved and a number of versions are available. For example, researchers need to make choices about the extent to which they will be involved with those who are the focus of their research and this is described on a continuum from non-participant to participant observation. Observation of human interaction raises important ethical and practical issues. For example, is it ethical to conduct research within sensitive environments such as hospital intensive care units (Seymour, 2001), and to what extent are behaviour and organizational practices changed in the presence of an observer?

Images

Finally, researchers may collect elicited or spontaneous images such as drawings, photographs and paintings (e.g., hospitalized children's artwork or family photographs). Technological developments mean it is also possible to record behaviour using video and digital cameras much more unobtrusively than in the past. These images represent useful ways to gather examples of elicited and spontaneous behaviour (Heath, 1997; May et al., in press).

7.3.3 Transforming data for processing

Qualitative researchers may become overwhelmed by the large volume of data collected. It is essential to establish consistent and reliable systems to manage data, whether data is to be stored electronically or in paper form. This ensures that during analysis, data can be retrieved when required and also provides an audit trail (part of the process of establishing quality, which will be discussed later). In my view all data, even that described by researchers as 'raw' (unanalysed) data have been transformed in some way. This is necessary because both talk and behaviour are ephemeral and need to be 'captured' to permit researchers to work on them. Elicited and spontaneous talk is generally audio-recorded, while behaviours may be video-recorded or written down by the researchers in field notes (May et al., in press).

Many textbooks on research methods devote little space to considerations about transcription but, in my view, this is the first stage of the analysis and critical decisions need to be made at this point about the style of transcription to be used. It is not merely something that is delegated to a secretary! O'Connell and Kowal (1995) highlight the decisions to be made about the extent of transcription to be undertaken. They define four elements:

- the *verbal* – the words (which are always included);
- the *prosodic* – the volume, pitch and intonation used in speech;

- the *paralinguistic* – for example, the coughs, laughter or crying which may accompany speech;
- the *extra-linguistic* – for example, hand, eye or body movements which accompany speech.

Decisions about how speech will be transcribed are dependent upon the nature of the analysis to be conducted. For example, if a grounded theory analysis is planned, it is important to transcribe both the speech of the interviewer and interviewee but not usually necessary to transcribe prosodic, paralinguistic or extra-linguistic elements. Likewise, in preparing text for interpretative phenomenological analysis (IPA), the same conventions would be used (Smith et al., 1999). Discourse analysis, however, requires more complete and detailed transcriptions because the researcher is often concerned with not only what is said but how it is said. Perhaps the most detailed, and therefore time consuming, transcription procedures are necessary for conversation analysis where specific and precise notation systems are available (see Sacks et al., 1974; Atkinson and Heritage, 1984; Psarthas and Anderson, 1990; Psarthas, 1995). In designing a qualitative study, an estimation of the cost and time needed to complete transcription procedures should be included.

I often suggest that novice researchers undertake at least a few transcriptions themselves because this allows them to become aware of the level of analysis required and gives an insight into the hard work involved. Even if the majority of transcriptions are done by others, it is helpful to listen to all the audio-tapes and carefully check through the transcriptions for errors and omissions. It has also been argued that researchers should conduct analysis directly from the spoken word rather than from transcriptions, because it allows access to the prosodic and paralinguistic features. For example, irony is difficult to 'capture' in written transcriptions, but the tone of voice or an accompanying giggle may indicate the intention of the speaker which is not directly evident from the words alone. There are also arguments about the use of punctuation and how the text is presented on paper. For example, Coffey and Atkinson (1996) suggested that parsing text into clauses retains more of the emotional resonance of the spoken words. This type of transcription gives the written text a poetic appearance. In conclusion, transformation of spoken language to written text should be regarded as the first stage in the interpretative process.

7.4 HOW ARE THESE DATA TO BE REGARDED?

In this section attention is directed to the status afforded to the responses of participants and the implications which are drawn from talk, and the purposes of the analysis of talk from differing perspectives. I will start by differentiating between two major conceptual approaches in qualitative methods of analysis:

- Those approaches which are concerned with inferring *meaning* from data and drawing inferences about what people think, feel and do. I will label these 'ethnographic' approaches. They include methods of analysis such as grounded theory analysis, IPA, narrative analysis and phenomenology.
- Those approaches which are concerned with how talk is *used* in social situations and that do not make inferences about how people feel or think. I will label these 'ethnomethodological' approaches. They include methods such as conversation analysis, analysis of institutional inter-action and discourse analysis.

For example, when undertaking a grounded theory analysis interview, responses are construed as evidence of what people think and feel and how they interpret their world (Strauss and Corbin, 1990; Glaser, 1992). These insights are assumed to have stability over time and are inferred as being characteristic of that individual. In comparison, the ethnomethodo-logical approach uses interview responses as evidence about how people use language to construct that particular situation at that particular time. This approach makes no assumptions about consistency of responses in other situations, no inferences about intra-psychic processes, and explains talk as representing a repertoire of ways that people have of dealing with questions in social situations, such as in an interview. In comparison, grounded theorists draw conclusions about the state of mind of individuals on the basis of their talk. They are interested in exploring the influence of previous experiences and personal understanding on the emotional and cognitive reactions displayed in talk. Thus, from this perspective, talk is seen as representing the contents of people's minds while, from an ethnomethodological stance, analysis of talk is concerned with individuals' attempts to deal with their current situation (for example in an interview). To illustrate these differences, I will use an example taken from an interview with a woman with advanced ovarian cancer (Payne, 1999):

> *Interviewer:* Can we start at the beginning of your treatment for cancer. How did you know that there was something wrong with you?
> *Interviewee:* Well, last August, I went up North, went on holiday up to Yorkshire and that was the first time. I had a job to sit down with it. I was constipated and I thought it was that. And of course, naturally, I didn't go to the doctor because I thought it was because I was constipated that it was pressing on it. Anyway, this went on. And I haven't been able to sit down

for quite a while, you know. If I have been sitting down in the evening, I have sat on the floor with my hands resting on the chair. Well, sitting on the side, you know, and if I have sat anywhere I have sat on my side and then, oh, when would it be about, well it was before Easter because I went to the doctor before Easter, didn't I?

Interviewer: Um.

Interviewee: And I told him, you know, about this that I was constipated and that. He gave me some Isogel and he said try it for a month.

An ethnographic approach to this interview, such as grounded theory analysis, might identify segments of text which could be labelled as categories. For example, it can be observed that the patient refers to a number of dates/times which locate her story in a temporal sequence, and this could generate a category called 'Significance of timing' and further instances of this category could be searched for in subsequent interviews. Her description of the symptoms of constipation is taken to represent a 'real' account of her experiences and her feelings *at the time* before diagnosis of cancer.

An alternative ethnomethodological approach to this interview might focus on the interactional aspects of the situation. A caveat is that interviews are not often used in ethnomethodological research, and that the transcription style in this example is inappropriate, because a much more detailed transcription indicating overlapping speech and other performance details would be required. However, returning to this example, the researcher sets the context with the key words 'beginning' 'cancer' and 'know'. This interview draws on a taken-for-granted understanding about 'medical' interviews such as the need to provide a history located in time and place, the description of (physical) symptoms and the justification of actions and non-actions. The analysis might identify how this is achieved in the interaction. For example, she justifies her actions by saying 'naturally, I didn't go to the doctor because I thought it was because I was constipated'. Thus the purpose of the analysis is to identify the way talk (*what* and *how*) is *used in the interview* situation to create an account; no inferences are made about underlying motives or feelings (*why*) experienced at the time.

This chapter cannot describe all the actual analytic procedures for the different types of qualitative analysis mentioned but an example of a type of process for a grounded theory analysis is shown in Table 7.1.

Most methods of analysis are dynamic and change over time. For example, grounded theory analysis has a number of competing versions (for a concise discussion of the different versions see Willig, 2001). Each of the major types of analysis (e.g., narrative analysis and discourse analysis)

Table 7.1 Procedures in conducting a grounded theory analysis

Process	Activity	Comments
1	Collect data	Any source of textual data may be used but semi-structured interviews or observations are the most common
2	Transcribe data	Full transcriptions of interviewer and interviewee talk
3	Develop initial categories – open coding	Categories are developed from the data by open coding of the transcripts. 'Open coding' means identifying and labelling meaningful units of text, which might be a word, phrase, sentence or larger section of text
4	Saturate categories	'Saturation' means gathering further examples of meaningful units as one proceeds through the transcripts until no new examples of a particular category emerge
5	Defining categories	Once the categories have been saturated, formal definitions in terms of the properties and dimensions of each category may be generated
6	Theoretic sampling	From the categories that have emerged from the first sample of data, choose theoretically relevant samples to help test and develop categories further
7	Axial coding – the development and testing of relationships between categories	During axial coding, possible relationships between categories are noted, hypothesized and actually tested against data that is being obtained in ongoing theoretical sampling
8	Theoretical integration	A core category (or in some cases more than one main category) is identified and related to all the other subsidiary categories to determine its explanatory power and finally links with existing theory are established and developed
9	Grounding the theory	The emergent theory is grounded by returning to the data and validating it against actual segments of text. A search for deviant cases may be used to test the emergent theory
10	Filling in gaps	Finally, any missing detail is filled in by the further collection of relevant data and hypothesis derived for further testing of the new theory

Source: Adapted from Bartlett and Payne, 1997.

has many sub-types. Probably the best-known qualitative methods of analysis in health psychology are grounded theory, IPA, phenomenology, narrative analysis, discourse analysis and conversation analysis. These should be regarded as generic terms rather than as labels for a particular method, with the exception of IPA (a type of phenomenology) which is a relatively new methodological approach closely associated with Smith and his colleagues (1999). Each method has its advantages and disadvantages, its adherents and opponents, but whatever method of analysis is selected it must be congruent with the research question and the methods of data collection.

7.5 HOW IS QUALITATIVE ANALYSIS PRESENTED?

According to Clark (1997, p. 166):

> Above all this is an approach in which the use of words and the expression of language are at a premium. In appealing for more rigour and methodological accountability, we must remember that pleasure in the written word is also something to be fostered. Poorly written qualitative research can be indigestible fare. Let us therefore look to qualitative researchers for a sense of poetry and a felicity of language which, in building on the insights of the method, create for us a brighter and more perceptive understanding of the world.

The literary ability to construct an argument is needed in writing up qualitative research. Generally the presentation of results is much less formulaic than experimental reports but the methods used and the processes undertaken during the analysis need to be made explicit to readers. Coffey and Atkinson (1996) suggest some novel ways to present the analysis, such as in poetic stanzas. In my view, there are two levels of data that require explanation: the analytical interpretations of the researcher in the form of codes, themes, discourses, turn-taking sequences, rules, essence and categories (the terms used will depend upon the actual method employed), and also excerpts of data such as text, images, field notes or interview transcriptions upon which the analysis is based. Researchers should be explicit in how they have selected the supporting excerpts to defend against the criticism that they have just found a few 'juicy quotes'. Excerpts should be clearly labelled with identifiers that allow readers to know that more than a single participant has been cited in support of a claim. In writing up qualitative research, a compromise is required between providing sufficient data for readers to draw alternative conclusions and enabling them to see how the interpretations have been arrived at, and an overly long account. The methods vary somewhat in presentation style but all aim to convey the analysis in text or graphical representations rather than numerically.

7.6 How Is Qualitative Analysis Judged?

There are a number of criteria for judging the quality of qualitative research (e.g. Guba and Lincoln, 1982; Henwood and Pidgeon, 1992; Silverman, 1993; Mason, 1996; Guba and Lincoln, 1998; Elliott et al., 1999; Yardley, 2000; Willig, 2001). In addition, there are published quality assessment criteria which relate to specific methods of analysis, such as different versions of discourse analysis (Potter and Wetherall, 1987; Parker, 1994) or IPA (Smith et al., 1999). None are perfect and some have been the focus of lively debate (see Reicher, 2000). The terms and concepts used to demonstrate rigour in quantitative psychological research including reliability, validity, representativeness, generalizability and objectivity, are problematic for many forms of qualitative research. Since most qualitative research methods of analysis are concerned with interpretation of data and the researcher's role in this is explicitly acknowledged, the notion of a split between subjectivity and objectivity is not supportable. Yardley (2000) has proposed four essential qualities for judging the quality of qualitative research:

- sensitivity to context;
- commitment and rigour;
- transparency and coherence;
- impact and importance.

I am not advocating any one set of criteria as the most appropriate. What I do suggest is that researchers need to recognize that they must demonstrate the methodological rigour of their work and be clear and explicit in the claims made when research is written up or presented. A number of devices have been proposed to enable researchers to do this, such as maintaining an audit trail (Appleton, 1995) of key analytical decision-making, often in the form of a research diary or in memo writing (in grounded theory analysis), and using reflexivity to allow the researcher to acknowledge their role in the creation of the analytical account. Triangulation has also been proposed to support the claims made (Foss and Ellefsen, 2002). This may take a number of forms such as methodological triangulation, theoretical triangulation or respondent validation but it should not be regarded as a panacea. In my view, it often just generates more data rather than establishing the validity of one particular perspective. Finally, researchers using qualitative methods need to address issues of transferability. What claims can be made for the research findings?

7.7 THE IMPACT OF QUALITATIVE APPROACHES ON PARTICIPANTS AND RESEARCHERS

Engaging in some types of qualitative research, especially those which seek to elicit data such as narrative analysis cannot be regarded as a neutral endeavour for either research participants or researchers. In this section, I will briefly highlight some of the issues which should be considered in designing and conducting qualitative research. All research designs should comply with ethical principles as described by professional bodies such as the British Psychological Society's Code of Conduct (2003). There are also special considerations that qualitative researchers need to be mindful of including the degree to which data collection is invasive in the life of the participant (e.g., some types of observation), may be construed as psychologically manipulative or exploitative of people when they are at their most vulnerable (e.g., following bereavement), or are believed (inappropriately) to be therapeutic (e.g. some types of in-depth life review). As far as possible, participants should be clear about the purpose and procedures of data collection.

7.7.1 Participants

Many qualitative methods take an explicitly participatory stance in engaging people with the design and analysis, such as action research and co-operative inquiry. Likewise, methods of data collection such as semi-structured or unstructured interviewing are often regarded as intuitively appealing because people generally like to talk and be listened to. From my experience of interviewing patients in hospitals and hospices, some of them report that it is one of the few times anyone has attentively listened to their story. It provides an opportunity for their 'voice' to be heard and for them to raise issues of salience which are not necessarily part of the research agenda. People may also find these interviews or focus group discussions to be helpful because they obtain additional information and social support from interaction with other participants or the researchers.

Researchers also need to be aware of the potential disadvantages of these methods of data collection and they should acknowledge problems such as power relationships. For example, analysing in-depth interviews or diaries may be intrusive and they may violate trust when such material becomes incorporated into published documents. Participants may feel used and 'let down' by researchers who establish relationships during data collection, especially in longitudinal designs, but abruptly terminate contact at the end of a study. There are confidentiality issues when sample sizes are small or data relates to identifiable aspects of individuals. For example, in reporting narrative analyses there are dilemmas in the extent to which individual stories may be made public. Researchers may not be able to use their 'best' data for these reasons. It has been argued that consent should be repeatedly negotiated throughout the research process as it may be difficult for people to understand what they are consenting to at the outset or they may reveal more than they intended during an interview (Seymour and Ingleton, 1999). It may be helpful for researchers to foster anonymity such as by asking them to select a pseudonym and agreeing which aspects of a narrative may be changed to hide identity. There are particular problems in reporting data from health professionals in small local studies where there may be only one or two members of certain professional groups or grades (e.g., social workers or medical consultants) or when a few people hold strong and divergent views. In such cases, it might be preferable to report collective data rather than accounts from individuals.

7.7.2 Researchers

It has been noted above that reflexivity, which means an awareness of self within the process of data collection and analysis, is often regarded as an important element in demonstrating the rigour of qualitative analysis. Some analytical methods offer specific procedures such as 'bracketing' (a cognitive process of explicitly becoming aware of and setting aside ones' taken-for-granted assumptions) which aims to address bias and pre-existing assumptions. It is thought that these procedures help to minimize the researcher's perspective in the interpretation of data. Alternatively, Willig (2001, p. 141) argues that 'the role of the qualitative researcher requires an active engagement with the data, which presupposes a standpoint'. This needs to be made explicit to readers so they may judge to what extent these presuppositions frame what data have been collected and how they have been interpreted.

Finally, there are safety issues for researchers engaged in 'real world' research whether qualitative or quantitative. Kenyon and Hawker (1999) have described the issues to be considered by field workers to ensure personal safety, such as leaving contact addresses, telephoning colleagues before and after interviews, arranging safe venues and times to meet participants. While certain types of research topics are acknowledged to be 'sensitive', such as working with bereaved people, seriously ill people, children and young people, in my view any type of research may be potentially challenging if it has emotional resonance for the researcher. For example, interviewing an ill or older person may trigger personal memories for that particular researcher because the interviewee is similar to a much-loved relative. Therefore I suggest that it is good practice to build in opportunities for support and personal supervision for researchers, especially in research with potentially vulnerable groups (Payne and Westwell, 1994).

7.8 Conclusions

It has been argued that qualitative research is more than a toolkit, and represents a range of methods of analysis based on different epistemologies. Even within broad categories of analytic methods, such as grounded theory analysis, there are many different types of approach to data analysis. Analytic methods should be regarded as dynamic and flexible. By this, I mean that methods may evolve over time and be adapted to particular contexts but all changes and modifications made by researchers should be made explicit and justified in presenting the research. They should also be congruent with the epistemological stance taken. This chapter provides a guide to the issues to be considered when designing and conducting qualitative research. It provides an example of the procedures that may be used in a grounded theory analysis. Health psychologists are rising to the challenge of developing and using qualitative research in innovative and exciting ways to understand the psychological processes underpinning health and illness.

7.9 Health Psychology Components of Competences Covered in this Chapter

This chapter, on designing and conducting qualitative studies, can help readers acquire the following 12 (of 73) core components included in stage 2 core units.

Unit 2.2 Design psychological research

2.2a Identify theoretical models and research findings relevant to proposed research questions

2.2b Generate testable research questions or hypotheses

2.2c Define the resources and constraints relevant to the conduct of the research

2.2d Identify and describe methods appropriate to proposed psychological research.

Unit 2.4 Analyse and evaluate psychological research data

2.4a Analyse data as specified by research protocols.

2.4b Interpret the results of data analysis.

2.4c Evaluate research findings and make recommendations based on research findings.

2.4d Write up and report research methods and findings.

2.4e Review the research process.

Unit 2.5 Initiate and develop psychological research

2.5a Conduct research that will advance existing, models, theories, instruments and methods in health psychology

2.5b Monitor and evaluate studies in relation to agreed protocols

2.5c Clarify and evaluate the implications of research outcomes for practice.

This chapter provides guidance for health psychologists in the UK completing stage 2 training. A good working knowledge of research design is essential to health psychology practice and all health psychologists need skills in selecting an appropriate research design. A range of research designs are needed to address different research questions and no one design is inherently superior to any other. Therefore health psychologists need to be aware of the full range of possible research designs and be able to provide a rationale to their selection of any particular design. This includes being aware of the advantages and limitations of all research designs.

A critical engagement with the literature provides the starting point for all research projects (unit 2.2). There are a number of ways to undertake this activity and the extent of the literature search will be influenced by the size of the anticipated proposal, the time and resources available. Electronic database searches have transformed the work of most health psychologists, providing a rapid way to access the world literature on a given topic. However, caution should be shown in selecting key terms to prevent either a deluge of inappropriate papers or failure to secure the relevant ones. A critical perspective is needed in reviewing previous research to identify and challenge assumptions that have constrained and shaped the way previous research questions have been framed or methods of data collection selected. It may be helpful to search outside conventional health psychology journals to see how other disciplines have framed research questions and explored topics (such as in *Social Science in Medicine*). In addition, health psychology researchers need to be aware of current policy, organizational and health technology developments. This ensures that research designs address current issues taking account of contemporary health and social care policies (for example, from the statutory and charitable sectors) and researchers are abreast of new health technology. All of this might sound a long way from developing research hypotheses from psychological theory, but applied research needs to take account of the socio-political context in which research occurs (unit 2.5). For example, helping a Chinese community group to develop an intervention to reduce smoking among its members may draw on psychological theories of behaviour change and be implemented in the context of a participatory research design such as action research. In comparison, a Department of Health funded project concerned with testing an intervention designed to increase adherence to post-operative chest physiotherapy may require a randomized control trial design. Each study design will be constrained by the expectations and wishes of the key players, including the research funders, the participants, the collaborating institutions and communities (unit 2.2c).

It has been argued in the chapter that the methods of data collection are not inherently quantitative or qualitative, it is how they are transformed and dealt with that matters (unit 2.4). If textual data such as interview transcripts are converted into numbers this enables them to be analysed in the same way as other numerical data. Typically qualitative methods of analysis use textual or other forms of data (e.g., photographs, images). Health psychologists need to be well informed about the range of possible qualitative methods of data analysis to ensure that the research question is addressed appropriately (unit 2.4a). For example, if you are interested in exploring how previous caring experiences impact on current caring activities and self-concept, eliciting the narratives (stories or autobiographies) of participants may be appropriate. There are many different types of narrative analysis – some focusing on the structure and presentation of the story as a rhetorical device – others concerned with making inferences about continuity and discontinuity in lifetime patterns of behaviour. A research question concerned with exploring how autobiographies of caring are portrayed may focus on the language used and the performance aspects of storytelling. The analytic procedures need to be rigorously applied and conform to published accounts of previous research (unit 2.4a). Modifications of analytic procedures are acceptable if they are fully justified and explained in the research reports (unit 2.4d).

The quality and rigour of any research design, data collection methods and analytic procedures are not self-evident. Health psychologists need to be familiar with research evaluation criteria and be able to demonstrate how their project has complied with these requirements (units 2.4 and 2.5). Within qualitative research, there is much debate about the usefulness and meaning of terms such as reliability and validity, so it is not possible to take a formulaic approach to assessing research quality. In addition, presenting and disseminating findings in a variety of formats and styles is required to ensure that implications for improvements in practice are derived from psychological research (unit 2.5c).

REFERENCES

Appleton, J. (1995). Analysing qualitative data: addressing issues of validity and reliability. *Journal of Advanced Nursing* 22, 993–9.

Atkinson, J.M. & Heritage, J. (1984). *Structures of Social Action: Studies in Conversation Analysis*. Cambridge: Cambridge University Press.

Bartlett, D. & Payne, S. (1997). Grounded theory – its basis, rationale and procedures. In: G. McKenzie, J. Powell & R. Usher (eds), *Understanding Social Research: Perspectives on Methodology and Practice*, London: Falmer Press, 173–95.

Birtwistle, J., Payne, S., Smith, P. & Kendrick, T. (2002). The role of the district nurse in bereavement care. *Journal of Advanced Nursing*, 38(5): 467–78.

Bradley, F., Wiles, R., Kinmonth, A.-L., Mant, D. & Gantley, M. (1999). Development and evaluation of complex interventions in health services research: case study of the Southampton heart integrated care project (SHIP), *British Medical Journal* 318, 711–15.

British Psychological Society Code of Conduct (2003). http://www.bps.org.uk/about/rules5.cfm

Clark, D. (1997). What is qualitative research and what can it contribute to palliative care? *Palliative Medicine* 11, 159–66.

Coffey, A. & Atkinson, P. (1996). *Making Sense of Qualitative Data*. Thousand Oaks, CA: Sage.

Denzin, N.K. (1997). *Interpretive Ethnography*. Thousand Oaks, CA: Sage.

Denzin, N.K. & Lincoln, Y.S. (2000). *Handbook of Qualitative Research* (2nd edn). Thousand Oaks, CA: Sage.

Elliott, R., Fischer, C.T. & Rennie, D.L. (1999). Evolving guidelines for publication of qualitative research studies in psychology and related fields. *British Journal of Clinical Psychology* 38, 215–29.

Floss, C. & Ellefsen, B. (2002). The value of combining qualitative and quantitative approaches in nursing research by means of method triangulation. *Journal of Advanced Nursing* 40(2), 242–8.

Glaser, B.G. (1992). *Emergence vs Forcing: Basics of Grounded Theory Analysis*. Mill Valley, CA: Sociology Press.

Greenwood, D.J. & Levin, M. (1998). *Introduction to Action Research: Social Research for Social Change.* London: Sage.

Guba, E.G. & Lincoln, Y.S. (1982). Epistemological and methodological bases of naturalistic inquiry. *Educational Communication and Technology Journal* 30, 233–52.

Guba, E.G. & Lincoln, Y.S. (1998). Competing paradigms in qualitative research. In N.K. Denzin & Y.S. Lincoln (eds), *The Landscape of Qualitative Research Theories and Issues.* London: Sage.

Hammersley, M. (1992). *What's Wrong with Ethnography? Methodological Explorations.* London: Routledge.

Hart, E. & Bond, M. (1995). *Action Research for Health and Social Care: A Guide to Practice.* Open University Press: Buckingham.

Heath, C. (1997). The analysis of activities in face to face interaction using video. In D. Silverman (ed.), *Qualitative Research: Theory, Method and Practice.* London: Sage, 183–200.

Hennick, M. & Diamond, I. (1999). Using focus groups in social research. In A. Memon and R. Bull (eds), *Handbook of the Psychology of Interviewing,* Chichester: John Wiley, 113–44.

Henwood, K.L. & Pidgeon, N. (1992). Qualitative research and psychological theorizing. *British Journal of Psychology* 83, 97–111.

Kenyon, E. & Hawker, S. (1999). 'Once would be enough: some reflections on the issue of safety for lone researchers. *International Journal of Social Research Methodology* 2(4), 313–27.

Kidder, L.H. & Fine, M. (1987). Qualitative and quantitative methods: When stories converge. In M.M. Mark & L. Shotland (eds), *New Directions in Program Evaluation.* San Francisco, CA: Jossey-Bass.

Kvale, S. (1996). *InterViews: An Introduction to Qualitative Research Interviewing.* London: Sage.

Mason, J. (1996). *Qualitative Researching.* London: Sage.

May, J., Ellis-Hill, C. & Payne, S. (in press). The use of video research techniques on a hospital ward for older people: ethical, practical and methodological issues. *Qualitative Health Research.*

O'Connell, D.C. & Kowal, S. (1995). Basic principles of transcription. In J.A. Smith, R. Harre & L. van Langenhove (eds), *Rethinking Methods in Psychology,* London: Sage, 93–105.

Parker, I. (1994). Reflexive research and the grounding of analysis: Social psychology and the psy-complex. *Journal of Community and Applied Social Psychology* 4(4), 239–52.

Payne, S. (1999). Interview in qualitative research. In A. Memon and R. Bull (eds), *Handbook of the Psychology of Interviewing,* Chichester: John Wiley, 89–102.

Payne, S. & Haines, R. (2002). Doing our bit to ease the pain: the potential contribution of psychology to palliative care. *The Psychologist,* 15(11), 564–67.

Payne, S., Horn, S. & Relf, M. (1999). *Loss and Bereavement.* Buckingham: Open University Press.

Payne, S. & Westwell, P. (1994). Issues for researchers using qualitative methods. *Health Psychology Update,* 16, 7–9.

Payne, S.A., Langley-Evans, A. & Hillier, R. (1996). Perceptions of a 'good' death: a comparative study of the views of hospice staff and patients. *Palliative Medicine*, 10, 307–12.

Potter, J. (1997). Discourse analysis as a way of analysing naturally occurring talk. In D. Silverman (ed.), *Qualitative Research: Theory, Method and Practice*. London: Sage, 144–60.

Potter, J. & Wetherell, M. (1987). *Discourse and Social Psychology: Beyond Attitudes and Behaviour*. London: Sage.

Psarthas, G. (1995). *Conversation Analysis: The Study of Talk-in-Interaction*. Thousand Oaks, CA: Sage.

Psarthas, G. & Anderson, T. (1990). The 'practices' of transcription in conversation analysis. *Semiotica* 78, 75–99.

Reicher, S. (2000). Against methodolatry: some comments on Elliott, Fischer and Rennie. *British Journal of Clinical Psychology* 39, 1–6.

Sacks, H., Schegloff, E.A. & Jefferson, G. (1974). A simplist systematics for the organization of turn-taking for conversation. *Language* 50, 696–735.

Seymour, J. (2001). *Critical Moments: Death and Dying in Intensive Care*. Buckingham: Open University Press.

Seymour, J. & Ingleton, C. (1999). Ethical issues in research at the end of life: two examples. *International Journal of Palliative Nursing*, 5(2), 65–74.

Silverman, D. (1993). *Interpreting Qualitative Data*. London: Sage.

Smith, J.A., Jarman, M. & Osborn, M. (1999). Doing interpretative phenomenological analysis. In M. Murray & K. Chamberlain (eds), *Qualitative Health Psychology Theories and Methods*. London: Sage, 218–40.

Strauss, A. and Corbin, J. (1990). *Basics of Qualitative Research: Grounded Theory Procedures and Techniques* Newbury Park, CA: Sage.

Willig, C. (2001). *Introducing Qualitative Research in Psychology*. Buckingham: Open University Press.

Yardley, L. (2000). Dilemmas in qualitative health research. *Psychology and Health* 15(2), 215–28.

SELECTED FURTHER READING

Denzin, N.K. & Lincoln, Y.S. (2000). *Handbook of Qualitative Research* (2nd edn). Thousand Oaks, CA: Sage. A major international textbook and resource.

Mason, J. (1996). *Qualitative Researching*. London: Sage. An excellent starting point for new researchers with guidance about addressing the difficult questions underpinning qualitative research methods.

Murray, M. & Chamberlain, K. (eds) (1999). *Qualitative Health Psychology Theories and Methods*. London: Sage. An edited collection of chapters by qualitative researchers who are health psychologists.

Silverman, D. (2000). *Doing Qualitative Research*. London, Sage. An easily accessible and practical book.

Willig, C. (2001). *Introducing Qualitative Research in Psychology*. Buckingham: Open University Press. An excellent introduction to a selection of methods of analysis commonly used in health psychology.

Chapter 8

PLANNING AND CONDUCTING SYSTEMATIC REVIEWS

Mark Petticrew and Simon Gilbody

Psychology researchers and practitioners are besieged by information. To take just one health behaviour as an example, up to 1,000 articles on smoking are added every year to the electronic database Psychlit, and another 6,000 to the medical database Medline. In many areas it is simply impossible to keep on top of 'the literature', yet hidden within that haystack of information may be several studies with important messages for practice or policy, obscured by the many irrelevant or flawed studies.

The traditional way of dealing with such information overload is to rely less on single primary studies, and more on literature reviews (including journal review articles and chapters in textbooks). These can help with the task of organizing and sifting the available evidence. Psychologists will be familiar with the traditional literature reviews, but a different sort of review, the *systematic literature review* can also be used as a method of scientifically testing hypotheses. This chapter gives an introduction to the main stages in carrying out a systematic literature review, including defining the review question, locating and selecting the studies, appraising and synthesizing them (by means of a meta-analysis if appropriate), and finally writing up the completed review.

8.1 BACKGROUND: THE UNCERTAIN NATURE OF RESEARCH

The problem with relying on research to tell us what to do is that single studies are rarely definitive, and are often inconsistent. It has not escaped the notice of the public that researchers tell them first that fast food and junk food are bad for their health (and teeth), while other researchers tell them that pizza and chocolate are good for them; or one set of researchers may tell them that the best way to deal with delinquents is to give them the 'short, sharp shock' of a spell in prison, while another lot suggest that the best way to deal with them is not to incarcerate them at all. Are both groups right? Is it possible that one group of researchers got it right, and the other wrong? Or are both right to some degree?

These are reasonable questions, and it is a fair criticism of scientific research that it is often difficult to know which study to believe. The traditional scientific approach to this problem is to carry out a literature review – often conducted by an expert in the field. We now know, however, that this traditional method of reviewing literature can be very biased. When we read such 'traditional' reviews we are often left unsure as to whether we are really reading an objective summary of the research evidence, or are reading about a selection of studies which have been assembled to suit the author's argument. Such reviews are sometimes disparagingly referred to as 'file-drawer' reviews – that is, they only include whatever the author happened to have in the file drawer.

There are also many other sources of bias in traditional literature reviews: one of the more notorious biases is introduced by the reviewer receiving funding from some organization (such as a pharmaceutical company) which has a vested interest in the results of the review. For example, in the medical field it has been shown that reviews of the effectiveness of drugs are more likely to reach positive conclusions if the authors are funded by or employed by drug companies (Lexchin et al., 2003). This is important because biased reviews can be harmful. They do not merely lead academics astray, but can also lead to treatments or other interventions being recommended which are not effective, or even harmful. The other real possibility is that people who could benefit from effective interventions do not receive them.

8.1.1 The need to assess the included studies

As suggested above, biased literature reviews may exclude relevant studies. However, even if we could be assured that the reviewer had identified all the relevant studies, we would want to be sure that the studies themselves were methodologically sound, and, because many studies are likely to be flawed to some extent, we want the reviewer to take this fact into account when summarizing them. Ideally, the studies which are most valid should contribute most to the conclusions of the review, while those which are least sound should contribute least. The assessment of methodological soundness (often referred to as 'critical appraisal') is an important part of a systematic literature review, and is discussed in more detail below.

Another problem with much primary research is that many of the studies of interest are small, and if the effects that they are also trying to detect are small, then there is a high risk of Type II error (a 'false negative' result). That is, the null hypothesis may be falsely accepted, simply because the study did not have the statistical power to detect the effect in question. Certain types of systematic reviews provide a solution to this problem, by using the statistical technique of meta-analysis to pool the results of two or more quantitative studies. The resulting increase in statistical power allows small effects to be detected reliably, even when the individual studies in the meta-analysis have reported statistically non-significant results (simple meta-analytic methods are described later in this chapter). Even where meta-analysis is not possible, systematic reviews are still valuable in helping to identify consistent patterns of findings among the primary studies. For example, if you read one small study that suggests that depression may be a risk factor for coronary heart disease in men, then you may not be entirely convinced that there is a real association; but if you find and review a number of studies carried out in different countries which show such an association, and on closer investigation find that the relationship is confirmed by large, methodologically rigorous studies, then you may be more confident that the association is a real one.

As the previous example implies, systematic reviews can be valuable for exploring questions about causation (that is, whether a particular psychological variable or factor is causally associated with another variable or event), as well as a means of determining the effectiveness of interventions.

8.2 DOING THE REVIEW

There are five main stages to conducting a systematic literature review. The following main tasks are discussed in this section:

- setting the review question;
- setting the inclusion and exclusion criteria for the review;
- planning the literature search;
- selecting and critically appraising the included studies;
- synthesising the studies.

8.2.1 Decide on the review question, and decide on your inclusion/exclusion criteria

A systematic review, like any piece of research, needs to start with a clearly specified review question. You can refine the question by thinking of (and talking to) the sorts of people you intend to read and/or use your review, to find out what their needs are. You can also refine it by reading some existing reviews, and consulting with experts in the area. A brief 'scoping' review may also be useful if you have time and resources. This involves a small-scale search of the literature to determine what sorts of studies have been carried out to date, where they are published and what sorts of outcomes they have assessed. This helps give you a feel for the nature and the scale of the review ahead of you, and it is acceptable to refine the review question in the light of what you have learned from this scoping exercise.

It also makes sense not to do a systematic review which has already been done before (unless you feel that previous systematic reviews were themselves significantly biased in some way). For that reason it is important to start any new review by searching for existing systematic reviews, to avoid duplication. If you identify an existing good quality review, then it may make sense to update it (if the authors are not already doing so) – that is, by including new studies completed since the review was completed. If you feel the review missed a significant proportion of the relevant literature, or was flawed in other ways, it may be appropriate to carry out a new, more rigorous systematic review.

Setting your inclusion/exclusion criteria: Deciding what types of studies to include

When you have decided on your review question, it should be easy to work out what sorts of studies you need to answer it. If the question is about effectiveness (such as, 'Do psychological interventions for preventing smoking really work?', or 'Are psychological interventions for drink-drivers effective?') then the review should seek to include randomized controlled trials (RCTs), as these represent the 'gold standard' study design for answering questions about effectiveness. If there are no RCTs, non-randomized controlled trials (that is, prospective studies with a control group) should be included. There will often be no controlled studies, and in that case it can be helpful to include before-and-after studies (sometimes called prospective cohort studies, or observational studies). These involve following a group of individuals before and after they receive some treatment or intervention, and assessing how the heath condition or behaviour has changed. These studies are more susceptible to bias than studies with control groups so their results should be treated with caution.

It may be that the review is not being carried out to assess the effectiveness of an intervention at all, but instead is asking a question about the causal association between some risk factor and some health or behavioural or psychological outcome. Examples of aetiological questions like this include, 'does Type A behaviour cause coronary heart disease?' 'Does having homosexual as opposed to heterosexual parents have an effect on the emotional wellbeing and sexual orientation of the child?' To answer such questions about causes and effects one usually needs to identify and review large observational studies, such as cohort and case-control studies.

Some research questions concern peoples' experiences, and other study designs may be more appropriate for this purpose. For example, qualitative studies are of relevance to researchers wanting to understand the process of implementing an intervention, what can go wrong, and what the unexpected adverse effects might be when an intervention is rolled out to a larger population. Qualitative research can also be systematically reviewed, though the approach to critical appraisal and synthesis of the included studies will be different to that used with quantitative studies (Popay et al., 1998). For example, the checklists which are used to assess quantitative studies cannot be applied to qualitative studies, and the means of synthesizing the findings of quantitative studies are also generally different. For example, in reviews of quantitative studies, statistical synthesis (meta-analysis) may be possible, but this approach is clearly not applicable to purely qualitative information. Instead, the systematic review of qualitative studies may involve identifying main themes within the studies, and comparing and contrasting those themes across the different studies. However, there are no standard approaches to the synthesis of qualitative research, though meta-ethnography is increasingly widely used. In this approach, the synthesis involves exploring the relationships and differences between the study findings, and exploring the extent to which they reflect common, higher order themes (Britten et al., 2002; Noblit & Hare, 1988).

In some systematic reviews, particularly those carried out by healthcare researchers, there is often some reference made to a 'hierarchy of evidence':

1 systematic reviews and meta-analyses
2 randomized controlled trials with definitive results
3 randomized controlled trials with non-definitive results
4 cohort studies

5 case-control studies
6 cross-sectional surveys
7 case reports.

This is simply a list range of study designs ranked in order of decreasing internal validity (bias). This list was developed initially to help decision-makers decide what sorts of studies they should prioritize when answering clinical questions, but it has been subsequently adopted more widely. However, the use of the hierarchy of evidence is contentious outside of clinical settings, and its purpose is often misunderstood. In particular, the fact that it only applies to studies of effectiveness is often overlooked; that is, it is not intended to be an absolute, fixed hierarchy – only a guide to determining the most appropriate study designs for answering questions about effectiveness. For other types of question (for example, questions about processes, or about the meanings of interventions), then qualitative study designs may be at the top of the hierarchy. For this reason, when carrying out a systematic review it may be more helpful to think in terms of typologies of evidence rather than hierarchies – that is, to consider which type of study is most appropriate for answering your review question. Sometimes controlled trials may clearly be appropriate, and sometimes surveys or qualitative studies, or other types of research are needed. Controlled trials are suitable for assessing whether an intervention works – whether Intervention A is 'better' than Intervention B. The interventions in question could be health promotion interventions (such as educational programmes) or drugs, or other therapies. Where controlled trials are impossible (such as when it proves impossible to withhold an intervention from a control group, for ethical or practical reasons) before-and-after studies (cohort studies) may be appropriate. Surveys or other types of cross-sectional study, however, do not provide robust information about effectiveness, though they are valuable methods of collecting other sorts of information – about the prevalence of health behaviours for example (smoking or drinking). Qualitative studies, however, provide much more detailed in-depth information about meanings and experiences – such as the experience of receiving an intervention, for example. They can also provide valuable information about processes, for example, about *why* an intervention worked (or did not work), though they do not provide robust information about *whether* an intervention actually worked. (Table 8.1).

Break the question down

If the review is attempting to answer a question about effectiveness, it is helpful to break the review question down into separate sub-questions.

Table 8.1 Appropriateness of different study designs for answering different types of research question[a]

Research question	Qualitative research	Survey	Case control studies	Cohort studies	RCTs	Systematic reviews
Effectiveness						
Does this work? Does doing this work better than doing that?				+	++	+++
Process of service delivery						
How does it work?	++	+				+++
Salience						
Does it matter?	++	++				+++
Safety						
Will it do more good than harm?	+		+	+	++	+++
Acceptability						
Will children/parents be willing to take up the service offered?	++	+			+	+++
Cost effectiveness						
Is it worth buying this service?					++	+++
Appropriateness						
Is this the right service for these children?	++	++				++
Satisfaction with the service						
Are users, providers and other stakeholders satisfied with the service?	++	++	+	+		+

[a] The example refers to the different questions which could be asked about an intervention aimed at children. (The larger the number of crosses, the greater the contribution which that particular study design can make to answering that particular question.)
Source: Adapted from Petticrew & Roberts, 2003; Gray, 1996.

First, what is the intervention that I am interested in? Second, what population am I interested in (Children? Women? Men? Older people? All of the above?); and third, what types of study are most appropriate to answer the question? (Trials? Surveys? Before-and-after studies? Qualitative studies?). Clear answers to these questions will be helpful when you start your literature search. It is very important to remember again that a systematic review is a hypothesis testing mechanism, so think of your review question as a hypothesis. It is *not* simply a review of 'everything that is known about X'.

It is crucial to get the review question very clear at the start of the review. If the question is not clearly defined, you will later be unsure what sort of studies you should be including, and you will risk becoming overwhelmed with irrelevant information. If this is the case, the review question may need to be changed – that is, broadened or (more commonly) narrowed. If the choice is between ploughing on with an unwieldy, unfocused review, or doing some judicious post-hoc adjustments, then the latter is preferable – just as long as you document the changes, and as long as the decision to revise the review question is not made on the grounds that the primary studies do not give the answers you want to hear. Make sure you document any changes you make.

8.2.2 The literature search

There are many potential sources of studies, but a search of electronic databases is probably the most important one. However, it is not the only one, and sometimes it is not even the most useful one.

Electronic databases

If you have worked on defining your review question clearly, then you should have been able to work out what sorts of studies you need to review in order to answer that question. So, if you are interested in answering a 'what works' question, then you might be interested in controlled studies, and uncontrolled prospective studies. You may, for example, know that there are some randomized controlled trials in the area you are interested in, and will wish to identify all those that have been carried out.

In many cases specific 'search strategies' have been developed by information scientists to help identify particular study designs in electronic databases. These have usually been designed to be used with specific databases, usually Medline, but they may also provide pointers on how to identify the type of study you are interested in while excluding a great deal of irrelevant literature. These search strategies work broadly in the same way. For an intervention, you need to list the different ways in which it can be defined, perhaps by drawing up a list of synonyms. Then specify the population in which you are interested, and finally the outcome of interest – again, including as many synonyms as relevant. These synonyms are combined (usually using the terms AND and OR and NOT) to allow only relevant studies to be retrieved. There is a particular skill in retrieving the relevant studies while excluding the irrelevant ones, which is why reviewers usually seek expert help from an information scientist or librarian at this stage in the review. They will know the most useful search terms for a range of databases, and how these can be combined to allow maximum yield of relevant articles while minimizing the numbers of titles and abstracts.

Search strategies

Information scientists have published a number of search strategies for identifying studies, usually trials. Most of these are designed for use in Medline, but provide useful pointers as to how to design a search strategy for other databases (such as PsycINFO). Some of these search strategies were developed by researchers working with the Cochrane Collaboration.

Identifying controlled trials and reviews

Highly sensitive search strategies have been developed for identifying controlled trials in Medline, and PubMed (Robinson & Dickerson, 2002). A list of search strategies for RCTs is also available on the web, at http://www.york.ac.uk/inst/crd/search.htm

This site also has a search strategy for identifying published systematic reviews and meta-analyses – an important first step in carrying out any review is to see whether it has already been done.

Identifying qualitative research

There is considerable interest in incorporating qualitative research into systematic reviews, particular reviews of social interventions. For most of its history the systematic review has been used to synthesize quantitative information (for example, on outcomes of interventions), but the answers to some key questions about interventions can only come from qualitative data. However, identifying qualitative studies for inclusion in reviews is more difficult than identifying trials. There is often no methodological information in the study's title or abstract to allow it to be clearly identified as a qualitative study, so it can be difficult to define specific search terms. The following terms may be useful, however, to construct a search strategy (for use with CINAHL): ethnography; qualitative; grounded theory; thematic analysis; content analysis; observational methods; constant comparative method; field notes; participant observation; narratives; field studies; audiorecording; focus group or focus groups.

You can run a simple check on the effectiveness of your search strategy by listing a few of the key studies that you would expect to identify for your review. If these studies have not been identified (for example, if your search of the main electronic databases does not locate them), then your search strategy is probably flawed and will need revision, preferably with the help of an experienced information scientist.

Other potential sources of information include bibliographies of review articles and primary studies, contacts with experts in the area, and citation searching. 'Best practice' also involves hand-searching particular key journals – that is, checking each paper in each issue of a particular journal to identify relevant primary studies. It is unwise to rely on electronic searches alone, and at a minimum one should examine bibliographies of other review articles, and primary studies. In some cases electronic searches fail to locate about half the relevant studies (for example, studies of the physical and mental health effects of transport, or of housing interventions may not appear on electronic databases). Searching for articles which themselves cite a key reference can be another useful way of widening the search. This can be done in Web of Science (a 'cited reference' search).

How do you know when to stop searching?

When one starts a new systematic review one often does not know just how comprehensive the search should be. Some reviewers suggest that it is necessary to search every last corner of 'the literature' in case a relevant study is missed. However, logic suggests that there must come a cut-off point, otherwise the review would never be completed. This cut-off point probably comes when you have identified so much of the relevant literature that any studies you fail to identify will not significantly affect your review's conclusions (see publication bias). The cut-off point sometimes becomes clear if you are monitoring the yield from your searches. If, having searched five of the main databases and bibliographies, additional searches of subsequent less well-known databases fail to add to the tally of included studies, then one can consider whether it is worth searching further.

The actual number of databases that one needs to search varies from topic to topic. For some clinical topics it has been shown that, for comprehensive searching, one needs to search a minimum of two or more databases, plus a hand search of selected journals (Suarez-Almazor et al., 2000). We would suggest that no search is complete without also searching the bibliographies of a selection of key traditional reviews and major discussion papers.

Do not omit books. In some social science areas, relevant literature may appear in book chapters, but not in refereed journal articles. Most importantly, keep a detailed record of where you identified the studies you have reviewed, and include this record in the report. This will help subsequent researchers identify the most efficient search strategies for identifying similar studies. It is also a requirement if you wish to publish the results of your review in some academic journals.

How far back should one search?

The answer to this question depends on the topic or the intervention, and the answer is arrived at logically, rather than by following hard and fast rules. If the intervention is a recently developed treatment, then the researcher can make the argument that the search should date from the publication of the first trial, or the first use of the treatment. For other types of intervention, the cut-off point needs to be decided and stated clearly in the protocol and methods section of the review, and an explanation given as to why that date was decided upon. As discussed earlier, if you are updating an existing good quality systematic review, then your search obviously needs to start from the end date of that review's searches. This information should be available from the methods section of that review. It may be sensible to allow some overlap, to allow for a margin of error – for example, if the methods section of the old review states that the literature was searched up until December 1997, then it would be sensible to include several months before that date in your own searches.

Where to search: Electronic databases

Box 8.1 includes a (non-exhaustive) list of some of the main databases which you may consider searching. There is some overlap in terms of actual content; some abstracts will appear on all of Medline, Embase, PsychInfo and ASSIA, for example. This is why it is useful to manage the results of your searches in a good bibliographic database such as Endnote or Reference Manager, which can help you to identify and delete duplicate entries. A librarian or information scientist will be able to advise you about access and coverage and about other databases available within other topic areas.

BOX 8.1 Some electronic databases which cover health and related literature

AMED: Database of articles on Allied and Complementary Medicine (1985–present).

ASSIA: Applied Social Sciences Index and Abstracts. Covers social sciences (1987–present).

BIOSIS: Life sciences database, includes Biological Abstracts.

Cancerlit: Database from the US National Cancer Institute containing more than 1.8 million citations and abstracts from over 4,000 different sources, including biomedical journals, proceedings, books, reports and doctoral theses. Free on the web at http://www.cancer.gov/

CCTR: Cochrane Controlled Trials Register. This is the world's largest database of controlled trials, and is searchable as part of the Cochrane Library (see below), which is available on CD and should be easily available at any academic library.

CINAHL: Database for nursing and allied health literature (1982–present). Includes literature from biomedicine, management, behavioural sciences, health sciences, education and consumer health.

DARE: The Database of Abstracts of Reviews of Effectiveness, held at the NHS Centre for Reviews and Dissemination at the University of York, UK. It is a database of systematic reviews of healthcare and other interventions. It contains details of over 7,000 reviews, with a commentary on the methodology of each. It mainly focuses on reviews of effectiveness, and most of the reviews are of clinical interventions. However, there are also many reviews of public health, health promotion, educational and other interventions. It is freely available at http://agatha.york.ac.uk/darehp.htm

Dissertation Abstracts: This contains details of dissertations from the UK (1988–present) and US (1861–present) along with selected MSc dissertations.

The Cochrane Library: This database contains details of completed systematic reviews and protocols of planned or ongoing systematic reviews carried out by the international Cochrane Collaboration. The database is available by subscription, and is also freely searchable on the web at: http://www.update-software.com/Cochrane/default.

HTM. It contains details of all Cochrane reviews of healthcare interventions (this includes reviews from nursing, public heath and health promotion).

ERIC: contains more than 1 million abstracts of documents and journal articles on education research and practice (1966–present).

EMBASE: Covers all aspects of human medicine and related biomedical research, including drugs and toxicology, clinical medicine, biotechnology and bioengineering, health affairs, and psychiatry. It includes data from 3,500 biomedical journals dating back to 1980.

Medline: This is the main international biomedical database, and is the electronic equivalent of Index Medicus, Index to Dental Literature, and the International Nursing Index (1966–present). About 40,000 abstracts are added monthly.

PsychINFO: Database produced by the American Psychological Association which includes over 1,300 journals from psychology and related disciplines including medicine, psychiatry, nursing, sociology, education, pharmacology, physiology, linguistics, and other areas (1887–present). It also includes book chapters. There is relatively little overlap with health databases like Medline and Embase.

SIGLE: System for Information on Grey Literature is a bibliographic database covering European non-conventional literature in the fields of pure and applied natural sciences and technology, economics, social sciences and humanities (1974–present).

Sociofile: This database contains sociological abstracts from about 2000 journals (1974–present). It includes abstracts of articles published in Sociological Abstracts, as well as books and book chapters.

SPECTR: Details of this database (compiled by the Campbell Collaboration, an international group which carries out systematic reviews) appear at www.campbellcollaboration.org. The website contains details of ongoing systematic reviews of social, educational and criminological interventions, as well as details of the SPECTR database of trials in these areas.

SPORTDiscus: Sport, fitness and sports medicine bibliographic database of articles, theses and dissertations (1975–present).

Box 8.1 also lists several databases which include so-called 'grey' literature, sometimes called 'fugitive' literature. This term tends to be used to refer to publications that are not peer-reviewed journals, and includes government reports, theses and other documents not published commercially.

It may also be useful to contact experts in the area to identify other studies they may be aware of. Hand-searching of journals can also be very also useful if time permits, as not all relevant studies may be well described on electronic databases – for example, if the title of an article is not very informative and does not include your search terms, it may be easily overlooked.

Checking for and minimizing publication bias

Searching electronic databases and grey literature sources will identify published studies. However, there is a danger in limiting your review to only published literature because of the problem of 'publication bias'. Publication bias involves the selective publication of positive research. Consequently, the results of reviews that do not take steps to minimize publication bias can be very misleading.

Publication bias arises for a number of reasons. For example, researchers tend to submit only positive or 'interesting' results for publication. Studies that show older interventions to be effective or equal in effectiveness, or that fail to demonstrate an association in aetiological research are also not considered interesting or publishable. Similarly, journal editors who are keen to publish new, interesting or newsworthy research will often actively discourage the submission of negative research. This problem has long been recognized in psychology (Shadish et al., 1989; Begg, 1994).

A number of steps can be taken to minimize this bias. Reviewers should seek out unpublished work – by contacting authors of already published research, or other experts, to see if they know of any other studies or have conducted unpublished research themselves. Reference lists and thesis databases can also be a source of unpublished research. Even when these steps are taken, however, it is still difficult to know whether this source of bias has been addressed.

Several techniques are available to check for and to correct for this source of bias – these include the construction of 'funnel plots' which reveal areas of missing research (NHS CRD, 2001). A funnel plot is a diagram on which the effect size (such as the mean, or odds ratio) for each quantitative study is plotted on the x-axis against a measure of the precision of the estimate, such as the standard error (which is usually plotted on the y-axis). If there is no publication bias, the plot will be approximately

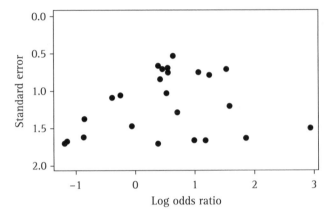

Figure 8.1 Example of a symmetrical funnel plot (Alderson & Green, 2002)

symmetrical, representing an upside-down funnel (Figure 8.1). However, in the presence of publication bias the plot is asymmetrical. This is sometimes because smaller, less precise studies with statistically non-significant findings are missing, perhaps because the author did not publish them, or because journals rejected them. However, asymmetry can occur for many reasons and, because of this, funnel plots should be used with caution.

8.2.3 Selecting and critically appraising the studies

Selecting the studies for review

Having carried out the searches and collated them in a database, the reviewer must screen the titles and abstracts in order to identify studies which appear to meet the review's inclusion criteria. It is usually seen as best practice for two reviewers to do this, as it has been shown that one reviewer working alone will miss about one in ten of the relevant studies. If the review is large, several thousands of abstracts may need to be screened in this fashion. Similarly, each paper that is being considered for possible inclusion in the review will need to be read carefully to identify whether it really meets the inclusion criteria. Again, it is best for two people to do this, working independently and keeping note of the number of papers on which they agree and disagree. Some journals also require reviewers to report Kappa statistics to show the level of agreement.

Having decided on the studies which meet the inclusion criteria and which need to be reviewed in detail, the reviewer needs to tabulate each study. The table should contain details of the study design, setting, number of participants, length of follow-up, and the main findings of the study. This information is sometimes extracted from each article on to a 'data extraction sheet', to ensure that relevant information is not missed, and to ensure accuracy.

Critical appraisal

Critical appraisal or 'quality assessment' of the included studies is a key component of a systematic review. Without this step the review cannot be said to be systematic. Checklists have been produced to assist with critical appraisal of a number of study designs (NHS CRD, 2001; Gray, 1996). These checklists highlight the main sources of bias for each type of study, and the reader uses this list to identify whether a particular study is affected by each of these biases in turn, and then uses this information to guide their overall assessment of the study's methodological soundness.

Randomized controlled trials

For randomized controlled trials (RCTs), the main sources of bias are well known. These are inadequate randomization, occurrence of dropouts after randomization, and lack of blinding. One of the most widely used scales for assessing RCTs is the Jadad Scale (Jadad et al., 1996). The scale includes the following items:

1 Was the study described as randomized?
2 Was the study described as double-blind?
3 Was there a description of withdrawals and dropouts?

Using this system, a trial receives one point for each positive answer, and a point can be deducted if either the randomization or the blinding/masking procedures described are felt to be inadequate. The total score is used to help decide which trials to include in the review or in a meta-analysis, and as an overall guide to the validity of the included studies.

Observational studies

Observational studies are those where no experimental manipulations have taken place, but where participants are followed up over time. These sorts of studies can be used to determine whether a treatment or other intervention is effective; for example, patients who received a particular form of counselling could be followed over time and the outcome of their treatment assessed. They may sometimes be compared to a control group. Observational studies can also help explore issues of causation. For example, a sample may be identified from the population, some psychological variables measured, and that sample followed up longitudinally to determine whether those variables are associated with the subsequent development of some illness. Studies of whether Type A behaviour and hostility are risk factors for CHD have used this design for example (i.e., prospective cohort studies). An alternative (and cheaper) study design involves identifying people who already have the illness in question and comparing them to a healthy group, and then assessing whether the possible risk factor is more common in the unhealthy group (for example, one could compare levels of hostility between healthy people, and CHD patients). This type of retrospective observational study is known as a case-control study. There are checklists available to help with critically appraising such studies (NHS CRD, 2001; Box 8.2). Two useful appraisal checklists are shown in Box 8.2.

BOX 8.2 Quality criteria for critical appraisal of observational studies

Cohort studies

1 Are the study participants adequately described (with adequate descriptive data on age sex, baseline health status and other variables as appropriate to the research question)?

2 If the study is an assessment of an intervention, is the intervention clearly described, with details of who exactly received it?

3 If the study is an aetiological study (e.g., does stress cause cancer?) were the independent and dependent variables adequately measured (that is, was the measurement likely to be valid and reliable)?

4 Are the health measures used in the study the most relevant ones for answering the research question?

5 If the study involves following participants up over time, what proportion of people who were enrolled in the study at the beginning, dropped out? Have these 'dropouts' introduced bias?

6 Is the study long enough, and large enough to allow changes in the health outcome of interest to be identified?

7 If two groups are being compared, are the two groups similar, and were they treated similarly within the study? If not, was any

attempt made to control for these differences, either statistically, or by matching? Was it successful?

8 Was outcome assessment blind to exposure status? (That is, is it possible that those measuring the outcome introduced bias?)

Case-control studies

1 Are the study participants adequately described (with adequate descriptive data on age sex, baseline health status and other variables as appropriate to the research question)?

2 If the study is an assessment of an intervention, is the intervention clearly described, with details of who exactly received it?

3 If the study is an aetiological study (e.g., does stress cause cancer?) were the independent and dependent variables adequately measured (that is, was the measurement likely to be valid and reliable)? Were they measured in the same way in both cases and controls?

4 Are the health measures used in the study the most relevant ones for answering the research question?

5 Are the two groups being compared similar, from the same population and were they treated similarly within the study? If not, was any attempt made to control for these differences, either statistically, or by matching? Was it successful?

(From NHS CRD Report 4, http://www1.york.ac.uk/inst/crd/report4.htm)

Qualitative research

There is much ongoing debate about the appropriateness of critical appraisal methods to qualitative research (Yardley, 2000). It is clear, however, that one still needs to be able to tell 'good quality' from 'poor quality' qualitative research, just as one does for quantitative studies. But there are as yet no widely accepted criteria as to how this may be done, though guidance as to the main criteria on which qualitative studies could be assessed is available (Box 8.3).

8.2.4 Summarizing the studies

Narrative synthesis of quantitative studies

If you have successfully critically appraised your primary studies you are in a position to synthesize their conclusions. Your overall goal is to

BOX 8.3 Some questions about quality that might be asked of a qualitative study (Mays & Pope, 2000)

Worth or relevance
- Was this piece of work worth doing at all? Has it contributed usefully to knowledge?

Clarity of research question
- If not at the outset of the study, by the end of the research process was the research question clear? Was the researcher able to set aside his or her research preconceptions?

Appropriateness of the design to the question
- Would a different method have been more appropriate? For example, if a causal hypothesis was being tested, was a qualitative approach really appropriate?

Context
- Is the context or setting adequately described so that the reader could relate the findings to other settings?

Sampling
- Did the sample include the full range of possible cases or settings so that conceptual rather than statistical generalizations could be made (that is, more than convenience sampling)?
- If appropriate, were efforts made to obtain data that might contradict or modify the analysis by extending the sample (for example, to a different type of area)?

Data collection and analysis
- Were the data collection and analysis procedures systematic?
- Was an 'audit trail' provided such that someone else could repeat each stage, including the analysis?
- How well did the analysis succeed in incorporating all the observations? To what extent did the analysis develop concepts and categories capable of explaining key processes or respondents' accounts or observations?
- Was it possible to follow the iteration between data and the explanations for the data (theory)? Did the researcher search for disconfirming cases?

Reflexivity of the account
- Did the researcher self-consciously assess the likely impact of the methods used on the data obtained?
- Were sufficient data included in the reports of the study to provide sufficient evidence for readers to assess whether analytical criteria had been met?

summarize the results, giving greater 'weight' to the methodologically more sound studies. A simple vote count (counting up which studies show the treatment is effective, and which show it is ineffective, and comparing the two numbers) is usually seen as inappropriate, as it can lead to bias. For example, if you have identified five trials, three of which suggest that a particular treatment is effective, and two of which suggest that it is ineffective, you might think that the balance of evidence (three trials) suggests that the treatment works. However, if these three trials had serious methodological problems, and the other two were more robust, then you might rightly come to the opposite conclusion. This is why 'vote counting' should be used with caution, because it fails to take account of the biases in the individual studies. Instead, you should be aiming to synthesize the results of the primary studies in a way that is informed by your critical appraisal.

In general, you should summarize the results of the studies you have included, summarizing the range and size of the associations these studies report, with a description of the important characteristics of the included studies (what populations they included, what questionnaires or other measures were used in the studies, and what interventions were assessed if your review is about effectiveness). In a separate section of the results you should also identify any major methodological problems you have identified which you feel may affect the study's conclusions. It is also helpful to highlight the higher quality studies in your review, and to explore how their results differ from the more methodologically biased studies. You may, for example, want to compare the results of the randomized studies with those of the non-randomized studies, which are more likely to be prone to bias. It is also helpful to the reader to explore how other study characteristics relate to study conclusions. Was the intervention more effective in children than in adults, for example? Were studies which carried out more rigorous outcome assessments (for example, those which used objective measures of success of treatment) more likely to report that the intervention was less effective? (This is often the case.) Finally, you should aim to produce a statement summarizing the results of your review, based on the methodologically most sound studies.

It may be helpful before attempting to do this to examine some short examples of the results sections of systematic reviews, to see how they have tackled the task of summarizing the methodological quality of the included studies.

EXAMPLE 8.1 Systematic review of individual behavioural counselling for smoking cessation (Lancaster & Stead, 2002)

'*Methodological quality*: Only three of the studies described a method of randomisation which could ensure that treatment assignment was blind until after allocation. In other trials randomisation was said to have been used but the method was not stated. One study has been included which has been described as a randomised trial (Meenan 1998). The primary report (Stevens 1993) makes it clear that the intervention was delivered to one of two hospitals, alternating on a monthly basis for 14 months. This design was used to avoid control patients hearing the intervention given to others in shared rooms. All eligible smokers in the intervention hospital were regarded as subjects whether or not the intervention was delivered, thus avoiding selection bias, and the intervention was not given by hospital staff. There were no significant differences between intervention and usual care groups at baseline; there were however a larger number of patients in the usual care group. As it seems unlikely that there would have been a high risk of systematic bias from this design, the study is included but with a sensitivity analysis of the effect of excluding it.'

EXAMPLE 8.2 Systematic review of interventions for preventing obesity in children (Campbell et al., 2002)

'Five of the seven long term studies were RCTs (Epstein 2001; Gortmaker 1999a; Mo-Suwan 1998; Mueller 2001; Sahota 2001). All of these five studies randomised by cluster, three by schools (Gortmaker 1999a; Mueller 2001; Sahota 2001), one by classes within schools (Mo-Suwan 1998), and one by families (Epstein 2001). However, only three of these RCTs statistically accounted for potential unit of analysis errors (Gortmaker 1999a; Mo-Suwan 1998; Sahota 2001). In addition, power calculations were only discussed in two of these studies (Gortmaker 1999a; Sahota 2001). Allocation of groups to intervention or control was concealed in two studies (Gortmaker 1999a; Sahota 2001), blinded outcome assessment was reported in one study (Gortmaker 1999a), and baseline differences between intervention and control groups were discussed in all studies. All studies reported follow-up data of more than 80% of the baseline sample.

The remaining long-term studies were non-randomised trials with concurrent control group (Donnelly 1996; Simonetti 1986). One study (Donnelly 1996) had very poor rates of follow-up over the two-year period of the study, while the other (Simonetti 1986) did not adequately describe attrition. None of these studies discussed the potential of contamination between study groups.'

Statistical synthesis of quantitative studies: Meta-analysis

In some cases it may be possible to statistically pool the results of the quantitative studies you have identified (meta-analysis). Meta-analytic techniques in their current form derive from Glass's work which began in the late 1970s (e.g., Glass et al., 1981). In its simplest form, meta-analysis involves statistically pooling the summary data from more than one study to produce a single overall effect size ('effect size' refers to a statistic which expresses the relationship between two variables – for example, the difference between two means or two percentages is an effect size, as is an odds ratio. Pearson's *r* is another). There are many approaches to conducting meta-analysis. A simple example will be discussed.

Fixed and random effects models

In reviews of effectiveness, we often need to pool effect sizes from several controlled trials, with the outcome data being continuous, expressed as the difference between two means. In this case, a simple statistic can be calculated for each trial to estimate the effect of the treatment. This statistic is the *d*-Index or *d*-statistic, which is calculated as the difference between the mean of the intervention and the mean of the treatment group $(X_1 - X_2)$, divided by their common standard deviation (SD). This *d*-index should be calculated for each trial in turn, and the individual *d* values are then combined. These should not simply be averaged, however, but each *d* should be weighted to take account of the fact that the *d*s derived from larger studies will be more reliable. The weighting factor for each *d* is given by W_i (Cooper, 1989):

$$W_i = \frac{2(n_{i1} + n_{i2})n_{i1}n_{i2}}{2(n_{i1} + n_{i2})^2 + n_{i1}n_{i2}d_i^2}$$

where n_{i1} and n_{i2} are the number of observations in each of the groups in the study, and d_i is the *d*-index for the individual study for which the weight is being computed.

The final step in producing a pooled effect size is to multiply each *d* by its corresponding weight (w_i), add these weighted *d*s, and then divide by the sum of the weights. This gives the combined, weighted effect size. The upper and lower 95 per cent confidence intervals around the pooled effect size are given by:

$$d \pm 1.96\sqrt{(\text{inverse of the sum of the weights})}.$$

The 'sum of the weights' referred to is just the sum of all the *w*is which have already been calculated above. Knowing the upper and lower confidence intervals allows us to determine whether the pooled effect size is statistically significant or not; in short, if the range from the lower to the upper confidence interval does not include $d = 0$, then the pooled effect is statistically significant (at the $p < 0.05$ level).

This is known as a 'fixed effects' model, because it assumes that each study included in the meta-analysis is attempting to estimate a single population effect size. However, random effects models can also be computed, which assume that the true population value is not fixed but itself varies. In this case the study weights will include a measure of inter-study variation. This variation can occur for many reasons – for example, in a meta-analysis of trials, we are interested in whether the treatment is similarly effective across all the studies. There is likely to be some variation that is simply due to chance, but if this variation is small then a fixed effects meta-analysis can be used. However, some variation between studies can occur because of differences in the population being studied, or in the way in which the treatment is delivered, or for many other reasons, and this may cause greater inconsistency between the study effect sizes. If this inconsistency (sometimes referred to as heterogeneity) is large enough, then a random effects meta-analysis, which incorporates an estimate of inter-study variation, is appropriate (Deeks et al., 2001).

Sometimes this heterogeneity among the study effect sizes can be detected by eye – for example, a plot of the effect size for each study may show one or more obvious outliers. However, it is usually more reliable to detect heterogeneity by statistical means, and this is commonly done using the Q statistic (sometimes called the Cochran chi-square). If there is no significant heterogeneity, then a 'fixed effects' meta-analysis is generally used. However, if the Q test is statistically significant, then this indicates that there is significant heterogeneity and a 'random effects' meta-analysis is indicated. It should be noted that the Q test has low power, so even if it is not statistically significant then some heterogeneity may still be present.

Even if the studies are not combined statistically, some exploration of heterogeneity should be carried out to investigate the reasons behind any variation in study findings. Variation may result from between-study differences in the sample, in the treatment, or in the study design. For example, a treatment may be more or less effective in women than in men, and some studies may involve single sex samples, or the actual details of the intervention may vary from study to study.

Combining different types of effect size

It would be convenient if, when synthesizing the results of many studies, the actual effect sizes were all measured in the same way; if all the studies reported means, or percentages, for example. Of course this is often not the case, and one often finds that a range of different types of effect size are used to describe the relationship between the variables of interest. For example, some studies may describe the effectiveness of an intervention to reduce obesity by comparing the percentage losing weight in the control group to the percentage losing weight in the intervention group, and then report the chi-square value describing the association. However, other studies of weight control in the same review may compare mean weight loss in the control and intervention groups by using a t test. Yet other studies may report an F value, but nothing else; and so on. Fortunately it is possible to convert all these effect sizes into a single common effect size, equivalent to Pearson's r, and all the individual r values can then be pooled (Cooper, 1989). The individual r values are first transformed to z-scores using statistical tables, and then combined to compute a weighted average effect size, with an associated confidence interval (Wolf, 1986).

A range of software programs, some free, are available to help with fixed and random effects meta-analysis. Such software generally includes statistical tests for heterogeneity. A comprehensive list of free and commercial software and macros appears on Dr William Shadish's webpage: http://willshadish.psyc.memphis.edu/

'Fail-safe' N (the 'file drawer' number)

Many systematic reviews include a 'fail safe' number, which is an estimate of the number of unpublished studies with statistically non-significant findings that would be required to overturn the results of the meta-analysis (that is, render its results statistically non-significant), but which may have been missed for whatever reason by the reviewer. If the number is large, then the assumption is that the review is unlikely to be biased through excluding these studies. Fail-safe numbers in the many thousands are sometimes reported. However, it is important to note that the accuracy of this number is dependent on the studies in the review being unbiased, and this is very often an unwarranted assumption. If the included studies are significantly biased, and the effect sizes are over-estimated as a result, then the fail-safe N is likely to be considerably exaggerated. If a fail-safe N is to be calculated, then it would be more appropriate to calculate it using only the methodologically sound studies in the review. Even then, the fail-safe N may still be susceptible to publication bias, as discussed above.

8.3 WRITING UP THE REVIEW

After you have synthesized your studies, considered the sources of hetero-geneity among them, and explored the possibility of publication bias, you will be in a position to write up the full review as an academic paper or report. Before doing this, however, it will be useful to obtain copies of some recently published systematic reviews as a guide. This will give you a clear idea of the sort of methodological information you need to report, as well as showing how to describe the process of identifying, appraising and summarizing research. It may be most useful to look through recent issues of the journals *Health Psychology*, *British Journal of Health Psychology*, *Psychology and Health*, and *Psychological Bulletin*, all of which regularly publish systematic reviews and meta-analyses. Systematic reviews are also a regular feature of general medical journals such as the *British Medical Journal* (www.bmj.com).

Because a systematic review involves a comprehensive survey of the existing research, and an assessment of its methodological soundness, a good review can be a very reliable indicator of future research needs. For this reason your review should end by describing any gaps in the evidence base which you have uncovered. This information generally forms part of the discussion. For example, if in a systematic review of psychological treatments for chronic pain you have identified an absence of adequately powered, rigorous trials, then it is important to point this out, and to suggest what sorts of interventions need to be evaluated, in which populations. You may also be able to identify other gaps in the literature; for example, you may have noted an absence of qualitative studies of patients' experiences of those treatments.

You should also be able to suggest areas where future systematic reviews are needed. For example, you may have found that existing systematic reviews are inadequate in some way and may need to be replicated, updated or extended – they may, for example, have missed relevant literature, or perhaps they have not assessed the quality of the included studies, which will render their conclusions suspect (a very common problem). In short, you should aim to end your review not just with a summary of the existing evidence, but also with clear pointers to what sort of evidence – whether new studies, or new systematic reviews – is needed in future.

8.4 CONCLUSION

Systematic reviews have become a common tool among social researchers, but many systematic reviews are themselves biased; unfortunately the phrase 'systematic review' in the title of a paper is not a reliable indicator of the quality of the rest of the paper. However if your own systematic review avoids the main methodological pitfalls you can expect it to be widely read, and can expect it to be seen as a valuable contribution to the health psychology evidence base. This chapter provides an overall guide to carrying out a reliable systematic review, but it is only a starting point. The next steps should involve consulting other more detailed literature on the subject, reading some examples of recent reviews, and ideally talking to someone who has actually completed one, to get an indication of what it is like to do a 'real life' systematic review.

8.5 CONDUCTING SYSTEMATIC REVIEWS

This chapter can help readers to acquire the following stage 2 core components:

2.1a Define topic and search parameters
2.1b Conduct a search using appropriate databases and sources
2.1c Summarize findings from the review.

8.5.1 Carrying out systematic reviews

Skills in systematic reviewing are essential for any social science or health researcher (unit 2.1). Systematic reviews allow one to assess the effectiveness of diagnostic, preventative, therapeutic, organizational and other interventions; allow one to assess the strength of evidence for causal relationships; and permit rigorous theory testing. Clearly these are all skills which are highly relevant to health psychologists seeking to attain stage 2 competences.

Systematic reviews are one among many methodological tools which health psychologists have at their disposal to answer research questions, but any piece of research needs to start with a clearly defined topic. In practice, this means that the researcher must clearly specify the question which the review is seeking to address, and from this identify the types of quantitative and/or qualitative studies (usually, primary research) which are most appropriate to review in detail (component 2.1a). Identifying these studies is often challenging, however, and when searches of electronic databases are employed, there is a need to balance sensitivity with specificity; that is, one needs to identify all the relevant studies, while excluding as many of the non-relevant studies as possible. Input from an information scientist can help with this task, but health psychologists will often be required to carry out limited searches themselves, and when reading other researchers' systematic reviews, to determine whether the search was likely to have been comprehensive enough. This requires a general understanding of the rationale and methods behind literature searching, as well as an awareness of how bias can be avoided (component 2.1b).

8.5.2 Synthesizing research evidence

Much of what health psychologists do in writing reports or papers involves drawing together different types of evidence (some of which is research evidence, and some of which is not), identifying any strengths and weaknesses in that evidence, and producing from this a defensible set of conclusions or recommendations. Systematic reviews also do this, but in a more formal way, usually following a review protocol. Their approach involves the systematic critical appraisal of the studies being reviewed, often using a checklist to aid in the identification of the methodological weaknesses in each study. This approach to validity assessment is an important prelude to summarizing the results of the studies. Without it, one risks placing more emphasis on flawed studies which are likely to produce over-optimistic conclusions – for example, it is known that methodologically weaker studies are more likely to suggest that treatments are effective when they are probably not. Where studies in a review are very similar (for example, if the study designs, interventions and populations being reviewed are homogenous), then statistical methods of summarizing studies can be employed (meta-analysis), otherwise narrative summary of the studies is appropriate (component 2.1c). A knowledge of these methods will also be helpful in understanding and using the results of the systematic reviews and meta-analyses which are increasingly published in health psychology journals.

8.5.3 Using systematic reviews to aid decision-making

Even if one never has to actually carry out a systematic review, it is highly likely that health psychologists will need to be able to understand what they are, how to use them and how to judge their strengths and weaknesses. Given that the early roots of the method are in psychology, it is also likely that non-academic users may turn to health psychologists to help interpret the findings of particular reviews. For example, reliable information on the effectiveness of treatments is likely to come from systematic reviews, but (as with any other type of study) systematic reviews vary in their methodological quality. It is important to be able to judge systematic review 'quality', because it can help one determine whether any review is likely to provide a sound basis for decision-making. This will be helpful when using systematic reviews as part of consultancy work (component 3.1b).

8.5.4 Systematic reviews and other competences

Elsewhere in this book (for example, in Chapter 4) there is an emphasis on the need to evaluate and make recommendations based on research findings (component 2.4c), and to review and evaluate relationships between current issues in psychological theory and practice (component 2.4f). Systematic reviews can aid in these tasks; while they are often referred to as a means of evaluating the effectiveness of services or interventions, they are equally able to shed light on other types of research question, and can be used to test the strength of relationships, and test models and theories (component 2.5a).

Finally, systematic reviews can contribute to be development of new research (unit 2.2). For example, it may be helpful before designing any new psychological study to investigate whether there have already been any systematic reviews carried out in the same topic area. This can help with the process of obtaining funding (component 2.3a); for example, a previous systematic review may suggest what sort of new primary research is needed, and may highlight some of the methodological problems which should be avoided in future work.

REFERENCES

Alderson, P. & Green, S. (eds) (2002). Cochrane Collaboration Open Learning material for Systematic Reviewers. Version 1.1.

Begg, C.B. (1994). Publication bias. In H. Cooper & L.V. Hedge (eds), *The Handbook of Research Synthesis*. New York: Russell Sage Foundation, 399–409.

Britten, N., Campbell, R., Pope, C., Donovan, J., Morgan, M. & Pill, R. (2002). Using meta ethnography to synthesise research: a worked example. *Journal of Health Services Research and Policy* 7(4), 209–15.

Campbell, K., Waters, E., O'Meara, S., Kelly, S. & Summerbell, C. (2002). Interventions for preventing obesity in children (Cochrane Review). In *The Cochrane Library*, Issue 2. Oxford: Update Software.

Cooper, H.M. (1989). *Integrating Research: A Guide for Literature Reviews*. Newbury Park, CA: Sage.

Cooper, H. & Hedges, L.V. (eds) (1994). *The Handbook of Research Synthesis*. New York: Russell Sage Foundation.

Crombie, I.K. (1996). *The Pocket Guide to Critical Appraisal*. London: BMJ Books.

Deeks, J.J., Altman, D.G. & Bradburn, M.H. (2001). Statistical methods for examining heterogeneity and combining results from several studies in meta-analysis. In M. Egger, G. Davey Smith & D.G. Altman (eds), *Systematic Reviews in Health Care: Meta-analysis in Context*. London: BMJ Publishing Group.

Glass, G., McGaw, B. & Smith, M. (1981). *Meta-analysis in Social Research*. Beverly Hills: Sage.

Gray, J.M. (1996). *Evidence-based Healthcare*. London: Churchill Livingstone.

Hemingway, H. & Marmot, M. (1999). Evidence based cardiology: Psychosocial factors in the aetiology and prognosis of coronary heart disease: systematic review of prospective cohort studies. *British Medical Journal* 318, 1460–67 (available free at www.bmj.com).

Jadad, A.R., Moore, A., Carroll, D. et al. (1996). Assessing the quality of reports of randomised clinical trials: Is blinding necessary? *Controlled Clinical Trials* 17, 1–12.

Lancaster, T. & Stead, L.F. (2002). Individual behavioural counselling for smoking cessation (Cochrane Review). In *The Cochrane Library*, Issue 2. Oxford: Update Software.

Lexchin, J., Bero, L.A., Djulbegovic, B. & Clark, O. (2003). Pharmaceutical industry sponsorship and research outcome and quality: systematic review. *British Medical Journal* 326, 1167–70.

Mays, N. & Pope, C. (2000). Assessing quality in qualitative research. *British Medical Journal* 320, 50–52 (available free at www.bmj.com).

NHS CRD (2001). *Report 4: UK Guidance on how to carry out a systematic review of effectiveness* (2nd edn). Essential reading for anyone contemplating carrying out a systematic review (available free at: http://www1.york.ac.uk/inst/crd/report4.htm).

Noblit, G.W. & Hare, R.D. (1988). *Meta-ethnography: Synthesizing Qualitative Studies.* Newbury Park: Sage.

Petticrew, M. & Roberts, H. (2003). Evidence, hierarchies and typologies: horses for courses. *Journal of Epidemiology and Community Health* 57(7), 527–29.

Popay, J., Rogers, A. & Williams, G. (1998). Rationale and standards for the systematic review of qualitative literature in health services research. *Qualitative Health Research* 8, 341–51.

Robinson, K.A. & Dickerson, K. (2002). Development of a highly sensitive search strategy for the retrieval of reports of controlled trials using PubMed. *International Journal of Epidemiology* 31(1), 150–3.

Shadish, W.R., Doherty, M. & Montgomery, L.M. (1989). How many studies are in the file drawer? An estimate from the family marital psychotherapy literature. *Clinical Psychology Review* 9, 589–603.

Suarez-Almazor, M.E., Belseck, E., Homik, J., Dorgan, M. & Ramos-Remus, C. (2000). Identifying clinical trials in the medical literature with electronic databases: MEDLINE alone is not enough. *Controlled Clinical Trials* 21(5), 476–87.

Yardley, L. (2000). Dilemmas in qualitative health research. *Psychology & Health* 15(2), 215–28.

Chapter 9

WRITING GRANT APPLICATIONS

Stanton Newman

Although a significant amount of research is done without seeking formal funding, such as student projects and some research degrees, there are costs associated with this which are met by the student and the supervisor under the umbrella of education. Much health psychology research that leads to publication requires additional funding and, therefore, leads to applications for funding.

This chapter introduces the process of writing grant applications. Researchers engage in a host of different writing tasks, including writing research papers, chapters, reports and grants. Each requires a different structure and style according to its purpose. The importance of grant writing as a specific academic activity is reinforced by the increasing emphasis in research evaluations (such as the UK Research Assessment Exercise) on researchers' ability to raise grant funding for their research.

9.1 CALLS FOR GRANT APPLICATIONS

Many public calls for grants are to be found in the daily press and on the internet. A more systematic accumulation of grants funding available is performed at many universities and some hospital Trusts where regular lists are provided for members of academic staff (for example, in e-mail 'alerts'). There are also external organizations where current calls for grants are listed.

9.1.1 Grant-awarding bodies

Many researchers think principally of major state-funded grant-awarding bodies (such as the UK Medical Research Council or the major charities, e.g., Cancer UK, British Heart Foundation, when considering an application for research funding. While these (especially the former) are considered the most prestigious grants to obtain, there are a number of other sources of funding that should be considered. These include National Health Service grants of various types, other government departments, minor charities, commercial grants, educational grants from commercial companies, wealthy benefactors, grants internal to universities, funding from a colleague's discretionary fund, etc. Each of these will have different requirements for writing and different techniques for costing the research activity. Some of these issues are discussed below.

For many grant-awarding bodies in the health field, there is a tension between basic science research, which focuses on processes of cause and maintenance, and clinical research, which considers issues around treatment and management of the condition. Historically, much of the research funding has gone to the former and only a small proportion to the latter. With the rise and increased acceptability of health services research more grant-awarding bodies consider health psychology research proposals on disease management or other aspects of the healthcare process.

There is a continuum of specificity requested in calls for grant proposals. Some ask for proposals to tackle a very specific question identified by the funding body (e.g., using a nurse-led intervention to improve adherence to diet in Type 2 diabetics); others specify a general subject area, (e.g., behavioural interventions to improve adherence to a diabetes regimen); and some are even more general (e.g., psychological research on diabetes). For specific calls, the justification of the importance of the research area is largely taken for granted while in more open-ended grant calls the importance of the specific area of the application will need greater justification.

Where one has a specific project in mind, finding the appropriate grant-giving body is a task in itself. Some successful researchers have focused on particular disease areas where they have sought repeat funding from the same source as they built up a body of research. For those whose interests extend across disease boundaries, different conditions need to be integrated in the same proposal. Many of the major and minor charitable organizations are grouped around a disease area, which makes it difficult to obtain funding from these sources for projects which cross illness boundaries. State-funded organizations and general health-related charities (e.g., the Wellcome Trust) are more likely to consider grants that incorporate a number of different conditions. There has been an increasing trend for grant-giving bodies to move towards 'directed programmes of research', that is, where the applicant has less freedom to specify the area they wish to study. This trend can be seen in the closure of the UK NHS responsive funding scheme and the more directed programmes adopted by the Medical Research Council.

For health psychologists, the behavioural and psychological interventions in different chronic diseases have tended to be less well funded than the biological ones seeking a medical cure. Carefully examining the statement of aims and objectives of the funding organization is one way of understanding what may be funded. These statements can, however, be vague and relatively unhelpful. Based on the principle that the best predictor of future behaviour is past behaviour, a clue as to where the grant-giving body tends to direct their funds can often be found in looking at what has been funded before. This is, however, no guarantee that the group deciding on grants has not changed or the committee members making the first sift of the proposals has altered its remit. Looking at the composition of the committee may be helpful.

Many grant-giving organizations have adopted a two-stage process for grant applications. The first application is often extremely brief (one or two A4 pages) and these applications are sifted and some selected to submit a full application. Brief applications require a very clear statement of the problem, the way in which it is to be addressed and why you are the person to address it. There is little scope for detail and most bodies are aware of the common strategies to include more information such as adding appendices or reducing the size of the text. A careful reading of the instructions is important to ensure that these are followed to avoid being excluded from consideration.

9.2 WRITING GRANT APPLICATIONS

9.2.1 Read the instructions

All grant-awarding bodies have instructions ranging from a specification of the size of the text through to the number of references allowed. They should be strictly followed and certainly no section should be omitted. Careful attention should be paid to eligibility criteria as many competitions have a nationality or age restriction and some require the principal applicant to be employed at a university or even a particular institution. Given the effort involved in writing a grant nothing is more disheartening than getting a rejection because of lack of eligibility.

9.2.2 Defining the question

A grant application should be directed to answering a particular question or set of questions and that question should be clearly stated. For the reviewer of the application, having this clarified early in the proposal is important. In some cases this can be achieved in the title. It is also helpful to restate the question at the conclusion of the review of previous research to indicate not only that the question is relevant and flows from previous research but also that it has not been addressed by others.

9.2.3 Provide adequate background information

All grant applications should provide evidence that the applicant is aware of the relevant, current literature on the topic. A common problem with unsuccessful grant proposals is that the applicants propose to review the literature at the first stage of the application. Most grant reviewers will not have confidence that the applicants know what the issues are in the area and, more importantly, what questions to ask if they cannot demonstrate an understanding of the literature at the time of making the grant application. One approach that has been adopted is to separately fund a systematic literature review with a view to a further application for the empirically based aspect of the study. In either case, a 'scoping' review should be provided.

It is important to assure reviewers that the applicants have a critical understanding of the current status of research in the field. An uncritical acceptance of previous research is unhelpful in indicating an understanding of the conceptual and empirical issues in the field. As the space allowed in most proposals is short, and it is important to be concise but comprehensive, clearly indicate that the issues reviewed are pertinent to the question. Avoid the pitfall of selectively quoting work that supports the direction you want to take in the research proposal. It is important to also cite evidence contrary to the approach you are suggesting in the proposal and to argue why your proposal deserves investment. The background information should link directly to the proposed question. It should provide evidence that the specific question or questions are relevant to the literature and have not been addressed before.

9.2.4 Specifying the hypotheses

The research questions addressed should lead directly to the hypotheses to be tested. Hypotheses should be well specified, clarifying the outcome measures that will be used to test them and the findings that will be critical to supporting or rejecting each hypothesis. Clarify how the study design actually tests the hypothesis, and how you will accept data that contradicts your and/or the prevailing view. If reviewers consider that the methods do not test the hypotheses (even if they shed some light on the question), the proposal is not likely to receive funding.

9.2.5 Defining the methods

The general and specific methods should be clearly laid out and justified as being the best to answer the question(s). The design of a study should be specific and efficient in tackling the question. The hypotheses should flow from the literature and in turn be tested by the proposed methods to be employed in the study. The nature of outcome measures should be seen to follow from the theoretical orientation of the research question although, in some cases, some specific outcomes not directly related to theory may also be appropriate. In the UK, there is an increasing trend towards involving service users or 'consumers' of the research at all stages of the research process.

9.2.6 Calculating sample size

It is a requirement of many grant-awarding bodies that a clear explanation of the power calculations is provided. Power calculations are important as they not only determine the sample size but also have a major impact on the costs and feasibility of conducting a study. A convincing argument for the basis of the power calculations should be provided (see Chapter 5 for details).

9.2.7 Ethical considerations

The design and conduct of all studies must be guided by ethical considerations. For example, the British Psychological Society has a clear statement of the ethical code that should govern psychological research (http://www.bps.org.uk/documents/Code.pdf). When performing collaborative research on individuals with a medical condition, the Declaration of Helsinki developed by the World Medical Association should also be reviewed as a guide to best practice (http://www.wma.net/e/policy/b3.htm).

9.2.8 Specifying the method of analysis

If relevant, techniques for statistical analysis must be described. Many grant-giving bodies require the applicants to consult a statistician to ensure adequate statistical expertise. Failure to consult could lead to a rejection of the application if there is doubt about the statistical analysis set out in the proposal. The need to be specific about the form of analysis also applies to qualitative data. It is insufficient to state that a qualitative analysis will be undertaken. The theoretical basis and the type of qualitative analysis planned should be clearly laid out in the proposal (see Chapter 7).

9.2.9 Qualities of the research team

Given the increasing competition for research funding, many grant-reviewing bodies will examine the past performance of the team that has been assembled for the study and its relative success in conducting and publishing prior research. Having a track record of successfully obtaining grants and following through to publication is an obvious advantage. New researchers might find it valuable to collaborate with others with such a record in the first instance, as this might assist them in obtaining their first grant.

Grant-awarding bodies frequently ask their review panels to comment on whether they feel the applicants have the relevant expertise, experience and access to the relevant material. Even a good proposal can fail without the right expertise in the proposed team. Therefore, careful attention should be given to constructing a team that has all the relevant expertise required for the conduct of the study. Since some studies in health psychology include clinical, biological and psychological measures, it may be necessary to seek collaborators with particular expertise. They may need to write a letter of collaboration to indicate that they will support the study. This is particularly necessary where only a limited number of applicants can be put on the application.

9.2.10 Costing the application

Grant application forms require applicants to justify expenditure requested. It is important not only to specify what the individuals employed on the grant are to do but also to identify major expenditure on equipment and to justify their need. Reviewers are particularly sensitive to the 'padding-out' grants for additional monies that are not strictly necessary to the application (for example, for computers or a large contingency fund). Most grant-giving bodies have expectations as to the level of support that should be provided by the universities in the conduct of research. For example, some expect the university to provide from their own resources the costs of housing the researchers and access to computer support and software. Others would expect these to be included in the requested funding (called 'overheads'). It is foolish to request support for something that is ruled out by the awarding bodies regulations. Charitable bodies in the UK tend not to provide overheads and believe that these should be covered by the institution, while the research councils do pay overheads at a specified rate.

The greatest complexity arises with commercial companies, for example pharmaceutical companies, as there is often no clear policy on overheads in these companies. Most institutions have some rules about the amount of overheads and what happens to overheads received. In this case the researcher may derive some secondary benefit where the institution devolves some of these overheads for the researcher to fund their research activities. Many UK universities have established separate groups to negotiate on the institution's costs on commercial grants. In many ways this is advantageous to the researcher, as the negotiations will be conducted by people experienced in dealing with commercial companies. This enables the researcher to remain at arm's length in financial discussions and to ensure their relationship with the commercial organization is not 'tainted' by discussions about money. The commercial companies are, however, aware of how overheads are calculated and the market for commercial grants has become very competitive. Sometimes, in their desire to obtain a grant, researchers apply for a sum of money that they know will be inadequate to conduct their research. Not only does this approach set unrealistic expectations in the grant-giving body, it also creates an additional burden of worry about obtaining further funding in order to complete the work. Going back to grant-giving bodies for extra money is to be avoided as it questions the competence of the researchers in their forecasts of needs and progress in the study and therefore their ability in designing and conducting research. However, the need to return to the grant-giving body for further funding does arise on occasion and, where it does, the justification for the extra funds needs to be clearly stated, including an explanation as to why the additional costs were not foreseen at the outset of the application.

9.2.11 Demonstrating feasibility

It is necessary to demonstrate that the planned study is feasible. This can often be significantly enhanced by means of having carried out a smaller scale pilot study. This indicates that (1) the project is feasible; (2) the research team has the capacity to conduct the research as defined; and (3) many of the potential difficulties of running the study will have been addressed in the pilot run. Enhancing the confidence of the reviewers in your ability to conduct the study may lay to rest a host of questions about your ability to deliver on the proposal. Pilot data can be obtained in a variety of ways, such as student projects, and is a worthwhile investment.

9.2.12 Plans for disseminating findings

Most grant-giving bodies require researchers to describe how the findings will be disseminated. The nature of the grant-giving body will often determine the relative importance that they attach to this. For example, if the study is being conducted for a charitable body that supports research in a particular medical condition, they will be keen to have findings that have a bearing on the provision of services for their client group well publicized, especially to those who may influence service delivery. Consequently, it may be insufficient for the researchers to say that they intend to publish their findings in learned journals. Some grant-awarding bodies may take the view that research publications benefit the researcher without having a real impact on policy or practice. It is, therefore, often advisable to include plans to present and publish findings widely.

9.2.13 Co-ordinating the grant application with obtaining ethics approval for the study

Many grant-giving bodies require an ethics application to have been made prior to the submission of the application. This frequently raises a problem regarding time, since ethics committees usually meet only on a monthly basis. The ethics committee requires details of the research proposal and the procedures to be used in it, and frequently have questions about the proposal which causes delays and therefore puts time pressure on any researcher hoping to meet a deadline to apply for a grant. Some grant-giving bodies will award grants subject to ethics approval but if there are elements in the proposal that might raise ethical questions, for example the use of potentially sensitive information, invasive procedures, etc., then it is important to try to address these with the ethics committee prior to submitting the proposal to avoid delay. Multi-centre studies are now required in the UK to go through an MREC (Multi-Centre Research Ethics Committee). Currently, if the proposal involves any more than three centres, it must go through an MREC and then an LREC (Local Research Ethics Committee) for each of the centres.

9.2.14 Specifying the timetable of work

Laying out a clear timetable for the work is helpful to the reviewers and to the applicants. Delay is a significant problem in conducting research as it has a knock-on effect, particularly on salaries. As salaries inflate with time, a delay of three months can add a significant sum to the study cost. Be realistic about the time it will take to obtain ethical approval, to recruit staff and participants. A good strategy is to leave extra time for preparatory work before initiating the study.

9.2.15 Naming potential referees

Many grant-giving bodies ask applicants to identify a number of potential referees for the grant proposal. It is useful to specify what their area of expertise is in relation to the proposal in order to justify the nomination. In some cases you may want to ask their permission and establish whether they would support the application.

9.2.16 Consult widely before submitting

Where grants involve many others, ensure that those with the expertise write the appropriate sections. One of the applicants, customarily the principal investigator, should take responsibility for assembling the full grant proposal. It is always helpful to invite others who have relevant knowledge but are not part of the team to comment on drafts of the application. Choosing when to send a draft application is advisable. First drafts are often a long way from the finished product and you may get the most useful comments when you have a draft that you are largely happy with.

9.3 RESPONDING TO GRANT APPLICATION REJECTIONS

Although you may be disappointed if your application is not funded, it is important to adopt a systematic and detailed analysis of the reviewers' comments. Also bear in mind that the rejection of a grant application is an extremely common event. Some grant-awarding bodies reject up to

90 per cent of the applications they receive. It is probably best to read the reviewers' response to your application and then leave it for a few days while you mull it over and discuss it with any co-applicants and collaborators.

Not all grant-awarding bodies allow resubmissions but, when you are constructing a resubmission for the same grant-awarding body, it is wise to assume that the application will be reviewed by the original referees. These reviewers would expect you to respond to each of the comments they have made in any reapplication. In a resubmission to the same grant-awarding body you should list your response to each point raised by the reviewers in a letter. In some cases they may have made a good suggestion and it is important to acknowledge this and amend your proposal accordingly. On re-reading your grant you may also find other aspects of the proposal that should be changed and these can be included in the changes you made with the rationale. When resubmitting the same grant to another grant awarding body the comments of the referees from the failed submission can be extremely useful in guiding the resubmission.

Writing grant applications takes a lot of time and effort and they are rejected for a host of different reasons. In some cases it may be because the grant-awarding body allocated their scarce resources to another application which took a different approach to yours. In the face of rejection it is necessary to persevere and not let a good idea die. It is worth remembering, in the face of a rejection, that the one way to ensure that you will not receive a grant is not to re-apply!

9.4 CORE COMPETENCES

The chapter on research grant writing and writing for publication addresses the issues of research competence in the stage 2 training. Consequently it covers the following competences:

2.2b Generate testable research questions or hypotheses
2.2c Define the resources and constraints relevant to the conduct of research
2.2d Identify and describe methods appropriate to the proposed psychological research
2.2f Prepare, present and revise research designs
2.3a Negotiate procurement of resources needed to conduct research and access to specified data and participants
2.3b Prepare to implement research protocol
2.3c Conduct preliminary investigation of existing models and methods
2.3d Collect data specified by research protocols.

Chapter 10

WRITING FOR PUBLICATION

Susan Michie and Robert West

Before putting pen to paper, or finger to keyboard, there are several questions to consider when writing a journal article:

- What is the article trying to achieve?
- Who is it aimed at?
- Which journal are you writing for?

It is important to be clear about the end product before you start. This will influence the material you include, the concepts and language you use and the format and style of presentation. It is always a good idea to look up guidelines for authors in the journal (see website www.mco.edu/lib/instr) you have selected and to refer to past examples of published papers. It may be useful to choose a very good article on which to base the structure of your article.

When selecting a journal, the first decision is whether it is appropriate for the content and format of your article. Journals have guidance notes for authors that outline this. Another criterion to take into account is whether the journal is widely read by the people you would like to know about your research. The higher the impact factor of a journal, the more widely read it is (and the more valued it is by the academic community i.e. it looks good on your CV!). See http://wos.mimas.ac.uk/jcrweb/ for indices of impact. Other factors to take into account are the quality of the service, for example, the time-lag for publication, and whether or not the journal charges for publication.

Before writing, be clear about who the authors are (ideally, this should be clarified before or during the research). The order of authorship depends on relative contribution both to the research and to the writing of the paper, and cannot always be determined in advance. However, the lead author should be identified in advance. Authorship is not a right: it must be earned.

This may be through contribution to either writing or to designing or carrying out the research on which a paper may be based. The issue of authorship can be a sensitive issue. Useful summaries of criteria for inclusion as an author are Game and West (2002) and Fine and Kurdek (1993). The latter is downloadable from www.apa.org/journals/amp/kurdek.html.

An important issue is the order of writing. It is usually unwise to begin at the beginning. When writing empirical papers, one approach is to start with the aims and the data tables (for quantitative data) or themes and illustrative quotes (for qualitative data). The data should be presented in such a way that, on their own, they tell the story of the paper. If the aims and results do not appear to be connected, you have a problem. It is useful to write the abstract before the paper. When you have a coherent abstract and summary of your data, you should have intellectual clarity of what you were trying to do, what you did, what you found and what it means. You are then in a good position to write the paper!

Remember that every article tells a story. Your job is to communicate that story simply, clearly and with enthusiasm. You must be convinced that the study and its conclusions are genuinely interesting, otherwise no one else will be. What is its main message? Your job is to communicate that message as concisely and simply as possible. A recent study of submissions to *Psychological Bulletin* found that the factor most strongly associated with acceptance for publication was the inclusion of clear and compelling arguments for major points that pertain to important conclusions. Scientific and technical quality was the next most predictive factor (Eisenberg et al., 2002).

The American Psychological Association has a useful electronic guide to preparing manuscripts for journal publication (http://www.apa.org/journals/guide.html) and a publication manual (APA, 2001). Another text that gives good practical advice to psychology authors is Sternberg (2000).

Below, we outline some pointers, section by section, for writing a good empirical paper.

10.1 WRITING A GOOD EMPIRICAL PAPER

10.1.1 Title

The title should concisely describe the essence of the paper. Ensure that the title does not promise more than the paper can deliver (e.g., using phrases such as 'The effect of ... on ...' when it should be 'Associations between ... and ...' and is succinct, avoiding redundant phrases (e.g., 'A study of ...'). Note any word limits.

10.1.2 Abstract

The purpose of the abstract is to communicate the subject of the paper to those who are deciding whether to read the paper or who have no time to read it. As the summary used in databases, the abstract and keywords will determine the extent to which people access your work appropriately. Ensure that the correct abstract format is used, e.g., structured. It should clearly summarize the aims, sample (e.g., the sampling strategy, sample size, response rate and main sample characteristics), the design, the measures used, the intervention(s) if present and the control if there is one, the main findings as they relate to the aims and the conclusions. The conclusions should avoid phrases such as 'The results are discussed' and avoid just repeating the summary of results.

10.1.3 Introduction

The introduction should 'set the scene' for the study. Begin with a statement of the main issues being addressed and make a clear case as to why the study was needed. This should include making reference to relevant literature. Literature is relevant if it shows why the research questions are important or gives an indication of how the result may turn out. It is essential to search for and give due credit to studies of a similar nature wherever they originate and whatever their conclusions. Selective citation is a common source of bias.

It is important not to be parochial: if the paper is to be relevant to a national or international audience, your study should be framed within this context. It is also important not to make absolute statements, when they apply only to the UK or the developed countries. Avoid colloquial expressions that would be confusing to an international readership.

The research questions or hypotheses should be clearly stated at the end of the introduction. This can be done with a numbered list, for easy reference. Also helpful is background information about the setting for the study, the choice of measures and the sampling strategy.

10.1.4 Method

Design

State the basic design and measurement strategy. Box 10.1 shows common designs. Where appropriate identify any interventions and controls and

BOX 10.1 Common types of research design

Cross sectional survey
A one-off assessment by questionnaire, interview or other means.

Longitudinal survey
Assessment by questionnaire, interview or other means undertaken on the same sample on a number of occasions.

Experiment comparing two or more groups
Random assignment of subjects into two or more groups who receive different intervention (or a control) and comparison between those groups on one or more measures.

Experiment comparing two or more conditions within the same subjects
Exposure of a group of subjects to two or more interventions on different occasions and comparison of measures taken with each intervention.

Experiment with a mixed design
An experiment where comparisons are made between different groups and between different conditions in the same subjects, all in the same study.

Randomized controlled trial (RCT)
Random assignment of subjects to a 'control' group and one or more 'intervention' groups, with comparison between the groups on one or more measures.

Quasi-experimental study
Non-random assignment of subjects to a 'control' group and one or more 'intervention' groups where the intervention aims to achieve a superior therapeutic effect, with comparison between the groups on one or more measures.

Case study
Description of one or a small number of 'cases' in which detailed information is provided to assist interpretation of the findings.

Qualitative study
Detailed, systematic analysis of information from in-depth interviews, text, focus groups or other sources.

measures taken. For clinical trials, most of the leading medical and psychology journals require the use of CONSORT guidelines for reporting their conduct, for example, randomization procedures, the flow of participants through various stages of the study design, and reason for attrition (Moher et al., 2001; Editorial in *Health Psychology*, 2003, 22(4)).

Sample

The total number of participants and the numbers in each group, if there are groups, should be stated with relevant demographic and other descriptive properties. The power calculation or rationale for the sample size should be provided. An account of how the sample was obtained and the response rate should be given in such way as to allow the reader to judge how representative the sample is. Some authors and journals prefer to report these in the results section.

Measures

The measures used should be clearly listed, indicating where possible indices of validity and reliability and giving a citation where possible. In randomized controlled trials, or other intervention studies, a primary outcome measure should normally be stipulated.

Procedure

This should be described in sufficient detail for replication, possibly backed up with an internet site or the offer of full details from the author. Ethical approval should be referenced here.

Statistical analyses

Any complex or unusual statistical methods should be explicitly described and citations given where appropriate. Some authors and journals prefer to report these in the results section.

10.1.5 Results

The results should be described in terms of the answers to the research questions or hypotheses presented at the end of the introduction, and presented in the same order. Descriptive data should be given in sufficient detail to enable readers to eyeball the data and judge whether the reported results of the statistical analyses make sense.

Avoid unnecessarily repeating material in both the text and tables or graphs. The text should summarize the data presented in tables or graphs. All tables and figures should be cited in the text, be numbered consecutively and have titles using a consistent format. Tables and figures should be cited in the text using a phrase such as 'Table 1 shows that . . .'.

Both in tables and figures and when referring to results from individual questionnaire items, use meaningful labels rather than just, for example, the question number.

Clearly state the numbers for every mean, correlation, proportion or other analysis and always give the numbers corresponding to percentages.

Avoid phrases such as 'The result was not significant', since only differences and associations can be statistically significant, not 'results'. State the test statistics (e.g., t value, F value or chi-squared value), degrees of freedom and p values. Even for p values greater than 0.05 it is helpful to show the exact p value. Avoid using $p = 0$ or $p = 0.000$ or $p < 0.0000$, since you cannot have a probability of zero or less. Use $p < 0.001$ or $p < 0.0001$ instead. Increasingly, journals (for example, *Health Psychology*) require the primary findings to be reported as effect sizes, in addition to statistical tests. Presenting effect sizes allows an assessment of the strength of relationships and will help any subsequent meta-analysis. Many journals require 95 per cent confidence intervals around important parameter estimates (e.g., means, proportions, correlation coefficients, regression coefficients).

10.1.6 Discussion

This section discusses the results within the context set out in the introduction. It should start with a summary of the main findings. You should not report or discuss results that have not been mentioned in the results section. They should then be related to previous research in terms of whether they support or fail to support the conclusions of that research. The findings should be considered within the context of the issues raised in the introduction. The implications of the findings for theory, practice, policy formulation and future research should be outlined. Explanation should be given for apparently anomalous findings

The strengths and weaknesses of the study should be assessed, addressing issues such as sample size, sample representativeness, measurement error, measurement bias, whether any intervention was successfully implemented, whether there was contamination between different intervention conditions and the extent to which the findings can be generalized. Finish with a paragraph summarizing the main conclusions. Ensure that the conclusions do not go beyond the data.

10.1.7 References

References follow a particular format, the Vancouver and Harvard systems being common. Ensure that your citations and references follow the journal's guidance to authors, e.g., 'Smith, Jones & Pike, 1998'. Check that your references are complete, in the correct order and match the citations in the paper. All non-English titles should be accompanied by an English translation. Avoid citing unpublished work, especially work reporting substantive findings.

10.1.8 Acknowledgements

Include an acknowledgements section stating the source of funding and thanking relevant people for their assistance and indicate any conflicts of interest.

10.1.9 Style

Journals usually have style manuals that should be followed. Use of past or present tense is partly a matter of personal preference, although past tense should be used when describing other people's findings and your own methods and results. Ensure that your formatting is consistent and appropriate (e.g., single blank lines between paragraphs, no indentations at the start of paragraphs, no multiple blank lines). Use arabic numerals (e.g., '12', '34') except for numbers below 10 and those beginning a sentence, in which cases spell the numbers out (e.g., 'three'). Ensure that all abbreviations are spelled out in full the first time they are used and avoid using shortenings such as 'don't' and 'it's'.

10.1.10 Before submission

Ensure that *all* the authors have read through the manuscript carefully to check it over. Critical reading and feedback by colleagues is invaluable.

A good paper has usually had many, many drafts before being ready to submit.

10.2 WHY PAPERS GET REJECTED OR RETURNED FOR REVISION

Below is a list of common reasons for editors to reject papers or to request revisions. This forms a useful checklist to use when assessing the quality of a paper before submission.

10.2.1 Rejection

- The research questions:
  - are not of sufficient importance;
  - have been addressed before;
  - appear muddled or ill-formed;
  - cannot be answered by the data (or even at all!).
- The findings are not clear or are just common-sense.
- Unwarranted assumptions have been made.
- The introduction fails to make a good case for doing the study or for the measures used.
- The sample size is too small, parochial or not representative.
- There is a low response rate or a high drop-out rate.
- There is reason to question the objectivity of the measurement.
- There are doubts about the reliability or validity of the measures.
- The measures do not seem appropriate to the research question.
- The follow-up may be too short or incomplete.
- Allocation of participants to the intervention may be biased.
- The intervention may be inadequately specified.
- There may be concern about the implementation of the intervention.
- There are inadequate controls.
- There is inadequate statistical control for possible confounding factors.
- The statistical analyses are wrong or wrongly presented.
- Insufficient account is taken of multiple statistical comparisons.
- The conclusions do not follow from the data.
- The editor suspects attempt at salami publication (i.e., a piece of work is chopped up in order to achieve multiple publications).

10.2.2 Revision

- The past literature is not adequately reviewed.
- The size of any effect or association is considered too small to be meaningful.
- The authors include interpretation of results in the results section.
- The language is inappropriate or poor.
- Important information on the methods is missing.
- The discussion overinterprets the findings.
- There is insufficient consideration of the study limitations.
- There is insufficient consideration of alternative interpretations of the findings.
- The paper is too long and/or repetitive.

10.3 RESPONDING TO EDITORS' LETTERS

The editor will communicate her or his decision in a letter and enclose copies of the reviews. The first important thing to remember is not to be disheartened: reviewers' comments often look more problematic to deal with than they turn out to be in practice. There are very few papers that cannot be improved to publishable standard. Regard the referees' comments as free consultancy and amend the paper accordingly. If the paper has been rejected, there are other journals. It may be that there are other, more suitable journals for the topic and type of study you are reporting. Remember, persistence pays in the publishing process!

If you have received a response of 'Revise and resubmit', that is good. Be positive about the comments and address them directly and clearly, even if they appear unreasonable or ill informed. If you disagree with a comment or recommendation, make an argued case, ideally referring to the literature. There are (rare) examples of successful challenges to editors who have rejected papers in an unfair fashion. However, if the referees' comments have merit (and most do), they should be attended to. Sometimes reviewers misunderstand a point: in such a case, explain the point, referring to your original report, and then revise the paper to clarify it. A covering letter should accompany the revised article, listing all the referees' points and outlining exactly what revisions you have made to address them, or making your case if you have decided not to revise a particular point.

10.4 COMPETENCE COVERED BY THIS CHAPTER

The competence covered by this chapter is:

2.4d Write up and report research methods and findings.

There are several reasons for writing up and reporting research methods and findings. The most important is that it may be useful to others. Methods should be written in enough detail to allow replication, and to allow lessons to be drawn, both in terms of methods that worked well and those that did not. If research findings are not reported, they will not contribute to the body of knowledge upon which scientific developments and practical applications are based. As well as writing for the social good, writing up research for publication helps to establish and develop careers.

The first step is to write, the second to write well. Poorly written articles will be less likely to be read, understood or incorporated into future thinking or practice. Writing is a key skill for academics and professionals, but one that is seldom taught directly. Attending courses and asking for critical feedback from colleagues are two obvious opportunities for developing this skill.

REFERENCES

American Psychological Association (2001). *Publication Manual* (5th edn). Washington, DC: American Psychological Association.

Eisenberg, N., Thompson, M.S., Augir, S. & Stanley, E.H. (2002). 'Getting in' revisited: An analysis of manuscript characteristics, reviewers' ratings, and acceptance of manuscripts in *Psychological Bulletin*. *Psychological Bulletin* 128, 997–1004.

Fine, M.A. & Kurdek, L.A. (1993). Reflections on determining authorship credit and authorship order on faculty-student collaborations. *American Psychologist* 48, 1141–7.

Game, A. & West, M.A. (2002). Principles of publishing, *The Psychologist* 15, 126–9.

Moher, M., Schulz, K.F. & Altman, D., for the CONSORT group (2001). The CONSORT statement: Revised recommendations for improving the quality of reports of parallel-group randomised trials. *Journal of the American Medical Association* 285, 1987–91.

Sternberg, R.J. (ed.) (2000). *Guide to Publishing in Psychology Journals*. Cambridge: Cambridge University Press.

Part III

CONSULTANCY AND INTERVENTIONS

Chapter 11

USING THEORY IN PSYCHOLOGICAL INTERVENTIONS

Gerjo Kok and Herman Schaalma

This chapter discusses the application of psychological theory to the development of health promotion programmes, such as those targeting HIV prevention, smoking cessation, and the self-management of chronic diseases. Evidence-based health promotion programmes are based on empirical data and theory. A broad range of social and behavioural science theories are available but the application of these theories to health promotion practice remains a challenge for health psychologists. *Intervention mapping* (IM) can help us to meet this challenge. IM describes a protocol for developing theory- and evidence-based health promotion programmes. This protocol provides guidelines and tools for the selection of theoretical foundations for health promotion programmes, for the application of theory, and for the translation of theory into programmes and materials. We shall describe the protocol and discuss appropriate use of theory in health promotion with illustrations from successful programmes.

11.1 DEVELOPMENTS IN HEALTH PROMOTION

Health education is any combination of learning experiences designed to facilitate voluntary actions conducive to health (Green & Kreuter, 1999). Health promotion is the combination of educational and environmental supports for actions and conditions of living conducive to health (Green & Kreuter, 1999), thereby including health education. These two definitions reflect a historical shift from more individual to more ecological approaches to health promotion. The role of the environment has acquired increased relevance in understanding and changing health.

Health promotion can be characterized by four other main developments: (1) the need for planning; (2) the importance of evaluation; (3) the use of social and behavioural science theories; and (4) the systematic application of evidence and theories in the development of health promotion pro-grammes. We will describe these developments and elaborate on the last two.

11.1.1 Health, environment and behaviour

In an ecological approach to health promotion, health is viewed as a function of individuals and their environments, including family, social networks, organizations, community and public policies. The presence of socio-economic differences in health is a clear example of environmental influences on health (Adler & Ostroff, 1999). At the same time, it also constitutes a major challenge. The central concern of health promotion is health behaviour. However, health behaviour refers not only to the indi-vidual's behaviour but also to the behaviour or actions of groups and organizations. Stress at work may be related to individual coping beha-viour, but also to managers' decision-making behaviour (organization). Richard et al. (1996) describe the various environmental levels as embedded systems. They indicate that individuals exist within groups, which are in turn embedded within organizations and higher order systems. The individual is influenced by, and can influence groups and organizations. The picture that emerges is a complex web of causation providing a rich context for intervention programmes. In the case of stress, the indi-vidual as well as the manager will both be targets for health promotion interventions. Moreover, at the societal level, programmes may target politicians' decision-making in relation to health at work. Thus, managers and politicians are seen as agents in the environment who serve as targets for health promotion programmes aimed at environmental changes (Bartholomew et al., 2001).

11.1.2 Health promotion planning

Health promotion is a planned activity. A widely used health promotion planning framework is Green and Kreuter's PRECEDE/PROCEED model (Green & Kreuter, 1999; McKenzie & Smeltzer, 2001). The model recom-mends that programme planners begin by assessing quality of life and health problems because these are key outcomes for many health promotion programmes. The model then guides the planner to assess the behavioural and environmental causes of reduced quality of life and health problems. In behavioural assessment, we typically ask what the individuals at risk are doing that increases their risk of a health problem. In environmental assessment, we ask what factors in the environment are (causally) related to the health problem directly or to its behavioural causes.

In the next phase of PRECEDE/PROCEED, the planner assesses the determinants (or correlates) of the behavioural and environmental factors. Green and Kreuter (1999) describe determinants affecting behaviour as predisposing, reinforcing, or enabling factors. Predisposing factors relate to the motivation of individuals or groups who may also be agents in one of the environmental levels, such as a manager or a politician. Such factors are usually psychological and include cognitive and affective dimensions of knowing, feeling, believing and valuing. Reinforcing factors are those consequences of a certain (healthy) action that determine whether the actor receives positive (or negative) feedback and is supported socially. They include social support, peer influences and advice/feedback by healthcare professionals. Reinforcing factors also include physical consequences of the behaviour such as wellbeing or pain, and emotional consequences such as pride or fear. Enabling factors, often conditions of the environment, facilitate the performance of an action by individuals, groups or organizations. Enabling factors include the availability, accessibility and affordability of healthy choices as well as healthcare and community resources. Enabling factors also include new skills that a person, organization or community needs to learn in order to make a desired behavioural or environmental change.

Subsequent phases of PRECEDE/PROCEED involve the administrative and policy assessment stages. Based on the identification of the causal pathways in the early phases of PRECEDE/PROCEED, plans are developed for health education and other health promotion interventions, such as policy, regulation or organizational change. The assessments include identifying potential barriers to be overcome in implementing a programme and policies that can be used to support the programme. The planner then proceeds to implementation. The final phases of PRECEDE/PROCEED refer to evaluation and distinguish between different levels of evaluation, that is, process, impact and outcome. Thinking about implementation and evaluation should start early in the planning process, not after intervention development. As we shall see, in the IM protocol, anticipating implementation and evaluation are steps in the development process.

11.1.3 Programme evaluation

It is important to evaluate the effect of a programme in terms of impact and process. If a programme fails, we need to know why it failed. Rossi et al. (1999) argue that it would be a waste of time, effort and resources to estimate the impact of a programme that lacks measurable goals or has not been properly implemented. They suggest four levels of evaluation:

1 Programme conceptualization and design refers to the planning process and the use of theory and evidence in the development of the programme.
2 Programme monitoring provides feedback on the implementation of the programme and its reception by the target population.
3 Impact evaluation assesses the extent to which a programme causes change in the desired direction.
4 Programme efficiency evaluation focuses on costs and effects, such as cost-benefits and cost-effectiveness analyses.

In health promotion impact evaluation rarely focuses on health or quality of life. However, if the proposed causal chain between intermediate factors and health is based on sound empirical evidence, it is appropriate to access impact in relation to intermediate factors, such as behaviour change. Indeed when a programme is designed to affect intermediate factors such as cognitions or behaviour it is important to measure effectiveness in terms of these targets. It is essential to clarify targets/expected outcomes and corresponding evaluation measures before programme implementation.

11.2 USE OF THEORY

A health promotion programme is most likely to benefit participants and the community when it is guided by social and psychological theories of health behaviour and health behaviour change (Glanz et al., 2002). Theory-driven health promotion programmes require an understanding of the components and processes specified by theory as well as an understanding of the operational and practical implications of these theories. Finding and applying relevant theories is a professional skill that health educators have to master (Bartholomew et al., 2001). Theories must be supported by empirical evidence and applied appropriately and correctly. Many interventions may profit from a multi-theory approach. For example, one theory may identify cognition targets while another describes psychological change processes. Many theories are potentially applicable at different levels: individual, interpersonal, organizational, community and societal. Such theories may also help us to understand the extent to which developed programmes are adopted and properly implemented. For example, the Theory of Planned Behaviour (Ajzen, 1991) has often been used to explain individual health behaviour (Godin & Kok, 1996) but it has also been applied to predict politicians' behaviour (Flynn et al., 1998) and the behaviour of implementers of health promotion interventions (Paulussen et al., 1994, 1995). Flynn et al. (1998) analysed the voting intentions of legislators for a cigarette tax increase and showed that the perceived impact on retail sales, public health and political support during the next election, along with perceived behavioural control in relation to getting a proposed bill through legislative committees, voting for it and passing it, were all associated with voting intention. Paulussen et al. (1994, 1995) analysed the determinants of diffusion, adoption and implementation of an HIV prevention programme by schoolteachers. They found that teachers' awareness of prevention programmes was associated with social influence of colleagues through professional networks, and that their decision to adopt a programme was associated with outcome expectations, such as expected student satisfaction. Programme implementation was strongly correlated with teachers' self-efficacy expectations about the proposed teaching strategies and their moral views on sexuality. Surprisingly, the documented effectiveness of the programme had no influence on teacher's implementation decisions. Such findings can help health promoters create persuasive messages that could promote a pro cigarette tax vote or decisions to adopt an HIV prevention programme in schools.

Some psychological theories of behaviour and behaviour change are health-specific while others are general. Health and health promotion oriented theories are often related to perceptions of health risks, for example, the Health Belief Model (Sheeran & Abraham, 1996; Janz et al., 2002) and Protection Motivation Theory (Rogers, 1983; Rogers & Prentice-Dunn 1997). Other theories have been developed in health settings, but have evolved into general theories such as the Transtheoretical Model of Stages of Change (Prochaska et al., 2002) or Relapse Prevention Theory (Marlatt & Gordon, 1985). Most general social psychological models were developed for a broad range of behaviours, but are easily applicable to health behaviours. For example, Learning Theory (Westen, 1996), Information Processing Theory (Hamilton & Chatala 1994), the Theory of Planned Behaviour (Azjen, 1991; Connor & Norman, 1996; Montaño & Kasprzyk, 2002), Social Cognitive Theory (Bandura, 1997), Goal Setting theories (Strecher et al., 1995), Attribution Theory (Weiner, 1986), Self-Regulatory theories (Clark & Zimmerman, 1990), Social Networks and Social Support theories (Heaney & Israel, 2002), the Persuasive-Communication Model (McGuire, 1985), the Elaboration Likelihood Model (Petty et al., 2002), and Diffusion of Innovations Theory (Rogers, 1995).

Health educators also draw upon various organizational change theories (Steckler et al., 2002) to consider policy development within organizations and to promote programme adoption and implementation. Organizational change theories focus on different aspects of organizations (Steckler et al., 2002): stages of change, organizational development, organizational culture interorganizational relationships and empowerment. The stage theory of organizational change is comparable to individual stages of change theory, but different because it is the organization and the agents in the organization that go through the stages:

- sensing unsatisfied demands on the system, and identifying a problem;
- searching for possible responses which provide solutions for the unsatisfied demand;
- evaluating alternatives and comparing potential solutions;
- deciding to adopt a course of action, in which one or a number of alternative responses is selected;
- initiating action within the system, which requires policy changes and resources necessary for implementation;
- implementing the change, that is, putting the proposed innovation into practice – this usually requires some organizational members to change work behaviours and relationships;
- institutionalizing the change by including it in strategic plans, job descriptions, and budgets so that it becomes a routine part of organizational operations.

The key actors involved in change differ from stage to stage. Senior-level administrators with political skills are important in the early stages and the institutionalization stage. Mid-level administrators are active during adoption and early implementation stages, when administrative skills involved providing training and resources to support organizational changes are critical. People who need to make changes in their working practices are the focus of the implementation process, for instance food service workers in the case of an innovation in cafeteria food preparation or company car drivers in the case of an innovation in fuel-saving driving. The focus here is on people's professional and technical skills. Of course, because agents and the behaviours are different at different stages, the determinants change as well. For example, at the decision stage organizational leaders might be persuaded by the characteristics of the innovation, whereas successful implementation may be determined by workers' skills and managers' feedback and reinforcement.

At the community and societal level, theoretical understanding can be provided by classic models of community organization and community development as well as the current community-level perspectives on health promotion (Minkler & Wallerstein, 2002). Issues of power, participation and goals, for instance, have been widely discussed among health educators in recent years. In selecting constructs to use for community change, planners must clarify their assumptions and values about the nature of the change process and select and implement strategies congruent with these. Finally, there are theories of policy-making that have been used primarily at the national, state and governmental level, such as Policy Window Theory (Kingdon, 1995).

Theories are important tools for those working in health education and health promotion. Theories are available to health promotion professionals through papers and textbooks (for good examples, see Connor & Norman, 1996; Glanz et al., 2002; Norman et al., 2000) and students usually study these theories in relation to pre-selected practical problems. However, in real life, the problem is given and the practitioner has to find theories that may explain or help change behaviours that are causally related to the problem (Kok et al., 1996). IM describes a process that facilitates the translation of theory into theory-based and evidence-based health education programmes (Bartholomew et al., 2001).

11.3 INTERVENTION MAPPING

Intervention mapping (see Figure 11.1) describes the process of health promotion programme development in five steps:

1 The definition of proximal programme objectives based on scientific analyses of health problems and causal factors.
2 The selection of theory-based intervention methods and practical strategies to change (determinants of) health-related behaviour.
3 The production of the programme components and production.
4 The anticipation of programme adoption, implementation and sustainability.
5 The anticipation of process and effect evaluation.

IM is not a new theory or model; it is a tool for the planning and development of health promotion programmes. It maps the path from recognition of a need or problem to the identification of a solution. Although IM is presented as a series of steps, Bartholomew et al. (2001) see the planning process as iterative rather than linear. Programme planners move back and forth between tasks and steps. The process is also cumulative: each step is based on previous steps, and inattention to a particular step may lead to mistakes and inadequate decisions.

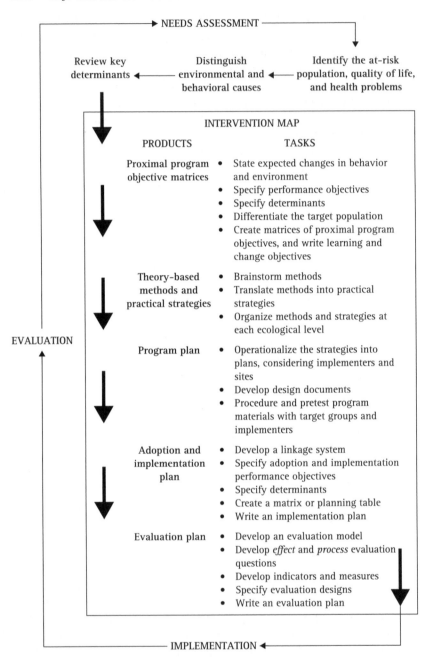

Figure 11.1 Intervention mapping (Bartholomew et al., 2001)

Bartholomew et al. describe three core processes for IM: searching the literature for empirical findings, accessing and using theory, and collecting and using new data. When planning intervention development for a specific problem the sensible thing to do is to search the literature to find out what others have written about possible explanatory factors and solutions. Reviews, including meta-analyses, are extremely useful at this stage. In many cases, however, a literature search will only generate provisional explanations and planners have to develop their own more comprehensive understanding. Useful theories and explanations may be added using three approaches, referred to as issue, concept and general theories approaches. An issue approach involves searching the literature again looking specifically for theoretical perspectives on the issue or problem one is facing. A concept approach involves mapping provisional explanations back to theoretical constructs and theories that may be useful, and a general theory approach involves identifications of general theories that may be applicable. In addition, it is important to identify gaps in the information obtained and collect new data to fill these gaps.

For example, if a health educator searched for predictors of delaying the onset of sexual intercourse in adolescents, the provisional list of determinants could include; knowledge, risk perceptions, group norms, gender, lack of confidence and sexual violence. From the empirical literature, one could refine this list and add: alcohol and drug use, and girls' lack of anticipation of a sexual encounter. Using an issue approach the Health Belief Model and the Theory of Planned Behaviour might be identified, adding determinants such as barriers, subjective norms and intentions. Theoretical descriptions of environmental influence could also be identified, such as living in a poor neighbourhood, or lack of parental supervision. Using the concept approach and tracking concepts from the provisional list of answers to theories, one could track lack of confidence to self-efficacy in Social Cognitive Theory. This could lead to identifying different types of self-efficacy, e.g. self-efficacy for negotiating non-penetrative sexual behaviours and self-efficacy for controlling sexual arousal. Social Cognitive Theory would also contribute other constructs, for example, skills, reciprocal determinism and modelling. Using a general theory approach could result in viewing the problem from the perspective of the Transtheoretical Model of Stages of Change, including consideration of awareness of personal risk from unsafe sex. This last approach may be limited to the theories the planner is familiar with. Consequently, IM recommends starting with a concept approach that involves searching for theories that planners are not familiar with, before adoption of a general theory approach.

11.3.1 Intervention mapping step 1: Proximal programme objectives

IM starts when the data from the needs assessments in the PRECEDE/ PROCEED model are known. Planners need to have insight into peoples' quality of life concerns and their health problems as well as the behavioural and environmental factors that cause the health problem, and the predisposing, reinforcing and enabling correlates of these factors. On the basis of these analyses planners should be able to define and select health promotion goals.

The first step in IM is the specification of the general programme goal into proximal programme objectives that explicate who and what will change as a result of the programme. Proximal programme objectives specify what individuals need to learn or what must be changed in the organization or community. IM describes a procedure for the specification of programme objectives, comprising four steps. First, planners specify the health promoting behaviours (for example, the promotion of condom use), into 'performance objectives'. Performance objectives describe the behaviours that we want the target group (or the environmental agents) to 'do', as a result of the programme. For example, in the case of HIV prevention, we would like the young people to buy condoms, have them available, negotiate with their partner about condom use, use condoms correctly and continue to use them during their teenage years (Schaalma et al., 1996; Schaalma & Kok, 2001).

Planners should then consider the determinants of performance objectives and map performance objectives on to their determinants and target groups, resulting in a matrix for proximal programme objectives. The determinants of one performance objective (for example, using condoms correctly) may be different from the determinants of other performance objectives (for example, always carry condoms). Determinants of behaviour can be cognitive (for example, outcome expectations, subjective norms and self-efficacy) or social (for example, social norms, social support). Target groups can be sub-groups, for instance, men/women, people in different stages of change. For example, one proximal programme objective for an HIV-prevention programme in schools could be adolescents (target population) express their confidence (determinant) in successfully negotiating with the partner about condom use (performance objective) (Schaalma & Kok, 2001). Proximal programme objectives may refer to individual level change (for example, adolescents will express confidence regarding negotiating condom use with a sexual partner), organizational change (for example, school administrators will acknowledge the advantages of condom distribution in the school), or community level change (for example, community leaders will approve of the sale of inexpensive condoms in schools and meeting places). A list of proximal programme objectives is usually long and should be ordered by determinant. Thus programme planners complete this first step with a series of lists of objectives per determinant, for instance, a list of all proximal programme objectives that have to do with skills and self-efficacy expectations.

11.3.2 Intervention mapping step 2: Theoretical methods and practical strategies

A 'theoretical method' is a specific change technique derived from theory and research. Such techniques can be used to realize a proximal programme objective. A 'practical strategy' is the application of that method in a particular context. For instance, a theoretical method for self-efficacy improvement could be modelling or observational learning, and a strategy could be the presentation of peer models in a video. An important task in this step is to identify the conditions or prerequisites that limit the effectiveness of theoretical models.

11.3.3 Intervention mapping step 3: Designing the programme

This step involves organizing practical strategies into a deliverable programme taking into account the characteristics of target groups and the constraints of settings within which the programme will be delivered. Planners have to integrate various strategies into one coherent programme; they have to make decisions on the programme structure, its theme, the sequence of strategies and the communication vehicles. Pilot materials need to be produced and tested. In this phase, planners usually collaborate with producers, such as text writers, graphic designers and video producers. Planners' major task is to convey programme intent to producers, and to ensure that final programme products adequately incorporate theoretical underpinnings.

11.3.4 Intervention mapping step 4: Anticipating implementation

A well-planned diffusion process is vital to ensure programme success. So, work on this step should begin early in programme planning and should involve the development of a linkage system that allows communication and collaboration between programme developers and programme users. A plan to promote adoption and implementation of the programme by the intended programme users should be developed. For example, in the case of a programme designed to change the behaviour of nurses, this might include a video modelling nurses using the programme and being reinforced because the programme is easy and the patients react positively. Step 4 is a re-run of the IM protocol aimed at identifying objectives, methods and strategies to promote the adoption and implementation of the intervention programme by the programme users.

11.3.5 Intervention mapping step 5: Anticipating process and outcome evaluation

Again, this process should begin early. For instance, adolescents express their confidence in successfully negotiating with the partner about condom use is an objective, but should also be operationalized as a measure of that objective, that can be applied in pre- and post-intervention tests with experimental and control group subjects. For example, self-report questionnaires might include the item, 'If you want to use condoms, to what extent do you feel confident that you can successfully negotiate with a future partner about condom use?'

11.4 APPLYING THEORY: ILLUSTRATIONS

The impact of theory is strongest in the process leading from programme objective to programme strategy, that is, between step 1 and the product of step 2. Theory provides method, or techniques, for the accomplishment of programme objectives; the prerequisites of the methods guide the translation of methods into practical strategies. However, things can go wrong if programmes fail to apply theory correctly. For example, an often-proposed strategy in prevention of drug use in schools is to have former drug users warn the students against the dangers of drugs. This strategy is very popular with students, teachers, parents, school boards and politicians. However, evaluation studies have shown that this strategy leads to increased drug use among the students (de Haes, 1987). Programme planners made two mistakes. First, former drug users provide a misleading model for students, suggesting that people who start using drugs can attain respectable positions, such as lecturing in schools. Second, the focus of the message is on the dangers of drug use while the most important determinants of the target behaviours are self-efficacy and skills in decision-making and resisting social pressure.

Theories are important for developing effective interventions and in the translation of theoretical methods into practical strategies. Below we discuss examples of adequate theory application using the IM protocol, starting with methods to improve self-efficacy and skills: modelling and active learning. The examples are from programmes found to be effective (Schaalma et al., 1996; Brug et al., 1998).

11.4.1 Modelling

One of the objectives in an HIV-prevention programme was that adolescents express their confidence in successfully negotiating condom use with a sexual partner (Schaalma & Kok, 2001). The determinant here is self-efficacy. To find methods for improving self-efficacy, we first turn to Social Cognitive Theory (Bandura, 1997). Suggested methods are modelling, guided practice and enactment. Other methods might be re-attribution, goal setting, and training in problem solving and stress management (Bartholomew et al., 2001). Modelling may be effective, but only within a number of prerequisites:

1 The target identifies with the model.
2 The model demonstrates feasible sub-skills.
3 The model receives reinforcement.
4 The target perceives the model as someone who is learning to cope with the real demands of the target situation. For example; 'I tried to negotiate condom use several times and was not successful, but now I can do it . . .' As opposed to a target who has already managed without dealing with the barriers salient to the target; e.g., 'I just mentioned that I wanted to have safe sex.'

Using modelling in the final programme will only be effective when the prerequisites are in place during the development of the practical strategies and materials. Schaalma et al. (1996) and Schaalma & Kok (2001) developed video scenarios as part of their programme in which models demonstrate sub-skills that are important when negotiating condom use with unwilling partners, namely, rejection, repeated rejection with arguments, postponement, making excuses, avoiding the issue and/or counterpose (derived from Evans et al., 1991). The models were carefully selected to serve as identifiable models for the target population. All scenarios had a positive ending, but the models clearly struggled with their task of persuading partners to use a condom. These scenes were only one part of the programme, in which a series of various methods for many objectives were translated into practical strategies within an integrated programme.

11.4.2 Active learning

Schaalma et al. (1996) and Schaalma & Kok (2001) presented their models in a context of active learning: video scenarios presenting high risk situations were stopped after the situation had developed. The students were then asked to elaborate on what they would do or advise the model to do, first individually, then in a group. After the break, the video was restarted and the students observed further development and ending of the scenario. Again, the group discussed the scenario. Active learning may be effective in almost any change method, as long as the situation provides enough motivation, information, time for elaboration and skills-related learning.

In the example below, taken from the video, a student resists social pressure from another student in relation to staying our late. Note that the student uses resistance techniques that had been introduced earlier in the programme (see above).

> Video scenario: In the discothèque
> *Boy*: Would you like another drink?
> *Girl*: No, I have to go home.
> *Boy*: Come on, don't be lame.
> *Girl*: No, I've got to be home at twelve.
> *Boy*: This is a great tune, let's dance.
> On screen: Assignment. Sasja really likes Mike. How does she make it clear that she still wants to be home at midnight? How will Mike react?
> Video stops, students discuss possible effective reactions. Video starts again.
> *Boy*: Don't you care about me any more?
> *Girl*: Yes, but that's not the point. They'll get on my case again if I don't get in before midnight.
> *Boy*: Come on, it can't be that bad.
> *Girl*: How do you know? I just want to go home. Besides, you'll ruin the whole evening if you're going to sulk.

Boy sinks to his knees in played apology.

Girl laughs: Come on, if I'm late, you'll be kneeling for my dad on Saturday.

Boy: So, you'll come on Saturday?

Girl: That's the plan.

Boy: Let's go.

This scenario uses role modelling in combination with active learning. All prerequisites of these methods are taken into account: identification, skills demonstration, reinforcement, coping model, information (on negotiation skills), and time for elaboration. One prerequisite for active learning may be underrepresented: motivation. Skills training often needs to be combined with methods to enhance motivation, in this case methods for increasing risk awareness and creating attitude change, anticipated regret and fear arousal.

11.4.3 Risk-scenario information

Another objective in the HIV-prevention school programme was that adolescents recognize the possibility of ending up in situations in which contracting HIV/STD cannot be ruled out. Here, the determinant is risk perception. We turn to theories on risk perception and risk communication for methods to improve personal risk perception. These theories suggest the provision of risk information and risk feedback, message framing, self (re-)evaluation, and fear arousal (Bartholomew et al., 2001). For instance, Hendrickx (1991) suggests that people may base risk judgements on information that facilitates representation of how particular outcomes may occur. An essential prerequisite for this method is that the information includes a plausible scenario with a cause and an outcome, not just an outcome. In their HIV prevention programme Schaalma et al. included peer models describing how they found themselves in situations that were risky (e.g., holiday love). By presenting causes as well as outcomes the scenarios make these contingencies seem more likely.

11.4.4 Changing attitudes and inducing anticipated regret

The anticipation of how one would feel after a risk behaviour, for instance having had unsafe sex, can promote attitude and intention change (Abraham & Sheeran, in press; Richard et al., 1995). Anticipated regret may be enhanced by asking people to imagine how they would feel after a risk behaviour. The prerequisite for anticipated regret is that they should stimulate imagery and anticipatory regret.

The Theory of Planned Behaviour (Ajzen, 1991; Connor & Sparks, 1996) suggests that changing relevant beliefs is the basis of attitude change. Witte (1995) organizes beliefs into categories, and identifies which beliefs need to be changed, which need to be reinforced and which need to be introduced. Schaalma and Kok (2001), for example, list the following objectives for attitude change, based on an earlier analysis of beliefs:

1 Adolescents perceive that condom use has advantages that are not related to health (to be introduced).
2 Adolescents have a strong perception of the health-related advantages of condom use (to be reinforced).
3 Adolescents recognize that the advantages of safe sex outweigh the disadvantages (to be changed).
4 Adolescents describe a plan to cope with the disadvantages of condom use (to be introduced).

Schaalma et al. used various methods for attitude change, including anticipated regret, active processing of information, linking beliefs with enduring values, and associating attitude object with positive stimuli. They combined the scenario information discussed earlier with the method of inducing anticipated regret.

11.4.5 Fear arousal

Many health promotion interventions use fear-arousing messages to promote preventative behaviour. Theories of fear-arousing communication (Eagly & Chaiken, 1993) and recent meta-analyses (Floyd et al. 2000; Milne et al. 2000) suggest that fear arousal may enhance the motivation to avert the threat, but that acceptance of health recommendations is dependent on people's outcome expectations regarding the recommendations (*'What will happen if I follow the recommendations?'*) and their self-efficacy (*'How confident am I that I can carry out the recommendations?'*). In addition, high levels of fear may inhibit persuasion through processes of denial and defensive avoidance (Ruiter et al., 2001), especially when response efficacy or self-efficacy is low (Witte & Allen, 2000). Consequently, when using fear arousal, coping methods for reducing the perceived threat should always be provided and targets should be taught skills necessary to employ such coping methods. The optimal strategy might be a combination of creating personal risk awareness, without arousing too much fear, and developing skills for the desired behaviour change.

Together, scenario information, anticipated regret and fear arousal may promote risk awareness and attitude and intention change. In the following example from the HIV prevention programme, the three methods are combined in one video scenario, again using modelling. This part of the video shows scenes in which students interview fellow students. The interview is introduced as a story told by a girl who was infected with Chlamydia. Her boyfriend is with her.

Girl: It wasn't with him last year. It was a boy I fell in love with on my holiday. So, we ended up in bed. I was prepared and brought some condoms, but he refused to use them. He kept saying: trust me, no AIDS. He was very persistent. It's okay to do it without one, just once. It was so stupid. But he was such a hunk. I wouldn't pass him up. I've got a much bigger hunk now (looks at her boyfriend). What's more, the boy looked very clean. But, it was very stupid of me. I slept with him without using a condom. I was on the pill at the time.

Interviewer: But why do it? It's risky as hell.

Girl: I didn't know what to think anymore. I thought: maybe it won't come to that. I thought, as long as I'm careful. And I was afraid I'd turn him off. I was doing it for him, basically. It was brought home to me later how stupid it was. I was pretty scared afterwards. And sure enough I got a discharge. I went to a doctor, who said I had a venereal disease. Chlamydia. I was petrified. It can make you infertile.

Interviewer: That would mean you could never have children!

Girl: I acted quickly, so it wasn't that bad. I was so angry with him afterwards. For saying he cared, but refusing to use a condom. Of course, I was angry with myself as well. I was stupid.

Interviewer: So, now you always use a condom?

Girl and Boyfriend: Yes!

Interviewer: So you don't agree with the holiday guy? (*to boyfriend*)

Boyfriend: No, I was glad she brought it up.

Interviewer: What do you mean?

Boyfriend: She mentioned it first. I don't talk about it very easy. I was afraid she'd think I jump into bed with any girl.

Girl: Nonsense, I think it's great if a boy brings it up. It means he really cares about you. I like boys who can talk about it. And sex is more fun if you know you are safe. No worries the next day.

Boyfriend: You bet. She takes care of the pill, and I take care of the condoms. We've got a nice condom joke (*both start laughing*).

Interviewer: Are you going to let me in on it?

Boyfriend: Before we make love . . . I say I've got to put a CD on!!

Interviewer: That's good. I've got to remember that.

In this example, the communication source is a peer, providing another example of modelling. Prerequisites of effectiveness have also been taken into account in designing the materials: Scenario imagery, cause and outcome, regret imagery, personal susceptibility, outcome expectations and self-efficacy enhancement and reinforcement of the desired behaviour.

Methods for increasing risk awareness and prompting attitude change need to be combined with methods to improve self-efficacy and skills. People need to be motivated to undertake active learning and skills training, but they also need to feel self-efficacious in order to accept unpleasant information (Bandura, 1997).

11.4.6 Behavioural journalism

Behavioural journalism is media-delivered behavioural modelling (McAlister, 1995) which makes use of role model stories based on authentic interviews with the target population. Within the target population, there will be some people who already perform the desired behaviours. These models give their reasons for adopting the new behaviour and highlight the reinforcing outcomes they experienced. The use of authentic interviews ensures that the content of the message is appropriate to the level of understanding of the target population and gives a realistic and credible picture of the target group's lifestyle. The challenge is to find the authentic story that corresponds to the recommendations of theory, without having to compromise the authenticity of the original interview.

Behavioural journalism can incorporate other methods, such as risk scenarios, anticipated regret and fear arousal. The holiday romance scenario is an example of behavioural journalism. In that case, behavioural journalism was combined with modelling, risk scenario information, anticipated regret, and fear arousal methods, taking into account the prerequisites: identification, skills demonstration, reinforcement, a coping model, cause-and-effect, stimulation of imagery, regret, personal susceptibility, outcome expectations and self-efficacy. This text is authentic because it was selected from an interview with an adolescent.

11.4.7 Personalized risk feedback by computer tailoring

Personal or tailored risk feedback in response to information provided by a target person has been identified as an effective method to motivate people to adopt healthier habits (DiClemente et al., 2001). Modern technology means that this need not involve individual counselling. Using computer tailoring or expert systems, personalized risk feedback can be provided to large groups of people at relatively low costs (Kreuter et al., 2000). Computer tailoring mimics the counsellor by first questioning the individual target person and then giving appropriate feedback messages, based on theoretical insights. In the work of Velicer and Prochaska (1999) on smoking cessation, messages were based on the Transtheoretical Model of Stages of Change and included processes of change tailored to the stage of the individual in regard to quitting smoking. Risk feedback included current status and stage of change, current use of change processes, suggested strategies and high-risk situations.

Computer tailoring may become more popular in the future and may be supplied using the internet (Brug et al., 2003). Various theories may be employed in computer tailoring and it is important that any theoretical prerequisites are included in the design of tailoring materials. For instance, in studies on determinants of dietary behaviours, it has been found that lack of awareness is a major barrier toward dietary change (Lechner et al., 1998). According to the Precaution Adoption Process theory (Weinstein & Sandman, 2002), risk feedback has been identified as a promising method to raise awareness. However, in order for risk feedback to be effective in raising awareness of personal intake levels it should include both personal risk feedback, comparison with a standard, and normative risk feedback, comparison with a reference group. Brug et al. (1998) provide an example of a computer-tailored intervention aimed at fat reduction. First, people are given personal risk feedback on their fat intake, usually indicating that it is higher than their self-rated level, to increase awareness. This personal risk feedback is followed by practical and personalized suggestions for behavioural change. People then receive feedback that their fat intake is higher than the recommended level. Lastly, people who are doing less well than the mean are given normative feedback so that those with higher than peer-average intake are informed of this fact. Normative feedback is especially effective in preventing people from rationalizing factual feedback. Later, feedback on people's progress can be provided.

11.4.8 Self-management of complex behaviours

Many health 'behaviours', for example increasing exercise, managing a chronic disease, or improving sexual health are complex because they involve sequences of different behaviours that need to be maintained over time. Dietary change, for example, may be quite different, in detail, from one person to another. Thus individual circumstances require different, that is, tailored messages.

Self-management is not a simple list of activities but is a flexible response to changing situations. Consider step 1 in an IM approach to designing a programme for asthma management by children (Bartholomew et al., 2000). The child must recognize threats and respond to them adequately. Self-management also involves self-correction which comprises three steps: (1) the monitoring of some aspect of behaviour or health; (2) evaluation: comparing one's observations with baseline or normal, and analysing the causes of the problem; and (3) action: trying a behavioural correction. Bartholomew et al. (2000) illustrated these steps for the target children in a rap song: Watch, Discover, Think and Act! The matrix of programme objectives for the children included for instance, identifies possible personal symptoms of asthma (skills/watch-discover), explains that medication work better if taken as described (outcome expectation/think), and describes and demonstrates the use of a peak flow meter (skills/act).

A self-management approach may help define and organize perform-ance objectives: monitoring, evaluation and action. For instance: monitor personal diet, evaluate problems and develop improvement plans, and act on these intentions. The actual content of the actions will be different for various people, but the systematic approach is the same. Of course, the performance objectives need to be completed by adding maintenance of behaviour change and maintenance of self-management. In this respect, the current interest in implementation intentions – that is, developing vivid ideas about when and where intended behaviour will be enacted – may lead to new ideas for effective interventions (Gollwitzer, 1999; Sheeran, 2002).

11.5 Conclusions

The systematic use of psychological theory in health promotion programmes has been neglected. More attention has been devoted to understanding health behaviour, than to understanding how to change it. Yet theories and empirical evidence form the basis for decisions made during the intervention planning process. Empirically supported theory can help answer questions about the health problem, behavioural and environmental causes, psychological determinants of relevant behaviours, appropriate objec-tives for intervention programme, appropriate methods and strategies, as well as the processes of programme implementation and evaluation. Often a multi-theory approach is required and theories must be applied at various levels (e.g., individual, group or society) because, for example, environmental change may depend on the behaviour of decision-makers. To change people's behaviour, whether they are students, teachers or politicians, the planner has to know about their motivation and skills.

IM (Bartholomew et al., 2001) is a protocol for systematically applying theoretical and empirical evidence when designing health promotion programmes. IM elaborates the programme development phase of the PRECEDE/PROCEED model for planning health promotion interventions (Green & Kreuter, 1999). IM involves: formulating programme objectives for the target group; selecting appropriate theoretical methods; translating methods into practical strategies within an integrated programme; and anticipating implementation and evaluation. In this chapter, we have concentrated on the application of theory in finding change methods and strategies for health promotion programmes. We have emphasized that planners need to faithfully translate principles and prerequisites specified by theory into techniques, methods and materials used in intervention programmes. We believe that use of the IM protocol can help bridge the gap between psychological theory and practice. It also highlights a number of the core skills that health psychologists need in order to practise competently.

11.6 CORE COMPETENCES

This chapter describes guidelines relating to (1) the identification of theories relevant to health promotion, (2) the translation of such theories into practical methods and materials in health promotion programmes, and (3) the evaluation of such programmes. Work of this kind requires health psychologists to have a good knowledge of psychological theory as well as the target health problem and related health behaviours. Health psychologists need to continually update and develop the knowledge they acquire during study for stage 1 of the British Psychological Society (BPS) qualification in health psychology. This is one aspect of core components unit 1.2 of the stage 2 qualification, that is, 'Contribute to the continuing development of self as a professional applied psychologist'.

The chapter should help readers understand and work towards the following core components of the BPS stage 2 qualification:

2.2a Identify theoretical models and research findings relevant to proposed research questions
2.2b Generate testable research questions and hypotheses
2.3c Conduct preliminary investigations of existing models and methods
2.5c Clarify and evaluate the implications of research outcomes for practice

2.5d Evaluate the potential impact of new developments on organizational functioning and healthcare practices

3.1a Identify, prioritize and agree expectations, needs and requirements of clients

3.2a Determine aims, objectives, criteria, theoretical frameworks and scope of interventions

3.2b Produce implementation plans for the consultancy

3.6a Identify evaluation needs and design evaluation

3.6b Implement planned evaluation

3.6c Assess the outcomes of the evaluation.

We have not discussed the process of reviewing relevant research literature but competence in this area is prerequisite to identifying useful psychological theories (see units 2.1 and 2.2). Research design competence (as specified by unit 2.2) is also relevant to applying theory to health promotion and to the evaluation of health promotion programmes. For example, component of competence 2.2a involves being able to 'identify, describe and evaluate the links between existing theoretical models and findings and the proposed research' (see guideline 2). This is essential to understanding the determinants of health behaviours and setting proximal programme objectives. Component 2.2b involves 'identifying areas of application (e.g., settings and populations) to which the developing research question is relevant' (guideline 1) and 'stating the purpose, aims and objectives of the research in relation to existing research findings' (guideline 3). Both tasks are crucial to applying theory appropriately in health promotion practice and to designing reliable and rigorous evaluation studies.

Unit 2.3, concerning the conduct of psychological research, is also relevant to developing theory-based health promotion materials and the evaluation of health promotion programmes. Core competence 2.3c involves being able to 'discuss the suitability and effectiveness of available psychological models and measures' (guideline 2) and 'undertake pilot studies capable of assessing the appropriateness and effectiveness of existing models, measures and techniques (guideline 3). Being able to guide others on the suitability and relevance of psychological models to health promotion and being able to pilot prototype materials are core skills for health psychologists working on development of effective health promotion.

Unit 2.5 specifies competences involved in initiating and developing psychological research. Components 2.5c and 2.5d are also important, involving, for example, 'assessing the applicability of new findings to particular areas of health psychology practice (e.g., health promotion)' (guideline 2.5c, 3), 'justifying developments in health psychology practice in relation to relevant and valid research findings' (guideline 2.5c, 5) and 'evaluating the impact of new practices suggested by research using valid and reliable methods' (guideline 2.5, 2). These are core skills in work involving the application of the research findings to the development to effective change programmes.

Research skills are essential to the development and evaluation of evidence-based health promotion programmes but this work also draws upon consultancy skills such as those specified by units 3.1 (assessment of requests for consultancy), 3.2 (planning consultancy) and 3.6 (evaluating consultancy). In this area of work, health psychologists collaborate with practitioners and the final product (e.g., the programme) must be both evidence-based and useful to practitioners who will implement it for it to have an impact. Hence core components 3.1a, 3.2a and 3.2b are all likely to be used in working with health promoters to design a health promotion programme. Components 3.6a, 3.6b and 3.6c all refer competence required to the design interventions and conduct evaluations thereof. These skills are as important to work in health promotion as to any other area of health psychology consultancy.

In addition to these core competences, the procedures described in this chapter are also relevant to three optional units of competence defined by the BPS stage 2 qualification. Units 5.1 (Implement interventions to change health-related behaviour) specifies competences necessary to deliver psychological change programmes. Unit 5.2 (Direct the implementation of interventions) specifies competences required to direct or manage the implementation of a change programme while unit 5.3 (Communicate the processes and outcomes of psychological interventions and consultancies) lists competences necessary to communicate effectively about and disseminate information about effective interventions.

REFERENCES

Abraham, C. & Sheeran, P. (in press). Deciding to exercise: The role of anticipated regret. *British Journal of Health Psychology*.

Adler, N.E. & Ostroff, J.M. (1999). Socioeconomic status and health: What we know and what we don't. *Annals of the New York Academy of Sciences* 896, 3–15.

Ajzen, I. (1991). The theory of planned behavior. *Organizational Behavior and Human Decision Processes* 50, 179–211.

Bandura, A. (1997). *Self-efficacy: The Exercise of Control*. New York: Freeman & Co.

Bartholomew, L.K., Parcel, G.S., Kok, G. & Gottlieb, N.H. (2001). *Intervention Mapping: Developing Theory- and Eevidence-based Health Promotion Programmes*. Mountain View, CA: Mayfield.

Bartholomew, L.K., Shegog, R., Parcel, G.S. et al. (2000). Watch, discover, think, and act: A model for patient education programme development. *Patient Education and Counseling* 39, 253–68.

Brug, J., Glanz, K., van Assema, P., Kok, G. & van Breukelen, G. (1998). The impact of computer-tailored feedback and iterative feedback on fat, fruit, and vegetable intake. *Health Education & Behavior* 25, 517–31.

Brug, J., Oenema, A. & Campbell, M. (2003). Past, present and future of computer-tailored nutrition education. *American Journal of Clinical Nutrition* 77 (4 Suppl), 1028S–34S.

Clark, N.M. & Zimmerman, B.J. (1990). A social cognitive view of self-regulated learning about health. *Health Education Research* 3, 371–9.

Connor, M. & Norman, P. (eds.) (1996). *Predicting Health Behaviour: Research and Practice with Social Cognitive Models*. Buckingham, UK: Open University Press.

Connor, M. & Sparks, P. (1996). Theory of planned behaviour and health behaviours. In M. Connor & P. Norman (eds), *Predicting Health Behaviour: Research and Practice with Social Cognitive Models*, 121–62. Buckingham, UK: Open University Press.

de Haes, W.F. (1987). Looking for effective drug education programmemes: Fifteen years exploration of the effects of different drug education programmes. *Health Education Research* 2, 433–8.

DiClemente, C.C., Marinilli, A.S., Singh, M. & Bellino, L.E. (2001). The role of feedback in the process of health behavior change. *American Journal of Health* 25, 217–27.

Eagly, A.H. & Chaiken, S. (1993). *The Psychology of Attitudes*. Fort Worth, TX: Harcourt Brace Jovanovich.

Evans, R.I., Getz, J.G. & Raines, B.E. (1991). Theory guided models in prevention of AIDS in adolescents. Paper presented at the Science Weekend at the American Psychological Association Meeting, San Francisco, August.

Floyd, D.L., Prentice-Dunn, S. & Rogers, R.W. (2000). A meta-analysis of research in protection motivation theory. *Journal of Applied Social Psychology* 30, 407–29.

Flynn, B.S., Goldstein, A.O., Solomon, L.J. et al. (1998). Predictors of state legislators' intentions to vote for cigarette tax increases. *Prevention Medicine* 2, 157–65.

Glanz, K.F., Lewis, F.M. & Rimer, B.K. (2002). *Health Behaviour and Health Education: Theory, Research and Practice* (3rd edn). San Francisco, CA: Jossey Bass.

Godin, G. & Kok, G. (1996). The theory of planned behaviour: A review of its applications to health related problems. *American Journal of Health Promotion* 11, 87–98.

Gollwitzer, P.M. (1999). Implementation intentions: Strong effects of simple plans. *American Psychologist* 54, 493–503.

Green, L.W. & Kreuter, M.W. (1999). *Health Promotion and Planning: An Educational and Ecological Approach*. Mountain View, CA: Mayfield.

Hamilton, R. & Chatala, E. (1994). *Learning and Instruction*. New York: McGraw-Hill.

Heaney, C.A. & Israel, A. (2002). Social networks and social support. In K.F. Glanz, F.M. Lewis & B.K. Rimer (eds), *Health Behavior and Health Education: Theory, Research and Practice* (3rd edn), 185–209. San Francisco, CA: Jossey Bass.

Hendrickx, L.C.W.P. (1991). *How versus How Often: The Role of Scenario Information and Frequency Information in Risk Judgment and Risky Decision-making.* Groningen, the Netherlands: Van Denderen.

Janz, N.K., Champion, V.L. & Strecher, V.J. (2002). The health belief model. In K.F. Glanz, F.M. Lewis & B.K. Rimer (eds), *Health Behavior and Health Education: Theory, Research and Practice* (3rd edn), 45–66. San Francisco, CA: Jossey Bass.

Kingdon, J. (1995). *Agendas, Alternative and Public Policies.* New York: Harper-Collins.

Kok, G., Schaalma, H., de Vries, H., Parcel, G.S. & Paulussen, T. (1996). Social psychology and health education. In M. Hewstone & W. Stroebe (eds), *European Review of Social Psychology,* 7, 242–82. Chichester, UK: Wiley.

Kreuter, M., Farell, D., Olevitch, L. & Brennan, L. (2000). *Tailoring Health Messages: Customizing Communication with Computer Technology.* Mahwah, NJ: Lawrence Erlbaum Associates.

Lechner, L., Brug, J., de Vries, H., van Assema, P. & Mudde, A. (1998). Stages of change for fruit, vegetable and fat intake: Consequence of misconception. *Health Education Research* 13, 1–11.

Marlatt, G.A. & Gordon, J.R. (1985). *Relapse Prevention.* New York: Guilford Press.

McAlister, A. (1995). Behavioral journalism: Beyond the marketing model for health communication. *American Journal of Health Promotion* 9, 417–20.

McGuire, W.J. (1985). Attitudes and attitude change. In G. Lindsey & E. Aronson (eds), *The Handbook of Social Psychology,* 2, 233–346. New York: Knopf.

McKenzie, J.F. & Smeltzer, J.L. (2001). *Planning, Implementing, and Evaluating Health Promotion Programmes.* Boston, MA: Allyn and Bacon.

Milne, S., Sheeran, P. & Orbell, S. (2000). Prediction and intervention in health-related behaviour: A meta-analytic review of protection motivation theory. *Journal of Applied Social Psychology,* 30, 106–43.

Minkler, M. & Wallerstein, N.B. (2002). Improving health through community organization and community building. In K.F. Glanz, F.M. Lewis & B.K. Rimer (eds), *Health Behavior and Health Education: Theory, Research and Practice* (3rd edn), 279–311. San Francisco, CA: Jossey Bass.

Montaño, D.E. & Kasprzyk, D. (2002). The theory of reasoned action and the theory of planned behavior. In K.F. Glanz, F.M. Lewis & B.K. Rimer (eds), *Health Behavior and Health Education: Theory, Research and Practice* (3rd edn), 67–98. San Francisco, CA: Jossey Bass.

Norman, P., Abraham, C. & Conner, M. (2000). *Understanding and Changing Health Behaviour: From Health Beliefs to Self-regulation.* Amsterdam: Harwood Academic Publishers.

Paulussen, T., Kok, G. & Schaalma, H. (1994). Antecedents to adoption of classroom-based AIDS education in secondary schools. *Health Education Research* 9, 485–96.

Paulussen, T., Kok, G., Schaalma, H. & Parcel, G.S. (1995). Diffusion of AIDS curricula among Dutch secondary school teachers. *Health Education Quarterly* 22, 227–43.

Petty, R.E., Barden, J. & Wheeler, S.C. (2002). The Elaboration Likelihood Model of Persuasion: Health promotions that yield sustained behavioural change. In R.J. DiClemente, R.A. Crosby & M.C. Kegler (eds), *Emerging Theories in Health Promotion Practice and Research*, 71–99. San Fransisco, CA: Jossey Bass.

Prochaska, J.O., Redding, C.A. & Evers, K.E. (2002). The Transtheoretical Model and Stages of Change. In K.F. Glanz, F.M. Lewis & B.K. Rimer (eds), *Health Behavior and Health Education: Theory, Research and Practice* (3rd edn), 99–120. San Francisco, CA: Jossey Bass.

Richard, L., Potvin, L., Kishuk, N., Prlic, H. & Green, L.W. (1996). Assessment of the integration of the ecological approach in health promotion programmes. *American Journal of Health Promotion* 10, 318–28.

Richard, R., Van der Pligt, J. & De Vries, N. (1995). Anticipated affective reactions and prevention of AIDS. *British Journal of Social Psychology* 34, 9–21.

Rogers, E.M. (1995). *Diffusion of Innovations*. New York: Free Press.

Rogers, R.W. (1983). Cognitive and physiological processes in fear appeals and attitude change: A revised theory of protection motivation. In R.E. Petty (ed.), *Social Psychophysiology: A Sourcebook*, 153–76. New York: Guilford Press.

Rogers, R.W. & Prentice-Dunn, S. (1997). Protection motivation theory. In D.S. Gochman (ed.), *Handbook of Health Behaviour Research*. I: *Personal and Social Determinants*, 1, 113–32. New York: Plenum Press.

Rossi, P.H., Freeman, H.E. & Lipsey, M.W. (1999). *Evaluation: A Systematic Approach* (6th edn). Newbury Park, CA: Sage.

Ruiter, R.A.C., Abraham, S.C.S. & Kok, G. (2001). Scary warnings and rational precautions: A review of the psychology of fears appeals. *Psychology and Health* 16, 613–30.

Schaalma, H. & Kok, G. (2001). A school AIDS-prevention program in the Netherlands. In K. Bartholomew, G.S. Parcel, G. Kok & N. Gottlieb (eds), *Intervention Mapping: Designing Theory and Evidence-based Health Promotion Programs*, 353–86. Mountain View, CA: Mayfield.

Schaalma, H., Kok, G.J., Bosker, R., Parcel, G.S., Peters, L., Poelman, J. & Reinders, J. (1996). Planned development and evaluation of AIDS/STD education for secondary school students in the Netherlands: Short term effects. *Health Education Quarterly* 23, 469–87.

Sheeran, P. (2002). Intention-behavior relations: A conceptual and empirical review. In W. Stroebe & M. Hewstone (eds), *European Review of Social Psychology*, 12, 1–36.

Sheeran, P. & Abraham, S.C.S. (1996). The health belief model. In M. Connor & P. Norman (eds), *Predicting Health Behaviour: Research and Practice with Social Cognition Models*, 23–61. Buckingham, UK: Open University Press.

Steckler, A., Goodman, R.M. & Crozier Kegler, M. (2002). Mobilizing organizations for health enhancement: Theories of organizational change. In K.F. Glanz,

F.M. Lewis & B.K. Rimer (eds), *Health Behavior and Health Education: Theory, Research and Practice* (3rd edn), 335–60. San Francisco, CA: Jossey Bass.

Strecher, V.J., Seijts, G.H., Kok, G.J. et al. (1995). Goal setting as a strategy for health behaviour change. *Health Education Quarterly* 22, 190–200.

Velicer, W.F. & Prochaska, J.O. (1999). An expert system intervention for smoking cessation. *Patient Education and Counseling* 36, 119–29.

Weiner, B. (1986). *An Attributional Theory of Motivation and Emotion.* New York: Springer.

Weinstein, N.D. & Sandman, P.M. (2002). The Precaution Adoption Process Model. In K.F. Glanz, F.M. Lewis & B.K. Rimer (eds), *Health Behavior and Health Education: Theory, Research and Practice* (3rd edn), 121–43. San Francisco, CA: Jossey Bass.

Westen, D. (1996). *Psychology: Mind, Brain & Culture.* New York: John Wiley & Sons.

Witte, K. (1995). Fishing for success: Using the persuasive health message framework to generate effective campaign messages. In E. Maibach & R.L. Parrott (eds), *Designing Health Messages: Approaches from Communication Theory and Public Health Practice,* 145–66. Thousand Oaks, CA: Sage Publications.

Witte, K. & Allen, M. (2000). A meta-analysis of fear appeals: Implications for effective public health campaigns. *Health Education and Behavior* 27 (5), 591–615.

Chapter 12

CONSULTANCY: WHAT IS IT, HOW DO YOU DO IT, AND DOES IT MAKE ANY DIFFERENCE?

Louise Earll and Julian Bath

12.1 INTRODUCTION

The world within which organizations have to survive is characterized by change. Technology is advancing, customer needs are changing, and pressures from the government are increasing. Within organizations, the needs and goals of employees are constantly under review. No longer can organizations rely on the methods and structures of yesterday. Constant change, and the need for effective management of change, has fuelled a rapid increase in the use of 'consultants' and the need for consultancy skills. It is therefore crucial that health psychologists have a clear focus and understanding of what consultancy is and how to do it in order that the skills involved can be clearly articulated and effectively marketed to a range of organizations.

Consultancy is not unique to health psychology, and principles of good consultancy can be found in other areas of psychology. Neither is the consultancy role a new one (Brunning et al., 1990; Earll et al., 1998). Michie (1998) makes the point that it has to a large extent been taken for granted, and it is only recently with the rapid and continuous pace of change that there has been a need to operationalize and identify this as a significant contribution that psychologists can bring to the workplace.

12.2 WHAT IS CONSULTANCY?

12.2.1 Definition of consultancy

The working definition of consultancy used in this chapter simply refers to 'a formal relationship where one party seeks help from another, the consultant's role being to facilitate the process whereby both the consultant and client arrive at a mutually acceptable solution'. That 'party' can be an individual, a group or an organization. The process of consultancy is similar whether it is undertaken for money or as part of one's job within the organization.

Many definitions of consultancy highlight the 'helping' nature of the relationship. It is imperative to ensure that the process of consultation is empowering for the client. Porter (2003) argues that the development of complex processes or 'technologies' and the elevation of the consultant to expert can lead to disempowerment, by making a simple process into a technique, which then becomes the specialized knowledge of a few experts.

12.2.2 A consultancy service

One of the authors (LE) has run a consultancy service within the UK National Health Service (NHS) Health Psychology Department since 1993. This arose out of necessity and was not part of the original job description under which the author was employed. The department had been set up on 'soft monies' and the short-term grants from a variety of sources were a significant, if insubstantial, source of funding. These grants enabled the department to 'subsidize' unfunded services to patients. With a change in NHS funding, which came about in a reorganization, this became untenable and only some of the services being provided were funded by the organization. To sustain the other patient services, and retain the psychologists employed to provide them, external funding needed to be found. A skills analysis of the psychologists in post identified consultancy as a viable and ethically acceptable activity which could be marketed effectively. Also, and importantly, the activity would bring in sufficient income to pay both for the time of those undertaking the consultancy and for the unfunded services. There were two main consultancy streams identified: providing expert opinion in the form of medico-legal reports in personal injury cases, and using research and facilitation skills to contribute to the planning and development of services to clients in other public sector and non-statutory organizations within the locality. This chapter focuses on the latter.

When developing the consultancy, it became increasingly clear that we needed to have some agreed parameters or 'values' which would guide us when making decisions as to whether or not to take on a contract. Consultancy needs to be embedded within a set of core values, and while such values have been explicitly incorporated into ethical guidelines, for example within research and the therapeutic relationship, this is less explicit in the area of consultancy. The British Psychological Society (2000), 'Code of Conduct, Ethical Principles and Guidelines' does not directly refer to consultancy but states that psychologists should, 'recognize and work within limits' of their professional competence and adhere to specific guidelines on conduct, consent and confidentiality.

Core underpinning values of consultancy should:

- maximize participation and minimize inequality;
- be solution focused, creating workable solutions to real-life problems;
- be transparent and inclusive;
- wherever possible, embed the work within existing organizational structures where those whose responsibility it is to implement the findings are empowered by the process and not de-skilled by it.

12.2.3 Consultancy competences

Consultancy includes the following stages:

- assess requests for consultancy;
- plan the work and negotiate the contract;
- establish, develop and maintain working relationships with clients;
- conduct and monitor the consultancy;
- evaluate the impact of the consultancy.

While it may appear from the above list that consultancy is a strictly linear process, with one stage logically leading to the next in a set order, the reality is that consultancy is an iterative process, where, depending on the level of participation, each stage informs the next. Initial plans, therefore, need sufficient flexibility to respond to either changing demands or unforeseen developments. It is therefore important that the consultancy contract reflects the fluid, and sometimes unpredictable, nature of the work.

Two examples from the authors' practices will be used to illustrate the consultancy competences: a relatively small-scale internal consultancy project, and a large external consultancy project. The former project, undertaken within the renal service of a District General Hospital, focuses on how research and training can be integral components of a consultancy project. The latter project, with older people, illustrates how consultancy was undertaken within a multi-agency framework. A variety of methods was used to address the current government agenda of involving older people in an active role in defining their own needs.

12.3 ASSESSMENT OF REQUESTS FOR CONSULTANCY

It is not unusual for the request for consultancy to come from an organization or area of work about which one has very little knowledge. This was certainly the case in the Older People's project, which involved working with community organizations that were themselves in the process of major change. In addition, the client group was not one that the consultant had had any previous experience of working with.

Harrison (1995) states that an accurate assessment (diagnosis) is the key to success. 'A good diagnosis is worth a thousand trial-and-error interventions. It permits people to achieve positive results with minimum effort, and prevents the harm that normally occurs as a result of change efforts which are not grounded.' When first approached with a request for help it is useful to have a checklist to guide you. For example:

- Who is the client?
- What is the question?
- What is the background and organizational context?
- Why has the client contacted you?
- What is the timeframe for the work?
- Does the client have a realistic appraisal of what you can achieve?
- What is the client's 'bottom line'?

12.3.1 Identify the client

While at one level this seems a relatively simple task, in reality the question of who the client is can be ambiguous and problematical. One can find oneself not knowing whom one is working for, or working with several clients whose goals are in conflict with each other. In order to clarify this, Schein (1987) categorizes clients into *contact, intermediate, primary* and *ultimate. Contact clients* approach the consultant initially, *intermediate clients* get involved in early meetings or planning next steps, *primary clients* own a problem for which they want help, and *ultimate clients* may or may not be directly involved with the consultant but their welfare and interest must be considered in planning further interventions.

In addition, one needs to identify the *stakeholders* and also the person who will *sponsor* the piece of work within the organization to ease the path for the consultant. *Stakeholders* can come from a wide group of people and organizations who relate to the client, and whose involvement with the organization will impinge on its success in both undertaking and implementing the outcomes of the work. The *sponsor* is the person within the organization who can act as the main point of contact with the consultant, and who will facilitate the necessary access and permissions needed to proceed with the work.

It is therefore essential to clarify the following early on:

- What authority does the client have to enlist your help?
- Are they sufficiently influential or powerful within their organization to implement and resource both the project and any outcomes?
- Who has budgetary responsibility for the work, and/or manages the people you will need to work with in order to undertake the work?
- Are there other clients you need to meet at this stage before proceeding?

In the case of the renal project, the initial contact was made by the lead Renal Consultant to the author (JB). It was clear that managerial involvement would be needed to develop this work, and a meeting was arranged with the management of the Haemodialysis Unit. This led to the wider involvement of the nursing staff and patients in the unit. The Older People's project was undertaken in collaboration with a co-consultant (Sue Porter, Sustainable Futures) with expertise in action research and participatory methodology. The client represented a collaboration of a local Health Improvement Partnership and a Primary Care Trust.

12.3.2 Clarify the question

The question addressed by the consultancy should be operationalized in terms of what outcomes need to be achieved and who will be responsible for making things happen. The objectives need to be specific, measurable, achievable, realistic and timely. The success of the evaluation of the consultancy depends on the clarity of the question.

The renal consultation came about as the result of a patient complaint concerning the care received from some of the staff in the haemodialysis unit. The initial formulation put forward by the lead renal consultant was that this might have been attributable to 'work stress' within the unit. The initial letter requested help to deal with this. A series of meetings resulted in reframing the question in terms of a need to identify what the nature and scale of the issues were for staff and patients in a way that could be taken forward by the management committee of the unit.

The initial question posed in the Older People's project was to provide the client with a clearer understanding of the needs of older people within a Gloucestershire borough. In particular, the client wanted to know what support was needed to enable older people to maintain their independence. With the publication of the UK Government's National Service Framework for Older People, this was modified to include 'in a way consistent with the aims and philosophy outlined in the NSF for Older People'.

12.3.3 Understand the background and organizational context

The first step to achieving an accurate assessment of the system is to understand the relevant background, using the following questions.

Is there significant organizational change, either current or planned? The commissioning agencies for the Older People's project were undergoing major organizational change, and thus organizational structures were unclear and roles not yet defined. In the course of the project, the project sponsor was promoted and there were many changes in the stakeholder group, necessitating work with staff new to the area. Within the renal unit, staff sickness and absence were high and, anecdotally, stress among the workforce was reported to be high. A particular problem with a senior staff member on long-term sick leave was placing the unit under considerable pressure and major building work being carried out at the unit was disrupting the normal working routine of the staff.

Where in the business planning cycle is the organization? The Older People's needs assessment had to be commissioned before the end of the financial year and some feedback provided for planning purposes within six months in order that the resources for any recommended action could be included in the business case.

What contribution is this work expected to make to the core business of the organization, e.g. achieving national targets, complying with government policy, meeting the local modernization agenda? The Older People's project was commissioned just prior to the launch of the National Service Framework (NSF) for Older People (Department of Health, 2001). A key aspect of the NSF was the involvement of older people in defining their own needs. The research recognized this and gave older people an active role in the research process by giving them the opportunity to volunteer as interviewers and to directly participate and influence service planning.

What is the anticipated or desired outcome of this work for the organization? Examples of outcomes are helping to meet government waiting list targets, enabling a change in existing work practices to facilitate speedier throughput of patients, and achieving a maximum two-week wait to see a breast cancer specialist. Within the renal service, improving the quality of the patient experience was a key driver for the work and a necessary outcome if the project was to be successful. With respect to the Older People's project, meeting as many targets as possible within the NSF was a clear objective.

At the assessment stage, it is neither realistic nor wise to allocate vast amounts of time and resources to undertaking a comprehensive literature search. However, it is necessary to be aware of the main issues and/or key documents, and to be able to identify and access colleagues with expertise in the given area to enable you to identify, where relevant, the appropriate theoretical frameworks.

12.3.4 Why has the client contacted the consultant?

The reasons clients give for contacting you can provide you with an idea as to their perception of what you can offer. This enables you to correct any misperceptions and gives you the opportunity to provide information about what you can do. Reasons given may vary widely and include familiarity with your work in other settings. For example, one of the authors (JB) was contacted with respect to the patient complaint within the renal service as he was the psychologist on the multidisciplinary team whose expertise in research and providing interventions within the team were recognized and valued. A frequent route to consultancy is the recommendation of a colleague or former client. LE was invited to collaborate in the Older People's project as previous collaborations had been fruitful and enjoyable.

With tight deadlines and a wide ranging remit, consultancy frequently requires a skill mix approach as no one person can reasonably profess to possess them all. Working in this environment is therefore a continual learning experience and a shared responsibility. In this project, there was a need to combine both qualitative and quantitative methodologies within a tight timetable. The consultant can take a proactive approach, contacting clients and marketing the skills he or she is offering. Boulton (2003) makes it clear that to achieve this you need vision coupled with a clear description of what it is that you do that people will pay for.

The consultant may well be aware of changes within their own organizations, or have identified areas where they feel their specific skills could be used to address clearly stated needs (e.g., achieving sustainable lifestyle changes in smoking, obesity and teenage pregnancies). A preliminary discussion is necessary to evaluate whether the potential client perceives the need for help and, if so, whether they consider you to be a potential source of that help. This must be based on a clear understanding of the problem, stressing the participative nature of the relationship. This ensures that the client does not perceive the offer of help to be potentially disempowering. In addition, a consultant might be used to deflect a potential unacceptable outcome from the client, thus preserving the client's positive standing within the organization.

12.3.5 Establish the timeline

If the work is to inform the planning process, or meet a specific deadline, then the timing of the output is crucial. This will, in many instances, inform both your decision to undertake the work, and the method adopted. There is invariably a need to feed back progress to the client at specified points and these need to be clearly established so that the consultant can allocate time flexibly to meet these needs. In many instances, if the work is not timely, then it is of no, or limited, use.

The initial timeline required by the client for the Older People's project was unachievable, since the request was for a comprehensive needs assessment within two months from start to finish. The work was reluctantly turned down. However, the client reconsidered and a compromise was reached regarding the provision of feedback at different stages to enable some timely input into the planning process.

12.3.6 What the consultant can offer

An assessment at an early stage can lead to a reframing of the problem or question, which may mean that the consultant does not need to be part of the solution. In this case, it is essential that the assessment can serve as an intervention in its own right and be a positive experience for both parties. This is equally true when working therapeutically with individuals. Schein (1987) states that, to get the most out of the initial consultation, it is helpful to think in terms of types of intervention:

Exploratory interventions: 'Can you tell me a bit more about the situation?'

Diagnostic interventions: 'Why is this an issue now?', 'Why do you want to bring in someone from outside the organization?'

Action alternative interventions: 'What have you tried to do about this yourself . . . has it worked and, if not why not?'

Confrontive interventions: 'Isn't this something you should be sorting out yourself?', 'You will need to be clearer about your desired outcomes before I can help you'.

There is a range of models available to the consultant dependent on the nature of the problem. The models described by Schein (1987) and discussed by Brunning et al. (1990), are outlined below and include providing:

- *Technical expertise*: e.g., setting up a database, analysing data;
- *Professional expertise*: frequently referred to as the doctor-patient model;
- *Process consultation*: this is less about providing solutions and more about using facilitation skills to develop equal partnerships between the consultant and the clients based on information, knowledge and empowerment (Rifkin & Pridmore, 2001);
- *Collaborative consultation*: this model is useful when faced with diverse and complex problems. As part of the assessment process, the consultant can become aware that not only do they not have all the necessary skills, but they neither have the time available to do the work within the client's required time frame. Working with colleagues (in LE's case, Professor Marie Johnston, Department of Psychology, University of Aberdeen, Scotland and Sue Porter, Consultant, Sustainable Futures) to complement their skills can mean that a successful outcome for the client is achievable. This model is the preferred modus operandi as it is a satisfying way of working and ensures that the piece of work enhances the learning experience and contributes to personal development by facilitating a more reflective approach to consultancy.

12.3.7 The bottom line

For external consultancy, the ability to pay for the work needs clarifying early in the process. For both internal and external work, the ability to deploy resources for the task within the given timeframe is crucial. It is not unusual for the client to expect the piece of work to provide solutions to a range of problems – yesterday. It is therefore essential that the 'bottom line' is clearly identified at the very beginning. A question it is always useful to ask of all clients is: 'For this piece of work to be successful/useful, what is the single most important thing that needs to be achieved and by when?' The bottom line for the Older People's project was that the process genuinely and actively engaged older people in identifying the issues and in taking part in solution-focused action planning.

In addition, the information had to feed into the planning cycle for the new organization.

12.4 PLAN THE WORK AND NEGOTIATE THE CONTRACT

Following the initial assessment, there will usually be some agreement as to whether to proceed to securing a contract. Negotiating the contract and planning the work is an iterative process and changes may be made to a draft contract as plans for the consultancy develop. It may be a learning experience for the client who may not have previously sought the help of a consultant. A shared understanding of the problem and of the potential solution, together with the development of a trusting relationship, is an important goal at this stage.

12.4.1 Identify the client's resources

The available 'ball park' budget for the piece of work needs to be ascertained at an early stage. This enables the consultant to allocate a proportionate amount of time researching the background and planning the work. There is little point working up a £200,000 piece of work, and spending three weeks doing it, if all that is available is £2,000. While the client might not always wish to disclose this piece of information, it helps to outline a range of cost-related options for undertaking the work, to enable the client to set realistic expectations. Projects undertaken by the author have ranged from £2,300 for a literature review to just under £250,000 to work over four years with all the statutory and non-statutory drug agencies in the county. The remit of the latter was to design, develop and implement a database to monitor people who access services for Class A drug misuse to inform the planning of services within the county. Most contracts have been around £12,000–£15,000 over a 12-month period. With respect to the Older People's project, it was not entirely clear how much money was 'on the table'. The funding was accessed from more than one funding source and, in addition, there was considerable uncertainty arising out of the organizational change.

Having identified the budget, it is important to be clear about whether the desired outcome can be achieved and which, if any, of the client's objectives can be met. If the available budget cannot meet all the objectives, those elements of the work that could be undertaken by the client need to be specified. The project team for the Older People's project agreed to identify and access older people for the research. Unfortunately, the organizational change made this difficult, with minimal continuity of staffing between each stage of the project.

It is sometimes helpful to 'stage' the project and cost each stage separately, so that the success of the first stage can support the request for additional funding. It is essential in this instance that each stage provides a 'stand-alone' contribution to the overall question, and that this is clearly stated in the proposal. The 'added value' of the additional stages needs to be clear. An understanding of the budgetary cycle is useful, since additional funds may be released if the work spans two financial periods. In addition, it can be helpful for organizations to invoice for the work before the end of the financial year, in advance of the work being undertaken. Clear accounting and financial procedures need to be adhered to, with a clear ring-fencing of funding for a given project.

Alternative, and frequently creative, ways of achieving the outcome without the use of the consultant should be explored. The client can be helped to consider different strategies which may include the deployment of existing staff, or organizing the work in a different way so that it can be incorporated into the existing agenda of the workforce or client. As part of this, the client's access to information, both paper and electronic, and the personnel who can facilitate that access, need to be identified.

12.4.2 Prepare a written proposal

The written proposal can form the basis for the contract and should be relatively brief (usually no longer than four to five sides of A4). For some external contracts, it is necessary to enter a tendering phase. This will involve being one of several consultants who are asked to prepare a written proposal for submission to the prospective client. It is also good practice to prepare a written proposal for internal contracts.

Having obtained a realistic appraisal of the resources available, it may be necessary to carry out some limited background work. This may involve a brief literature search, meeting with selected key personnel, and ensuring that the methodology you propose is understood by and acceptable to the client and the culture of the organization. More detailed background work, including in some cases a systematic review, needs to be included in the methodology and costed, and only undertaken once the contract is secured, as this can take a substantial amount of time.

The proposal needs to include an introduction outlining the background to the piece of work, both national and local. In the case of the Older

People's project, the introduction had to clearly refer to the NSF for Older People and to national and local population trends. Reference was also made to the key functions of Primary Care Groups including improving the health of the local community, reducing inequalities, developing primary care and community services and commissioning from secondary care to meet patients' needs.

Measurable aims and objectives need to be clearly specified. The aim of the Older People's project, 'to seek the views of older people living in a Gloucestershire borough in order to obtain a clearer understanding of their needs', was accompanied by the following objectives; to:

- clarify the issues of importance to older people and to identify their concerns;
- find out how older people view the services currently available to them;
- identify which services are working well, which need to be improved, and the gaps in service provision;
- recommend ways to provide services;
- involve users in both undertaking the research and planning solutions;
- disseminate the findings to service planners.

The method should be clearly linked to the objectives, explaining why the particular method has been selected. For this project, the criteria for the assessment method were that the team:

- listen to, and understand, people's views, and how people make sense of their experiences;
- deal with the 'unexpected' from participants;
- undertake the work in a way consistent with the aims and philosophy outlined in the NSF for Older People;
- use robust and credible methodology, and employ triangulation of method;
- be data driven rather than theory driven;
- give a picture of the 'here and now';
- be solution focused;
- inform the delivery team;
- work cost effectively.

Consideration needs to be given to ensure compliance with confidentiality, human rights, the identification of patient information (Caldicott Committee, 1997), data protection and ethics requirements. Local procedures, policies and regulations need to be taken into account in offering such advice. Some pieces of work require recommendations to be made, others do not. If recommendations are required, the responsibilities of the consultant and that of the client need to be delineated. It is usually appropriate to discuss the recommendations at a meeting with the project team if one wants to maximize action. The Older People's project involved the feedback from a public 'making sense' meeting.

A clear description of how the results will be analysed, reported and disseminated should be provided. The Older People's project relied heavily on qualitative data. It was clearly stated that this would be content analysed, involving the identification of common themes such as transport, which would then be split into sub-themes, such as private and public transport. The use of two independent raters was also specified, with the requirement for a minimum of 80 per cent inter-rater agreement. It was also specified that representative quotes would be used to illustrate the themes. A dissemination strategy should be included at this stage, to include the scope (e.g. local and/or national) and specification of the quality and quantity of the final reports (e.g., copied/printed, ring bound/ stapled, black and white/colour).

A transparent unambiguous programme of work should be linked to outcomes, costs and timeline.

- Identify those undertaking the work with, or on behalf of, the consultant. In this instance, the research team was specified, including the partnership between the two consultants.
- Clearly delineate the consultant's and client's areas of responsibility, making explicit the implications for the project should either party fail to deliver their agreed actions within the agreed timeframe. In this case, this was fortunate, as the original project team were unable to complete their agreed task of identifying older people from within their services due to organizational change. This delayed the project by several months, but was very clearly not the responsibility of the research team.
- Identify a project team. The client needs to identify a group of people, frequently stakeholders and key people in the organization, with responsibilities for planning and delivering services. It may be necessary to extend the membership of the group for the duration of the project, but this needs to be negotiated with the existing team once the contract is secured. The timing and frequency of these meetings should be used to guide the reporting and monitoring framework. In the Older People's project, this comprised a group of statutory and voluntary organizations who were already meeting to plan better health and social care services.

12.4.3 Presentation to the client and project team

Presentation to the client is part of the contract negotiation and planning, and is often the first step in the implementation of the work. It is also a valuable opportunity to secure the commitment of the organization and project group, who are key in any implementation of findings. Such a meeting enables the client to feel confident about the proposal and establishes the client and project team as equal partners in the work, with equal responsibility for the outcome. This meeting should be interactive: the consultant needs to facilitate discussion, and establish the need for active involvement from the team. The team needs to agree a project sponsor as the main point of contact for the consultant; this is usually, but not necessarily always, the contact client. The consultant needs to ensure that notes of the meeting are taken as a public record and circulated to members for verification.

12.4.4 Amend the proposal

Some modifications are usually necessary to the original proposal following the initial project team meeting. It is important to specify any additional team members who may be co-opted onto the existing team for the duration of the project, or at times when the consultant reports back to the team. Any amendments need to be acknowledged in writing from the project sponsor (email will suffice as long as a copy is kept). Ensure that a covering letter goes with the proposal and refers to the main changes agreed, clearly stating any implications for timeline or costs. This should be copied to the project team and include the amended proposal.

12.4.5 Specify the monitoring and reporting framework

Regular meetings should be set up with the sponsor and project team. Where possible, these should form part of the agenda of existing meetings. Trying to set up additional meetings with a wide range of senior personnel is an onerous and time-consuming task. Informal reporting arrangements need to be agreed, such as updates by email when each of the stages outlined in the proposal have been completed. There needs to be clarity as to how this will be undertaken, that is, interim reports, verbal updating at meetings, formal presentations, feedback at specific stages of the project, updates if the project deviates from the agreed parameters.

For the end of the project, potential dissemination opportunities such as national and/or local conferences to which the client may wish to present should be identified. It is likely that the client may wish to disseminate the results to a wide range of groups within the client's organization. This can be done in conjunction with the consultant, or the consultant may furnish the client with a Powerpoint presentation together with handouts. The consultant may also suggest assisting the client in facilitating workshops as part of the action planning stage within the client's organization.

12.5 UNDERTAKE AND MONITOR THE WORK

Collaborative planning and thorough preparation pay off in the implementation of the work, enabling it to proceed as smoothly as possible. However, despite the work put into preparing the proposal and establishing a relationship with the client, an agreement to take the work forward might not be forthcoming. This can happen as a result of organizational changes, changing priorities, funding 'drying up', or a reappraisal on the part of the consultant as to the 'do-ability' of the project. The most frequent reasons are too short a timeline and unrealistic funding.

12.5.1 The renal service

In both examples outlined in this chapter, the research methods used followed from the original question posed (see Chapter 5). In the case of the renal consultation, a needs analysis was carried out using both qualitative and quantitative research methods. When the results were analysed, it became apparent that the patients at the Haemodialysis Unit were generally satisfied with the care that they received from the staff. However, the majority of the staff reported that they would benefit from further training in communication skills, in what they perceived to be a very stressful environment. This was within the job remit of the internal consultant, and did not incur additional costs for the organization.

In discussion with the manager of the renal unit it was felt that a 'rolling' programme of four one-hour teaching sessions covering a variety of psychological issues was the most appropriate intervention for this group of staff. This training included active listening and basic counselling skills and was carried out by a health psychologist. A follow-up assessment several months after the training had finished showed that both staff and patient satisfaction had improved. Interventions like this enable the role of the internal consultant to develop flexibly in response to identified need.

12.5.2 The Older People's project

The needs assessment for this project was the beginning of a process of collecting information to make a plan for action, and not an end in itself. The distinct feature of this consultancy was that the consultant worked with those being researched, both to design the questions and to optimize and implement solutions. The disadvantage is that generalizability may be compromised; the advantage is that the likelihood of appropriate implementation may be enhanced. While representative sampling is often the preferred choice for conducting quantitative surveys, this is rarely an appropriate method for carrying out an in-depth needs assessment. In this context, the primary consideration is the selection of specific people with relevant experiences and an awareness of issues relevant to their group or community.

The project was divided into five stages, each stage informing the next:

- *Stage 1:* Consultation with the project team. This involved a mapping exercise with 15 stakeholders to identify key existing services available to older people in the area.
- *Stage 2:* A free-text questionnaire. This was completed at the consultation meeting and sent to those services identified within the mapping process.
- *Stage 3*: Recruitment and training. Older people were recruited via a media campaign. The project was publicized widely by local radio and newspapers and by posters in public places such as libraries and leisure centres. Fifty-two people volunteered to be interviewed, and 10 people joined the research team as interviewers. The training took the form of a half-day workshop, with the time and place arranged to be convenient to the older people taking part. Expenses were paid and lunch provided. The training was interactive, with the participants invited to contribute both to the scope and wording of the questions as well as to a discussion of the skills needed as an interviewer.
- *Stage 4:* Interviews. Thirty-one of the 52 interviews were undertaken by older people. This involved a small number of questions to which free-text replies were sought. These interviews were analysed by the research team, and then fed back to the interviewers to seek clarification and ensure that they accurately reflected their perceptions at the time.

- *Stage 5*: 'Making sense' meeting. The team fed back to a publicly advertised meeting consisting of older people, those organizations working in the area, interviewees and interviewers, plus other interested stakeholders. The meeting gathered further information on the issues identified and the formulation and action planning of possible solutions.

Data analysis was undertaken on completion of each stage to inform the planning and execution of the next stage of the project. The questionnaires and interviews were content analysed to identify common themes. Comments concerning a broad issue such as transport may fall into a number of sub-categories such as public and private transport. Full descriptions of these themes were developed and comments categorized by two independent coders. Results from the quantitative and qualitative data and comments made from the public meeting were reported and included representative quotes. A brief summary was produced and sent to all those involved in the project, with a contact number for those wishing to obtain the full report. Recommendations were made and organized to facilitate identification and ownership by the respective organizations responsible for providing services for older people.

12.6 Evaluate the Impact of the Consultancy

The evaluation of a project needs to be clearly linked to the aims and objectives. This can take many forms and include:

- *A measure of client satisfaction.* In the case of the renal service, the project team agreed that baseline measures of staff and patient satisfaction and wellbeing should be taken as part of the initial stage of the project. Satisfaction measures repeated at the end of the project clearly showed that there was a significant improvement in both patient and staff satisfaction with general functioning of the dialysis unit. On the basis of this outcome, a rolling teaching programme has been developed. In addition, the psychology service identified the need to provide cover for the single-handed psychologist at times of annual leave and sickness to ensure that these initiatives could be sustained.
- *Influence on decision-making.* With the Older People's project, one of the aims was to impact on decision-making that would result in policy changes or actions. The report and its recommendations have been

widely used to influence policy-making, the development of local planning strategies, and the allocation of resources. In addition, the more generic recommendations have been applied to other boroughs within the Primary Care Trust.

- *Scope of dissemination.* As part of the Older People's project, a published report and executive summary were produced and agreed with the project team. Verbal presentations were given to a wide audience and the information disseminated at a public meeting. A press briefing was also arranged by the sponsor and covered by the local media.
- *User involvement.* One of the major requirements of the NSF for Older People was the need to actively engage older people in both identifying their needs and contributing to the solution at a strategic level. Of the 10 older people who interviewed their peers, four now represent older people on four of the six NSF planning sub-groups. Service users or ultimate clients were also involved in interpreting and making sense of the outcomes of the work by facilitating the process of developing action plans during the public meeting.
- *Client empowerment.* The process has empowered the client to behave and think in different ways. The client/project sponsor for the Older People's project has now taken on wider responsibilities for services to older adults across both health and social services, thus ensuring that the recommendations contained in the report can be implemented. The process also empowered the interviewers to represent their peers in influential planning arenas.
- *A learning experience.* The process was a learning experience for the research team who were, (with the exception of the authors!), young psychology assistants and trainee health psychologists with little prior knowledge or understanding of this client group. In addition, their previous research experience had been in the traditional academic setting of undergraduate research projects. For many of them it was the first time they had been involved in action research undertaken collaboratively.

In conclusion, the opportunities for consultancy are increasing. To benefit from these, the consultant needs to be clear about the skills they have which can be marketed. In addition, good time management and financial skills are essential, as is the ability to listen carefully to what the client wants and to be clear about the facilitators and barriers to achieving the stated aims and objectives of the consultation process. At the end of the day, successful consultancy depends on the ability to deliver a high-quality project on time and in budget.

12.7 CORE COMPETENCES

This chapter on consultancy addresses the following competences:

Unit 3.1 Assessment of requests for consultancy
3.1a Identify, prioritize and agree expectations, needs and requirements of clients
3.1b Review psychological literature and other information sources for relevant advice, research findings, research methods and interventions
3.1c Assess feasibility of proposed consultancy.

Unit 3.2 Plan consultancy
3.2a Determine aims, objectives, criteria, theoretical frameworks and scope of interventions
3.2b Produce implementation plans for the consultancy.

Unit 3.3 Establish, develop and maintain working relationships with clients
3.3a Establish contact with clients
3.3b Develop and maintain consultancy contracts with clients
3.3c Develop and maintain working relationships with clients
3.3d Monitor and evaluate working relationships and practices with clients.

Unit 3.4 Conduct consultancy
3.4a Establish systems or processes to deliver the planned advice, research, interventions or activities
3.4b Implement the planned advice, research, interventions or activities
3.4c Close the consultancy.

Unit 3.5 Monitor the implementation of consultancy
3.5a Review the consultancy
3.5b Implement changes identified by the monitoring process
3.5c Review client expectations, needs and requirements within the consultancy
3.5d Implement quality assurance and control mechanisms.

Unit 3.6 Evaluate the impact of consultancy
3.6a Identify evaluation needs and design evaluation
3.6b Implement planned evaluation
3.6c Assess the outcomes of the evaluation.

Although consultancy may appear as linear in the regulations for stage 2 (units 3.1–3.6) it is unlikely to be so in practice. Unit 3.1 considers the

'Assessment of requests for consultancy'. An 'assessment' will generally be the starting point for most consultancy projects and, if done well, is the key to carrying out successful consultancy. The format of the assessment will depend on the individual circumstances of each project. Identifying the client with whom you will be working, assessing their needs and agreeing a written contract of work, that satisfies the requirements of both yourself and your client is reflected in component 3.1a, 'Identify, prioritize and agree expectations, needs and requirements of clients'. It is crucial that a written contract is drawn up and agreed, however flexible the terms may be within the contract, as this will act as the basis for ongoing work (component 3.3b, 'Develop and maintain consultancy contracts with clients').

Before a contract is agreed with a client, there should be a plan of at least the first stage of the project. For this to be done effectively, it is necessary to have a clear understanding of the aim of the consultancy and the question that is being asked by the client. Operationalizing the question in terms of outcomes and objectives is an important first stage and, as ever, the objectives will need to be SMART (Specific, Measurable, Achievable, Realistic and Timely). To develop a plan that can be presented to the client and agreed upon (component 3.2b, 'Produce implementation plans for the consultancy') it will be necessary to research the given subject area in which the consultancy will take place (component 3.1b, 'Review psychological literature and other information sources for relevant advice, research findings, research methods and interventions'). This might involve literature reviewing and database searches to inform testable hypotheses (component 3.1b, guideline 6). The stage 2 trainee may not have a firm knowledge base of the organization with whom he/she will be working and it is essential that there is an understanding of the 'context and critical influences that may affect clients' (component 3.1a, guideline 1). Without thoroughly researching the area and client group with whom he/she will be working, the consultant may be in danger of providing an inappropriate intervention.

Throughout any consultancy project, it is essential that the consultant maintains a close working relationship with the client (component 3.3c, 'Develop and maintain working relationships with clients'). This requires listening to, reviewing and acting upon any feedback, advice or suggestions that the client may present (component 3.5c, 'Review client expectations, needs and requirements within the consultancy'). This may arise through research undertaken as part of a given project or it may be part of a formal or informal feedback procedure. There is a need for flexibility in developing the intervention, as it is likely that an intervention that the consultant has tentatively in mind at the beginning of a project may not be the final intervention that is implemented (component 3.4b, 'Implement the planned advice, research, interventions or activities').

The impact of the consultancy should be evaluated (component 3.6). Many of the skills that the health psychology trainee will be putting into practice when fulfilling the research competence (units 2.1–2.5) will be evident when planning and implementing the evaluation. The evaluation should form part of the initial plan and be put into place before, or run alongside, the implementation of the intervention. It is essential that consultant and client negotiate and agree on the 'evaluation criteria to be used' (component 3.6a, guideline 4). Assessing the outcome of the evaluation is generally the final part of the consultancy process and will normally involve feedback to the client through presentation and report (component 3.6c, guideline 1). Reflection is advisable at the end of the consultancy project to consider what has been learnt from the process, any action that needs to be taken immediately (component 3.6c, guidelines 2–4) and how things could be done better in the future.

REFERENCES

Boulton, E. (2003). Turning crisis into opportunity: Consultancy for allied health professionals. *Health Psychology Update* 12(2), 16–21.

British Psychology Society (2003). Regulations for the Qualification in Health Psychology (Stage 2). The BPS Board of Examiners in Health Psychology.

Brunning, H., Cole, C. & Huffington, C. (1990). *The Change Directory: Key Issues in Organisational Development and the Management of Change.* Leicester, UK: British Psychological Society.

Caldicott Committee (1997). *Report on the Review of Patient Identifiable Information.* Department of Health.

Department of Health (2001). *National Service Framework for Older People.* London: HMSO.

Earll, L., Morrison, L., Giles, M., Wyer, S. & Johnston, M. (1998). Consultancy as an integral part of the profession of health psychology: examples of practice. Workshop at the BPS Division of Health Psychology Annual Conference. Abstracts, p. 2.

Harrison, R. (1995). *Consultant's Journey: A Professional and Personal Odyssey* (ed. M. Pedler). London: McGraw-Hill.

Michie, S. (1998). Consultancy. In A. Bellack & M. Hersen (eds), *Comprehensive Clinical Psychology*, 153–69. Amsterdam and New York: Pergamon.

Porter, S. (2003). From the margins to the mainstream and back again – searching for legitimacy without compromise. PhD in progress.

Rifkin, S.B. & Pridmore, P. (2001). *Partners in Planning: Information, Participation and Empowerment.* London: Macmillan Education Ltd.

Schein, E. (1987). *Process Consultation.* Vol. 2. *Lessons for Managers and Consultants.* Reading, MA: Addison-Wesley.

Chapter 13

HEALTH PSYCHOLOGY WITHIN ORGANIZATIONAL CONTEXTS

Eamonn Ferguson and Máire Kerrin

13.1 INTRODUCTION

There are a number of growing and important overlaps between health and occupational psychology. Understanding organizations is important as they provide health services and are places where health professionals work. In order to improve health service provision and to make for healthier work, it is necessary to understand how organizations function. Two major related areas of academic inquiry are addressed in this chapter: (1) the nature of organizational change and (2) the impact of organizational change on employee health. Organizational change, by its very nature, often involves some form of intervention, either as part of the process of change (e.g., organizational restructuring) or managing that change (e.g., stress management). Lipsey and Cordray (2000) argue that understanding and interpreting interventions aimed at social change (e.g., smoking reduction, support at work) requires consideration of two main theoretical domains: social and organizational change. Social change refers to models designed to explain the 'causal chain' of change (e.g., the trans-theoretical model: Prochaska et al., 1992). In contrast, Lipsey and Cordray (2000) highlight how little theory from organizational change is applied to social interventions despite most interventions being organizational. They argue that organizational theory holds considerable potential for helping to explain outcomes and for planning programme improvements. In this chapter, the role of organizational theory and its potential integration with practice and work in health psychology will be structured around three main areas: theory in organizational change and interventions, theories focusing on stress management at work and improving safe working practice, and practical issues of working as an external consultant in organizations.

13.2 Understanding Organizational Change

What do we mean by organizational change and development? Roughly defined, 'change' is the outcome, and 'development' is the mechanism by which this change is brought about. Organizational change is something most organizations face (Peters & Waterman, 1982). Since such change may be stressful, theories of change and how to manage it are important guides for the development of interventions (see Ferguson & Cheyne, 1995).

The organizational change and development literature is diverse and many disciplines, other than psychology, have contributed. Applied psychology has been involved in contributing to three key questions from both an academic and applied perspective:

- Why carry out organizational change and development?
- What do organizations change?
- How do you manage change?

13.2.1 The 'why' of organizational change and development

There are multiple reasons for organizational change. The rapidly changing economic environment means that it is vital for organizations to adapt to changing circumstances. Dawson (1994) notes that the external triggers to change include political, legal, economic, technological and socio-cultural factors. Internal triggers include personal development (i.e., changes in attitudes and skills), and changes in the scale of activities and organizational tasks, organizational strategy and structure, reward systems or use of technology. Much of the work within the area of the 'why' of organizational change is not just about identifying causes but involves analysing the relationships between them to understand the complex dynamics of change. This can illuminate the 'knock-on' effects that change in one part of the system has for other parts. It can also clarify which part of a system or organization needs changing, and how this can be managed.

13.2.2 What do organizations change and develop?

In deciding what to change in an organization, a number of features are likely to be targeted. These may include (1) products and services (e.g., from selling bio-engineered to organic produce), (2) strategy and structure (e.g., hierarchical to a flatter structure), (3) people and culture (e.g., recruitment and retention), and (4) technology (e.g., use of information technology). Applied psychologists have tended to focus on the people and cultural aspects of organizational change. What is targeted will depend on how change is managed and the approach used within the organization to carry out the change process.

Organizational structure can play a key role in change and is often the most frequently identified aspect of an organization which managers decide to change. It is often viewed as the visible or formal part of the system, which can be changed in response to, or ahead of, a change programme. However, it is recognized that there is an invisible part of the 'organizational iceberg' (French & Bell, 1990). This consists of elements such as employees' values, attitudes and beliefs which form part of the organizational culture and which influence the power and 'norms' of behaviour that are unique to any organization.

13.2.3 How do you manage change?

A distinction is often made between organizational change that is planned and change that emerges over time (Cummings & Worley, 1993).

Models of planned change

The most influential psychological theory of planned change is Lewin's (1951), based on the laws of physics that states that change only occurs when there is disequilibrium in favour of the forces for change. The model consists of three basic steps. The first, unfreezing, consists of reducing resistance to the proposed change and developing the perception of a need for change (similar to a performance gap analysis). The second step is the change itself and the third, refreezing, ensures that the new state of the organization is stabilized, with activities and policies in place.

Developmental and planned change is concerned with improving the efficiency or effectiveness of the organization within its existing framework, that is, changing the mode of organizing and values that are already in place. This includes approaches to change that involve management development programmes, improvements in technology, job re-design and teambuilding. The scale of the change within this approach is important to consider and may include the whole organization, or sub-systems such as the individual, group, inter-group or department.

Models of emergent change

Transformational or emergent change lies at the other end of a dimension of approaches to change and is designed to have an impact on the strategy, structure, people, process and values in a *fundamental* way. This may be carried out by changes to organizational structure or culture. Proponents of this approach to change argue that, because of the complexity of the changing environment, it is not possible to clearly plan change in a developmental way as put forward by Lewin, and that there can be no simple prescription (Dawson, 1994). Therefore, while the planned approach is based on clear time lines and linear events, the emergent approach is viewed as a continuous process. Johnson (1993) suggests that the strategic management of change is essentially 'a cultural and cognitive phenomenon' rather than an analytical, rationale exercise that can be planned and managed.

Case study 13.1 describes how the process of organizational change is implemented.

CASE STUDY 13.1 Organizational changes within the NHS – Selection and retention in medical training programmes

Why change? There is a need to select the right people for the right courses, careers and specialities to reduce drop out rates, reduce stress and to improve both doctor and patient satisfaction.

What can be changed? There is more to being a doctor (both in terms of undergraduate and post-graduate training) than just good academic skills. A variety of personal qualities or competences (e.g., empathy, ability to cope with stress) are important and these need to be reflected at the initial selection (see Ferguson et al., 2002; 2003a). Furthermore, these qualities may also go some way to fulfil guidelines on broadening access.

How was change implemented? Change can be implemented through developing new selection procedures. For example, to aid the selection of the 'right' candidates for GP training, new assessment procedures have been developed on the basis of a comprehensive job analysis leading to GP competence models (see Patterson et al., 2000). General Practice assessment centres (a combination of exercises and tests) were developed, validated (both internally and externally) and run within one health authority (see Patterson et al., 2001; 2003). Once success is shown within a region, such programmes can be considered for implementation nationally.

13.2.4 Politics and power in organizational work

Awareness of politics and power within organizations is crucial for carrying out organizational research and understanding the impact of interventions (Currie & Kerrin, in press; Buchanan & Badham, 1999). Power concerns the capacity of individuals to exert their own will over others, while political behaviour is the practical domain of power in action, worked out through the use of techniques of influence and other, more or less extreme, tactics (Kakabadse, 1983).

For example, some index (e.g., via confidential interview) of how different key stakeholders in an organization feel about an intervention may be useful when evaluating why, in some areas of an organization, an intervention was successful and in others it was not (cf. Silvester et al., 1997). For example, if key stakeholders in one part of an organization support and view an intervention as worthwhile, they may be likely to convey a positive attitude to their employees and give them time and support to take part. On the other hand, if stakeholders in another part of the same organization do not support the intervention, they may not do this. In such an organization, an intervention may not appear to be effective due to these organizational pressures rather than anything fundamental about the intervention. Lipsey and Cordray (2000) refer to these types of influence as 'within programme effects' and argue that they should be measured and their effects evaluated.

13.3 HEALTH PSYCHOLOGY'S POTENTIAL CONTRIBUTION TO UNDERSTANDING ORGANIZATIONAL CHANGE AND DEVELOPMENT

A number of theoretical models have been used and developed within health psychology that can be applied to issues of organizational change and intervention (see Ferguson, 2001), for example, managing occupational stress and improving safe working practice.

13.3.1 Occupational stress and health

Models of occupational stress

While Lazarus and colleagues (see Lazarus & Folkman, 1984) have developed a general model of stress, two occupationally specific models of occupational stress have been proposed: the demand–control model and the effort–reward model (Karasek & Theorell, 1990 and Siegrist, 1996, respectively). Short scales for measuring their parameters are available (Kuper et al., 2002; Smith et al., 1997).

The demand–control model proposes an interaction between work demands (e.g., pressure) and job control (e.g., skill utilization), where those in high demand–low control working conditions will be more susceptible to work-related ill-health (the strain hypothesis). This model has been developed to include social support, such that low social support increases strain, and a combination of high demands, control and support increases motivation and learning (the learning hypothesis). The effort–reward model is based on an imbalance between effort put into work (e.g., extrinsic work in terms of physical and psychological effort) and rewards received (e.g., money, esteem and career opportunities). A large imbalance (i.e., high effort for little reward) results in increased occupational ill-health. There are similarities between these two models, in that both are based on an imbalance and the idea of extrinsic effort and perceived demands are similar (see Ostry et al., 2003).

There is evidence for the utility of both models (see Kuper et al., 2002; Karasek & Theorell, 1990). For the demand–control–support model, there is good support for the main effects and less for the interactions (e.g., Van der Doef & Maes, 1999). Two recent studies comparing the two models (Kivmaki et al., 2002; Ostry et al., 2003), found evidence that the effort–reward imbalance was predictive of both objective and subjective health outcome. The pattern was less consistent for the demand–control model, with one study indicating that perceived control added predictive power (Ostry et al., 2003) and the other finding demands to be predictive (Kivmaki et al., 2002).

Stress management interventions

Health and clinical psychologists have tended to examine this area, both theoretically and practically, from an individual perspective, whereas occupational psychologists have tended to take a more macro-organizational perspective. Cox (1993) has distinguished between individual and organizational level interventions and how these might be addressed using primary (preventing or eliminating the cause of stress), secondary (damage limitation

– reducing the impact of an existing problem but not eliminating it) or tertiary (therapy – trying to cure any consequences of the stressor) interventions (see Cox, 1993).

There is evidence for the relative effectiveness of interventions at both the individual and organizational levels (Briner & Reynolds, 1999; Reynolds, 1997). Organizational and individual level interventions should not necessarily be viewed as mutually exclusive. For example, developing organizational level systems designed to anticipate problems may also incorporate individualized therapy. Health and occupational psychologists could join forces to develop interventions that are tailored to individual and organizational needs.

Case study 13.2 describes a secondary level intervention aimed at both the individual and the organization.

CASE STUDY 13.2 Keeping Pub Peaceful (Lawrence et al., 1999)

The problem. Violence is a major stressor in some working environments. How can psychology help to reduce the escalation of violent incidents in public houses?

An intervention. Lawrence et al. (1999) describe how they developed and evaluated their Keeping Pub Peaceful (KPP) campaign. The intervention was based on a package of training delivered to licences and area managers through a series of organized workshops. The aim of the training was to highlight possible strategies for reducing the escalation of violence in conflict situations. Both licences and managers were included to indicate that violence was an issue that was needed to be understood and responded to at all levels in the organization. The training was reinforced by an organizational policy statement and developed through extensive rounds of survey information and an examination of incident report forms.

Evaluation. Workshops were evaluated using a basic pre-post quasi-experimental design with a control group. Trainees were assessed on knowledge and attitudes with respect to (1) reducing the risk of violence, (2) conflict resolution and (3) managing the aftermath of conflict. The results showed that the trainees had more positive attitudes towards conflict resolution and more knowledge after training than before.

Behavioural versus organizational outcomes

As well as focusing on individual behavioural and emotional outcomes, organizational psychologists are interested in organizational effects (e.g., turnover) and financial utility (cost-benefit of an intervention). This has led to particular hierarchical models of evaluation (see Kirkpatrick, 1967; Hamblin, 1974). The following four levels influence the higher ones: (1) the lowest level, reactions (e.g., the extent to which the intervention was liked); (2) learning (e.g., the acquisition of new skills); (3) job-behaviour (e.g., transfer of learning); (4) ultimate values (e.g., profit). These models have been criticized for the implication that success at one level aids success at another (Alliger et al., 1997; Kraiger et al., 1993). Within healthcare settings, demonstrating the financial success of an intervention is an important step in convincing government bodies of its utility.

13.3.2 Health behaviours, risk communication and reducing injuries at work

A central question in health psychology focuses on how best to communicate information to promote health protective behaviours (e.g., using sun block) (Rothman & Salovey, 1997). The same issue applies in the occupational setting where it is important for employees to think positively about and adopt new safe working practices. For example, recent studies have examined how to effectively design risk communication leaflets with respect to the appropriate use of manual handling and the use of ear defenders (Ferguson et al., 2003a). Case study 15.3 provides a brief summary of Ferguson et al. (2003a).

CASE STUDY 15.3 Developing risk communications for occupational risk behaviour (Ferguson et al., 2003a)

The problem. People in organizations often do not act in accordance with health and safety information and therefore may experience occupationally related injury and disease. Two large occupational health issues are back pain, from inappropriate manual handling, and hearing loss, related to not wearing ear protection.

The theoretical background. This is based on message framing, as a means of developing effective risk communications (see Kahneman & Tversky, 1984). Frames were designed to reflect losses (e.g., what you will lose by not doing the behaviour) or gains (e.g., what you will gain by performing the behaviour). Framing was studied in this context as Rothman and Salovey (1997) argue that this interacts with the type of behaviour to be changed. They distinguish between detection behaviours (e.g., breast self-examination) and prevention behaviours (e.g., smoking cessation, using sun block). Similarly, occupational risk behaviours can be designated either as detections (e.g., radiation counter, safety checks) or preventions (e.g., wearing ear defenders). Other theories of risk communication and decision-making do not take into account the type of behaviour targeted for change. Framing theory makes predictions about the role of past behaviour (see Ferguson et al., 2003a; Rothman & Salovey, 1997). Specifically, gain frames should be more effective with regular (habitual) users of the behaviour and loss frames for occasional users (cf. Ferguson & Bibby, 2002).

The interventions. This case study used these constructs to examine the effectiveness of message framing to influence employee's intentions to act in accordance with safe working practice, once other traditional predictors had been controlled (e.g., optimistic bias, past behaviour, subjective norms, self-efficacy). Framing materials were developed through interviews with staff to enhance the relevance of the messages. The gains and losses referred to in the messages were written with regard to the language used by workers n these occupations. A series of experimental and quasi-experimental studies were conducted.

Populations examined. Samples were recruited from a number of NHS trusts as well as the mining and foundry industries. Health and safety, occupational health and personnel staff were contacted to set up the studies and help to design the materials.

Findings. Results indicated that workers exposed to messages framed as gains were more likely to express higher intentions to follow safe working practices. This was moderated by past behaviour such that gain frames were more effective for regular/committed users of safe working practices and loss frames for occasional users.

Feedback. Feedback was provided to all participating organizations through formal feedback meetings and reports.

13.4 Practical Issues and Potential Barriers to Organizational Research

There are a number of issues specific to conducting research in organizational settings. This section focuses on working as an external consultant/researcher (see Chapter 12 for details of internal consultancy). Psychologists working as external consultants/researchers should ensure that their work is well grounded in theory and evaluated. Sufficient time has to be allocated to negotiating access to the organization. This will normally follow a number of stages: (1) identifying the appropriate key areas in the organization to approach; (2) a series of initial presentations and meetings; (3) negotiating the pragmatics of the research; and (4) data collection and feedback.

13.4.1 Identifying the appropriate personnel areas in the organization to approach

This will be determined, in part, by the nature of the study, as well as the structure of the organization. For example, the first line of contact might be in occupational health or personnel, or the director of training. Not all organizations have all these types of departments. Homework on the organization is important and initial contact needs to set out clearly what the project is about, who is funding it and why it is important. Having a 'champion' in the organization is extremely useful in getting things moving. Organizations may move slowly and there may be quite a time lag between initial contact and the organization responding.

13.4.2 Initial presentations and meetings

Usually a series of meetings follows a successful initial contact. Issues will arise at the first meeting that organizations may wish to address by involving other members of the organization or by seeking their advice. Trade union support and approval can be crucial and should be actively sought. Initial presentations should be simple and to the point.

One of the main issues raised by organizations will be to ask what is in it for them, and for their individual employees (both management and trade unions will have issues here). There should be no hidden costs to the organization and the benefits should be explained. For example, in terms of stress research, the organization may get a free stress audit. The cost of having a private consultancy to do this could be used as a comparison. The researcher will usually be asking for employees' time. If this involves employees stopping working, this will result in lost productivity to the organization and a detailed justification for this should be given.

It is important for the researcher to emphasize their independence if they are working on an externally funded project. This is important when discussing the project with the management and the unions, as it allows you to show to both parties that you are impartial with respect to the organization, and that the research is not driven by any organizational political agenda. At this point, it is also useful to try and spend some time in the organization talking to key individuals and observing organizational practices to gain a familiarity with the organization and its culture.

13.4.3 Negotiating the pragmatics of the research

The next stage of data collection needs to be done as efficiently as possible, with minimal inconvenience to the organization. Be guided by the organization on ways to do this. For example, sending survey materials out with payslips is a procedure that is reasonably effective and widely used.

Once agreed, it is important to advertise the project widely to employees. This may be done through emails, listings, posters, company and trade union newsletters, as well as through team and management briefing documents. These communications should be short and cover the key issues. Contact details of research staff should be provided for employees to use for further information.

13.4.4 Collecting data

There are a number of options for collecting data. For surveys, it is possible to (1) arrange for the data to be returned directly to the researchers using pre-paid reply envelopes; (2) have collection sites around the organizations; or (3) have them returned to a specified person in the organization. This should be negotiated. Option 1 is often preferred as it maintains the researcher's independence, especially in the eyes of the employees who might be asked to comment on sensitive topics. Study information sheets (to be retained by the participants) and consent forms (to be returned separately, so as to maintain anonymity) should be distributed to all employees. Monitor response rates and send out reminder communications to the organization to try and boost response rates.

13.4.5 Feedback

Feedback should aim to be as inclusive as possible. Presentations should include senior management, trade unions and employees, and should be complemented with a brief executive summary (one page) that all employees can have access to. No individuals should be identifiable through this process.

13.4.6 No guarantees

Organizational research has its own set of problems associated with the nature of organizations. Always have a contingency plan and try to work with more than one organization. Organizations can go bankrupt, there can be management and organizational change, the project may lose favour, your champion(s) in the organization might leave or be replaced, or very few people may participate.

13.4.7 Ethics

Psychologists acting as consultants or researchers are bound in the UK by the BPS code of ethics (www.bps.org.uk), and projects should be conducted professionally and have ethical approval. In the light of increasingly rigorous research governance, any UK project that involves data collection, with outcomes that are generalizable beyond the immediate setting, will require ethics approval (www.corec.org.uk). All data should be stored and managed with respect to the Data Protection Act (http://www.dpa.lancs.ac.uk/, www.hmso.gov.uk/acts/acts1998/19980029.htm).

13.5 Conclusions

Health psychologists have much to offer in terms of (1) developing theory and practice within organizational settings, especially with respect to organizational change and development and (2) collaborating with occupational psychologists.

13.6 Stage 2 Competences Addressed in this Chapter

Health psychologists working within organizational contexts may be involved in providing advice, conducting research, designing and evaluating interventions and training staff. Consequently, work within organizations can potentially draw on all the competences specified by the BPS stage 2 training. The challenge of working in organizations is that psychologists need not only to draw upon a range of professional competences, but to use these in a manner that is sensitive to specific organizational values, policies and structure within which the work is undertaken. This can be illustrated with respect to the consultancy cycle (getting in, getting on and getting out).

'Getting in' involves establishing contact, developing trust, deciding on a programme of work and securing contracts. Managing this stage successfully will involve consultancy competences such as those specified by units 3.1 (Assessment of requests for consultancy) and 3.3 (Establish, develop and maintain working relationships with clients). See especially components 3.1c (Assess feasibility of proposed consultancy), 3.3a (Establish contact with clients) and 3.3.b (Develop and maintain consultancy contracts with clients). Health psychologists may need to draw upon professional competences such as those specified by units 1.1 (Implement and maintain systems for legal, ethical and professional standards), unit 1.3 (Provide psychological advice and guidance) and unit 1.4 (Provide feedback to clients). See especially components 1.1a (Establish, maintain and review systems for the security and control of information), 1.1b (Ensure compliance with legal, ethical and professional practices for self and others), 1.3a (Assess the opportunities, need and context for giving psychological advice), 1.3b (Provide psychological advice), 1.4a (Evaluate feedback needs of clients) and 1.4d (Present feedback to clients). At the end of this stage, clear objectives and deliverables, as well as clearly defined roles and boundaries should be established.

'Getting on' includes competences specified by unit 3.4 (Conduct consultancy). The psychologist may be required to design (see unit 2.2) and conduct research (see unit 2.3) as well as analyse and evaluate the data (see unit 2.4). Research projects also require management and competences specified by unit 2.5 (Initiate and develop psychological research) and monitoring research progress and ensuring that difficulties and problems do not escalate can be crucial to success (component 2.5b, Monitor and evaluate studies in relation to agreed protocols).

If the work involves training for employees then the psychologist may draw upon competences specified by units 4.1 (Plan and design training programmes) and 4.2 (Deliver training programmes). However, if the work involves design and evaluation of an intervention, then a psychologist who has the competences specified by optional units 5.1 (Implement interventions to change health-related behaviour) and 5.2 (Direct the implementation of interventions) may be best qualified to undertake the work.

'Getting out' refers to closing the 'psychological' and actual contract with the organization. Unit 3.4 (Conduct consultancy) specifies this competence as component 3.4c (Close the consultancy). This involves having a set of agreed deliverables produced in a specific form for a specific date and an establishing agreement that the work is complete. This means that the psychologist will not be asked to undertake any other work unless a new contract is agreed. Contracts should be checked carefully at the planning stage, including ensuring that it details how the contract will be closed (see unit 3.2, Plan consultancy).

REFERENCES

Alliger, G.M., Tannenbaum, S.I., Bennett, W. Jr, Traver, H., & Shotland, A. (1997). A meta-analysis of the relationship among training criteria. *Personnel Psychology* 50, 341–58.

Briner, R.B. & Reynolds, S. (1999). The costs, benefits and limitations of organisational level stress interventions. *Journal of Organisational Behaviour* 20, 647–64.

Buchanan, D. & Badham, R. (1999). Politics and organisational change: the lived experience. *Human Relations* 52, 609–29.

Cox, T. (1993). *Stress Research and Stress Management: Putting Theory to Work.* HSE Contract Research Report No. 61. Sudbury: HSE Books.

Cummings, T.G. & Worley, C.G. (1993). *Organisation Development and Change,* 5th edn. St Paul, MN: West Publishing.

Currie, G. & Kerrin, M. (in press). The limits of a technological fix to knowledge management: Epistemological, political and cultural issues in the case of intranet implementation. *Management Learning.*

Dawson, P. (1994). *Organisational Change: A Processual Approach.* London: PCP.

Ferguson, E. (2001). The roles of contextual moderation and personality in relation to the knowledge-risk link in the workplace. *Journal of Risk Research* 4, 323–40.

Ferguson, E. & Bibby, P.A. (2002). Predicting future blood donor returns: past behavior, intentions and observer effects. *Health Psychology* 21, 513–18.

Ferguson, E., Bibby, P.A. & Leaviss, J. (2003a). *Effective Design of Workplace Risk Communications.* HSE Research Report (RR) 093. Sudbury, UK: HSE Books.

Ferguson, E. & Cheyne, A. (1995). Organisational change: main and inter-active effects. *Journal of Organisational and Occupational Psychology* 68, 101–7.

Ferguson, E., James, D. & Madelely, L. (2002). Factors associated with success in medical school: systematic review of the literature. *British Medical Journal*, 324, 952–7.

Ferguson, E., James, D., O'Hehir. F., & Sanders, A. (2003b). A pilot study of the roles of personality, references and personal statements in relation to perform-ance over the 5 years of a medical degree. *British Medical Journal* 326, 429–31.

Ferguson, E., Sanders, A., O'Hehir, F., & James, D. (2000). Predictive validity of personal statements and the role of the five factor model of personality in relation to medical training. *Journal of Occupational and Organisational Psychology* 73, 321–44.

French, W.L. & Bell, C.H. (1990). *Organisation development: Behavioral Science Interventions for Organisation Improvement.* Englewood Cliffs, NJ: Prentice Hall International.

Hamblin, A.C. (1974). *Evaluation and Control of Training.* Maidenhead: McGraw-Hill.

Johnson, G. (1993). Processes of managing strategic change. In C. Maybey & B. Mayon-White (eds), *Managing Change.* London: PCP.

Kahneman, D. & Tversky, A. (1984). Choices, values and frames. *American Psychologist* 39, 341–50.

Kakabadse, A. (1983). *The Politics of Management.* Aldershot: Gower.

Karasek, R. & Theorell, T. (1990). *Healthy Work: Stress, Productivity, and the Reconstruction of Working Life.* New York: Basic Books.

Kirkpatrick, D.L. (1967). Evaluation of training. In R.L. Criag and L.R. Bitle (eds), *Training and Development Handbook.* New York: McGraw-Hill.

Kivmaki, M., Leino-Arjas, P., Luukkonen, R., Riihkami, H., Vahtera, J. & Kirjonen, J. (2002). Work stress and risk of cardiovascular mortality: prospective cohort study of industrial employees. *British Medical Journal* 325, 857–60.

Kotter, J.P. (1985). *Power and Influence.* New York: Free Press.

Kraiger, K., Ford, J.K. & Salas, E. (1993). Application of cognitive, skill-based and affective theories of learning outcomes to new methods of training evaluation. *Journal of Applied Psychology* 78, 311–28.

Kuper, H., Singh-Manoux, A., Siegrist, J. & Marmot, M. (2002). When reciprocity fails: effort-reward imbalance in relation to coronary heart disease and health functioning within the Whitehall II study. *Occupational and Environmental Medicine* 59, 777–84.

Lawrence, C., Beale, D., Leather, P. & Dickson, R. (1999). Violence in public houses: An integrated organisational approach. In P. Leather, C. Brady, C. Lawrence, D. Beale & T Cox (eds), *Work-related Violence: Assessment and Intervention,* 127–44. New York: Routledge.

Lazarus, R.S. & Folkman, S. (1984). *Stress, Appraisal and Coping.* New York: Springer.

Leavitt, H. (1965). Applied organisational change in industry: structural, technological and humanistic approaches. In J.G. March (ed.), *Handbook of Organisations*, 1114–70. Chicago: Rand McNally.

Lewin, K. (1951). *Field Theory in Social Science*. New York: Harper and Row.

Lipsey, M.W. & Cordray, D.S. (2000). Evaluation methods for social intervention. *Annual Review of Psychology* 51, 345–75.

Ostry, A.S., Kelly, S., Demers, P.A., Mustard, C. & Hertzman, C. (2003). A comparison between the effort–reward imbalance and demand control models. *BMC Public Health*, 3(10), 27 February, available at http://www.biomedcentral.com/1471-2458/3/10

Patterson, F., Ferguson, E., Lane, P., Farrell, K., Martlew, J. & Wells, A. (2000). A competency model of general practice: Implications for selection, training and development. *British Journal of General Practice* 50, 188–93.

Patterson, F., Lane, P., Ferguson, E. & Norfolk, T. (2001). A competency based selection system for general practitioner registrars. *British Medical Journal* 323 (7311), 2–3.

Patterson, F., Norfolk, T., Ferguson, E. & Lane, P. (2003). Predicting work performance of GPs: A criterion-related validation study of a new selection system. *Proceedings of the British Psychological Society's Occupational Psychology Conference*. Published by the Division of Occupational Psychology, 39–42.

Peters, T.J. & Waterman, R.H. (1982). *In Search of Excellence: Lessons from America's Best-run Companies*. New York: Harper and Row.

Pfeffer, J. (1992). Understanding power in organisations. *California Management Review* 34, 29–50.

Prochaska, J.O., DiClemente, C.C. & Norcross, J.C. (1992). In search of how people change: Applications to addictive behaviors. *American Psychologist* 47, 1102–14.

Reynolds, S. (1997). Psychological well-being at work: Is prevention better than cure? *Journal of Psychosomatic Research* 43, 93–102.

Rothman, A., and Salovey, P. (1997). Shaping perceptions of motivate healthy behavior: The role of message framing. *Psychological Bulletin* 121, 3–19.

Siegrist, J. (1996). Adverse health effects of high-effort/low-reward conditions. *Journal of Occupational Health Psychology* 1, 27–41.

Silvester, J., Ferguson, E. & Patterson, F. (1997). Comparing spoken attributions by German and British engineers: Evaluating a culture change programme. *European Journal of Work and Organisational Psychology* 6, 103–17.

Smith, C.S., Tisak, J., Hahn, S.E. & Schmieder, R.A. (1997). The measurement of job control. *Journal of Organisational Behavior* 18, 225–37.

Van der Doef, M. & Maes, S. (1999). The job-demand–control (–support) model of psychological well-being: A review of 20 years of empirical work. *Work and Stress* 13, 87–114.

Chapter 14

CHANGING BEHAVIOUR TO IMPROVE HEALTH

Paul Bennett, Mark Conner and Gaston Godin

This chapter focuses on the nature of health behaviours and the contributions that health psychologists can make to changing such behaviours. Gochman (1997), in the *Handbook of Health Behavior Research*, defined health behaviours as 'behavior patterns, actions and habits that relate to health maintenance, to health restoration and to health improvement' (Vol. 1, p. 3). Behaviours within this definition include the use of medical services (e.g., physician visits, vaccination, screening), adherence to medical regimens (e.g., dietary, diabetic, anti-hypertensive regimens), and self-directed health behaviours (e.g., diet, exercise, smoking, alcohol consumption). In describing health behaviours, it is common to distinguish health-enhancing from health-impairing behaviours. Health-impairing behaviours have harmful effects on health or otherwise predispose individuals to disease. Such behaviours include smoking, excessive alcohol consumption, high dietary fat consumption, or less than maximal adherence to medical regimens. By contrast, engaging in health-enhancing behaviours confers health benefits or otherwise protects individuals from the onset of disease or disease progression. This class of behaviour includes exercise, condom use, and effective efforts at managing disease.

Interest in behaviours that impact on health and wellbeing is based upon two assumptions: (1) that a significant proportion of the mortality from the leading causes of death is caused by the behaviour of individuals; and (2) that such behaviour is modifiable (Conner & Norman, 1996). Behaviour is held to exert its influence on health in three basic ways: by producing direct biological changes; by conveying health risks or protecting against them; or by leading to the early detection or treatment of disease (Baum & Posluszny, 1999). This chapter focuses on a number of approaches to changing health behaviour to reduce risk for disease, enhance control over the impact of diseases, or to ameliorate negative emotional reactions occurring in the context of illness.

14.1 BEHAVIOURAL APPROACHES

Behavioural approaches consider behaviours, including those influencing health, to be learned and controlled by external factors within the social and physical environment in which they occur. According to learning theory (see Kazdin, 2001), behaviour is acquired and changed through interaction with the social and physical environment by one of two processes: operant and classical conditioning. Conditioning may also occur to mental representations of stimuli, a process known as covert sensitization.

14.1.1 Operant conditioning

Based on Skinnerian psychology (e.g. Skinner, 1953), operant conditioning explains behaviours that are voluntary and purposive. Skinner's basic premise was that behaviour that is rewarded (reinforced) will increase in frequency or be repeated; that which is not rewarded or punished will decrease in frequency or not be repeated. Cues within the environment may come to elicit such behaviours by signalling later reinforcement. Behaviours that are perceived to be a direct consequence of illness may, in fact, be maintained and shaped by operant processes. Pain and disability may result in avoidance of undesired activities (e.g., going to work, social events) and an increase in positive consequences (e.g., help and attention from family and friends). Cardiac patients, for example, may fear that overexertion will result in cardiac problems, and as a consequence their partners may take on all responsibilities to avoid them being 'stressed' within the home. Here, two reward systems may operate – one in which the patient feels relief from the fear of overexerting themselves, and one in which they avoid unrewarding tasks they may otherwise have to do – an outcome known as secondary gain (Skinner, 1953). Perhaps the most powerful, and the most frequent, reinforcement schedule is known as intermittent reinforcement. In this, behaviours are reinforced in an apparently random fashion. Behaviours rewarded by this type of reinforcement schedule may take longer to establish than those rewarded by continuous reinforcement as it takes longer for the relationship between the behaviour and reinforcement to become obvious. Once established, however, they are resistant to extinction, as the individual is used to periods of non-reinforcement and will continue their behaviour over many episodes in which it is not rewarded in the expectation that it will ultimately be so. This may occur, for example, in the context of pain behaviours, where patients may learn that if they persist in making requests from healthcare professionals they will, on occasion, be given pain medication.

Operant conditioning interventions

Pain interventions often use operant procedures. The originator of this approach, Fordyce (e.g., 1988), was clear that operant procedures are not designed to lessen the pain. Rather, they are designed to control excessive responses to pain which may include inappropriate demands for pain relief, avoidance of activity that should be within patients' physical limits, wincing and other facial expression designed to elicit sympathy, and so on. Operant procedures do not punish such behaviours. Instead, they change their outcomes to ones that are less rewarding (usually by ignoring them) and reward the individual for engaging in 'appropriate' behaviours, such as engaging in appropriate levels of exercise or not making excess complaints about pain.

Identification of factors that influence target behaviours, such as the pain-related behaviours identified above, involves a process known as functional analysis. This may involve detailed interviews with the individual and relevant others or the use of diaries which note the antecedents and consequences of the behaviours. If the behaviours occur in a hospital setting, diaries may be based on observation of events by healthcare staff. Once the relationships between specific behaviours and any environmental cues and rewards have been identified, where possible these are removed or modified. Fordyce, for example, moved a patient who was engaging in excessive pain behaviours into a single room within a ward, the door of which could be closed if necessary. This prevented the patient trying to attract the attention of nurses. Withdrawal of reinforcement for pain-related behaviours and rewards for non-pain behaviours were achieved by staff leaving the room if the patient inappropriately demanded pain medication or staying for a social chat if they did not do so. Despite its apparent lack of humanity, Fordyce obtained the patient's consent for this type of treatment approach and it proved highly effective (Fordyce & Steger, 1979).

Operant procedures are frequently used in group interventions for people with chronic pain. The methods used include positive reward of healthy behaviours, withdrawal of attention or other rewards that were previous responses to pain behaviours, and providing analgesic medication at set times rather than in response to behaviour (e.g., Kole-Snijders et al., 1999). Depending on the nature of the presenting problem, these processes may be augmented by other interventions. In the case of lower back pain, for example, where disuse may result in a weakening of the back muscles and reduced exercise capacity, patients may take part in exercise pro-grammes in which they engage in progressively more demanding exercises, with the pace of progress being determined by the health professionals involved rather than by the patient. Summarizing the effectiveness of this approach in the treatment of lower back pain, Van Tulder et al. (2003) concluded that there was strong evidence that behavioural treatments had a positive effect on reported pain, the degree to which individuals regained function of their back, and on behaviour away from the clinic.

14.1.2 Classical conditioning

Classical conditioning has its roots in Pavlovian psychology (e.g., Pavlov, 1927). The basic premise of this approach is that an initially neutral stimulus present at the same time as a stimulus that evokes a basic emotional or physiological response can become associated with that stimulus and comes, in turn, to elicit an identical conditioned response. That is, an initially neutral stimulus becomes a conditioned stimulus and elicits a conditioned response, identical to the unconditioned one. In the case of dental phobia, for example, the experience of pain and distress in the dentist's chair may result in a conditioned association between an initially neutral stimuli such as dental surgeries (and particularly instruments such as the 'drill') and distress. As a result of this fear, the individual may avoid going to the dentist – a process that may result in a prolonga-tion of the conditioned fear response as the individual has no experience of pain- or distress-free dental visits. Interventions to change this behaviour include repeated presentation of the conditioned stimulus (dental surgery) in the absence of the unconditioned stimulus (pain) which result in a gradual fading of the fear response – a process known as extinction.

Classical conditioning interventions

Classical conditioning provides a good explanation for the development of conditioned, or anticipatory, nausea associated with chemotherapy. In this, the severe nausea and vomiting associated with chemotherapy become conditioned to a variety of stimuli associated with the treatment (e.g., Redd et al., 2001). These may include the room in which the indi-vidual receives the chemotherapy, the bed, or the drip through which the chemotherapy is administered. Even the sight of the car that takes a patient to treatment can be sufficient to trigger this response. The nausea experienced at such times can be so intense that a small, but significant, percentage of people refuse to continue chemotherapy as a consequence

(Redd et al., 2001). A number of factors moderate the risk that any one individual may have for experiencing anticipatory nausea. The most obvious is the type of drug with which they are being treated – some may trigger more nausea than others. A more psychological factor is the level of anxiety or physiological arousal the individual feels at the time they receive their chemotherapy: higher levels of arousal increase the degree to which an individual becomes conditioned to aversive stimuli and/or more likely to experience the vomiting reflex. This suggests that teaching patients to relax prior to and at the time of their initial chemotherapy will reduce their risk of developing conditioned nausea. The relaxation process most commonly taught in doing this is a derivative of Jacobson's deep muscle relaxation technique (Jacobson, 1938). This involves alternately tensing and relaxing muscle groups throughout the body in an ordered sequence. As the individual becomes practised in its use, they may use relaxation without prior tension.

An alternative approach that may help people cope with anticipatory nausea once instigated, is to teach people to relax in the presence of stimuli that trigger the nausea reflex. This may best be incorporated into a programme of systematic desensitization (Wolpe, 1958). Systematic desensitization was initially used to help people cope with specific fears or phobias. In this context, the patient is repeatedly exposed to a series of stimuli initially somewhat distant from, and then increasingly like, the feared stimulus. Each stimulus is presented to the patient while they are fully relaxed. They then try to remain or become relaxed in the presence of the feared stimulus. Once this relaxation has been achieved, they indicate this to the therapist. The feared stimulus is then removed. This process is repeated on a number of occasions, starting with the least feared stimulus, until the individual no longer experiences fear at the time of its presentation. At this point, they progress to the next feared stimulus and repeat the same procedures, progressing through a hierarchy until they no longer feel anxious in the presence of their target stimulus. This should ideally be conducted in the presence of the conditioned stimuli (a process known as in vivo desensitization). Where this is not possible, either because of problems of access or the patient finding such stimuli too overwhelming, they may work through a hierarchy of stimuli in their imagination, a process known as imaginal exposure. This procedure can be modified for working with people who have anticipatory nausea. In this, patients are systematically exposed to a variety of stimuli which trigger their nausea, starting with stimuli that trigger a relatively mild feeling of nausea and fairly quickly working up to stimuli that trigger more severe reactions. On each occasion they use relaxation to help them relax and to control any feelings of nausea. This approach has proven effective in reducing the degree of nausea and vomiting experienced prior to chemotherapy, and has helped to maintain people within chemotherapy programmes (Morrow & Hickok, 1993).

14.1.3 Covert conditioning

A technique developed from both classical conditioning and operant principles is known as covert sensitization. The approach is based, in part, on more recent developments of operant theory developed by Bandura (1977) which acknowledges the role of cognitions as mediators between behaviour and external factors. People choose between behaviours which bring potentially competing outcomes. As a general principle, the closer an outcome is to a behaviour in time, the more influential it is likely to be. A simple example of this can be found in many people's eating habits, where the short-term pleasure of eating a high-fat snack may overwhelm any negative expectations of long-term weight gain or negative health consequences. Covert conditioning attempts to make these longer-term outcomes more salient at the time of key behavioural choices. The patient focuses on the negative consequences of engaging in target behaviours, such as smoking or excess eating, and then uses a simple conditioned stimulus to evoke these behaviours. One simple technique is to wear a loose elastic band around the wrist. During conditioning trials, the patient flicks the elastic band gently while thinking of these negative consequences, until there is a learned association between flicking the elastic band and thoughts about the negative consequences of a particular behaviour. Once this association has been established, patients are asked to flick the elastic band to evoke these thoughts at the time they face relevant behavioural choices. This approach is infrequently used, but has proven moderately effective in the treatment of a number of conditions including smoking cessation (Lowe et al., 1980).

14.2 COGNITIVE APPROACHES

Cognitive approaches consider internal processes, cognitions, to mediate the relationship between environmental events and behaviour. Historically, cognitive approaches to changing health behaviour have been informed by a number of theoretical perspectives including communication theory (Murphy & Bennett, 2004), social learning theory (Bandura, 1997), cognitive models of psychopathology and therapy (Beck, 1977; Ellis, 1977), and social cognition theory (Conner & Norman, 1996).

Relatively few studies have explicitly used social cognition theories in interventions designed to change behaviour: most have not gone beyond trying to change intentions to either change behaviour or adopt new behaviours. Godin et al. (2003), for example, developed a programme to promote the adoption of safe sexual practices among adolescents with social adaptation difficulties. The programme was based on the theories of reasoned action and planned behaviour (Ajzen & Fishbein, 1980; Ajzen, 1991) and social learning theory (Bandura, 1977: see below). It targeted changes on a number of variables including intentions to use condoms, self-efficacy, normative beliefs, attitude towards safer sex practices, and knowledge. The programme involved 10 sessions, each dealing with one or more of the following issues: the meaning of sexual intercourse; unsafe and safer sexual activities; pros and cons of condom use; values and sexuality; negotiation of safer sex; communication skills; self-affirmation; and arguing to overcome obstacles to safer sex behaviour. Learning activities included group discussions, brainstorming, role-playing, problem-solving, demonstrations, condom manipulation, improvisation, and audio-visual documents. The intervention proved successful in changing intentions to use a condom with a new sexual partner, confidence in using condoms, attitudes towards using a condom with a new partner, and knowledge about STD/AIDS and prevention modes.

Other relevant studies have been reviewed by Rutter and Quine (2002) and Hardeman et al. (2002). These reviews identified a diverse literature, but few studies that have explicitly stated how the theory had been applied. Of the 12 identified studies that used the theory of planned behaviour to inform a behaviour change intervention, for example, four were found to change behaviour: none investigated whether behaviour change was mediated by the psychological changes proposed by the theory. Accordingly, although numerous studies demonstrate that the theory of planned behaviour can predict health behaviours (e.g., Godin & Kok, 1996), the theory has not been systematically evaluated as an explanation of behaviour change (see Michie and Abraham, 2004, for more discussion of this point). Accordingly, we focus here on a number of approaches for which there is a stronger empirical base to evaluate their utility in changing behaviour.

14.2.1 Social learning theory

Social learning theory (Bandura 1977, 1986) suggested that both skills and personal efficacy necessary for behavioural change can be gained or increased through a number of simple procedures, including observation of others performing relevant tasks, practice of tasks in a graded programme of skills development, and active persuasion. The effectiveness of learning is increased by observing people similar to the learner and by observing them cope with, rather than master the behaviour or skill. This gives the observer confidence that they too are able to acquire the behaviour. Learning is also increased by observing the acquisition of components that make up complex behaviours, rather than just observing a complete, complex behaviour. The process of demonstrating the behaviour to others is called 'modelling'.

One way of applying these principles is through the use of video or other media programmes. One of the first large-scale interventions which utilized this approach was the Stanford Three Towns coronary heart disease prevention programme (Farquhar et al., 1977). This seminal study aimed to reduce risk behaviours for coronary heart disease including smoking, high fat diet, and low exercise levels in two communities around the University of Stanford in California, with a third community acting as no intervention control area. The interventions included education provided through media channels including television, radio, leaflets and magazines. The initial programme provided risk information to alert people to the need to achieve change. The second phase showed people how to achieve change. A significant element of this phase included televised smoking cessation groups, images of people taking part and enjoying exercise, and cooking demonstrations to show viewers how to change key behaviours linked to coronary heart disease. The programme proved highly effective in changing population levels of risk behaviours, although the specific impact of each element of the intervention was not examined (Farquhar et al., 1977).

More specific programmes involving the use of videos based on social learning theory have also proven effective: including attempts to change sexual behaviour. O'Donnell et al. (1998), for example, monitored over 2,000 people who attended Sexually Transmitted Disease (STD) clinics who were randomly allocated to a control or intervention group. The intervention comprised a video that provided information about STDs and their prevention, portrayed positive attitudes about condom use, and modelled appropriate strategies for encouraging condom use in different sexual relationships. Attendance at further clinics for both groups was tracked for an average of 17 months following the intervention. Over this time, the rate of new infection was significantly lower among those shown the educational video than among controls (22 per cent compared with 27 per cent). Among a sub-group of individuals with a relatively high number of sexual partners, infection rates were 32 per cent among controls and 25 per cent among those who saw the video; a significant difference. Video interventions may be further enhanced by the use of other techniques. O'Donnell et al. (1995) compared the effectiveness of showing a video combined with a problem solving skill-building session, showing a video on its own, and a no treatment control in an intervention attempting to promote safer sexual behaviour among attenders at a STD clinic. Both active interventions were more effective than no intervention, with the combined intervention proving most effective. Levels of redemption of a voucher at a local pharmacy for free condoms were 40, 28 and 21 per cent respectively.

14.2.2 Self-management training

A more complex intervention based on social learning theory is known as self-management training (Lorig, 1996). This aims to teach people how to manage their illness in a way that maximizes control over their symptoms and maximizes their quality of life. It draws on a variety of cognitive behavioural techniques, including learning skills from practice and from watching others, setting goals, planning action, problem solving and proceeding in a structured, progressive fashion. This ensures success at each stage before progression to the next and the development of a sense of control that leads, in turn, to increased confidence and continued application of new skills.

Summarizing evaluation studies of self-management training in the mid-1990s, SuperioCabuslay et al. (1996) reported that, compared to drug treatment alone, self-management interventions provided additional benefits of 20–30 per cent on measures of pain relief in both osteoarthritis and rheumatoid arthritis, 40 per cent in functional ability in rheumatoid arthritis, and 60–80 per cent in the reduction in tender joint counts in rheumatoid arthritis. Self-management programmes have also been developed to help people cope with HIV and AIDS. Gifford et al. (1998), for example, randomly assigned men with symptomatic HIV or AIDS to either a seven-session group self-management programme or to usual care. The intervention used interactive methods to provide information about living with HIV/AIDS and a number of disease self-management skills, including symptom assessment and management, medication use, physical exercise and relaxation skills. Over the course of the study, participants who did not enter the programme reported increases in the number of 'troubling symptoms' they experienced and an increased feeling of lack of control over their health. By contrast, participants in the self-management condition both reported more control over their health and less 'troubling symptoms'.

In a further refinement of this approach, a number of programmes have moved from a 'one size fits all' intervention in which all participants take part in the entire programme regardless of their particular needs and skills. Tailored programmes provide a number of modules which participants can select according to need – ensuring that they focus on elements of the programme that will be of benefit and do not waste time on less useful elements. Evers et al. (2002) evaluated the effectiveness of one such programme targeted at people with rheumatoid arthritis. Modules were targeted at helping people to cope with fatigue, negative mood, pain, and maintaining or improving social relationships. The programme resulted in mid- to long-term gains on a number of psychological measures including use of active coping strategies, mood, fatigue and helplessness in comparison to a no treatment condition.

14.2.3 Cognitive therapy

The basic premise of cognitive therapy developed by clinical psychologists such as Beck (1977) and Ellis (1977) is that the fundamental determinant of mood, behaviour and our physiological state is our cognitive response to events that impact on us. We make hypotheses about events, which may include attributions about the cause of an event and expectations about its potential outcome. In reality, the relationship between cognitions, emotions, behaviour and physiological state is more complex than this simple model – there are reciprocal relationships between each element of the cognitive, emotion, behavioural and physiological systems. Changes in behaviour, for example, may influence our beliefs about ourselves and the world, just as changed beliefs may influence behaviour. Beck (1977) referred to the thoughts that drive negative emotion and behaviours as automatic negative assumptions. They come to mind automatically as the individual's first response to a particular situation and without logic or grounding in reality. Despite this, their very automaticity means they are unchallenged and taken as true. Beck identified a number of categories of thoughts that lead to negative emotions, including:

- *Catastrophic thinking*: considering an event as completely negative, and potentially disastrous: 'That's it – I've had a heart attack . . . I'm bound to lose my job, and I won't be able to earn enough to pay the mortgage'.
- *Over-generalization*: drawing a general (negative) conclusion on the basis of a single incident: 'That's it – my pain stopped me going to the cinema – that's something else I can't do . . .'.

- *Arbitrary inference*: drawing a conclusion without sufficient evidence to support it: 'The pain shows I have a tumour . . . I just know it'.
- *Selective abstraction*: focusing on a detail taken out of context: 'OK, I know I was able to cope with going out, but my joints ached all the time, and I know that will stop me going out in future . . .'.

Cognitive therapy involves identifying and changing the cognitions that drive negative emotions and related behaviours. Key cognitions in healthcare settings may be inappropriate beliefs about the nature of an illness, its treatment, and depressive or anxiety-provoking thoughts – all of which may interfere with appropriate self-care or behavioural change. A cognitive approach to the management of pain would, for example, target cognitions that increase anxiety and/or interfere with an individual engaging in appropriate behaviours. These may, for example, include beliefs that the experience of pain is indicative of physical damage and that avoiding painful movements will prevent further physical damage. People who have had a myocardial infarction (MI) may be inhibited from engaging in appropriate levels of exercise as the result of a belief that their heart is 'worn out' and should not be placed under any further stress, or a fear that they will have a further MI if they take part in excessive physical activity.

Perhaps the simplest method of changing cognitions is known as self-talk or self-instruction training (Meichenbaum, 1985). This involves interrupting the flow of stressful or negative thoughts by replacing them with pre-prepared realistic or 'coping' ones. These typically fall into one of two categories: reminders to use stress coping techniques that the person has practised (e.g., 'Relax . . . that will get me through it'), and reminders that negative beliefs may be inaccurate ('Remember – you exercised like this before without any problems . . . you can do it again').

A more complex approach, known as cognitive challenge (Beck, 1977), involves identifying and challenging the reality of the negative assumptions an individual is experiencing. In this, the person is taught to 'catch' their thoughts and identify the association between thoughts, emotions and behaviour. They then learn to treat their immediate negative cognitive response to particular situations as hypotheses or guesses, not reality; to challenge their veracity, and to replace them with more appropriate and less emotionally disturbing or behaviourally maladaptive thoughts. This skill can be practised within controlled situations before being used in the 'real world'. Rehearsal can be used with a variety of skills prior to their use in the 'real world', often through the use of role-play. The skills taught will depend on the needs of the individual, but may include self-management, emotional regulation, assertive communication and problem-solving. Behavioural rehearsal frequently involves a graded approach in which complex skills are broken down into smaller components which are practised alone, before being integrated into a larger set of skills, as suggested by Bandura (1977).

A third approach, cognitive behaviour therapy (CBT), combines cognitive and behavioural approaches. Behavioural challenge, for example, involves setting up behavioural experiments within a training session or as homework to directly test the negative or more positive beliefs that patients may hold – in the expectation that negative beliefs are disconfirmed and more positive ones affirmed. Success in these tasks – which validates patients' new ways of thinking – brings about longer-term cognitive, behavioural and emotional changes than pure cognitive work (see Bennett-Levy et al. 2004).

Cognitive therapy has proven particularly effective in the treatment of stress-related health problems including diabetes (Mendez & Belendez, 1997), irritable bowel syndrome (Chalder, 2003) and others (see Bennett, 2000). Perhaps the most impressive use of cognitive therapy as a means of reducing risk for disease progression was in the Recurrent Coronary Prevention Program (Friedman et al., 1986). This targeted men high on a measure of Type A behaviour (an excess of time urgency, competitiveness, and easily aroused anger thought to be associated with CHD) who had experienced an MI. An evaluation study allocated participants into one of three groups: cardiac rehabilitation, cardiac rehabilitation plus Type A management, and a usual care control. The rehabilitation programme involved small group meetings over a period of four and half years, in which participants received information on medication, exercise and diet, as well as social support from the group. The Type A management group received the same information in addition to engaging in a sustained programme of behavioural change involving training in relaxation, cognitive techniques and specific behavioural change plans in which they reduced the frequency of their Type A behaviours. Evidence of the effectiveness of this process was compelling. Over the four and a half years of the intervention, those in the Type A management programme were at half the risk for further infarction than those in the traditional rehabilitation programme, with total infarction rates over this time of 6 per cent and 12 per cent respectively. A later follow-up study (Friedman et al., 1987) reported the outcomes of a group of patients who had previously been in the control group and took part in a year-long intervention programme. This group also showed a significantly reduced intensity of type A behaviour and a significant decrease in both the cardiac mortality and morbidity rate over this follow-up period.

14.3 USING THE THEORIES: DEVELOPING HEALTH PROMOTION PROGRAMMES

Each of the theories considered in this chapter have differing historical antecedents, but most can inform both individually based interventions and large-scale population interventions. However, care should be taken in their use. Developing health promotion intervention programmes to change individual health behaviour is far from easy. If it were, car drivers would all wear their safety belts, swimmers would all use sunscreen, and dentists would be unemployed! But that is not the case, and for good reason. Schaalma et al. (1996) differentiated three generations of programmes designed to change individual health behaviours. Programmes of the first generation were based on the premise that providing knowledge would be sufficient to change behaviour (i.e., that knowledge of the health risks of a behaviour would be sufficient to produce behaviour change). Although first-generation programmes were generally successful in increasing knowledge, only a few such studies reported attitude modification following these programmes (Schaalma et al., 1996; Damond et al., 1993) and most had little impact on behaviour change. Among the criticisms addressed at this type of programme, their narrow view of the complex relationships between knowledge, attitude and behaviour has been particularly emphasized (Kirby et al., 1994; Oakley et al., 1995). Such programmes appear to have only limited usefulness in changing individual health behaviours.

Second-generation programmes recognize that proper knowledge is a necessary but not sufficient condition in order to modify behaviour. These programmes included education strategies addressing values, attitudes, social influences, decision-making processes and communication skills. The majority of second-generation programmes were inspired by theoretical frameworks such as the health belief model (Rosenstock, 1974) and the social learning theory (Bandura, 1977). However, evaluation of these programmes indicated considerable inconsistency across studies. Some evaluations have reported positive effects on knowledge acquisition only, while others have noted an impact on attitude and intention to adopt preventative behaviours (Schaalma et al., 1996).

Programmes of the third generation differ from the previous two by the utilization of a systematic three-step approach in their development (see Chapter 11). In the first step, a needs assessment is made to identify the determinants of the behaviour under study in the targeted population. In the second step, intervention contents, methods and material are developed, based on formal theoretical frameworks and on research eliciting intervention strategies and needs that are specific to the groups. In the third stage, collaboration between health educators, staff and other key people is employed to ensure the efficiency of the programmes. These programmes are likely to be more successful strategies in producing individual health behaviour change since they are inspired by a theoretical explanation of the links between behavioural determinants that also indicate how interventions should be implemented (Collins et al., 1996; Bennett & Murphy, 1997). In short, such programmes allow targeting of specific health behaviours by specific populations in specific contexts (Sanderson & Jemmott, 1996). However, greater specification of interventions are necessary if causal mechanisms are to be better understood, allowing the development of more effective interventions (Michie and Abraham, 2004).

14.4 HEALTH PSYCHOLOGY COMPETENCES COVERED IN THIS CHAPTER

This chapter has focused on how to change individual health behaviours using cognitive behavioural and social-cognitive approaches. As such, the chapter is mostly obviously related to competence unit 5: Implement interventions to change health-related behaviour. The chapter addresses the need to define the environmental contingencies which have led to and maintain the behaviour (5.1c.1), to identify the influence of past and current behaviours on target behaviours (5.1c.2) and to elicit cognitions and underlying beliefs associated with the current behaviour (5.1c.3). We also addressed part of competence unit 5.1d: develop a behaviour change plan based on cognitive-behavioural principles. Critical issues here are the need to identify cognitive, behavioural and situational barriers to, and facilitators of, change (5.1d.1/2) and to identify the motivators and rewards for behaviour change (5.1d.3). Also important are the need to develop cognitive-behavioural strategies to deal with possible setbacks (5.1d.6). Inherent within the interventions outlined are the need to ensure monitoring and support for behaviour change plans (competence 5.1e). Any intervention should select appropriate methods for monitoring behaviour change (5.1e.1), obtain baseline data (5.1e.2), and teach clients the skills of self-monitoring and responding appropriately (5.1e.3). This is perhaps most obvious in the self-management programmes such as those led by Lorig and colleagues, but should also form the key element of any behavioural or cognitive behavioural intervention. Finally, we addressed competence unit 5.1f: evaluate outcomes. This indicates the need to maximize the effectiveness of any intervention by identifying how effective any intervention is (5.1f.1) and identifying the effective components within it (5.1f.2). Equally important is the identification of ineffective elements of an intervention (5.1f.3) and any unintended consequences of behavioural change (5.1f.4). It cannot be assumed that any intervention will only affect the targeted behaviours.

The chapter has largely focused on the theoretical underpinnings of cognitive behavioural and social cognition based interventions. It has not considered some of the key practical skills required. However, any intervention will require a number of practical skills relating to both the organization of the intervention, communicating with other professionals with regard to its implementation, or perhaps advising or training others to provide the intervention. As such, the competences involved in designing and implementing interventions will also address other areas of competence including those related to directing the implementation of interventions (5.2). These competences include ensuring that there are necessary resources for the effective implementation of any programme (5.2a), that those running any intervention are competent (5.2b), and advising and guiding the activities of designated others in running any programme (5.2c). Clearly relevant are also the competences involved in communicating the process and outcomes of interventions (5.3).

REFERENCES

Ajzen, I. (1991). The theory of planned behavior. *Organizational Behavior and Human Decision Processes* 50, 179–211.

Ajzen, I. & Fishbein, M. (1980). *Understanding Attitudes and Predicting Social Behaviour*. Englewood Cliffs, NJ: Prentice-Hall.

Bandura, A. (1977). Self-efficacy: Toward a unifying theory of behavioural change. *Psychological Review* 84, 191–215.

Bandura, A. (1986). *Social Foundations of Thought and Action: A Social Cognitive Theory*. Englewood Cliffs, NJ: Prentice-Hall.

Baum, A. & Posluszny, D.M. (1999). Health psychology: Mapping biobehavioral contributions to health and illness. *Annual Review of Psychology* 50, 137–63.

Beck, A. (1977). *Cognitive Therapy of Depression*. New York: Guilford Press.

Bennett, P. (2000). *An Introduction to Clinical Health Psychology*. Buckingham: Open University Press.

Bennett, P. & Murphy, S. (1997). *Psychology and Health Promotion*. Buckingham: Open University Press.

Bennett-Levy, J., Butler, G., Fennell, M.J.V., Hackmann, A., Mueller, M. & Westbrook, D. (2004). *Oxford Guide to Behavioural Experiments in Cognitive Therapy*. Oxford: Oxford University Press.

Chalder, T. (2003). Cognitive behavioural therapy and antispasmodic therapy for irritable bowel syndrome in primary care; a randomised controlled trial. Paper presented at 'Psychological interventions in physical health' invited expert conference, Roratonga.

Collins, J., Rugg, D., Kann, L., Banspach, S., Kolbe, L. & Pateman, B. (1996). Evaluating a national program of school-based HIV prevention. *Evaluation and Program Planning* 19, 209–18.

Conner, M.T. & Norman, P. (eds) (1996). *Predicting Health Behaviour: Research and Practice with Social Cognition Models.* Buckingham: Open University Press.

Damond, M.E., Breuer, N.L. & Pharr, A.E. (1993). The evaluation of setting and a culturally specific HIV/AIDS curriculum: HIV/AIDS knowledge and behavioral intent of African American adolescents, *Journal of Black Psychology* 19, 169–89.

Ellis, A. (1977). The basic clinical theory of rational-emotive-therapy. In A. Ellis & R. Grieger (eds), *Handbook of Rational-emotive Therapy.* New York: Springer.

Evers, A.W., Kraaimaat, F.W., van Riel, P.L. et al. (2002). Tailored cognitive-behavioral therapy in early rheumatoid arthritis for patients at risk: A randomized controlled trial. *Pain* 100, 141–53.

Farquhar, J.W., Maccoby, N., Wood, P.D. et al. (1977). Community education for cardiovascular health. *Lancet* 1, 1192–98.

Fordyce, W.E. (1988). Pain and suffering. *American Psychologist* 43(4), 276–83.

Fordyce, W.E. & Steger, J.C. (1979). *Behavioral Medicine: Theory and Practice.* Baltimore: Williams and Wilkins.

Friedman, M., Powell, L.H., Thoresen, C.E. et al. (1987) Effect of discontinuance of type A behavioral counseling on type A behavior and cardiac recurrence rate of post myocardial infarction patients. *American Heart Journal* 114, 483–90.

Friedman, M., Thoresen, C.E., Gill, J.J. et al. (1986) Alteration of type A behavior and its effect on cardiac recurrences in post myocardial infarction patients: Summary results of the recurrent coronary prevention project. *American Heart Journal* 112, 653–65.

Gifford, A.L., Laurent, D.D., Gonzales, V.M., Chesney, M.A. & Lorig, K.R. (1998). Pilot randomized trial of education to improve self-management skills of men with symptomatic HIV/AIDS. *Journal of Acquired Immune Deficiency Syndrome and Human Retrovirology* 18, 136–44.

Gochman, D.S. (ed.) (1997). *Handbook of Health Behavior Research* (Vols. 1–4). New York: Plenum.

Godin, G. & Kok, G. (1996). The theory of planned behavior: A review of its applications to health-related behaviors. *American Journal of Health Promotion* 11, 87–98.

Godin, G., Michaud, F., Alary, M. et al. (2003). Evaluation of an HIV and STD prevention program for adolescents in juvenile rehabilitation centers. *Health Education and Behavior*, 30, 601–14.

Hardeman, W., Johnston, M., Johnston, D.W., Bonetti, D., Wareham, N. & Kinmonth, A.L. (2002). Application of the theory of planned behaviour in behaviour change inteventions: A systematic review. *Psychology & Health* 17, 123–58.

Jacobson, E. (1938). *Progressive Relaxation.* Chicago: Chicago University Press.

Kazdin, A.E. (2001) *Behaviour Modification in Applied Settings.* London: Wadsworth, Thomas Learning.

Kirby, D., Short, L., Collins, J. et al. (1994). School-based programs to reduce sexual risk behaviors: A review of effectiveness. *Public Health Reports* 109, 339-60.

Kole-Snijders, A.M., Vlaeyen, J.W., Goossens, M.E., Rutten-van Molken, M.P., Heuts, P.H., van Breukelen, G. & van Eek, H. (1999). Chronic low-back pain: what does cognitive coping skills training add to operant behavioral treatment? Results of a randomized clinical trial. *Journal of Consulting and Clinical Psychology* 67, 931-44.

Lorig, K. (1996). *Patient Education: A Practical Approach.* Newbury Park: Sage.

Lowe, M.R., Green, L., Kurtz S.M., Ashenberg, Z.S. & Fisher, E.B. Jr (1980). Self-initiated, cue extinction, and covert sensitization procedures in smoking cessation. *Journal of Behavioral Medicine* 3, 357-72.

Meichenbaum, D. (1985). *Stress Inoculation Training.* New York: Pergamon.

Mendez, F.J. & Belendez, M. (1997). Effects of a behavioral intervention on treatment adherence and stress management in adolescents with IDDM. *Diabetes Care* 20, 1370-5.

Michie, S. and Abraham, C. (2004) Identifying techniques that promote health behaviour change: Evidence based or evidence inspired? *Psychology and Health* 19, 29-49.

Murphy, S. & Bennett, P. (2004). Health psychology and public health: Theoretical possibilities. *Psychology and Health* 9, 13-27.

Morrow, G.R. & Hickok, J.T. (1993). Behavioral treatment of chemotherapy-induced nausea and vomiting. *Oncology* 7, 83-9.

Oakley, A., Fullerton, D. & Holland, J. (1995). Behavioral interventions for HIV/AIDS prevention, *AIDS* 9, 479-86.

O'Donnell, L.N., Doval, A.S., Duran, R. & O'Donnell, C. (1995). Video-based sexually transmitted disease patient education: its impact on condom acquisition. *American Journal of Public Health* 85, 817-22.

O'Donnell, C.R., O'Donnell, L., San Doval, A., Duran, R. & Labes, K. (1998). Reductions in STD infections subsequent to an STD clinic visit. Using video-based patient education to supplement provider interactions. *Sexually Transmitted Diseases* 25, 161-8.

Pavlov, I.P. (1927). *Conditioned Reflexes* (ed. and trans. G.V. Anrep). New York: Dover (reprinted 1960).

Redd, W.H., Montgomery, G.H. & DuHamel, K.N. (2001). Behavioral intervention for cancer treatment side effects. *Journal of the National Cancer Institute* 93, 810-23.

Rosenstock, I.M. (1974). Historical origins of the Health Belief Model. *Health Education Monographs* 2, 328-35.

Rutter, D.R. & Quine, L. (eds) (2002). *Changing Health Behaviour: Intervention and Research with Social Cognition Models.* Buckingham: Open University Press.

Sanderson, C.A. & Jemmott, J.B. (1996). Moderation and mediation of HIV-prevention interventions: Relationship status, intentions, and condom use among college students. *Journal of Applied Social Psychology* 226, 2076-99.

Schaalma, H.P., Kok, G., Bosker, R.J., Parcel, G.S., Peters, L., Poelman, J. &t Reinders, J. (1996). Planned development and evaluation of AIDS/STD education for secondary school students in the Netherlands: Short-term effects. *Health Education Quarterly* 23, 469–87.

SuperioCabuslay, E., Ward, M.M. &t Lorig, K.R. (1996). Patient education interventions in osteoarthritis and rheumatoid arthritis: A meta-analytic comparison with nonsteroidal antiinflammatory drug treatment. *Arthritis Care and Research* 9, 292–301.

Skinner, B.F. (1953). *Science and Human Behavior.* New York: Macmillan.

Van Tulder, M.W., Ostelo, R.W.J., Vlaeyen, J.W.S. et al. (2003). Behavioural treatment for chronic low back pain (Cochrane Review). *The Cochrane Library*, 1. Oxford: Update Software.

Wolpe, J. (1958). *Psychotherapy and Reciprocal Inhibition.* Stanford, CA: Stanford University Press.

Chapter 15

STUDYING AND CHANGING HEALTHCARE PROFESSIONALS' BEHAVIOUR

Anne Walker

15.1 HEALTHCARE AS BEHAVIOUR

Healthcare is delivered through services that aim to improve the health of the population by prevention, treatment or palliation of illness. Donabedian (1980) identifies two criteria for good quality healthcare: first, that it is generally effective in improving the health of the population; and second, that it meets public and professional standards about how care should be provided. Most current commentators accept that good quality healthcare should be safe, effective (and often cost effective) and equitable (see Crombie and Davies, 1996 for a discussion of these terms). Health services can be organized in a variety of ways to deliver good quality healthcare. The focus in this chapter will be on the UK healthcare system, which is predominantly delivered through the National Health Service (NHS) which is funded through taxation, and free at the point of delivery. This system creates a closer relationship between health policy decided at government level and healthcare delivery than is the case in some other countries.

The NHS is often characterized as involving doctors and nurses working in hospitals to treat acute conditions. While this is an important aspect of healthcare, in reality the majority of healthcare is provided in the community (see Lipman, 2000) and is concerned with management of chronic conditions or prevention of ill health. Even within hospitals, care is provided in a range of settings (e.g., operating theatres, specialist in-patient units, day case units, out-patient clinics), and the range of facilities varies between hospitals. Similarly, doctors and nurses are not the only healthcare professionals. Healthcare involves a wide range of people with differing qualifications, for example health visitors, physiotherapists, radiographers, dentists, pharmacists, psychologists, dieticians. Often these professionals work together, either directly or indirectly, in multidisciplinary or multi-agency teams (e.g., to provide care for stroke patients or to deliver a heart–lung transplant).

Often healthcare is thought of only in terms of these interventions, leading to debates about 'rationing' of drugs and waiting times for various procedures, for example. From a psychological point of view, however, healthcare not only involves effective treatments and procedures, but also the processes that result in the appropriate use (or non-use) of interventions. From this perspective, the use of existing treatments and procedures results from a sequence of clinical decisions and actions taken by healthcare professionals alone or in combination with others (e.g., patients, patients' relatives, other professionals). These decisions and actions may be influenced by a wide range of factors, such as the knowledge, skills, attitudes and experience of the healthcare professional; communication between professional(s) and patient; patient preferences and medical history; available resources and facilities; the effects of stress and time or work pressures on healthcare professionals; the possibility of errors, lapses or mistakes; and organizational factors. Thus psychological theories that help us to understand decision-making and action regulation are likely to be relevant to understanding the behaviour of healthcare professionals and, therefore, healthcare practice.

15.2 Interventions that Have Been Used to Change Healthcare

A wide variety of interventions have been used within healthcare settings to improve the quality of healthcare. The development of many of these interventions has been driven by a growing expectation that decisions about treatments and procedures should be based on information about an individual person's needs and on the best research evidence about available treatments. This is often described as 'evidence-based healthcare' (e.g., Sackett et al., 1996; see Trinder & Reynolds, 2000). Each patient has a unique set of needs and circumstances, so variations in healthcare are inevitable. However, the research evidence relating to available treatments and procedures is the same for all patients, and so it is often possible to identify the most appropriate treatment for most patients with a particular diagnosis. For example, the research evidence shows that most adult patients with a sore throat will not receive any benefit from taking antibiotics, and generally it would be considered inappropriate to prescribe one (Del Mar & Glasziou, 1997). However, it may be appropriate to prescribe an antibiotic for a particular patient if the doctor feels that there is a risk of developing a secondary bacterial infection, for example a chest infection.

There are numerous reports of inappropriate care across different healthcare settings, countries and specialities (e.g., NHS Centre for Reviews and Dissemination, 1999; Schuster et al., 1998; Grol, 2001). One reason for this may be that healthcare professionals vary in their awareness and evaluation of the available research evidence. The evidence-based healthcare movement has reacted to this problem by synthesizing research evidence and improving its availability to clinicians. For example, the Cochrane Collaboration is an international organization which co-ordinates systematic reviews of the best available research evidence on specific healthcare issues (Bero & Rennie, 1995; Clarke, 2002). The development and dissemination of evidence-based clinical guidelines is another response to the problem of digesting research findings and making them available to practising clinicians (e.g., see Woolf et al., 2000).

Providing information is only one approach to improving healthcare, although it is the most widely used intervention (NHS Centre for Reviews and Dissemination, 1999; Grimshaw et al., 2001). There are a number of other interventions that may be used. These range from the more 'top down' government-led types of interventions, such as legislation, target setting (e.g., waiting list initiatives, National Service Frameworks) or structuring of health services (e.g., the creation of Primary Care Trusts); to local or professionally driven initiatives, such as educational workshops or the development of local guidelines. The most commonly used approaches in the UK are summarized in Box 15.1.

BOX 15.1 Strategies used to implement clinical guidelines: The Cochrane Collaboration Effective Practice and Organization of Care (EPOC) module taxonomy

Interventions orientated towards health professionals

- Distribution of published or printed educational materials
- Conferences, lectures, workshops or training sessions
- Local consensus processes
- Educational outreach visits
- Local opinion leaders
- Patient-mediated interventions
- Audit and feedback
- Reminders (including computerized decision support)

- Tailored interventions that target specific barriers to change identified by health professionals
- Peer review
- Combined strategies.

Financial interventions
- Provider interventions, e.g., fee-for-service, capitation, incentives for the health professional or their organization
- Patient interventions, e.g., premiums, user fees, incentives for patients.

Organizational interventions
- Structural interventions, e.g., changes in the setting of service delivery, telemedicine, changes in medical record systems, changes in facilities or equipment; introduction of quality assurance mechanisms
- Staff oriented interventions, e.g., changes in professional roles, multidisciplinary teams, case management, interventions to relieve staff stress.

Regulatory interventions
- Changes in medical liability
- Management of patient complaints
- Licensing and accreditation.

(Adapted from the Cochrane Collaboration Review Group on Effective Practice and Organization and Delivery of Care (EPOC) checklist of interventions. For more details see http://www.epoc.uottawa.ca)

New ideas for improving the quality of healthcare have proliferated in recent years, and the effectiveness of many of these has been evaluated and summarized in systematic reviews (e.g., NHS Centre for Reviews and Dissemination, 1999; Grimshaw et al., 2001; 2002; in press). One review included 235 rigorous evaluations of guideline dissemination and implementation strategies published up to 1998 (Grimshaw et al., in press). This review concludes that the majority of interventions achieve modest to moderate improvements in care (the median absolute improvement in performance ranges from around 6 per cent to 13 per cent). Few studies provided any rationale for their choice of intervention and most include only limited descriptions of the interventions and context. As a result, it is difficult to assess the likely generalizability of these findings. Researchers may have chosen interventions that they think are likely to be effective within their study context; thus there may be important differences in the context, barriers or targeted behaviour between studies that assessed, for example, printed educational materials and educational outreach. At present there is no widely accepted theoretical perspective from which to make sense of these issues.

Healthcare is complex so it is unlikely that a single theoretical (or disciplinary) approach can provide a panacea for choosing interventions to improve the quality of care, or for understanding why they are effective. Ferlie and Shortell (2001) suggested four levels at which interventions to improve the quality of healthcare might operate: (1) the individual health professional; (2) healthcare groups or teams; (3) organizations providing healthcare (e.g., NHS Trusts); and (4) the larger healthcare system or environment in which individual organizations are embedded.

15.3 USING PSYCHOLOGICAL THEORY TO UNDERSTAND HEALTHCARE AND DESIGN INTERVENTIONS

This chapter focuses on the use of theories from social and health psychology to understand variability in healthcare practice and to design or evaluate interventions. Clearly, this is not the only body of relevant theory, and health psychologists will often need to seek advice from and work collaboratively with other disciplinary specialists (e.g., health economists, organizational specialists). Organizational theories are likely to be particularly useful (see Chapter 13; and Iles & Sutherland, 2001, for a useful overview).

Psychological theories have been used primarily to understand factors influencing practice; to understand why an intervention may have made a difference or not ('process evaluation'); and, to design and evaluate interventions aimed at health professionals as individuals or groups. Examples of some studies using these different approaches are described in Case studies 15.1–15.3. All of these studies are based on the same underlying logic – that is, that interventions to change practice are more likely to be effective if they address the reasons why health professionals are behaving in a particular way. These studies generally use theories that have been of value in understanding potentially comparable types of behaviour, for example health preventative behaviour and patient treatment adherence.

CASE STUDY 15.1 GPs' intentions to prescribe antibiotics

Problem. Over-prescribing of antibiotics for minor and/or viral infections in UK primary care.

Behaviour. Prescribing an antibiotic for an adult patient with an uncomplicated sore throat.

Theory. Theory of planned behaviour (TPB).

Study design. Assessment of the current situation to identify psychological factors predicting GPs' intentions to prescribe antibiotics for patients presenting with a sore throat.

Methods. Literature reviews, non-participant observation and interviews with general practitioners were used to develop a questionnaire to measure constructs specified in the TPB. Measures of the constructs used scales and items recommended by Ajzen (1991) and Conner and Sparks (1996). The questionnaire was distributed by post to a 1 in 2 random sample of GPs in the Grampian region of Scotland. Analysis used descriptive statistics, multiple linear regression to assess the relative importance of the theoretical constructs in predicting behavioural intention, and *t*-tests to compare the strength of salient beliefs between GPs who intended to prescribe and those who did not.

Key findings.

- Two-thirds of the GPs returned the questionnaire ($N = 126$, 68 per cent).
- The majority of GPs indicated that they intended to prescribe for less than half of the patients presenting with an uncomplicated sore throat in the next two weeks ($N = 69$, 55 per cent).
- The variables specified in the TPB predicted 48 per cent of the variance in intention, with attitude and control beliefs being the most important predictors. Past behaviour added a further 7 per cent to the model.
- Doctors who intend to prescribe are more likely to believe that:
  - antibiotics will reduce the risk of developing minor complications
  - prescribing an antibiotic is cost-efficient
  - an antibiotic will reduce the time taken for a sore throat to resolve
  - they will prescribe an antibiotic if a patient specifically asks for one
  - they will prescribe an antibiotic to avoid missing something

- they will be inclined to prescribe an antibiotic for patients of a lower social class
- patients will finish a prescribed course of antibiotics.
- Doctors who intend to prescribe antibiotics are less concerned about the problem of antibiotic resistance.

Key implications. Interventions to strengthen GPs' intentions to avoid prescribing antibiotics should focus on the beliefs that distinguish between doctors who intend to prescribe and those who do not.
Report of outcome. Walker et al. (2001).

CASE STUDY 15.2 Evaluating tailored strategies to implement guidelines for management of depression in general practice

Problem. Failure to implement guidelines for the management of patients with depression in UK primary care.

Behaviour. Seven behaviours indicating adherence to the guideline (e.g., assessing patients for risk of suicide at diagnosis, referring patients with major depression for cognitive behaviour therapy, prescribing anti-depressants for patients with major depression).

Theory. Various, including 'stages of change' (preparedness to change), self-efficacy, social influence theory, cognitive dissonance theory.

Study design. Cluster randomized controlled trial of an individually tailored guideline implementation intervention versus no intervention.

Methods. All 1,239 GPs in five central English counties were invited to participate, and 69 agreed (6 per cent). The practices of those GPs who agreed to participate were randomly allocated to intervention and control groups (no practice included a doctor in both study groups). Guidelines were disseminated by post to both groups. GPs in the intervention group participated in an in-depth interview to identify their obstacles to implementing the guidelines. For each comment indicating a particular obstacle to change, a psychological theory (or construct) to explain the observed obstacle was proposed. The theory was then used to select the implementation method. For example, if a GP reported being uncertain about their ability to assess suicide risk, the implementation method would be designed to increase self-efficacy. The implementation method might include provision of scripts of questions for assessing suicide risk for use in consultations.

Key findings.

- Sixty practices (64 GPs) completed the study (34 GPs in intervention group, 30 in control group).
- The most frequent obstacles to change were explained by the constructs of preparedness to change and self-efficacy.
- Levels of adherence to 3/7 of the guideline recommendations were 70 per cent or above in both groups at baseline and post intervention.
- Of the remaining four recommendations assessed, adherence after the intervention was significantly higher in the intervention group for only one (assessment of suicide risk at diagnosis – 26.5 per cent of eligible patients assessed in the control group compared to 66.5 per cent in the intervention group).

Key implications. Interventions based on theoretical principles that take individual obstacles to change into account are feasible in general practice and may be effective.

Report of outcome. Baker et al. (2001).

CASE STUDY 15.3 Changing dentists' intentions to extract third molars

Problem. Dentists were not following clinical guideline to reduce third molar extractions.

Behaviour. Extraction of third molars ('wisdom teeth') in patients presenting with third molar related pain and swelling.

Theory. Theory of planned behaviour.

Study design. Randomized controlled trial of an intervention (rehearsing alternative actions) to change dentists' intentions to extract third molars.

Methods. A random sample of 205 dentists in Scotland was randomly allocated to intervention or control groups. Both groups were sent a postal questionnaire assessing knowledge and intention to extract third molars. The intervention was an open question asking participants which alternative treatments to extraction they would consider for patients with third molar related pain and swelling. This item appeared before the intention items in the intervention group questionnaire only.

Key findings.

- Ninety-nine (of 205) dentists participated (66 in the control group, 33 in the intervention group).
- The intervention group had significantly less intention to extract than the control group (control group mean z score = 0.39 (sd 1.99), intervention group mean z score = −0.78 (sd 1.89), $t(1,97)$ = 2.79, p = 0.006), despite similar knowledge of management alternatives.

Key implications.

- Behavioural intention is known to be a predictor of behaviour, and may be a useful proxy measure in studies of practice change.
- The results suggest that this relatively simple intervention successfully influenced a proximal predictor of behaviour, and therefore would result in improved practice.

Report of outcome. Bonetti et al. (in press).

Theoretically based evaluations have three important advantages. First, they reduce the number of possible variables and mechanisms under consideration. This is important for both pragmatic and ethical reasons, given the limited time that health professionals have to participate in research. Second, they can cast some light on causal processes because theories generally specify relationships between variables, which allows some assessment of how the important variables may impact on practice. Third, theories provide a common language and methodology across studies, allowing findings in different areas to be accumulated and built upon. Of course, theory limits the potential mechanisms and variables that are considered and researchers need to take care to ensure that crucial factors are not missed. Similarly, if the theory chosen is weak or not applicable to health professional practice, then there is a high risk of 'rubbish in – rubbish out'. To limit these potential disadvantages, any study requires a careful survey of the existing research literature before selecting which theory (or theories) to use, and wherever possible, some preliminary observation or interview based work to identify which broad categories of theories are likely to be appropriate.

15.4 A STEP-BY-STEP APPROACH

Steps involved in applying psychological theories to healthcare practice include the following: specify the problem; assess the behaviour; select a theory or theories to use; design the study; develop a protocol and budget; consider ethical and research governance issues; assess the determinants or predictors of behaviour; develop a behaviour change plan; implement a behaviour change plan; evaluate the process and outcome; report the outcome (see Bartholomew et al., 2001). There is some overlap between these steps, and they may not always be considered in this order, but most will need to be considered for the majority of projects. As a consultant, you may be approached by a manager or senior health professional whose main concern is to implement a particular clinical guideline or service framework, and the following discussion assumes that this is the case. Slightly different (although related) issues arise in large-scale trials of implementation strategies (see Grimshaw et al., 2000 for discussion) and in implementation of more generic or structural changes (e.g., waiting list initiatives, or creation of primary care trusts).

15.4.1 What's the problem?

The most crucial, and often the most difficult, part of any project that applies psychological theories to healthcare improvement is to describe the problem in terms of what people are currently doing and what needs to change. The problem may be that people are doing too much of something (e.g., over prescribing of antibiotics for minor infections), too little of something (e.g., hand washing) or the right amount but not always in the right circumstances (e.g., use of dental sealants). The change may require people to stop doing something (completely or partially), to introduce a new behaviour (in all circumstances or some), or to substitute one behaviour for another. Each of these may require different approaches to assessment and intervention, so it is important to be clear about what the problem is. Unfortunately for psychologists, most clinical guidelines cover a broad area of care for patients with a particular diagnosis or group of diagnoses and contain numerous evidence-based recommendations for practice. For example, the Royal College of Obstetrics and Gynaecology guideline on care of women requesting induced abortion contains over 30 separate practice recommendations (RCOG, 2000); the Scottish Intercollegiate Guidelines Network guideline on prophylaxis of venous thromboembolism contains around a hundred (SIGN, 2002). In most circumstances, studying adherence by healthcare professionals to all of these recommendations in detail will not be feasible and you will have to choose a small number to focus on. Which are chosen (and how many) will depend on a number of issues including:

- the frequency with which the practice occurs – it is difficult to demonstrate significant changes in practice for rare conditions or infrequently used aspects of care unless the study is conducted over a lengthy period or includes a very large geographical area;
- whether there is any evidence of poor adherence to the recommendation – it is difficult to demonstrate improvements if adherence is already high, that is, there is no problem;
- whether it is feasible to measure or assess the degree of adherence to the recommendation – in most cases it is easier to assess adherence to aspects of care that are documented in some routine way than those that are not (e.g., prescribing, laboratory test requests, blood pressure measurement);
- whether it is possible to identify which individuals or groups of health professionals are responsible for delivering care relevant to any particular recommendation – if this is not possible, then it will be difficult to be certain that the study includes the appropriate participants;
- the clinical importance of the recommendation.

15.4.2 Assessing the behaviour

Having decided which recommendations to focus on, the next step is to define what adherence or non-adherence to the recommendation means in terms of behaviour, and to establish what the current level of adherence is. Defining adherence may seem straightforward at first glance, but often requires some skilled interviewing of key informants, or even observation of practice, to identify what is actually happening and who is responsible for doing it. For example, in a study of prevention of deep vein thrombosis (DVT) among hospital in-patients, it was clear that patients in particular risk categories should receive intravenous heparin injections, but not at all clear whether the behaviour was the decision to give the injection (generally made by the consultant), or the administration of the injection (generally by the senior house officer).

Applying models such as the theory of planned behaviour (Ajzen, 1991) requires detailed specification of the behaviour in terms of who is doing what in which circumstances and over what period of time (e.g., general practitioners prescribing antibiotics for adult patients presenting with an uncomplicated sore throat in the next month – see Case study 15.1). Not all studies will require this level of specificity, but they will all require a description of the behaviour of interest, who is performing it and the desired change.

Closely related to this is the issue of measurement (see also Section 15.4.1). In order to assess adherence to a guideline, it is necessary to measure the behaviour of interest. There are a variety of ways of doing this. The most efficient method is to use data that are collected in routine information systems or recorded in patient case notes. However, these data are generally collected for different reasons and do not always provide the level of specificity that some studies require. For example, the researchers conducting the study described in Case study 15.1 (Walker et al., 2001) thought that rates of prescribing of particular classes of antibiotics would provide a good measure of prescribing practice among GPs. However, routine prescribing data is collected largely for financial reasons and does not have to be accurate at the level of the individual GP, so it was unusable for this study. The use of routine data also raises issues of data protection and confidentiality (see Section 15.4.5). Patient case notes are a valuable source of information about many areas of clinical practice, but these data can be costly and time consuming to collect and it is best done by trained clinical audit staff. As with routine data, the use of case notes raises issues of confidentiality and data protection (see Section 15.4.5). Other sources of information about practice are patient surveys and observational data. These have their own strengths and limitations (see Adams et al., 1999) but both can be valuable sources of information. In some circumstances, responses to simulated patients can be used. For example, in a recent study trained actors were used to assess the response of staff in community pharmacies to customers describing symptoms that might be suggestive of vulvovaginal candidiasis (Watson et al., 2002).

Finally, probably the most widely used measure of practice is self-report. Self-report is often used in studies of health behaviour, generally using responses to validated behaviour assessment questionnaires. There are no instruments of this type available to measure health professional practice and most studies either rely on statements of behavioural frequency or on responses to patient scenarios. The relationship between these measures and objective measures of practice varies between studies, from very good to quite poor (Adams et al., 1999). In addition, statements of behavioural frequency and responses to patient scenarios can be difficult to interpret if they are assessed in questionnaires that also include measures of knowledge and behavioural intention. For these reasons, it is recommended that objective measures are used wherever possible, although there will always be circumstances in which self-report is the only feasible measure. If self-report is to be used, then some preliminary work may be required to develop a measure and to assess its reliability and validity (if possible).

15.4.3 Which theories to consider

Once you have established that there is a measurable behaviour, and that there is good reason to think that it may need to change, the next step is to choose the theory or theories to use from the various possibilities. A number of theories have been used to investigate health professional practice and/or to design or evaluate interventions (see Davies, 2003), but there are not enough good quality studies to assess the applicability of these theories to health professional practice. The most popular theories relate to information processing (e.g., the vividness heuristic), social cognition (e.g., theory of planned behaviour), social influence (e.g., diffusion theory), persuasion (e.g., elaboration likelihood model), theories used in health promotion (e.g., precede–proceed) and organizational models (e.g., total quality management, organizational development).

Selection of theories should be based on careful thought about the specific situation in which the theory is to be applied. The theories that are most likely to be useful are those that:

- have demonstrated effectiveness in predicting and explaining behaviour change in other settings, such as health promotion in community populations;
- explain behaviour in terms of factors that are changeable (e.g., knowledge, beliefs, attitudes, motivation, actual or perceived external constraints). Some factors are difficult to change (e.g., age, personality and intelligence), even though they may be important predictors of behaviour;
- include non-volitional components, that is, they should assume that individuals working in healthcare do not always have complete control over their actions and allow an examination of the influence of individuals' perceptions of external factors, such as patient preferences or organizational barriers and facilitators, on their behaviour (Eccles et al., in preparation).

On the basis of these criteria, the following six psychological theories might be expected to be useful in this area. They are social cognitive theory, theory of planned behaviour, operant conditioning, implementation intention formation, the self-regulatory model, and the precaution adoption process model (or a similar stage-based model).

15.4.4 Design the study

As in any research or consultancy situation, the study design depends upon the questions that are being asked. The most likely questions in this situation are:

- What is currently happening (and why)?
- What is likely to be the best way of achieving change?
- Is the chosen method of achieving change effective?
- How does it work?

The first, second and last of these questions are most suited to descriptive or predictive study designs, predominantly using survey methods. The third requires an evaluative study design.

What is currently happening (and why)?

Some assessment of the current situation will be required in almost all studies. From a psychological perspective, this assessment has two components: what are people doing, and why are they doing it. Both of these are necessary if the ultimate aim is to develop an intervention to change practice. Investigation of what people are doing has been discussed in Section 15.4.2 above. This section will focus on study designs seeking to provide insight into why current practice is as it is.

Broadly speaking, theories can either be used from the 'top down' or the 'bottom up' to gain insight into the factors associated with current practice. In a top-down approach, the theory (or theories) are chosen at the beginning of the study and are used to drive the data collection and analysis. In a bottom-up approach, the data are collected first and then either analysed or interpreted with reference to theoretical constructs. Alternatively, the data may be used to generate a new or context specific theory as in a grounded theory approach (Strauss & Corbin, 1990). Both of these approaches have their strengths and limitations. Which is chosen will depend largely on how much is known about the situation already, your own philosophy of science, and pragmatic factors such as the time and resources available.

In a top-down approach, the key stages are selecting a theory or theories (see Section 15.4.3) and then operationalizing the theory. Generally this will mean developing measures to assess the various constructs identified in the theory. This is done in exactly the same way as it would be if the behaviour of interest was healthy eating, smoking or safe sex. For example, when using the theory of planned behaviour, preliminary interviews may be required to establish the salient beliefs about the behaviour. The responses to these interviews would be used to generate survey items, using question stems and formats appropriate to each of the theoretical constructs and specific to the behaviour of interest (e.g., see Conner & Sparks, 1996). The questionnaire would be piloted and amended as necessary, and then administered to an appropriate sample of participants. Ideally, an objective measure of the actual behaviour of interest would also be obtained (see Section 15.4.2). The responses would be analysed in two ways: descriptively, in order to identify which beliefs are most strongly held; and predictively, in order to identify which constructs (and/or beliefs) best predict behavioural intentions and the actual behaviour. Crucial things to think about in this approach are the need to be as precise and specific as possible about the behaviour of interest and the need to match survey items to this specific behaviour. This can be difficult, especially if the behaviour is part of a larger 'care package' for a patient (e.g., giving prophylaxis against DVT is part of a larger package of care for patients undergoing surgery to remove gall stones).

A bottom-up approach is likely to make greater use of qualitative methods such as interviews and participant or non-participant observation (see Chapter 7) and data that are already available (e.g., audit data, statistics on hospital performance). The task of the researcher is to gather all this data together and interpret it, either by making reference to existing theory or by developing a context specific explanation. The latter of these requires the development of skill in qualitative analysis, and can be a major undertaking.

What is likely to be the best way of achieving change?

Understanding the factors underlying practice is prerequisite to thinking about the best way of achieving change. For example, if a preliminary study suggests that health professionals are unaware of a guideline or do not know the latest research evidence, then an educational intervention would provide a good start (although knowledge enhancement is unlikely to change behaviour by itself). On the other hand, if preliminary work suggests that health professionals know what they should be doing but do not have the skills or resources needed to follow the recommendation, then specific training may be needed or interventions to address goal conflicts and deployment of resources within the organization. Baseline work may suggest that factors beyond the health professional's control are the most important, in which case a different type of intervention may need to be developed – for example, involving system redesign (e.g., reorganization of an out-patient clinic) or targeted at different groups (e.g., managers or patients). These interventions may be designed to be delivered at a 'population level' (i.e., the same intervention for all participants) or at an 'individual level' in which the intervention is tailored to meet the needs of each participant separately (see Case study 15.2).

Some interventions are more likely to be practical in the NHS than others, and in a consultancy situation you may often find that you are asked to refine or adapt an existing (or acceptable) intervention rather than design a new one from scratch. Educational workshops and training sessions are familiar and can be adapted to achieve different aims (e.g., to increase knowledge, change attitudes, address specific beliefs, develop self-efficacy, develop action plans, consider how to resolve conflicting goals, practise communication skills, etc). Integrated care pathways (care plans that outline the sequence and timing of tasks for all the professional staff caring for a specific patient group) can be adapted in a variety of ways. For example, to incorporate reminders if cognitive overload is an issue, or to make the recommended practice easier to perform if perceived behavioural control or self-efficacy are key factors. Over recent years, clinical audit has become a common feature of most healthcare settings, and this can be combined with feedback to develop an effective intervention (Grimshaw et al., 2001). At present there are few evaluations of different types of feedback or the frequency of feedback, but standard behavioural principles suggest a range of different methods that might be useful (e.g., giving positive feedback for appropriate practice, using a variable feedback schedule, etc.).

Whether you are developing an intervention from scratch or adapting an existing one, the next step is to implement it (see Chapter 12). Different practical issues will arise in different situations, but you will need to think about issues such as what does the intervention actually involve; how will it be delivered and who will deliver it; do the people delivering it require special skills or training; what are the financial costs of the intervention; when is the best time to deliver the intervention; are there any other ongoing initiatives that need to be accommodated; and so on.

Is the chosen method of achieving change effective?

A wide range of study designs can be used to assess the effects of an intervention – from case studies through to randomized controlled trials. The evaluation of interventions to change professional practice is more complicated than evaluation in other areas of health psychology because interventions are often introduced at an organizational or even national level. For example, you might be asked to design and evaluate an intervention for local implementation of a National Service Framework, or an integrated care pathway, involving many different health professionals in one Trust. Case studies and quasi-experimental designs will often be more appropriate than experimental designs in this setting.

Quasi-experimental designs, which compare groups that have been allocated 'naturally' in some way, are often possible (Shadish et al., 2002). For example, an intervention may be introduced in one geographical region before another, allowing a comparison between them. Similarly, interrupted time-series designs, which compare behaviour in the same unit or organization before and after the introduction of an intervention (Campbell & Stanley, 1966), can be very useful. These are intuitively straightforward to design, but can be complex to analyse because they need to take into account any time-related trends present in the data before and after the intervention (Shadish et al., 2002). For example, if an intervention is introduced at a time when practice was changing anyway then a simple before and after comparison may suggest that it was effective, when in fact it had no effect on the underlying trend. Similarly, comparing average performance before and after an intervention might underestimate its effects if the underlying trend was in the opposite direction. A good interrupted time series design requires repeated measures of the behaviour of interest at regular intervals before and after the intervention using a measure that it is not affected by repeated use. For example, monthly prescribing rates for a year before and after dissemination of a guideline collected from routine information systems and not from self-report.

Health professionals rarely work in isolation, so when randomization is possible a cluster randomized trial is generally the most appropriate study design. In cluster randomization, groups of professionals (e.g., clinical units, primary care practices) are randomized to intervention and control groups, rather than individuals. Conceptually cluster randomized trials are identical to individually randomized trials. However, sample size calculations and data analysis need to take into account the effects of clustering and may require specialist statistical input (see Boruch & Foley, 2000; Grimshaw et al., 2000).

How does it work?

Knowing that an intervention works is important, but it doesn't necessarily imply that it will work in different circumstances or for different types of behaviour. An understanding of how the intervention functions is also important (Michie & Abraham, 2004). In an ideal world, this would come from extensive preliminary research to develop interventions and understand their mechanisms of action before testing them out in the real world (as there might be in the development of new drugs, for example). Many behaviour change technologies have been through this process. For example, cognitive behaviour therapy developed from theories originating in the early twentieth century. It was modelled and refined in analogue studies and exploratory trials in the 1960s (e.g., Lang et al., 1970) with definitive trials being conducted in the 1970s (e.g., Sloane et al., 1975), and long-term implementation studies conducted after this (e.g., Shapiro & Shapiro, 1982; Hollon & Beck, 1994). However, few of the interventions routinely used to improve the quality of healthcare have been developed in this way. As a consequence, it is important to build in some assessment of the process of change into any study.

Process evaluation is a term that can be used in a variety of ways. In trials of interventions to improve healthcare, it is often used to refer to an assessment of practical factors that might influence the effectiveness of the intervention (Pawson & Tilley, 1997). For example, was the intervention delivered as planned; did all of the target audience participate; were there any extraneous factors that might alter the effects of the intervention (e.g., the introduction of a new drug partway through the study). The aim here is to identify factors that might modify the effect of the intervention (usually called effect modifiers – or more often in psychological literature, mediators and moderators). Theoretically based process evaluation is an extension of this, and aims to identify psychosocial processes that mediate or moderate the effect of an intervention. In order to do this, the study usually needs to measure potential intermediate variables before and after the intervention is administered, or to compare intervention and control groups post intervention. For example, imagine that an intervention has been designed to strengthen positive attitudes towards hand-washing among hospital nurses. The theory of planned behaviour would propose that any effect of this intervention on behaviour would be mediated through behavioural intention. The process evaluation would require measurement of behavioural intention and behaviour before and after the intervention to investigate whether the effect of the intervention on behaviour was mediated by its effect on intention.

Process evaluation can also be used to mean the development of an understanding of how an intervention operates and how the outcome is produced, drawn usually from detailed observation and analysis of naturally occurring situations (Calnan & Ferlie, 2003). From this perspective, the process evaluation may be the whole study. This form of process evaluation is quite different and much more detailed. It is often used to study particularly complex situations or settings and is particularly useful for investigating the implementation of a complex guideline or practice initiative (e.g., a National Service Framework involving a large number of different professionals and aspects of care), in a single setting (e.g., one NHS Trust). The research methods used in this form of process evaluation include ethnographic methods and action research but the most common approach is either the single or comparative case study (see Ferlie, 2001). Case studies usually use a number of different types of data (e.g., in depth interviews, information from records, observation of practice, small scale surveys) to explore a particular situation in detail (Dopson, 2003). From this perspective, theory might be built from the data or existing theories might be used to make connections with the published literature, or to provide different angles for interpreting the data (see Calnan & Ferlie, 2003).

15.4.5 Developing a protocol and budget

A protocol is a description of the planned study (see Chapters 5 and 10). Usually introduced by a brief summary of the background and a rationale, the main purpose of the protocol is to describe and justify all the separate components of the study (e.g., the data collection methods to be used, any measures involved, the study design, sample size calculations, planned analysis, etc.). A protocol will be essential if you are applying for research funding or ethics committee approval – but even if you are not, it is good practice to write a protocol because it can often identify problems at an early stage. As part of the protocol development, seek advice from as many sources as possible, and where appropriate form collaborative relationships. In particular, talk to relevant clinicians, R&D managers, people with specific methodological expertise (e.g., a statistician or an ethnographer), secretarial staff who may be involved in questionnaire production or interview transcription, people who may control access to routine measures of practice (e.g., Health Authority/ Health Board Medical Prescribing Advisers) and interested colleagues. The protocol is the most important part of the study – expect to go through several drafts.

A detailed protocol provides the basis for costing the study. It is important to be realistic about the costs of aspects such as producing questionnaires (e.g., remember to cost in enough to send out a second copy with each reminder), transcribing interviews, and the detailed costs of the intervention itself (e.g., everything from room hire to printing of reminders). It is also important to be realistic about which aspects of the work you will be doing yourself and which you need help with. It is very unusual for studies in this area to be undertaken by a single researcher, so you may need to include salary costs for people to collect the data, deliver the intervention, analyse the data and provide administrative support. If your study uses quantitative methods, think about the analysis at an early stage and if possible consult a statistician. You may need to include salary costs or consultancy fees for a statistician if you are not undertaking the analysis yourself. In some institutions, you may have access to specialist research funding advisors. These staff can be invaluable, especially if you are applying for funds from research councils or charities and costing in your own time.

15.4.6 Ethics, permissions and research governance issues

The British Psychological Society has its own Code of Conduct, Ethical Principles and Guidelines by which all members are bound. This sets out useful guidelines for research conduct (see also Chapter 9).

The main ethical issues in this type of study arise from the method of collecting information and its potential impacts on patient care as well as the potential for coercion of health professionals to participate. Practice information may require access to patient identifiable material (e.g., case notes or observation) which raises issues of confidentiality and data protection for patients as well as health professionals. Health professionals may feel under pressure to participate, especially if the proposed practice change is being introduced by senior management, raising the need to ensure that they can provide informed consent. For these reasons, it is now essential to seek ethics committee approval for all studies concerned with health professional practice. This is true even if the study has limited ethical implications (e.g., a preliminary interview study to develop questionnaire measures).

In addition to ethical issues, research undertaken in healthcare settings needs to be sensitive to the potential costs to the organizations involved in terms of staff time or changes in the nature of the care provided (these latter costs may persist after the study has ended). For these reasons, the Directors of Research and Development with NHS Trusts need to be aware of any research studies that involve staff in their organizations, and usually have the right to refuse permission for their Trust to be involved. This is now true for Primary Care Trusts as well as Secondary and Tertiary Care Trusts. It is good practice to discuss any study that you are planning with the relevant R&D managers at an early stage. You may also want to enlist the help of these staff in recruiting participants to the study, for example by co-signing letters of invitation.

The third group of potential gatekeepers is the people who control access to any routine information systems that you may be planning to use to assess practice. Who this is will depend on the nature of the data you plan to collect. For example, in an ongoing study we are seeking permission from clinical directors of radiography in secondary care trusts in order to access the number of lumbar spine x-rays requested by GPs who refer to those hospitals. Other studies involve permission to access anonymous data held by the health boards or health authorities.

In addition to these 'gatekeepers', there will be a range of potential stakeholders, who can help or hinder the process of the study (see Walker et al., 2000). For example, senior staff within the Trust(s) involved, professional organizations, patient groups and so on. It is generally worthwhile discussing your planned research with interested parties at an early stage, inform anyone who may have an interest and enlist their help wherever possible. When in doubt, it is generally better to inform senior staff than not to (e.g., through circulating a brief information sheet or email about the project).

Research governance is a process for preventing fraud within research and protecting the interests of participants (e.g., Scottish Executive, 2001). Research governance procedures vary between organizations, but are generally concerned with issues such as accountability for the research, ownership of any data collected, establishing who is responsible for standards of data management, archiving, access to data and so on. In a research setting, these issues may be straightforward, but they can become confused in consultancy settings. For example, if you have been asked to design and analyse a process evaluation as a consultant, do you own the data at the end of the study – or does it belong to the organization that employed you? Who has the right to prevent publication of the data? Who is required to store the data? It is important to discuss these issues at an early stage, and, bearing in mind that there can sometimes be a considerable turnover of staff over the time of a project, to keep records of any agreements in writing.

15.4.7 Reporting the outcome

The final stage of any project is the report of the outcome. Studies of healthcare improvement may need to be reported in several ways. First, there will almost always be a report for whoever commissioned the research (e.g., the research funding body, the NHS trust or health authority). This will usually need to be produced to a deadline in a pre-specified format and will need to be written for a general audience. You may be asked to make recommendations at the end of the report. Second are any academic or professional publications that may arise from the work. If your study can make a contribution to this literature it is worth trying to publish it. There are few journals that are read by both psychologists and health services researchers, so papers in this area may need to be written for different audiences (e.g., for health psychologists and GPs).

15.5 FINAL THOUGHTS

Applying psychology to healthcare improvement raises a host of challenges. The number of things to think about described in this chapter may seem a little daunting. However, as Marteau and Johnston pointed out over ten years ago (Marteau & Johnston, 1990), health professional practice is one of the most important (and often unrecognized) sources of potential variance in health outcomes. From the ordinary everyday activities such as hand-washing to less common activities such as the skilled use of laparascopic procedures, or the decision to prescribe a new drug, health professionals have great potential to make a difference to the health of their patients. To date, most of the efforts that have been made to enable health professionals to offer the best care that they can, have been based on the assumptions that sub-optimal care results from either ignorance or incompetence (Michie & Johnston, 2003). So, the major approaches to improvement have been through education and professional regulation. Both of these are important, but ignorance and incompetence are not the only mechanisms that limit the effectiveness of healthcare practice. Health psychologists have an opportunity to develop an understanding of other mechanisms and of how to intervene to change them. Such work may be of practical benefit and also help develop the science of health psychology.

15.6 CORE COMPONENTS ADDRESSED
BY THIS CHAPTER

This chapter on studying and changing health professionals' behaviour and the additional recommended reading will help readers to acquire 10 (of 73) core components included in the stage 2 core units.

1.3a Assess the opportunities, need and context for giving psychological advice

2.3b Prepare to implement research protocols

2.3c Conduct preliminary investigations of existing models and methods

2.3d Collect data as specified by research protocols

2.4c Evaluate research findings and make recommendations based on research findings

2.5c Clarify and evaluate the implications of research outcomes for practice

2.5d Evaluate the potential impact of new developments on organizational functioning and healthcare practices

3.4a Establish systems or processes to deliver the planned advice, research, interventions or activities

3.4b Implement the planned advice, research, interventions or activities

3.6a Identify evaluation needs and design evaluation.

Healthcare is the result of decisions and actions made by health professionals (and organizations) and their patients (or clients) in order to prevent or alleviate ill health. It has the potential to have a major impact on health outcomes. Until recently, healthcare practice has been something of a neglected area in health psychology, with more attention being paid to health promotion and the behaviour of people experiencing ill health. At present, there is a limited research literature on the behaviour of people and organizations that provide healthcare. Consequently, we know less than we might about how to change such behaviour. Health psychology has much to offer in developing this understanding.

Health psychologists are increasingly being asked for advice and help in relation to health professional practice because the quality and safety of healthcare has become a major international concern. UK governments have established systems to ensure that NHS patients receive the most cost effective and best quality care possible (e.g., Department of Health, 1997, Scottish Executive Health Department, 2001). These include the reorganization of hospital and community care trusts, establishment of bodies to evaluate treatments used in the NHS (e.g., National Institute for Clinical Excellence, Health Technology Board for Scotland), and bodies to assess clinical performance (e.g., Commission for Health Improvement, Clinical Standards Board for Scotland). Recommendations made by quality improvement bodies often require changes in the everyday decisions and actions taken by health professionals.

Health psychologists can provide advice on how to implement quality standards and clinical guidelines. To do so they need to:

- have a thorough knowledge of the theories used in health psychology, and to be able to apply these to professional practice and healthcare organizations;
- have a good knowledge of healthcare practices in the area that they are concerned with and available evidence relating to their effectiveness;
- be able to undertake consultancy within the health service, to investigate the practice of interest and evaluate methods of quality improvement, including behaviour change interventions;
- be able to undertake research studies that can contribute to the development of theory and interventions.

The underlying competence in research and consultancy is the same as that in other areas of health psychology, but healthcare behaviour does raise a number of important issues that require further development of these skills. This chapter aims to provide a basis for developing these skills, and to complement supervised practice with a health psychologist experienced in this area.

The specific core components addressed by the chapter are outlined above. They relate particularly to units 2 and 3. Psychologists working in this area need to be able to implement research protocols (component 2.3b), conduct preliminary investigations (component 2.3c) and collect data as specified in the research protocol (component 2.3d). In this area more than many others, health psychologists will be required to clarify and evaluate the implications of research outcomes for practice (component 2.5c). Although in this case it is research findings *about* practice and their implications for how to change practice that will need to be clarified. Additionally the ability to evaluate the potential impact of new developments on organizational functioning and healthcare practices (component 2.5d) will be especially important. For example, a health psychologist may undertake work to investigate the potential impact of a proposed service redesign on professional practice (e.g., what effects would the replacement of a conventional out-patient system with an open-access out-patient clinic have on the practice of urologists? Would they see more or fewer patients? Undertake more or fewer investigations? Be more or less likely to take a full medical history? Offer different treatments? Be more or less likely to discuss all the treatment options with the patient? Would GPs be more or less likely to refer patients to an open-access clinic? And so on).

Most of the work that health psychologists undertake in this area is likely to be undertaken as consultancy, to provide advice on how to implement a particular quality standard or clinical guideline in a particular NHS organization – for example, how best to implement the National Service Framework on Coronary Heart Disease within a particular NHS Trust. So, health psychologists must be able to assess the opportunities, need and context for giving psychological advice (component 1.3a). In addition, they must be able to establish systems to deliver and implement the planned advice, research interventions and activities (components 3.4a, 3.4b), and they must be able to identify evaluation needs and design evaluations where appropriate (component 3.6a). All the other components of consultancy competence are also relevant in this area (all of unit 3), but these are covered in more depth in Chapters 12 and 13 and not discussed here.

ACKNOWLEDGEMENTS

Many of the ideas in this chapter have been developed through my work with the Medical Research Council (MRC) Implementation Research Group and other collaborators and PhD students. I would particularly like to acknowledge Jeremy Grimshaw, Martin Eccles, Marie Johnston, Nigel Pitts, Philippa Davies, Liz Smith, Debbie Bonetti, Margaret Watson and Robbie Foy. Members of the British Psychological Society Research Seminar series on 'Psychological processes involved in the implementation of evidence based practice' have also been influential – in particular Susan Michie, Charles Abraham, Diane Parker, Rebecca Lawton, John Weinman and Marie Johnston.

I am grateful to the MRC Health Services Research Collaboration for funding meetings of the Implementation Research Group, and to the British Psychological Society for funding the research seminars. The Health Services Research Unit is funded by the Chief Scientist Office of the Scottish Executive. The opinions expressed in this chapter are those of the author and may not be shared by the funding bodies.

REFERENCES

Adams, A.S., Soumerai, S.B., Lomas, J. & Ross-Degnan, D. (1999). Evidence of self-report bias in assessing adherence to guidelines. *International Journal for Quality in Health Care* 11, 187–92.

Ajzen, I. (1991). The theory of planned behaviour. *Organisational Behaviour and Human Decision Processes* 50, 179–211.

Baker, R., Reddish, S., Robertson, N., Hearnshaw, H. & Jones, B. (2001). Randomised controlled trial of tailored strategies to implement guidelines for the management of patients with depression in general practice. *British Journal of General Practice* 51, 737–41.

Bartholomew, L.K., Parcel, G.S., Kok, G. & Gottlieb, N. (2001). *Intervention Mapping: A Process for Designing Theory- and Evidence-based Health Education Programs.* Mountain View, CA: Mayfield.

Bero, L., & Rennie, D. (1995). The Cochrane Collaboration. Preparing, maintaining and disseminating systematic reviews of the effects of health care. *Journal of the American Medical Association* 274, 1935–8.

Bickman, L. (ed.) (2000). *Validity and Social Experimentation: Donald T Campbell's Legacy,* Thousand Oaks, CA: Sage.

Bonetti, D., Johnston, M., Pitts, N. et al. (in press). Can psychological models bridge the gap between clinical guidelines and clinician's behaviour? A randomised controlled trial of an intervention to influence dentists' intention to implement evidence-based practice. *British Dental Journal.*

Boruch, R. & Foley, E. (2000). The honestly experimental society: Sites and other entities as the units of allocation and analysis in randomised trials. In L. Bickman, (ed.), *Validity and Social Experimentation: Donald T Campbell's Legacy,* 193–238. Thousand Oaks, CA: Sage.

Bowling, A. (2002). *Research Methods in Health: Investigating Health and Health Services,* 2nd edn. Buckingham: Open University Press.

Calnan, M. & Ferlie, E. (2003). Analysing process in healthcare: the methodological and theoretical challenges. *Policy and Politics* 31(2), 185–93.

Campbell, D.T. & Stanley, J.C. (1966). *Experimental and Quasi-Experimental Designs for Research.* Chicago: Rand McNally.

Clarke, M. (2002). The Cochrane Collaboration: Providing and obtaining the best evidence about the effects of health care. *Journal of Evaluation in the Health Professions* 25, 8–11.

Conner, M. & Sparks, P. (1996). The theory of planned behaviour and health behaviours. In M. Conner & P. Norman (eds), *Predicting Health Behaviour,* 121–62. Buckingham: Open University Press.

Crombie, I.K. & Davies, H.T.O. (1996). *Research in Health Care: Design, Conduct and Interpretation of Health Services Research.* Chichester: Wiley.

Davies, P. (2004). The Use of Psychological Theories in Clinical Guideline Implementation Research. Unpublished doctoral thesis University of Aberdeen.

Del Mar, C.B. & Glasziou, P.P. (1997). Antibiotics for the symptoms and complications of sore throat. In R. Douglas, C. Bridges, C. Webb et al. (eds), *Acute*

Respiratory Infections Module of the Cochrane Database of Systematic Reviews. The Cochrane Collaboration, Issue 3. Oxford: Update Software.

Department of Health (1997). *The New NHS: Modern Dependable,* London: Department of Health.

Donabedian, A. (1980) *Explorations in Quality Assessment and Monitoring.* Vol. 1. *The Definition of Quality and Approaches to its Assessment.* Ann Arbor, MI: Health Administration Press.

Donner, A. & Klar, N. (2000). *Design and Analysis of Cluster Randomisation Trials in Health Research,* London: Arnold.

Dopson, S. (2003). The potential of the case study method for organisational analysis. *Policy and Politics* 31, 217–26.

Eccles, M.P., Grimshaw, J.M., Walker, A.E., Johnston, M. & Pitts, N. (in preparation). Changing the behaviour of health professionals: The use of theory in promoting the uptake of research findings.

Ferlie, E. (2001). Organisational studies. In N. Fulop, P. Allen, A. Clarke & N. Black (eds), *Studying the Organisation and Delivery of Health Services: Research Methods,* 24–39. London: Routledge.

Ferlie, E.B. & Shortell, S.M. (2001). Improving the quality of health care in the United Kingdom and the United States: A framework for change. *The Milbank Quarterly* 79(2), 281–315.

Grimshaw, J.M., Campbell, M., Eccles, M. & Steen, I. (2000). Experimental and quasi-experimental designs for evaluating guideline implementation strategies. *Family Practice* 17, S11–S18.

Grimshaw, J.M., Eccles, M.P., Walker, A.E. & Thomas, R.E. (2002). Changing physicians' behaviour: What works and thoughts on getting more things to work. *Journal of Continuing Education in the Health Professions* 22(4), 237–43.

Grimshaw, J.M., Shirran, L., Thomas, R.E. et al. (2001). Changing provider behaviour: An overview of systematic reviews of interventions. *Medical Care,* 39 Supplement 2, 2–45.

Grimshaw, J.M., Thomas, R.E., MacLennan, G. et al. (in press). Effectiveness and efficiency of guideline dissemination and implementation strategies. *Health Technology Assessment.*

Grol, R. (2001). Successes and failures in the implementation of evidence-based guidelines for clinical practice. *Medical Care* 39, 1146–54.

Hollon, S.D. & Beck, A.T. (1994). Cognitive and cognitive-behavioural therapies. In A. Bergin & S. Garfield (eds), *Handbook of Psychotherapy and Behaviour Change,* 4th edn, 428–66. New York: John Wiley & Sons.

Iles, V. & Sutherland, K. (2001). *Organisational Change: A Review for Health Care Managers, Professionals and Researchers.* London: National Co-ordinating Centre for NHS Service Delivery and Organisation R&D.

Lang, P.J., Melamed, B.J. & Hary, J. (1970). A psychophysiological analysis of fear modification using an automated desensitisation procedure. *Journal of Abnormal Psychology* 76, 220–34.

Lipman, T. (2000). Evidence-based practice in general practice and primary care. In L. Trinder & S. Reynolds (eds), *Evidence-Based Practice: A Critical Appraisal,* 35–65. Oxford: Blackwell Science Ltd.

Marteau, T. & Johnston, M. (1990). Health professionals: A source of variance in health outcomes. *Psychology and Health* 5, 47–58.

Michie, S. & Abraham, C. (2004). Interventions to change health behaviours: Evidence-based or evidence inspired? *Psychology and Health* 19, 29–49.

Michie, S. & Johnston, M. (2003). Constructing an integrative theoretical framework for evidence-based practice. British Psychological Society, Division of Health Psychology Annual Conference, University of Staffordshire, September.

NHS Centre for Reviews and Dissemination (1999). Getting evidence into practice. *Effective Health Care* 5, 1–16.

Pawson, R. & Tilley, I. (1997). *Realistic Evaluation*. London: Sage Publications.

Royal College of Obstetrics and Gynaecology (2000). *The Care of Women Requesting Induced Abortion*. London: RCOG (www.rcog.org.uk/guidelines/abortion).

Sackett, D.L., Rosenberg, M.C., Muir Gray, J.A., Haynes, R.B. & Scott Richardson, W. (1996). Evidence based medicine: What it is and what it isn't. *British Medical Journal* 312, 71–2.

Schuster, M., McGlynn, E. & Brook, R.H. (1998). How good is the quality of health care in the United States? *Milbank Quarterly* 76, 517–63.

Scottish Executive Health Department (2000). *Our National Health: A Plan for Action, a Plan for Change*. Edinburgh: Scottish Executive Health Department.

Scottish Executive Health Department Chief Scientist Office (2001). *Research Governance Framework for Health and Community Care*. Edinburgh: The Scottish Executive. (www.show.scot.nhs.uk/cso)

Scottish Intercollegiate Guidelines Network (2002). *Prophylaxis of Venous Thromboembolism: A National Clinical Guideline*. Edinburgh: SIGN (www.sign.ac.uk).

Shadish, W.R., Cook, T.D. & Campbell, D.T. (2002). *Experimental and Quasi-experimental Designs for Generalized Causal Inference*. Boston, MA: Houghton-Mifflin.

Shapiro, D.A. & Shapiro, D. (1982). Meta-analysis of comparative therapy outcome studies: a replication and refinement. *Psychological Bulletin* 92, 581–609.

Shortell, S., Jones, R., Rademaker, A., et al. (2000). Assessing the impact of total quality management and organisational culture on multiple outcomes of care for coronary bypass graft surgery patients. *Medical Care* 38, 207–17.

Sloane, R.B., Staples, F.R., Cristol, A.H., Yorkston, N.J. & Whipple, K. (1975). *Psychotherapy versus Behaviour Therapy*. Cambridge, MA: Harvard University Press.

Strauss, A. & Corbin, J. (1990). *Basics of Qualitative Research: Grounded Theory Procedures and Techniques*. London: Sage.

Trinder, L. & Reynolds, S. (eds.) (2000). *Evidence-Based Practice: A Critical Appraisal*. Oxford: Blackwell Science Ltd.

Walker, A.E., Campbell, M.K., Grimshaw, J.M. & the TEMPEST group (2000). A recruitment strategy for cluster randomized trials in secondary care settings. *Journal of Evaluation in Clinical Practice* 6, 185–92.

Walker, A.E., Grimshaw, J.M. & Armstrong, E. (2001). Salient beliefs and intentions to prescribe antibiotics for patients with a sore throat. *British Journal of Health Psychology* 6, 347–60.

Walker, A.E., Johnston, M., Grimshaw, J.M., Abraham, S.C.S., Campbell, M.K. &
the TEMPEST study group (1998). When do clinicians follow guidelines? Using the
theory of planned behaviour to predict intentions to prescribe prophylaxis for
patients at risk of deep vein thrombosis (abstract). *Journal of Epidemiology and
Community Health* 52(10), 676.

Watson, M.C., Bond, C.M., Grimshaw, J.M., Mollison, J., Ludbrook, A. & Walker, A.E.
(2002). Educational strategies to promote evidence-based community pharmacy
practice: a cluster randomised trial. *Family Practice* 19(5), 529–36.

Woolf, S., Grol, R., Hutchinson, A., Eccles, M.P. & Grimshaw, J.M. (2000). An
international overview. In M.P. Eccles & J.M. Grimshaw (eds), *Clinical Practice
Guidelines*, 31–48. Oxford: Radcliffe Medical Press.

FURTHER READING AND RESOURCES

Booth, A. & O'Rourke, A. (2000). *Getting Research into Practice: An Optional
Self-study Module for the Unit GMH 6050 – Literature Review and Critical
Appraisal*. Sheffield: University of Sheffield, School of Health and Related
Research (URL http://www.shef.ac.uk/~scharr/ir/units/resprac/index.htm).

Cochrane Collaboration Review Group on Effective Practice and Organisation and
Delivery of Care (EPOC) (URL http://www.epoc.uottawa.ca).

Fulop, N., Allen, P., Clarke, A. & Black, N. (eds) (2001). *Studying the Organisation
and Delivery of Health Services: Research Methods*. London: Routledge.

NHS Centre for Reviews and Dissemination (1999). Getting Evidence into Practice.
Effective Health Care 5, 1–16 (URL http://www.york.ac.uk/inst/crd/ehcb.htm).

Part IV

TRAINING AND TEACHING

Chapter 16

DEVELOPING AND EVALUATING TRAINING AND TEACHING

Helen Winefield

16.1 INTRODUCTION: TEACHING AND TRAINING IN HEALTH PSYCHOLOGY

The role of the health psychologist as teacher and trainer means sharing knowledge and skills with a wide range of others, from psychologists to medical and other healthcare professionals, students of all these disciplines, and members of the public. This chapter aims to specify the knowledge, skills and abilities which health psychologists need to teach and train others.

Teaching and training are closely related concepts, the main difference between them being the strongly vocational implication of 'training'. This term refers to acquiring capacity for improved work performance. With today's rapid expansion of professional knowledge and information technology, health workers need constant training and retraining (described as professional development or continuing education).

Psychologists, with their scientist–practitioner model of professional practice and their familiarity with psychometrics and research design, have sound preparation for teaching others about the evidence base for psychosocial aspects of health and healthcare. Those they teach will gain not only useful knowledge and skills to apply to their own practices but also understanding of the possible contributions of psychology and how to make appropriate requests for psychological intervention. The need for health psychologists to undertake an educative role with regard to other health professionals is widely recognized (Garcia-Shelton & Vogel, 2002; Gatchel & Oordt, 2003).

16.1.1 Content of teaching and training

The areas of knowledge and skill which a health psychologist might seek to teach to others are very diverse (see Johnston & Johnston, 1998). Basic knowledge to be taught may include the biopsychosocial model of health, statistics and research methods and the principles of behaviour change. Skills to be trained may include medical communication or 'interviewing' skills, chronic pain management, promoting adherence to medical treatments and healthy lifestyles, and management of health professional work stress. Health psychologists should also be able to teach about teamwork and interprofessional collaboration – increasingly valued skills in the modern multidisciplinary healthcare context (Belar et al., 2001; Bray & Rogers, 1997; Gatchel & Oordt, 2003; Singh & Martin, 2001; Winefield & Chur-Hansen, 2003).

Health psychologists may not have complete freedom to choose what to teach, or how, or to whom. However, the principles of trying to establish what the learners want to know, what goals they have in seeking teaching or training, and what the possibilities are for time, format and assessment method, need to be kept in mind even when they cannot be fully applied.

16.1.2 Who are the learners?

When health psychologists teach other psychologists or psychology students, the shared background will reduce the obstacles to clear communication. Problems become more likely where multidisciplinary teaching occurs, and these will receive particular attention in this chapter. Some aspects of health psychology knowledge will readily be translatable for other health professionals, while others may be much more difficult to convey. In addition to teaching and training other health professionals, health psychologists may find themselves conveying health-related knowledge and skills to people in the community, for example self-help groups, service and charity organizations, and the mass media.

Psychological concepts are not necessarily well understood in the community despite the large amount of 'pop psychology' in magazines and television shows. Many members of the public do not understand the differences between psychologists, psychiatrists, and counsellors – and many members of other health professions share that confusion. Therefore health psychologists need to start from this basis and not assume that audience expectations or knowledge match yours.

Apart from knowing who the learners are, and what they already know, the size of the learner group will influence how the health psychologist plans to conduct teaching and training. Strategies for providing and assessing training for large groups, small groups, individual learners and the general public are discussed below.

16.2 ADULT LEARNING PRINCIPLES

The teaching methods which the health psychologist adopts must suit both the content and the audience. In general this chapter will assume that learners are more-or-less motivated adults. Such teaching is problem directed rather than subject directed, student centred rather than teacher centred, aims for internalized rather than superficial rote learning, is interactive rather than didactic, and utilizes peer support. Kaufman (2003, p. 215) has usefully outlined the following principles for when the learners are adults, and therefore likely to be at least somewhat self-directed:

- learners should contribute actively to the educational process;
- learning should closely relate to solving real-life problems;
- it is critical to take the learners' current knowledge and experience into account;
- learners should have the opportunity and support to use self-direction in their learning;
- learners should have the opportunity and support to practise, assess their work, and receive feedback from teachers and peers;
- learners should be given opportunities to reflect on their own practice.

Kolb (1984) outlines the cycle of how adults assimilate useful information into their 'experience bank', by reflecting on experience, relating these observations to past experience or knowledge, and testing them in new situations. Accordingly, 'learning by doing' acquires high priority for adults, and learning will be more efficient when people are aware of a need for new information, have a chance to try it in practice, and then get feedback. Theory and practice are seen as mutually interdependent, rather than theory being seen as prior to practice (Foley, 1995), and there is much interest in the beneficial role of reflection, the process through which experience becomes learning (Boud et al., 1985).

Professional trainees and practitioners should be encouraged to reflect on their work. This implies not a random process of reverie, but a purposive and critical review to integrate the cognitive and affective aspects of experiences and to extract meaning and new understanding from them.

Reflection can be promoted by scheduling time for learners to process their experiences, perhaps through discussion, debriefing with others, or keeping a reflective log or journal. Teachers can best assist by helping the learner to describe their experiences objectively, to pay attention to their associated feelings, and then to integrate what has been learned with the application context (Boud et al., 1985).

As Candy (1987) points out, the active rather than passive nature of adult learning does not mean that people always prefer to find out for themselves rather than to *be taught*. However, the need to engage in reflection to optimize the learning value of new experiences does indicate the importance of engaging learners motivationally. Wlodkowski (1999) has identified four stages in this process: (1) inclusion (engender a feeling of connection and a climate of respect, among the learners); (2) attitude (build positive attitudes, self-concepts and expectancy, create relevant learning experiences); (3) meaning (maintain learners' attention, interest and engagement); and (4) competence (engender competence with both assessment procedures and the perceived authenticity of the learning).

16.2.1 Learner goals

Learners may be motivated by the requirements of their professional bodies and registration authorities to demonstrate participation in continued professional education. The increasing regulation of healthcare practice by outside authorities and insurers has increased the formality of professional development. It will be useful therefore to find out what professional development obligations your audience may have, so that you can offer teaching or training that is congruent with those goals and requirements.

Some learners may want to acquire skills they can use at work, some may want to learn the concepts and terminology so that they can continue learning independently, and some may just want to know that health psychologists have expertise about certain questions and how to contact them. In preparing educational information for the public, it is important to be aware of the range of motivations from simple curiosity to desperate need to understand what is happening to oneself or a loved one. For listeners who are distressed or confused, you need to establish your credibility by demonstrating empathic understanding as well as conveying facts and knowledge.

Numerous health workers need to be able to carry out simple counselling procedures including advising and listening. Fewer in number are those at the middle level, with more training and more skill, who can apply more specialized psychological techniques by following a manual (Richards, 1994). Fewer still are those health psychology specialists who consult about complex cases, devise innovative procedures based on their understanding of the underlying scientific principles, and critically evaluate their own and others' programmes. A highly valued component of health psychologists' professional role is their teaching and training of other health professionals, and the performance of this role is likely to increase the respect accorded to psychology.

16.2.2 The adult learning model applied to training by health psychologists

The model for adult learning is of an iterative cycle of planning, doing, assessing and improving (see above). The literature on adult educational methods is not characterized by high methodological rigour, due partly to the difficulties of measuring outcomes such as improved quality of work performance. The literature from occupational psychology provides another useful perspective on training and development (Salas & Cannon-Bowers, 2001).

Traditionally, a training needs analysis adopts the tripartite perspectives of the organization, the job or task, and the person. Training is a means to an end, and factors that facilitate the translation of training into workplace outcomes are at least as important to consider as the training itself, and constitute a new focus for research (Muchinsky, 2000, ch. 6; Salas & Cannon-Bowers, 2001). Thus the climate and needs of the organization, and the level of managerial support for new ways of doing things, become as crucial to analyse in preparing to undertake training, as are the analyses of what needs to be taught and the relevant trainee characteristics. This systemic view of possible obstacles to the transfer of training into work practice offers an exciting extension of previous more limited orientations, and has obvious applications in thinking about the impact of training new skills in workers within multidisciplinary and hierarchical healthcare systems.

In medicine, considerable attention is paid to doctors' educational responsibilities, as shown by journals, books and conferences devoted to medical education, and the maxim 'see one, do one, teach one'. Less attention has been paid to education as a task for health psychology, but there is no reason to suppose that the experiences of medical educators are irrelevant to health psychology teachers and trainers. It is to be hoped that in the future there may be a distinctive scientific literature on the educational activities of health psychologists. In the meantime, this chapter has adopted findings and concepts from several disciplines (educational psychology, adult learning, medical education, work-related training and development). A key message is that health psychologists need to accept responsibility for continuous monitoring of their own teaching and training efforts.

The relevant research paradigm for health psychologists to monitor their own success as teachers and trainers, is that of Action Research (Kemmis & McTaggart, 1992). The action research model lays great emphasis on participation by all the stakeholders, so as to facilitate not only their active co-operation but the sustainability of the changes suggested by the researchers (Altman, 1995). This model has developed for field situations where experimental control is very limited, and where the research participants need to feel ownership of the project. The crucial concept is that of a continuous spiralling process. Its successive components are realistic plans, their implementation, the observation of their effects (*all* of the effects: some will be unintended), reflection and discussion among all those affected (the planners and their colleagues, the changees), then formulation of further plans and the iteration of the cycle.

16.2.3 Facilitating your own learning about teaching and training

Health psychologists should seek opportunities to attend training courses in how to teach and train, and should also make use of the opportunities they have as trainees and as learners themselves, to reflect on the observational evidence of successful and unsuccessful techniques. The fact that the health psychologist is also a professional learner, and may recently have undergone tertiary-level professional training, is very relevant. Spend some time recalling and reflecting upon the following issues, and if possible discuss them with colleagues:

• What sort of teaching do you find most engaging and memorable?
• How long can you concentrate on a lecture especially if feeling tired and/or resentful of being required to attend by someone else?
• What is the best way that a teacher can help you to learn?
• What gives you confidence in transferring newly acquired information into daily practice?

A general recommendation is that health psychologists form small groups for the purpose of peer support and shared learning. These will be especially helpful to those who are isolated due to working in rural areas, so some alternatives to face-to-face meetings may be needed (e.g., an internet discussion group, videolink, or telephone conference). Together, you can devise for yourselves exercises and mini-assignments to develop your understanding and confidence. Examples of these practical exercises might include questions to ask others (including your trainee peers), self-tests, and ways to arrange rehearsals in safe environments, in addition to topic-based reading and group discussions.

16.3 PREPARATION FOR TEACHING AND TRAINING

The first step in preparing to teach or train is to clarify the objectives, and establish the learner goals. Why has the health psychologist been asked to teach, and how do the learners envisage using what they learn? Second, what do they already know or think they know? As psychology is sometimes seen as 'common sense', the degree of preparation needed to understand some concepts may be underestimated.

Methods for deciding on the appropriate content and format of the teaching or training offered will include interviews, surveys and questionnaires. A less familiar form of data collection for psychologists, though one widely accepted in business and human service settings, is the focus group. It provides a credible method of information-gathering about learner goals, expectations, and prior knowledge, outlined below.

16.3.1 How to conduct a focus group

A focus group is a group of 8–12 similar people who are encouraged to provide information through a discussion (Duffy, 1993). Normally, discussions take one to two hours and are tape-recorded.

- Try to get a representative sample: you may need to sample several hospital wards or community clinics. Be aware that, if the groups include people of different status levels, there is a risk of the least-powerful members contributing less.
- Prepare for the group session by formulating a few open-ended questions, then aim to funnel the talk towards the key issue as quickly as possible, as the best information tends to surface at the end of the session (Duffy, 1993). It is usual to use a U-shaped seating arrangement and to have a co-facilitator. Once individuals begin to talk, they are likely to continue contributing, so it becomes essential to get all the group members participating actively in discussion from the beginning

(Duffy, 1993). Those who come late and do not hear the introductory material may disrupt the process and should be excluded.

- Start the session with a welcome and outline how members have been selected, the overall objective, and clear ground rules re confidentiality, privacy, acceptance of all contributions ('no right and wrong answers', etc.).
- After the session(s) you will need to collate the information and make sense of it using techniques such as thematic analysis (Boyatzis, 1998).

16.4 TEACHING LARGE GROUPS

Health professional education has long been conducted by academics and clinicians who have themselves had no specific training in how to teach effectively. However, there is a rich literature on how to do it (e.g., Newble & Cannon, 1994). One of the commonest media for teaching, which survives despite widespread condemnation of its usefulness, is the lecture. Its resilience may be due to the apparent efficiency of one expert imparting knowledge to a hallful of learners. Because of this, and its similarities to the conference presentation, it is worth reiterating some guidelines for good lecturing. The most crucial is the caution against trying to convey too much information for your audience to be able to understand, let alone remember. The lecture situation invites a passivity on the part of the audience which must be counteracted if lasting learning is to occur.

16.4.1 How to prepare an interesting and memorable lecture

Some specific pointers follow (for more detail, see Race, 1999).

- Before you decide the outline of your presentation, find out how this lecture fits into the overall learning experience of the audience, and what their existing knowledge is.
- The inexperienced should write down what they want to say, then practise saying it in an interesting tone of voice. Leave extemporizing until later, especially if you're nervous at first. But speaking from notes is not the same as reading; try recording yourself doing different styles if you need proof. Taping your lecture and/or asking a colleague to comment can provide useful feedback to you afterwards.
- Start by saying why the topic is important and what the lecture will cover, and end with a summary of both these. Give opportunities for

questions at least once, and after difficult sections of the material, and whenever you see hearers looking bored, confused or irritated. Use concrete examples relevant to the audience's own experience.

- Plan to make two or three main points which the audience will remember even after they lose their notes. Give lists of backup references and suggested readings in a separate handout for later possible perusal. Some note-taking by the audience does encourage them to process the information which assists later recall, but provide handouts of complex diagrams, with space for student-added material.

- Rehearse your timing, not by reading the lecture to yourself, but by practising the actual delivery alone or in front of someone else. The visibility and clarity of any audio-visual aids should be assessed, for example by getting a colleague to review your preparations. Too little information is better than too much, and no audience ever complained that a lecture ended a few minutes early.

16.4.2 Lecture delivery and evaluation

- Break up the lecture with audiovisual aids, relevant jokes or anecdotes, brief discussion among groups of three to five, questions (by the lecturer or from the audience), or role plays. Never forget the rather brief human attention span – especially if audience members are not particularly well motivated to listen/learn. Adopt a 20-minute limit for continuous lecturer talking.

- Audio-visual aids can enliven a presentation, but can also bore and discourage engagement. Too much information per slide or overhead, or too fast or slow a rate of presentation, can turn off attention, particularly in a darkened lecture hall. Too much reliance on special effects, such as animation in a Powerpoint presentation, may distract rather than maintain concentration (Murray, 2002; Race, 1999). Distributing copies of overheads or the output from a software presentation program like Powerpoint can be extremely useful for students, who can add their own notes as the lecture proceeds.

- Flipcharts or whiteboard markers can be useful despite their primitive character – use lots of contrast, large, clear but quick writing and rough diagrams – but do not turn your back on the audience for more than a few seconds.

- Speak to be heard at the back of the room: imagine your voice arching over the front rows to land at the back, and vary the volume and intonation. Express enthusiasm for the topic and convey your own emotional involvement. Act it to some extent if necessary.

- Speak in headlines (with short words and sentences) and with some drama; be as concrete as possible rather than abstract and complicated.
- Continually scan the audience, making eye contact. If the audience is inattentive, try asking someone whether they'd like you to clarify a point, or what they're thinking about the lecture. This responsiveness to the audience is very hard to do at first because it requires a lot of familiarity with the material and confidence in your communication skills. Expect to improve with practice.
- In all cases you need to respond to overt disruptions and talking rather than to pretend that they are not happening. Others in the lecture hall are likely to be irritated by thoughtless noise and the lecturer's consequent pauses waiting for quiet, and hopefully will attempt to influence the offenders.
- If the audience appears rude or rejecting, its members may be tired or distracted. Try to see their point of view, shorten and simplify, don't take it personally.
- Ask to see some student lecture notes as a way to determine how successfully your lecture conveyed information (Cantillon, 2003). This can be a very disheartening experience, though one likely to reinforce the principles of focus and interactivity stressed above.

The main difference between lectures and conference presentations is the length. It is a real challenge to present complex ideas and findings in the 10–15 minutes commonly allocated, so practice with informed feedback from colleagues becomes even more important.

Some health psychologists may have severe performance anxieties about addressing large groups of their professional colleagues, which may need to be specifically extinguished. If self-desensitization by starting with small groups of friends does not work, consult a behaviour change specialist.

Technology now allows a rapidly expanding array of options for distance education, by using video conferencing, video discs, and online internet courses. Validated distance training methods still require development, however. A host of questions requires research about the best level and nature of interaction between the instructor and the trainees, how much learner control over pace is desirable, and how best to respond to questions (Salas & Cannon-Bowers, 2001).

16.5 SMALL GROUP TEACHING AND TRAINING

A variety of small working groups acts as learning environments, even if this is not specified as their primary function. One is the medical ward round or case conference, which can develop a routine format with functions such as skills modelling, information sharing, and providing peer support in dealing with challenging clinical problems (Patterson et al., 2002). These settings offer opportunities for health psychologists to educate their colleagues from other disciplines in a less formal manner.

Team training is one specific concern of occupational psychologists which has clear applications to healthcare work. Salas and Cannon-Bowers (2001) conclude that strategies such as crew resource management, used for 20 years in the aviation environment, improve teamwork and reduce mistakes in the cockpit, and that practice and feedback are essential to achieve behavioural effects in the workplace.

16.5.1 Conveying new theories, concepts or research findings

The tutorial is a time-honoured teaching method, with extensions beyond the classroom to work settings and training environments. Its advantage is the possibilities of interaction and monitoring of process not only between the leader and the group but also among the group members. These advantages are lost if the leader speaks for too much of the time and thus fails to stimulate both independence and cohesion in the group members. The leader should be sensitive to non-verbal aspects of group process and creativity, such as seating arrangements, to gain the optimum benefits of this learning experience (Jaques, 2000; Tiberius, 1999).

A group discussion on prepared key questions is a good way to reveal areas of misunderstanding or gaps in knowledge. A collegial rather than competitive atmosphere will be more enjoyable, and is usually more productive of engagement in the learning task. This format can be motivating and enjoyable for students, though it takes a relatively large amount of teacher time (McDonough & Marks, 2002).

A group-based instructional method which has become popular in health sciences education in recent years is Problem-Based Learning (PBL). In this model a group of learners is confronted with a patient care problem in life-like concrete detail, then group members go through systematic steps to define what they need to know in order to understand the problem, and to synthesize and test the new information (Kaufman, 1985; Newble & Cannon, 1994; Schmidt, 1989). The group leader needs to understand the learning process, but an important difference from traditional teaching is that the person does not need to have expertise in the area of the problem. The supposed benefits of 'deep learning' and student engagement have been difficult to demonstrate in terms of graduate skill levels (Dean et al., 2003).

16.5.2 Skills training in a workshop format

Small to medium groups (up to about 25) are ideal for the training of complex skilled performances such as motivational interviewing, establishing a self-care routine in chronic illness, or facilitating a support group. Within a safe learning environment, trainees are guided through the identified and manageable steps. The trainer needs to ensure active participation and processing of the information by all members, encourage practice and testing, and give plenty of constructive feedback (not only verbal but performance oriented, e.g., using role plays and videos).

In healthcare, the use of simulated patients or consumers of the service has gained a respected role. Actors are trained volunteers who present a standardized history and set of problems, allowing rich feedback on trainee skills and also a method of assessment. The methods of assessment, like the method of training, call for behavioural demonstrations of the skill rather than written accounts and offer remediation and extra practice where necessary. Students are required to reach a clearly defined criterion for successful skill performance.

16.5.3 Facilitating peer support and reflection in stressful workplaces

Another small group training situation arises where healthcare professionals want to know how they can address work stress issues. Peer support, which happens best through a group medium, is very helpful for stress management, and health psychologists may be asked to teach relevant knowledge and skills in order to facilitate that support.

Many healthcare settings are chronically stressful (Griffiths et al., 2003; Le Blanc & Schaufeli, 2003; Winefield, 2003), with prominent causes being the long hours, lack of feedback about success, poor management by people promoted for other reasons, and altruism, even amounting to 'workaholism', which is common in healthcare culture. Understanding from others facing the same challenges is an invaluable source of information that one is not isolated in feeling overwhelmed, that others struggle and may have developed coping strategies, and might be able to offer advice or tips. Peer support groups may also result in shared initiatives to improve organizational procedures and a realization that the individuals' problems are due to a psychologically toxic work environment, which may be modifiable with concerted staff action. The stress management group may start to think about and press systemically for better management practices or a fairer distribution of resources. Those trying to establish such a support mechanism need also to cope with practical issues such as who will pay for participants' time.

16.6 SKILLS TRAINING IN A ONE-TO-ONE FORMAT

Healthcare settings are often the scene for individual supervision of skill acquisition by one or a very small number of trainees over quite prolonged periods of time, for example several months. This kind of supervised training is given detailed consideration in Chapter 17.

16.7 TEACHING THE PUBLIC AND HEALTHCARE CONSUMERS, RATHER THAN PROFESSIONALS AND STUDENTS

Some of the teaching and training which health psychologists do may be aimed at increasing the knowledge and skills of people with no professional educational background in health and healthcare, but who may nonetheless know or need to know quite a lot about their own health issues. This sector may include those suffering from serious or chronic illness and also their family caregivers and others giving emotional support. Most of the health psychologist's teaching role here has a health promotional goal or involves training the caregivers in basic listening and communication skills (see Chapters 14 and 15 of this volume). Issues of language, especially the avoidance of jargon, and cultural sensitivity are extremely relevant in effective communication with this group. Family caregivers often act as unpaid and untrained health workers, and the training they receive from a health psychologist may well improve their capacity for the work of caregiving (Winefield, 2000). Assessment of this training needs to include consumers' self-reported satisfaction.

The internet offers new possibilities for conveying health information to the public and for setting up support groups for people suffering from chronic illnesses (Neuhauser & Kreps, 2003; Rice & Katz, 2001; Wright & Bell, 2003). Evaluation of the success of the health psychologist's teaching and training efforts will be particularly difficult where, as is the case with the internet, the consumer audience is of unknown size and composition.

16.8 How to Assess Learning Outcomes

It is useful to draw a distinction between assessing students' learning, by reviewing and grading their assignments, exam papers or other test products, and evaluating your own teaching. The latter implies a longer time perspective and a wider perspective on what are the important outcomes. Some assessment methods are considered below.

16.8.1 Using written products

Essays, multiple choice exams and assignment predominantly indicate knowledge rather than skills. Their assessment in a reliable, valid, timely and equitable way is a demanding task. It is informative, and can be motivating for those assessed, if the marker adds encouraging as well as critical comments to potentiate the learning experience and suggests what could make the product better, especially for those on or below the borderline of a satisfactory grade.

Common criteria are the depth and breadth of knowledge demonstrated by the examinee. Assessors need to become familiar with local standards and procedures.

16.8.2 Satisfaction and confidence ratings

Anonymous ratings of student satisfaction can provide useful feedback to the teacher or trainer. Many educational institutions routinely collect student evaluations of teaching, and answers to their standardized questions about the teaching materials, quality of delivery and perceived relevance of the teaching can be helpful. Professional development also often requires participants to complete similar evaluative ratings about the teaching or training received. To overcome 'death by questionnaire' (Race, 1999), open questions which invite a more thoughtful response can be added. Examples are asking for respondents to nominate the most and least useful aspects of the teaching or to offer suggestions for improvement.

While learner ratings can also provide information about the confidence levels or gains which follow skills training, interviews and observations of task performance are also relevant and these begin to overlap with ways to evaluate your training methods.

16.8.3 Practical tests such as the Objective Structured Clinical Examination (OSCE)

Standardized simulated patients are used in the Objective Structured Clinical Examination (OSCE), to assess skills and their components. The high face validity of this method comes at considerable cost of time, resources (such as trained standardized patients) and organization, as predictive validity is only reasonable when a wide range of skills has been assessed (Martin & Jolly, 2002; Mavis & Henry, 2002). The OSCE can also be modified as a teaching situation (Brazeau et al., 2002). Developed initially in medical educational settings, the OSCE offers a potentially valid approach to the assessment of skills such as history taking, psychosocial assessment and treatment formulation.

16.8.4 Feedback from the intended beneficiaries of the new learning

The ultimate test of the success of your training is, in principle, the amount of improvement shown in patients' health outcomes as a result of your learners' improved knowledge and skills. However, such evaluation requires extremely large numbers to detect differences at this level, and proximal outcome measures are often used such as waiting times, staff courtesy and information comprehensibility. The need to take positive biases into account is important: few patients will risk overt criticism of a service that they may need again soon (Molnar & Stup, 1994).

16.9 How to Build in Evaluation

The ultimate goal of teaching other health professions is likely to be changes in how they carry out their work. The first step in assessing work performance is to define exactly the components of skilful performance. Hays et al. (2002) identified the following five desirable qualities of assessment of healthcare performance: validity, reliability, feasibility, educational impact and acceptability. They noted further that there is little empirical evidence available that bears on competence assessment using these criteria. Direct or videotaped observations of practice, covert simulated patients, surveys, interviews and patient-record analyses all have advantages and weaknesses. Some aspects of high quality practice, including teamwork ability, patient empowerment, keeping up to date, and insight into learning needs remain a challenge to assess (Hays et al., 2002).

Evaluation may be at several levels, for example changed learners' reactions, changed attitudes and perceptions, new knowledge and skills, changed organizational practices, and patient benefits (Morrison, 2003). Some feedback about your success or otherwise as a teacher may arise spontaneously from your audience. Possibilities include positive comments made to you informally, invitations to continue/expand/return, increased referrals, requests for consultancies or co-investigatory partnerships, and invitations to join decision-making committees.

Some feedback you need to seek out for yourself. Focus groups may give more depth of information than do attitude and satisfaction ratings. Another possible method is to use the vignette. One way to do this is to write brief descriptions of events or situations, varying their key dimensions, and use these as stimuli for data collection. Another approach is to ask participants (for example, in some change process), to write vignettes which reflect representative experiences with various questions about what happened, the participant's role, the consequences, and the most significant aspects. Clarification and elaboration may be needed afterwards, for example through a telephone interview. Jochums and Pershey (1993) describe this method and advocate the collection of serial vignettes during a change-oriented intervention. Evaluators then use the material to learn about the strengths and weaknesses of the programme and, by feeding results back to participants and seeking further comment, to formulate recommendations for programme modification. Training skills development over a period of time would lend itself to this method of evaluation.

16.9.1 How to collect evidence of your competence

As adult learners themselves, trainee health psychologists will benefit from collecting information about their own competences using multiple sources, then considering how to interpret it, discussing it with peers and supervisors, and experimenting with variations.

The extent to which teaching and training is regarded by other decision-makers as a core business of health psychologists will vary. Therefore the trainee may need to express preparedness to undertake such tasks, in tactful ways, in order to get opportunities to collect the needed evidence of competence. A side-effect may be wider recognition of health psychologists' competence as teachers and trainers of other health professionals.

16.10 HEALTH PSYCHOLOGY COMPETENCES COVERED IN THIS CHAPTER

The British Psychological Society has defined the competences needed for qualification as a chartered health psychologist. To specify health psychologist qualifications in terms of explicit competences implies behavioural definitions of skills. The behavioural framework is a familiar and well-tested one within health psychology; indeed it is a distinctive feature of our discipline and profession, and the source of much of the evidence for the efficacy and effectiveness of our techniques (Compas et al., 1998).

The competences addressed in this chapter include those constituting the British Psychological Society's stage 2 Regulations 4.1a to 4.4c. These four units on teaching and training competence include 16 core components which in brief refer to planning, delivering and assessing teaching/training activities, and to the evaluation of the success of such efforts. In principle, the sub-units as detailed below form a logical sequence and this is the order in which the chapter has addressed each one. The process of gaining overall competence in teaching and training is likely to be an iterative one where the health psychologist needs to continually update his or her own knowledge through reading, critical observation of, and feedback on, one's own efforts, and systematic commitment to improvement. The case study, video, log, teaching plan and evaluation required in the BPS Regulations all fit within this model.

The first step (unit 4.1) is to plan and design training programmes that enable students to learn about psychological knowledge, skills and practices (see Section 16.3 of this chapter). Components include assessing training needs (4.1a), identifying training programme structures and content (4.1b), selecting training methods and approaches (4.1c), producing training materials (4.1d) and using appropriate media to deliver training materials (4.1e). The delivery of such training programmes involves implementing the chosen training methods (4.2a) and facilitating learning (4.2b) (see Sections 16.4–16.7 of this chapter).

It is useful to distinguish between activities designed to assess the outcomes of the training programme for the recipients (unit 4.3), and activities designed to evaluate the training programme in a wider sense (unit 4.4). The first of these goals involves identifying assessment methods (4.3a), selecting assessment regimes (4.3b), establishing the availability of resources for assessment procedures (4.3c), producing assessment materials (4.3d), ensuring a fair appreciation of assessment methods (4.3e) and producing relevant records of progress and outcomes (4.3f). The latter, evaluative goal includes evaluating training programme outcomes (4.4a), identifying factors contributing to training programme outcomes (4.4b), and identifying improvements for the design and delivery of training for implementation in future programmes (4.4c). Description of these competences is mainly woven through Sections 16.8–16.9 of this chapter.

REFERENCES

Altman, D.G. (1995). Sustaining interventions on community systems: On the relationship between researchers and communities. *Health Psychology* 14, 526–36.

Belar, C.D., Paoletti, N. & Jordan, C. (2001). Assessment and intervention in a medical environment. In J. Milgrom & G.D. Burrows (eds), *Psychology and Psychiatry: Integrating Medical Practice.* Chichester: Wiley, 65–92.

Boud, D., Keogh, R. & Walker, D. (eds) (1985). *Reflection: Turning Experience into Learning.* London: Kogan Page.

Boyatzis, R.E. (1998). *Transforming Qualitative Information: Thematic Analysis and Code Development.* California: Sage.

Bray, J.H. & Rogers, J.C. (1997). The Linkages Project: Training behavioural health professionals for collaborative practice with primary care physicians. *Families, Systems & Health* 15, 55–63.

Brazeau, C., Boyd, L. & Crosson, J. (2002). Changing an existing OSCE to a teaching tool: The making of a teaching OSCE. *Academic Medicine* 77, 932.

Candy, P. (1987). Increasing learner-control in the instructional setting. In D. Boud and V. Giffin (eds), *Appreciating Adults Learning: From the Learners' Perspective.* London: Kogan Page, 159–78.

Cantillon, P. (2003). Teaching large groups. *British Medical Journal* 326, 437–40.

Compas, B.E., Haaga, D.A.F., Keefe, F.J., Leitenberg, H. & Williams, D.A. (1998). Sampling empirically supported psychological treatments from health psychology: Smoking, chronic pain, cancer, and bulimia nervosa. *Journal of Consulting and Clinical Psychology* 66, 89–112.

Dean, S.J., Barratt, A.L., Hendry, G.D. & Lyon, P.M.A. (2003). Preparedness for hospital practice among graduates of a problem-based, graduate entry medical program. *Medical Journal of Australia* 178, 163–6.

Duffy, B.P. (1993). Focus groups: An important research technique for internal evaluation units. *Evaluation Practice* 14, 133–9.

Foley, G. (ed.) (1995). *Understanding Adult Education and Training.* St Leonards Australia: Allen & Unwin.

Garcia-Shelton, L. & Vogel, M.E. (2002). Primary care health psychology training: A collaborative model with family practice. *Professional Psychology: Research and Practice* 33, 546–6.

Gatchel, R.J. & Oordt, M.S. (2003). *Clinical Health Psychology and Primary Care: Practical Advice and Clinical Guidance for Successful Collaboration.* Washington DC: American Psychological Association.

Griffiths, A., Randall, R., Santos, A. & Cox, T. (2003). Senior nurses: Interventions to reduce work stress. In M.F. Dollard, A.H. Winefield & H.R. Winefield (eds), *Occupational Stress in the Service Professions.* London: Taylor & Francis, 169–90.

Hays, R.B., Davies, H.A., Beard, J.D. et al. (2002). Selecting performance assessment methods for experienced physicians. *Medical Education* 36, 910–17.

Jaques, D. (2000). *Learning in Groups* (3rd edn). London: Croom Helm.

Jochums, B.L. & Pershey, E.J. (1993). Using the vignette method in formative evaluation. *Evaluation Practice* 14, 155–61.

Johnston, D.W. & Johnston, M. (eds) (1998). *Health Psychology.* Vol. 8 in *Comprehensive Clinical Psychology* (eds. A.S. Bellack & M. Hersen). Amsterdam: Elsevier.

Kaufman, A. (ed.) (1985). *Implementing Problem-based Medical Education.* New York: Springer.

Kaufman, D.M. (2003). Applying educational theory in practice. *British Medical Journal* 326, 213–16.

Kemmis, S. & McTaggart, R. (1992). *The Action Research Planner* (3rd edn). Geelong: Deakin University Press.

Kolb, D.A. (1984). *Experiential Learning.* New York: Prentice-Hall. Cited in Adult Learning Theory and Model <http://www.arl.org.training/ilsco/adultlearn.html> accessed 21 January 2003.

Le Blanc, P.M. & Schaufeli, W.B. (2003). Burnout among oncology care providers: Radiation assistants, physicians and nurses. In M.F. Dollard, A.H. Winefield and H.R. Winefield (eds) *Occupational Stress in the Service Professions.* London: Taylor & Francis, 143–67.

Martin, I.G. & Jolly, B. (2002). Predictive validity and estimated cut score on an objective structured clinical examination (OSCE) used as an assessment of clinical skills at the end of the first clinical year. *Medical Education* 36, 418–25.

Mavis, B.E. & Henry, R.C. (2002). Between a rock and a hard place: Finding a place for the OSCE in medical education. *Medical Education* 36, 408–9.

McDonough, M. & Marks, I.M. (2002). Teaching medical students exposure therapy for phobia/panic: Randomized, controlled comparison of face-to-face tutorial in small groups vs. solo computer instruction. *Medical Education* 36, 412–17.

Molnar, J. & Stup, B. (1994). Using clients to monitor performance. *Evaluation Practice* 15, 29–35.

Morrison, J. (2003). Evaluation. *British Medical Journal* 326, 385–7.

Muchinsky, P.M. (2000). *Psychology Applied to Work* (6th edn). Belmont, CA: Wadsworth/Thomson Learning.

Murray, B. (2002). Tech enrichment or overkill? *Monitor on Psychology*, April, 42–4.

Neuhauser, L. & Kreps, G.L. (2003). Rethinking communication in the e-health era. *Journal of Health Psychology* 8, 7–23.

Newble, D. & Cannon, R. (1994). *A Handbook for Medical Teachers* (3rd edn). Lancaster: Kluwer.

Patterson, J., Peek, C.J., Heinrich, R.L., Bischoff, R.J. & Scherger, J.S. (2002). *Mental Health Professionals in Medical Settings: A Primer.* New York: Norton.

Race, P. (1999). *2000 Tips for Lecturers.* London: Kogan Page.

Rice, R.E. & Katz, J.E. (2001). *The Internet and Health Communication.* Thousand Oaks, CA: Sage.

Richards, J. (1994). Giving psychology away? A comment on 'Health care, psychology, and the scientist-practitioner model' by James (1994). *Australian Psychologist* 29, 12–14.

Salas, E. & Cannon-Bowers, J.A. (2001). The science of training: A decade of progress. *Annual Review of Psychology* 52, 471–99.

Schmidt, H.G. (1989). The rationale behind problem-based learning. In H.G. Schmidt, M. Lipkin, M.W. deVries & J.M. Greep (eds), *New Directions for Medical Education: Problem-based Learning and Community-oriented Medical Education.* New York: Springer-Verlag, 105–11.

Singh, B.S. & Martin, P.R. (2001). Teaching, training and research: Future directions. In J. Milgrom & G.D. Burrows (eds), *Psychology and Psychiatry: Integrating Medical Practice.* Chichester: Wiley, 279–96.

Tiberius, R.G. (1999). *Small Group Teaching: A Trouble-shooting Guide.* London: Kogan Page.

Winefield, H.R. (2000). Stress reduction for family caregivers in chronic mental illness: Implications of a work stress management perspective. *International Journal of Stress Management* 7, 193–207.

Winefield, H.R. (2003). Work stress and its effects in general practitioners. In M.F. Dollard, A.H. Winefield & H.R. Winefield (eds), *Occupational Stress in the Service Professions.* London: Taylor & Francis, 191–212.

Winefield, H.R. & Chur-Hansen, A. (2003). Working with a multidisciplinary staff. In L.M. Cohen, D.E. McChargue & F.L. Collins (eds), *The Health Psychology Handbook: Practical Issues for the Behavioral Medicine Specialist.* Thousand Oaks: Sage, 28–41.

Wlodkowski, R.J. (1999). *Enhancing Adult Motivation to Learn* (rev. edn). San Francisco: Jossey-Bass.

Wright, K.B. & Bell, S.B. (2003). Health-related support groups on the Internet: Linking empirical findings to social support and computer-mediated communication theory. *Journal of Health Psychology* 8, 39–54.

Chapter 17

SUPERVISING EFFECTIVELY

Sandra Horn

In this chapter, supervised practice as an effective way of gaining professional competences, will be discussed. The discussion will include the practical aspects of setting up supervision, the nature and process of supervision, the supervisory relationship, and the rights and responsibilities of supervisors and trainees.

17.1 SUPERVISED PRACTICE

An extended period of supervised practice has been adopted as a model for training in a range of professions. Here, 'extended' means the equivalent of a minimum of two years of full-time work. The *practice* or experiential learning element takes place in the context of work. In this model, learning, including the acquisition of skills and competences, takes place through the interaction between experience and reflection. The learning process is enabled by the other element of the model: *supervision*, in which a suitably qualified and experienced colleague works with a trainee to guide their experiential learning and facilitate the development of professional competence.

17.2 THE STRENGTHS OF THE MODEL

The practice of acquiring skills and undergoing professional development via supervised practice is well established in professional training in many fields. With support and guidance from one or more experienced colleague, a trainee will gain direct experience of the realities of professional working in relevant contexts, develop practical skills and the ability to integrate theory into practice. Through keeping a reflective diary of experiential learning and discussing it during supervision, trainees will become aware of the processes which are taking place and enabling learning. This is what Gardiner (1989) calls *level two learning*, which focuses on process rather than content *(level one)*. As trainees progress through their training and take more responsibility for determining the way in which supervision sessions are run, they will be moving to *level three learning:* learning to learn. Thus, effective supervised practice provides a means of personal and professional development and is an integral part of the preparation for effective independent working.

At the end of the period of supervision, professional competences will be assessed, and only those achieving agreed standards will be eligible to become professional practitioners.

This mechanism protects the public, employers, and other members of the profession who have a right to expect that those who have achieved recognition from their professional body will show consistently high and appropriate standards in the delivery of services.

Professional training is designed to ensure that health psychologists are able to meet a range of work demands, to an appropriate standard, within their particular contexts of employment. Many practitioners have moved beyond a narrow focus on work with individual clients or highly specialized research into areas such as organizational consultancy, multidisciplinary working, and the support and enhancement of the work of other staff.

In the UK, health psychology training is based on the acquisition and demonstration of competences applicable across a variety of work settings and tasks. This allows considerable flexibility and means that most, if not all, professional development can take place in the normal work setting. It also encourages depth in exploration of contextual and practical issues in several areas of work by requiring trainees to gain experience and demonstrate competence with a variety of clients, recipient groups and settings, to produce extensive and detailed documentation, to keep reflective logbooks and to undertake regular supervision.

The approach maintains a clear emphasis on what the health psychologist in training actually does and on the understanding and demonstration of good practice, whatever the setting. This aids the transferability of skills across different and complex contexts. Such versatility is itself an important characteristic of being a professional.

17.3 WHAT IS SUPERVISION?

Supervision is an interactive method of teaching and learning, usually carried out on a one-to-one basis, between a trainee and an experienced and skilled colleague (supervisor), in which by discussion, reflection and guided discovery the trainee is facilitated by the supervisor to develop the skills and knowledge of an effective, self-aware learner. It is a developmental process, and one in which responsibility for the learning is shared. Supervision is a familiar concept in the 'helping' professions, and is the process by which supervisees are educated, supported and managed (Kadushin, 1976) as they develop, explore and reflect on the skills they need to carry out their work effectively.

The supervisor's role is multifaceted. A supervisor is a source of information, a teacher, a mentor, a modeller of effective, professional practice and a manager.

At its most basic level, supervision involves the exchange of information. Initially, this might focus on identifying what the trainee needs to know and how that knowledge may be gained. The trainee will need to know, for example, what the ethical issues are and the procedures for obtaining ethical committee permission, in carrying out research. Some of these issues and procedures are matters of fact, which the supervisor might know or know where to find; for example, who is the NHS contact for the Local Research Ethical Committee (LREC)? Where can a copy of the ethical application form be found? Other issues are matters for discussion and clarification; for example, is LREC approval needed? What are the issues around informed consent for children? In the early days of supervision, when the trainee is setting up a system of working, a great deal of information might be needed from the supervisor. In the main, and as time goes on, however, learning will be experiential and reflective.

Woolfe (1992) talks of experience as a potential asset; a means of enhancing understanding of oneself and the external world. However, experience alone is not enough to promote such understanding; there is 'an interactive relationship between experience, reflection and learning'. This is obviously true of a range of experiences. Reflection as a solitary activity, however, carries with it the danger of distortion. Both triumphs and failures may be magnified or minimized by things like fatigue or emotional state. Sharing reflections with a supervisor, who should be neutral but supportive, is a way of counteracting such distortions and enabling a clearer and more productive view. Revisiting reflections during supervision should not only help to consolidate experiential learning, but also to extend it. It is an opportunity to give and receive feedback on the trainee's performance, to consider how learning might be applied in other situations, to think through alternative approaches that might have been taken and their possible consequences. This habit of evaluative reflection is one of the main ways in which competence as a professional health psychologist is ensured and developed.

By giving trainees the opportunity to take progressively more responsibility for managing the process, supervisors will facilitate trainees' ability to manage their own learning and professional relationships and practices. The process of reflecting on learning and practice will become a habitual way of working as trainees progress. Effective supervision will give them the tools they need for incorporating best practice into their work. It will enable them to take the good habits they have learned under supervision with them, after they qualify as professional health psychologists. These habits include critical self-evaluation, the evaluation of knowledge and feedback, the effective utilization of competent consultation and advice, and the seeking and evaluating of opportunities for continuing self-development.

17.4 THE RIGHTS AND RESPONSIBILITIES OF SUPERVISORS AND TRAINEES

Supervision is a demanding undertaking for both supervisor and trainee. It is essential, therefore, to ensure that the responsibilities and rights of trainees and supervisors are made explicit and are understood and accepted by both parties. The supervisor's and trainee's responsibilities operate on at least two levels:

- a generic responsibility for their part of the supervisory relationship;
- specific, agreed responsibilities for the process of supervising while the trainee attains, documents and presents evidence of competence.

17.4.1 Generic responsibilities in the supervisory relationship

The cornerstone of an effective supervisory relationship is trustworthiness. Egan (1985, p. 19) has described the components of a trustworthy relationship in the helping professions as confidentiality, credibility, consideration in the use of power, and understanding:

- *confidentiality*: what the supervisor is told by the trainee will not be disclosed to others without the trainee's express agreement;
- *credibility*: the trainee can believe what the supervisor says;
- *consideration in the use of power*: the trainee has entrusted him or herself and career to the supervisor, who will be careful with them;

- *understanding*: the supervisor will make an effort to understand the trainee.

Trustworthiness must be mutual. Trainees also must maintain appropriate confidentiality, be open and truthful, be careful of their supervisors' time and feelings and reputation, and make an effort to be understanding. The adoption of trustworthy attitudes and behaviours will be crucial in all the trainee's future working relationships, be they with colleagues (peers, managers, those needing guidance and training, etc.) or clients.

The supervisor's responsibilities include:

- discussing with the trainee and agreeing the supervision plan, work placement arrangements and training needs; advising on attendance at seminars and other learning opportunities;
- ensuring that the formal arrangements for the work placement are documented fully;
- giving appropriately detailed and prompt feedback on the trainee's progress every month (either in person, verbally or in written form) and countersigning the records of experience and supervision;
- maintaining contact with the work placement contacts as appropriate, and assisting in the resolution of any difficulties the trainee may experience in the workplace;
- agreeing completion dates for components of the training;
- where the workplace does not provide opportunities for all the competences to be attained, giving advice and information about voluntary or other opportunities the trainee might pursue, and assisting the trainee in negotiating such additional placements if appropriate;
- reading written work as appropriate and returning it to the trainee in a reasonable time with constructive commentary;
- maintaining contact with the trainee throughout the period of supervised practice;
- being accessible to the trainee at other reasonable times when advice is needed;
- monitoring the trainee's work, discussing and giving advice on progress;
- ensuring that the trainee is made aware, as quickly as possible, if progress is not adequate or the standard of work is below that expected, and to work with the trainee to develop a constructive plan for its improvement;
- arranging as appropriate for the trainee to present their work to others (e.g., at graduate seminars or conferences) and to have practice in oral examinations;
- encouraging publication of the trainee's work as appropriate;

- drawing the trainee's attention to safety, ethical and other statutory procedures;
- if necessary, arranging for the trainee to receive supplementary advice from appropriate colleagues;
- overseeing the preparation of assessed work and advising about the nature of work and the standard expected;
- advising the trainee on procedures and preparation for examination.

The trainee's responsibilities include:

- ensuring that there is a written agreement with any workplace contact;
- with the supervisor, drafting a supervision plan and job description, discussing and agreeing the final formats and agreeing the amount of time to be devoted to the various aspects of the work;
- seeking and negotiating other opportunities to attain competences if the workplace cannot provide them all, in discussion with and with the agreement of the supervisor;
- making an appropriately detailed progress report (verbal or written) once each month and keeping logs of supervision and work experience;
- discussing with the supervisor their preferred type of guidance and agreeing a schedule of meetings;
- agreeing with the supervisor their personal training needs and participating fully in any arrangements made;
- taking the initiative in raising problems or difficulties, however elementary they may seem, and indicating at an early stage if supervision is not meeting needs;
- maintaining the progress of their work according to the plan, including the presentation of written materials as required, in sufficient time to allow for comments and discussion before proceeding to the next stage;
- deciding when to submit work for assessment, taking into account the supervisor's opinion – which is, however, advisory only;
- informing the supervisor immediately if there is any medical or other difficulty which may be affecting their work and progress;
- informing the supervisor in good time of any impending change in the supervision plan, discussing and agreeing a revised version with the supervisor before it is submitted for formal approval.

The supervisor and the trainee also have *rights*. The following points are given as reminders about those rights. Consideration should be given to the rights and responsibilities of both parties in a formal letter of agreement.

The supervisor has the right to:

- expect the trainee to fulfil all the agreed responsibilities, and to be notified in good time if there is a reason why that cannot happen;
- limit the demands made on his/her time, in accordance with the agreement;
- receive work in good time and in good condition (legible and presented well and correctly);
- be given due notice, wherever possible, of necessary changes in arrangements;
- be listened to attentively, and to have due consideration given to advice; if advice is not taken, to have the reasons explained;
- be *consulted* by the trainee about joint authorship of papers for publication arising from work carried out under supervision (note: there is no automatic right of joint authorship; it depends on the relative contribution of supervisor and trainee).

The trainee has the right to:

- expect the supervisor to fulfil all the agreed responsibilities and to be notified in good time if there is a reason why that cannot happen;
- limit the demands the supervisor makes on his or her time, in accordance with the agreement;
- be given due notice, wherever possible, of necessary changes in arrangements for supervision;
- be listened to attentively and to have reasons for decisions the supervisor may make, fully explained and discussed.

17.5 THE SUPERVISORY RELATIONSHIP

Establishing and maintaining an effective relationship between the supevisor and trainee is a centrally important part of professional and personal development throughout the period of supervised practice. The trainee and supervisor undertake to work together, closely, on areas of mutual interest, over an extended period of time. There is, therefore, a need for the boundaries between their professional and personal lives to be recognized and respected. Maintaining appropriate boundaries is important for both parties, but because there is unequal power in the relationship, it is the supervisor's particular responsibility to protect the interests of the trainee, to respect the trust involved in the supervisor–trainee relationship and to accept the constraints and obligations inherent in that responsibility (see http://www.calendar.soton.ac.uk/sectionXV/part10.html). Meetings are best held in neutral, professional venues, and if there is social contact outside supervision sessions, due consideration should be given to its potential impact on the relationship, and this should be discussed between them.

The following ways of working can facilitate effective supervision.

17.5.1 Planning and preparing

Keeping a practice logbook is a requirement for stage 2 health psychology training. It should be kept up to date, so that it can be discussed with the supervisor and used as a basis for reviewing the supervision plan together, and is one obvious way in which supervisory contact can be planned and prepared for. Another is to set an agenda for the meeting, whether it is face-to-face or distant, and let the supervisor have it in good time so that the topics can be agreed between them. Each supervision session will be recorded in the supervisory log, and it is good practice to include items for action by the trainee and the supervisor, with agreed dates by which the actions will be taken. This systematic approach to preparing for and recording meetings is good practice for professional working and also a good model for meetings concerned with undertaking consultancy, where a formal agenda and minutes for each meeting are the norm.

17.5.2 Self-awareness

The logbook and diary encourage trainees to reflect on their work and what and how they are learning. They should also help to identify trainees' needs and difficulties – the gaps in their learning and experience. It is crucial to record these perceived needs and difficulties, and not just to make optimistic entries about all the things the trainee has achieved (although of course that must be done too!). Identifying and bringing these needs to supervision meetings will enable the effective planning of the trainee's time and workload, especially with the benefit of a dispassionate but interested supervisor's view on how the work is progressing and how best to proceed. It is not possible to do everything all at once, and mistakes will probably be made, so it is important for both supervisor and trainee to accept that the trainee is *in the process* of personal and professional development.

17.5.3 Openness

It is important for trainees to be open about the work and how it is going. A full and honest account of it, warts and all, is essential in supervision. This is only possible if the trainee trusts the supervisor to give a calm and frank appraisal and to offer guidance with any aspects of the work that are not going well. There is nothing to lose by being open.

17.5.4 Feedback

Trainees must be open to receiving feedback from supervisors. If trainees feel the need to justify or defend themselves when feedback is being given, it may be best not to respond at that moment, but to reflect on those feelings later and try to work out why there was a defensive reaction. If, on mature reflection, the trainee still thinks there is an issue about the way the feedback was given, or its content, they should contact the supervisor and explain why.

Trainees should also give supervisors feedback about how they feel supervision is going, and the extent to which it is meeting, or failing to meet, their needs. A mechanism for this should be set up at the outset of the supervisory relationship, and a mutually acceptable way of doing it should be found. An evaluation section could be added to the supervision log, for example.

17.5.5 Progression

The supervisory relationship should mature as the trainee gains in knowledge, skills and confidence. Supervision is a collaborative enterprise, and responsibility for the good management of the process is shared. At the outset, the supervisor might need to take the lead in some respects, where he or she will have more knowledge and/or skills, but trainees will take an increasing amount of responsibility for the supervision sessions as they become more aware of their needs and begin to feel free to ask for what they want from the sessions. Trainees are in the process of becoming independent practitioners and, by the end of their training, they will be fully accountable for themselves and their work.

All the aspects of professional development mentioned above are enshrined in the supervisory process, in which health psychologists in training will take an active part in planning and organizing their learning and work experience. This active engagement begins with the supervision plan and develops throughout the time of supervised practice as the trainee records and reflects on work experiences and how they have contributed to the attainment of competences in the logbook and reflective diary, and collects, collates and presents appropriate documentation for evidence of competence.

17.5.6 What happens if there is a problem in the relationship with the supervisor or in the workplace?

If difficulties are encountered in the relationship between the trainee and the supervisor, they should both take all reasonable steps to resolve them. Because the power balance tends to be weighted in favour of the supervisor, it is crucial to consult an independent adviser if the difficulty cannot be resolved easily. In academic supervision, it is usual practice for the trainee to have such an adviser, who is appointed to support the trainee, attend progress meetings and keep an overall eye on the trainee's welfare. Similarly, in supervised practice, it is good practice for the trainee to have an adviser to perform a similar supportive role. If, however, the difficulty cannot be resolved at a local level, either the trainee or the supervisor may refer the matter to the chief supervisor, who may approve or sometimes suggest a new supervisor. If the issue is one involving serious malpractice or professional misconduct, the professional body's disciplinary procedure may be invoked by the supervisor or the trainee or another party. Such difficulties are rare, but it is important to recognize that there are protective mechanisms in place should relationships break down.

17.6 THE PRACTICAL ASPECTS OF SUPERVISION

In identifying a suitable potential supervisor, it is important to ensure that:

- the person has the necessary qualifications and experience;
- there is sufficient commonality between the interests and experience of the supervisor and the trainee's needs to permit effective facilitation and guidance of experiential learning. The supervisor should be knowledgeable and enthusiastic about the trainee's proposed research and other work plans;

- a formal letter of agreement about the rights and obligations of both parties is drawn up and signed.

Hunt (1986) discusses the value of having a clear supervisory agreement covering such issues as goals, methods and responsibilities, in helping to ensure that supervision is both effective and satisfying to trainee and supervisor alike. Mutually agreed expectations need to be transparent, explicit and detailed in order to avoid misunderstanding and disappointment by either party. The letter of agreement may seem unnecessarily fussy, but its function is to protect trainees' interests and also those of the supervisor. Those interests are not best served by the assumption that they get on well and like each other at the outset, so they can work the details out as they go along. Trainees must know what is, and what is not, expected of them, and so must supervisors. Even though the supervisor will be experienced, and trainees will have had experience of being supervised for previous research projects, professional supervision is different in that it has elements of both academic and practical work over a wide range of competences.

The following points should be covered in the letter of agreement.

- *The recommended minimum level of supervision.* Supervision takes place during personal interactions between the trainee and the supervisor, and includes face-to-face meetings, telephone conversations, verbal or written feedback on reports, and email communications. The trainee should make an appropriately detailed progress report (verbal or written) once each month, and the supervisor should give appropriately detailed and prompt feedback on this report every month (either in person, verbally or in written form). The minimum number of face-to-face meetings per year may vary according to specific needs, but in order to maintain a satisfactory level of continuity it should not usually be fewer than six.
- *Method and times of contact.* As much of the supervision may take place at a distance, it is helpful to treat the telephone and email contacts as if they were face to face; that is, to timetable them. In that way, frustrating failed attempts at contact will be avoided. As it may also be necessary to make contact at other times, both parties should specify times during which contact may be made and times during which contact should be avoided. It might be helpful to exchange timetables. There should be an agreement between the trainee and supervisor about whether telephone, email or other forms of communication are preferred.

- *Fees.* The amount and timing of any fees and, how they are to be paid and what they cover, should be made explicit, as should the consequences of failing to meet the fees. Written receipts should be provided promptly.

17.7 CORE COMPETENCES

In this chapter, the process of supervision has been described, and the roles of the supervisor and trainee have been clarified. Participation in supervision should facilitate appropriate and effective ways of working in order to ensure competence in implementing and maintaining systems for legal, ethical and professional practice (unit 1.1) and in ongoing professional development as a health psychologist (unit 1.2).

Unit 1.1 includes the competences of establishing, maintaining and reviewing systems for the security and control of information (1.1a); ensuring compliance with legal, ethical and professional practices for oneself and others (1.1b); and establishing, implementing and evaluating procedures to ensure competence in psychological practice and research (1.1c). All supervisors will have experience of developing systems to manage the safe and secure storage of data, issues around the Data Protection Act, and of dealing with Ethical Committee requirements.

Unit 1.2 includes the competences of establishing, evaluating and implementing processes to develop oneself as a professional health psychologist (1.2a); employing methods of self-evaluation to determine learning needs and consolidate competences (1.2b); eliciting, monitoring and evaluating knowledge and feedback to inform practice (1.2c); organizing, clarifying and utilizing access to competent consultation and advice (1.2d); and incorporating best practice into one's work (1.2e). The process of identifying and engaging with a supervisor, and undertaking the model of supervised practice in which the acquisition of competences is documented, reflected upon and brought to supervision, plays a major role in the continuing development of a professional health psychologist. Self-evaluation and supervisor evaluation are enshrined in the process, as are eliciting, monitoring and evaluating knowledge and feedback. The supervisor as a model and a mentor will assist in developing best practice and professional ways of working. The managerial aspect of supervision is most evident in the supervisor's role as a placement tutor, concerned with setting up and monitoring the work placement and ensuring that the trainee has appropriate opportunities to gain and document all the relevant competences of a professional health psychologist.

ACKNOWLEDGEMENT

The above text was taken, extended and adapted from the BPS document 'Standards of Supervised Practice in Health Psychology (2001) to which Professor Lucy Yardley, past Chair of the DHPTC, made a major contribution.

REFERENCES

Egan, G. (1985). *The Skilled Helper: A Systematic Approach to Effective Helping* (3rd edn). Monterey, CA: Brooks/Cole Publishing.

Gardiner, D. (1989). *The Anatomy of Supervision: Developing Learning and Professional Competence in Social Work Trainees.* Buckingham: SRHE and Open University Press, 128–58.

Hunt, P. (1986). Supervision, *Marriage Guidance*, Spring, 15–22. Quoted in P. Hawkins and R. Shohet (2000) *Supervision in the Helping Professions* (2nd edn). Buckingham: Open University Press, 31.

Kadushin, A. (1976). *Supervision in Social Work*, New York: Columbia University Press.

Woolfe, R. (1992). Experiential training in workshops. In T. Hobbs (ed.), *Experiential Training: Practical Guidelines*. London, Tavistock/Routledge, 1–13.

FURTHER READING

Cryer, P. (2000). *The Research Trainee's Guide to Success* (2nd edn). Buckingham: Open University Press.

Gardiner, D. (1989). *The Anatomy of Supervision: Developing Learning and Professional Competence in Social Work Trainees.* Buckingham: SRHE and Open University Press.

Hawkins, P. & Shohet, R. (2000). *Supervision in the Helping Professions* (2nd edn). Buckingham: Open University Press.

Hobbs, T. (ed.) (1992). *Experiential Training: Practical Guidelines.* London: Tavistock/Routledge.

Laurillard, D. (1993). *Rethinking University Teaching.* London: Routledge.

Issues in Postgraduate Supervision, Teaching and Management, published by The Times Higher Education Supplement and Society for Research into Higher Education:

No. 2: Handling Common Dilemmas in Supervision, Pat Cryer (1997).

No. 3: Developing Postgraduates' Key Skills, Pat Cryer (1998).

No. 4: Supervising Trainees on Industrial-based Projects, Alan Smith and John Gilby (1999).

No. 7: Delivering Core Training for Postgraduate Research Trainees over the Web, Sue Clegg and Margaret Alexander (2001).

Part V

PROFESSIONAL ROLES
AND PRACTICE

Chapter 18

HEALTH PSYCHOLOGY WITHIN HEALTH SERVICE SETTINGS

Claire N. Hallas

This chapter discusses the competences that health psychologists (HPs) require to practise professionally and effectively within healthcare services. It illustrates professional and ethical challenges that arise when striving to implement evidence-based psychological practice in a multidisciplinary setting.

HPs' competences are employed at all levels of healthcare systems. At the level of direct patient care, HPs may work on assessing and enhancing psychological adjustment to illness and treatment, minimizing distress associated with medical procedures, delivering health education, facilitating patient decision-making and implementing psychological interventions to promote healthy behaviours. HPs are employed to train healthcare professionals so they have a better understanding of the psychological impact of illness and treatment and professional–patient communication. HPs can provide support to staff individually and on a group basis, for example, by developing organizational stress management interventions (see Wren & Michie, 2003). HPs can also use research competence to take on in-house research projects (e.g., to evaluate a new patient education programme) or assist with audit (e.g., advising on how to assess how well a particular health guideline is being adhered to by healthcare professionals). HPs work within public health and primary care departments based in regional health authorities or in national agencies (such as the National Institute for Clinical Excellence [NICE]). Their roles may include development and evaluation of health promotion, including health education materials and community-based interventions. Finally, HPs are employed to research and assess the efficacy of healthcare systems and policies and to advise on policies that promote evidence-based practice.

This chapter will focus on five key areas of HP healthcare practice: (1) direct patient care and education; (2) training of healthcare professionals; (3) research and consultancy in healthcare; (4) service development and healthcare policy; and (5) supporting and advising other healthcare professionals. Although examples are generally provided for within hospital settings they are also applicable for primary care, community and organizational services.

18.1 DIRECT PATIENT CARE AND EDUCATION

Health psychologists offer a combination of hospital and community-based psychological services to prevent and reduce the incidence of illness and to reduce mortality. HPs provide services at all stages, from the initial diagnosis to offering advice on emotional support in palliative care.

Psychological assessment provides insight into patients' experiences of illness and treatment and determines the need for psychological interventions. HPs may be asked to assess patients to identify processes involved in coping and adjusting to illness and treatment, to assist with psychological preparation for surgery, to facilitate pain management and symptom control and to understand and enhance motivation to adhere to treatments and rehabilitation.

Assessment interviews vary according to the patients' healthcare needs but will usually focus on a series of interviews assessing mood and affective state, perceptions, attitude and emotional reactions towards illness and treatment, social support, coping style, cognitive capacity, culture and their response to the healthcare system/environment. Assessments may involve psychometric questionnaire measures (e.g., the Hospital Anxiety and Depression Scale; the Illness Perception Questionnaire), pictorial maps (e.g., the McGill body pain locations diagram), visual analogue scales, patient diaries describing behaviours and thoughts, observations by the HP or proxy (e.g., family reports) and psychophysiological measures (e.g., blood pressure reactivity to a stress test). A combination of measures can maximize understanding of the patient's perspective and experience.

HPs should be skilled at eliciting information in patient interviews and communicating this information clearly to other healthcare professionals. For example, information about patients' cognitive capacity to perceive, retain and understand medical information can guide healthcare professionals' communication with a patient and provide vital information on a patient's capacity to consent to treatment. Psychological assessments may also guide referrals to liaison psychiatry, clinical psychology and social services.

HP interventions can be delivered within primary or secondary prevention services and are often employed as part of hospital outpatient programmes. HPs working with individual patients and groups design and implement goal-directed cognitive–behavioural interventions to modify risk factors for chronic illness such as obesity, smoking and stress and to change unhealthy behaviours including excessive alcohol consumption, poor nutrition and non-adherence to medical treatments.

For example, cognitive interventions to change patients' negative perceptions following a heart attack have been found to be effective in significantly reducing cardiac symptoms (Petrie et al., 2002) and in improving prognosis (Cossette et al., 2001). Other types of HP interventions include hospital surgical rehabilitation programmes, community health promotion clinics to motivate individuals to exercise, manage their health and adjust their lifestyle, self-efficacy enhancing interventions using health education materials and the promotion of adherence (e.g., among individuals diagnosed with long-term chronic conditions). A variety of techniques are incorporated into such interventions including cognitive behavioural therapy (White, 2001), stress/anger management (Mostofsky & Barlow, 2000), desensitization, cognitive restructuring and distraction (Deffenbacher & McKay, 2000; Smith, 2002), biofeedback (Schwartz & Andrasik, 2003), relaxation (Smith, 1999) and guided imagery, skills training and modelling (Hill, 2001).

Evidence-based interventions may be structured by models of the psychological determinants of health-related behaviours. For example, when encouraging patients to exercise following surgery, cognitive (e.g., fear of falling), behavioural (e.g., poor mobility) and environmental barriers (e.g., physiotherapy shortages) can undermine motivation, self-efficacy and setting specific goals (e.g., '*patient walks to the hospital canteen two times a day*', rather than e.g., '*patient is more mobile*') as well as highlighting positive consequences (e.g., going home to family) to facilitate change. Such interventions should be developed with the patient so that they are acceptable (e.g., not overly exhausting). In addition, the goals of healthcare professionals involved with the case need to be taken into consideration. For example, does the HP's advice involve taking up more physiotherapy time and, if so, how will this be funded?

HPs working in healthcare services must understand, and be able to skilfully negotiate, their particular healthcare system in order to maximize the impact of their work. The first point of contact with a patient may be a referral request. Maximizing referral information lays the foundation for a good understanding of the requested work and so enhances effectiveness. Of course, sometimes accepting a referral will necessitate a rapid decision but it is important to assess the appropriateness of a referral, just as it is important to understand and assess a consultancy request. For example, an HP could be asked, '*Will you go and see Mrs A . . . ? She needs to see you because she didn't turn up to clinic yesterday . . .*'. Asking for more thorough background medical and psychological information might reveal that the patient did not turn up to clinic because she was unwell and had been admitted to hospital. In this example, the person referring the patient had not investigated the cause of her non-attendance and the referral to a psychologist was premature. HPs must manage inappropriate referrals of this kind in a professional and efficient manner. They may also be used as an opportunity to educate professionals about referral criteria and the appropriateness of requests. In addition to receiving referrals, HPs will also be required to make appropriate and informative referrals to other agencies and professionals (see below).

CASE STUDY 18.1 Referral

A 54-year-old man on a respiratory hospital ward who had been recently diagnosed with Chronic Obstructive Pulmonary Disease was referred to the HP by a doctor. The patient's medical history was conveyed but the reason for the HP referral remained unclear. The referral information was conveyed verbally in a rush in a hospital corridor. The patient was said to be 'difficult' and it was noted that 'there's something not quite right about him'. When the HP asked about how the patient was coping, how he had responded to medical treatment and whether he accepted his diagnosis, the doctor revealed that the patient had denied the severity of his illness. He had been refusing treatment because he did not perceive a need for it. Specific questioning clarified a key feature of the case at the referral stage. The next stage, prior to contact with the patient, would be to establish whether the patient was aware of the referral and wanted a referral.

Professionals may also refer a patient to determine whether there are any psychological determinants of the patient's symptoms. Professionals will recognize their limitations for assessing this problem and so contact a psychologist who may subsequently take over the responsibility of care for the individual. HPs should work in liaison with other professionals, however, to determine whether there is a need for dual care responsibility and whether additional medical consultation may be recommended if psychological assessments are inconclusive.

In addition, during the course of any assessment or intervention, HPs should be observant and aware of the need for further medical investigation. HPs must balance a lack of medical expertise and their professional boundaries with the need to ensure that biological and physiological changes and symptoms are properly investigated even though there are psychological issues relating to the patient's health and wellbeing. HPs should not convey health-related information to patients that lies outside their area of expertise or that authorizes patients to change their treatment plan without consultation.

HPs can sometimes find themselves in a position that requires them to be an advocate for their patient, helping them to negotiate and facilitate services with professionals and organizations. HPs may receive referrals for patients who are unwilling to undergo surgery, change their lifestyle or agree with a treatment plan. Other professionals may assume that the HPs role is to 'persuade' the patient to follow the medical advice. However, the role may become one of advocating the patient's position and negotiating with the healthcare team on the patient's behalf (e.g., when a cancer patient accepts that they are terminally ill and decides not to have further treatment). Psychological assessment and communication skills are essential in this role.

CASE STUDY 18.2 Advocacy

A 24-year-old woman was admitted to hospital with acute heart failure and refused to have intravenous medication or be taken to intensive care. The medical team made an urgent referral to an HP stating that she could die if she did not get to intensive care within 48 hours. An extended assessment was conducted to assess the patient's capacity to make decisions about her care and future. This involved conducting brief tests of cognition, interviews with the patient and her family to assess their perceptions of the illness and treatment and the impact of socio-cultural beliefs on decision-making. Discussions were also conducted with the liaison psychiatrist regarding the implications of the assessment from a medico-legal perceptive. From the assessment it was clear that the woman and her supportive family had accepted that her genetic heart condition would eventually lead her into this position and she wanted to be supported at home to live out the remainder of her life. There were no surgical options for this woman and the thought of prolonging her death in intensive care was abhorrent to her religious and family beliefs. The woman was cognitively intact (e.g., had not suffered any brain injury/insult resulting in an ability to make decisions or understand information) and had made her decision over many months of deteriorating health. However, the multidisciplinary team involved in her care found it difficult to accept this decision. Following liaison between the patient, the family and the team, a sense of resolution developed and the team were able to make the transition from crisis management to supportive care.

HPs must communicate effectively with patients, carers, families and with other healthcare professionals. Communicating with patients involves acknowledging and understanding the unique circumstances in which they find themselves and, in the initial meeting, establishing what preparation they had for a meeting with a psychologist and what expectations they have of the HP. Negotiating mutually acceptable and realistic goals is often central to work with patients.

Communications with the healthcare team can vary from precise entries in medical records to regular multidisciplinary team meetings. Accurate confidential record-keeping and notes of correspondence demonstrate professional competence and assist careful planning and delivery of services. Good documentation is also important to HPs in the case of complaints. Written reports should be informative but succinct. Otherwise they may not be understood or even read.

Regular feedback on the outcome of assessments and interventions maintains good co-ordination between the team, helps to deliver efficient patient care and respect for the HP, and maintains the reputation of health psychology within healthcare services. There may also come a time when these are needed as evidence of appropriate and professional conduct in defence against complaints or serious allegations against a HP.

18.2 DELIVERING HEALTH PSYCHOLOGY TRAINING TO HEALTHCARE PROFESSIONALS

There are many opportunities to deliver training to professionals on an individual, group or organizational level, for example:

- An undergraduate medical degree director requests a course on health psychology for the intercalating medical students.
- A surgical ward nurse asks a HP to develop a training session on coping with 'tearful' patients.
- A director of an MSc course in Health Psychology requests a session from a HP to discuss professional practice skills in healthcare.
- The education and training manager of a hospital requests a communication skills session for a course on bereavement that is open to all staff.
- A HP develops a web-based training package to teach community nurses how to cope with the worries of newly diagnosed people with lung cancer.

- A HP writes an educational leaflet for a lay population on the service that HPs offer to hospital patients.
- A postgraduate psychology student on a practice placement requires HP supervision in a healthcare setting.

When preparing a training programme for students, the materials and content must be tailored to their learning objectives. Additional training materials, such as simple flow diagrams, can provide a quick way of communicating service delivery pathways or theoretical models. Case study presentations and discussions can demonstrate the application of psychological knowledge and skills in medical practice. It can be difficult to persuade students to engage with role play but this method can create opportunities for observational learning and skills rehearsal. Finally, problem solving enables students to use cognitive abilities in bringing together knowledge from different sources. Such active learning is more likely to be remembered and so influence future practice.

HPs may also use their competence in intervention design and delivery to support other healthcare professionals in delivering interventions and developing their own intervention design competence. For example, an HP could supervise a group of hospital-based physiotherapists conducting a cognitive-behavioural intervention to improve patients' motivation to exercise following coronary bypass graft surgery. Alternatively, an HP could train a group of rehabilitation nurses to implement anxiety management techniques with patients undergoing radiotherapy.

18.3 RESEARCH AND CONSULTANCY IN HEALTHCARE

Healthcare practice involves implementation, evaluation and revision of practice, policies and standards as well as the measurement of patient care and outcomes. During this process, questions and problems arise that require further investigation to promote evidence-based practice. This provides opportunities for HPs to influence standards of practice by drawing upon their research and consultancy competence (see Figure 18.1). HPs can be employed as researchers or consultants on medical or public health projects, in clinical audit or research departments in hospitals or as research or clinical governance officers in health authorities or NHS Trusts. HPs primarily involved in delivering patient care may also undertake research. For example, an HP working in a general hospital may be asked by the occupational health department to develop an organizational intervention to reduce workplace stress and improve staff sickness and absenteeism, or a medical consultant may ask an HP *'Why do only some of my patients panic when they have an asthma attack . . . could you find out?'*

HPs should assess their interests, resources and opportunities for psychological research and consultancy, and consult the organization's research strategy to identify those areas that are prioritized and financially supported. Consulting with relevant research committees within the organization can help establish collaborative networks for projects and raise the profile and funding of psychological research.

Submission of research projects to an ethics committee requires preparation of a research protocol and supporting materials (e.g., study information sheets, consent forms, questionnaires). In healthcare contexts the majority of the reviewers are not psychologists and therefore HPs must avoid the use of HP jargon and counter lay interpretations of psychology materials. For example, an ethics committee might object to a standardized, psychometrically validated HP questionnaire because *'it might make people depressed'*, unless they are reassured that the instrument has been used successfully with similar patients in the past and that the researcher has planned how to respond to patients who are upset by the questions. Communicating clearly with ethics and research committees is an important skill. It is also necessary to identify whether there are any other organizational structures or systems that should be informed of the project or that need to be involved in the development of the protocol (e.g., research services or clinical governance department, Department of Health steering group or advisory board, occupational health or human resource department). Gaining advice and support from these may help to prioritize HP research within often hierarchical and medical healthcare infrastructures.

It is important to consider whether ethical or practice issues are related to, or are a possible outcome of, the project, particularly where vulnerable groups of patients or medically unwell populations are being investigated. It is imperative to consider how to respond if patients become psychologically or medically unwell and its impact on the implementation of the project/study and its outcomes. It is good practice to discuss possible ethical and professional issues prior to commencement of the study/project and to adopt a policy of referring patients on if necessary, while documenting and acknowledging the impact on study results and recommendations. The HP's research/consultancy manager or professional adviser should be consulted if an ethical issue develops that is outside the HP's competence or experience to deal with.

CASE STUDY 18.3 Implementing HP research within existing services and systems

A consultant cardiologist approached an HP to request that a research project be designed to assess whether patients' beliefs about their medication and their adherence to anti-heart failure medication had a significant impact on their quality of life. The HP decided that it was necessary to determine whether this project was feasible within existing psychology services. The feasibility analysis indicated that it was not possible for the HP to collect the data although it would be possible for the HP to be involved in the analysis of the data. Therefore, as the project could be undertaken within a short time-frame and would not be costly in time or money it appeared appropriate to consider training another healthcare professional who would have the remit within their existing job description to implement this project. A nurse consultant in the hospital's heart failure out-patient clinic was trained by the HP to administer and score psychological measures and enter them into a SPSS database. The nurse also collated the pharmacological and medical data. The HP supervised this process and subsequently analysed the data. Then, in consultation with the nurse consultant and the consultant cardiologist, the HP wrote a report that recommended services and strategies designed to enhance management of patients' concerns regarding anti-heart failure medication and adherence to treatment. The HP then took the lead in writing up the study for publication.

CASE STUDY 18.4 Implementing HP consultancy within healthcare

The protocol

The Director of Nursing and Quality contacted a HP and asked for advice about how the Trust meets the emotional needs of physically ill patients admitted to hospital for treatment. The HP was asked to co-ordinate a project to review Trust policies, guidelines and practice and to recommend areas of improvement in line with the Department of Health's National Service Frameworks. The HP was required to develop the protocol, plan the feasibility and time-scale of the project and manage, analyse and report on the project outcomes and recommendations. The feasibility analysis of the time and resources required indicated that a variety of professional skills would be required. The protocol identified the need for a working party incorporating psychology, nursing, medical and administrative professionals to collate the relevant policy, guidelines and clinical practice knowledge. The protocol also included the responsibilities of each member of the working party, the time-scale for delivering an interim and final report and the Trust committees and services to be consulted on the outcomes. The project outcomes evaluated: (1) the multidisciplinary team's procedures for assessing the emotional needs of patients and their possible causes; (2) the process and efficacy of making an appropriate HP referral; (3) the outcome and impact of a HP referral; and (4) the extent to which individual medical directorates were able to financially and practically access HP services.

The implementation and outcome

The project took six months to complete. The working party met every three weeks to report on and evaluate their individual responsibilities and to review the project outcomes and time-scale. An interim report highlighted areas of practice that were unknown previously, in particular respiratory medicine psychology services that had been established through medical business plans rather than via the psychology service development plans and were managed within the medical directorate rather than by psychology. The HP circulated the final report within the Trust and, as a result, there were further suggestions to facilitate the implementation of the recommendations. The HP presented the final report at a Trust Directors' meeting. Two of the recommendations included the introduction of a psychology referral system that was generic for all medical directorates to reduce confusion regarding where services were accessed and multidisciplinary care plans were amended to include a screening assessment of patients' emotional state. A new budget to support the recommended changes was negotiated.

CASE STUDY 18.5 Implementing outcomes into healthcare practice

Results are presented from a longitudinal, HP research study investigating the impact of illness perceptions and mood on quality of life for patients with heart failure (see Figure 18.1). Figure 18.1 shows one way in which the recommendations of research are applied to hospital multidisciplinary practice and organization practice and policy.

When developing the rationale for healthcare research and consultancy it is important to identify relevant National Service Framework targets and standards and to draw upon NICE or Department of Health guidelines to support the need for conducting the project/study. Standards and targets for the delivery of healthcare are prioritized and so conducting research or consultancy to improve the efficacy of services and meet these standards is highly valued.

HPs must ensure availability of appropriate resources before embarking on research or consultancy. Resources can include additional personnel (administrative or clinical staff), space (notoriously difficult to find in most organizations), equipment (clinical or technical), time and funds. For example, where will interviews with patients be conducted if there is no room in an outpatient clinic? Resources and space within healthcare organizations are often scarce and need to be booked well in advance. HPs cannot assume that research can be conducted within the remit of existing roles and responsibilities. Staff time should be realistically costed and budgeted for before projects begin. Funding may be sought from a variety of sources (see also Chapter 9). These may include Primary Care Trusts (PCTs are the main budget holder for most funds associated with patient-focused services), healthcare charities, government councils, patient support groups or industrial medical companies (e.g., drug or medical equipment companies). The status of the project should also be considered, that is, whether it should be classified as research, clinical audit or consultancy. This may influence funding eligibility and the availability of staff to work on the project.

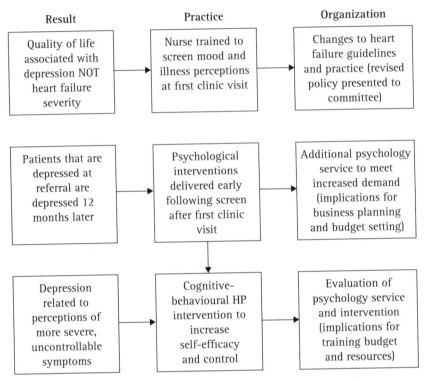

Figure 18.1 Applying recommendations of research to hospital multidisciplinary practice and organization practice and policy

18.4 SERVICE DEVELOPMENT AND HEALTHCARE POLICY

Health service managers and public officials routinely revise policies on service delivery and standards as a result of Department of Health studies and guidelines. HPs may be approached to assist in the revision of existing policies, which may involve the evaluation of a policy, or providing professional advice. In some cases, these may refer directly to the implementation of psychology services but sometimes they may affect psychological services or staff training indirectly. For example, if an extra hospital surgical theatre is built to accommodate more cardiac surgery patients then existing psychological services in cardiology may become inadequate. Thinking through the implications of organizational change for psychological services and for the psychological wellbeing of staff and patients is one of the responsibilities of HPs working in healthcare services.

18.5 SUPPORTING AND ADVISING OTHER HEALTHCARE PROFESSIONALS

HPs in healthcare settings are often asked to assist, advise or consult on a variety of issues. Much of this is informal. Below are five examples of the type of advice that can be requested.

- A diabetes specialist nurse asks for advice on how to assess a patient's emotional state.
- A hospital consultant requests regular advice on the psychological issues relevant to transplantation.
- An occupational therapist asks for advice on the type of measure that may be suitable for assessing patients' activities of daily living and quality of life after chemotherapy.
- A director of public health requests advice on the best psychological model to reduce drug addiction.
- A clinical psychologist in a community mental health team seeks advice regarding a useful psychometric assessment for a patient referred with chronic pain.

As with formal consultancy (see Chapter 12), it is necessary to assess what the person wants, whether as an HP you can provide appropriate advice and, if so, whether you have the resources to do so and how best to do so. It is useful to consider the following:

- What is the context of the request for advice (e.g., its purpose/value/outcome)?
- Is it appropriate for an HP to provide the advice?
- What form should the advice be provided in?

In providing advice, HPs must be clear about their own expertise in an area and the professional and ethical boundaries within which they work.

Often advice can be provided in an informal manner on a one-to-one basis. On the spot requests for information and guidance on patient care may require immediate responses. For example, a HP may be able to advise on the skills and tools that professionals could employ to assess and support the emotional state of patients. This advice could be given on the telephone, in person or through multidisciplinary ward meetings. However, more formal advice may be required when a need is identified. This could involve staff training such as a teaching session for nurses on the emotional consequences of surgery or the preparation of new guidelines. These more formal interventions may require additional resourcing to be agreed by management. A request for 'regular advice' may imply a change in the role of the HP and needs to be considered carefully in terms of resources and expertise. Providing such advice may highlight contradictions between psychological standards and professionals' expectations of psychological practice. Psychologists must provide evidence-based advice but the format of that advice should be negotiated with the team of involved professionals and a combination of formal and informal verbal and written advice is often required.

18.6 STAGE 2 HEALTH PSYCHOLOGY COMPETENCES COVERED IN THIS CHAPTER

This chapter discusses a range of HP work in healthcare settings and highlights the competences required to practise independently and efficiently. This chapter will help the reader acquire 19 of the 73 core competences:

1.3a Assess the opportunities, need and context for giving psychological advice
1.3b Provide psychological advice
1.3c Evaluate advice given
1.4a Evaluate feedback needs of client groups
1.4b Prepare and structure feedback to meet the needs of clients
1.4c Select method of communicating feedback to the needs of clients
1.4d Present and evaluate feedback to clients
2.5a Conduct research that will advance existing models, theories, instruments and methods
2.5b Monitor and evaluate studies in relation to agreed protocols
2.5c Clarify and evaluate the implications of research outcomes for practice
2.5d Evaluate the potential impact of new developments on organizational functioning and healthcare practices
3.4a Establish systems of processes to deliver the planned advice, research, interventions or activities in consultancy
3.4b Implement the planned advice, research, interventions or activities in consultancy
3.4c Close the consultancy
3.6a Identify evaluation needs and design evaluation to evaluate the impact of consultancy
3.6b Implement planned evaluation
3.6c Assess the outcomes of the evaluation

4.2a Implement training methods
4.2b Facilitate learning.

The core competences provide a framework for practising skills that can be utilized according to the demands and responsibilities of the individual working role. It should be clear that within applied practice many competences and skills are often practised simultaneously to deliver patient care and research and service development. The provision of direct patient care and the training of multidisciplinary professionals in psychological techniques are highly valued, as they are necessary to meet national targets for reducing health inequalities and improving treatment outcomes. Research competences (units 2.1–2.5) and evidence-based consultancy practice (units 3.1–3.6) are also highly valued and are integral to the objectives of the NHS Modernization Agenda, particularly to improve support for healthcare professionals and the standards of care and practice. Consultancy practice is developing in healthcare and there are examples of HPs being specifically commissioned to conduct consultancy work (see Quine, 1998). However, the resources available to conduct research and consultancy may not be readily available in all organizations and the project may need to be externally funded to support the extent of the time involved conducting the work. However, the opportunity to conduct this work should be maximized where possible as valuable experiences, skills and collaborations can be established and many professionals acknowledge the versatile skills of HPs.

HPs must be able to flexibly apply competences for multiple purposes. For example, when assessing the opportunity and need for giving advice (component 1.3a), HPs could consider giving advice regarding a patient's ability to cope with treatment or, in contrast, consider the need for giving advice about how a psychological service could be implemented within an existing cardiac rehabilitation programme. HPs working in healthcare services also need to be able to direct and implement high standards of research (component 2.5a) and apply them to their organization's policy and their own individual practice delivering patient care (components 5.3b, 5.4b).

Competences that are especially valuable when applying health psychology within a healthcare setting are those which facilitate the advancement of existing models, theories, instruments and methods (component 2.5a), assist in the development, evaluation and revision of healthcare policy and services (components 2.5c, d) and in the assessment (components 5.1a, b, c), delivery (components 5.1d, e) and the evaluation of behaviour change interventions to promote adjustment to treatment and care (components 5.1f, g).

HPs are also required to conduct needs-led and appropriately tailored training programmes for a range of multidisciplinary healthcare professionals (components 4.2a, b). Teaching sessions invariably focus on the psychological experience of illness and treatment, strategies for other professionals to conduct health behaviour change or psychological assessment, and the delivery of stress management techniques to support professionals. Competent HPs should be able to differentiate the needs of different professional groups and consider the healthcare outcomes and consequences of sessions.

18.6.1 Stage 2 optional competence units

In addition, many of the optional competence units have been identified as crucial to the application of HPs to deliver and evaluate patient care, services and healthcare policies. These are:

5.1 Implement interventions to change health-related behaviour
5.2 Direct the implementation of interventions
5.3 Communicate the processes and outcomes of psychological interventions and consultancies
5.4 Provide psychological advice to aid policy decision-making for the implementation of psychological services
5.5 Promote psychological principles, practices, services and benefits
5.6 Provide expert opinion and advice, including the preparation and presentation of evidence in formal settings
5.7 Contribute to the evolution of legal, ethical and professional standards in health and applied psychology.

Competences and skills relating to the practice of seven of the eight optional units, 5.1–5.3 (see Section 18.1), 5.4 (see Sections 18.3 and 18.4), 5.5 (see Section 18.2) and 5.6 and 5.7 (see Section 18.5) have been explored in various sections of this chapter. Optional units 5.1 and 5.2 are particularly useful for HPs who wish to work in the delivery of patient care. These units develop skills associated with assessing the cognitive behavioural elements of unhealthy behaviours, the identification and negotiation of goals to change behaviours and the development and implementation of a behaviour change plan. These skills are extremely useful to a variety of primary and secondary care healthcare practices although particularly in the areas of rehabilitation and health promotion. Directing and implementing interventions designed to change maladaptive and unhealthy behaviours such as reducing unhealthy eating and obesity, reducing teenage pregnancy and improving patients' adherence to medication are skills that HPs are extremely competent in and that health services desperately need. Other optional competences utilized in healthcare management roles involve the assessment and analysis of health policies to aid service decision-making (for unit 5.4 see Section 18.4). Policy revision and service development are a constant and ongoing task for health authorities. In addition, there are independent national organizations commissioned to measure and rate healthcare systems and so these types of roles are more prevalent and valued than ever before (e.g., NICE).

The reader should also have a clear insight into other competences that are relevant to working in healthcare systems and environments and that are not specifically tested in the stage 2 qualification. For example, HPs will need to understand the professional systems and culture of any health service they work in. HPs should also be aware of and study government healthcare policies and the reports of national organizations and institutes with a remit to evaluate health outcomes. The reference section of this chapter gives relevant UK websites, papers and books that will assist this process (e.g., Llewellyn & Kennedy, 2003).

REFERENCES AND ADDITIONAL READING

Belar, C.D., & Deardorff, W. (1996). *Clinical Health Psychology in Medical Settings: A Practitioner's Guide* (3rd edn). Washington: American Medical Association.

Bennett, P. (2000). *Introduction to Clinical Health Psychology*. Buckingham: Open University Press.

Boll, T., J. Bennett, Johnson, S., Perry, N. & Rozensky, R. (eds) (2002). *Handbook of Clinical Health Psychology: Medical Disorders and Behavioral Applications.* Volume 1. Washington, DC: American Psychological Association.

Clayton, S., & Bongar, B. (1994). The use of consultation in psychological practice: ethical, legal, and clinical considerations. *Ethics and Behavior* 4(1), 43–57.

Cossette, S., Frasure-Smith, N., & Lesperance, F. (2001). Clinical implications of a reduction in psychological distress on cardiac prognosis in patients participating in a psychosocial intervention program. *Psychosomatic Medicine* 63(2), 257–66.

Deffenbacher, J. & McKay, M. (2000). *Overcoming Situational and General Anger: A Protocol for the Treatment of Anger Based on Relaxation, Cognitive Restructuring, and Coping Skills Training.* New Harbinger Publishers.

Elliott, H. & Popay, J. (2000). How are policy makers using evidence? Models of research utilisation and local NHS policy making. *Journal of Epidemiology & Community Health* 54(6), 461–8.

Gatchel, R.J. & Oordt, M.S. (2003). *Clinical Health Psychology and Primary Care: Practical Advice and Clinical Guidance for Successful Collaboration.* Washington: American Psychological Association.

Harries, U. & Higgins, A. (1999). Evidence-based policy-making in the NHS: exploring the interface between research and the commissioning process. *Journal of Public Health Medicine* 21(1), 29–36.

Hill, C.E. (ed.) (2001). *Helping Skills: The Empirical Foundation*. Washington, DC: American Psychological Association.

Llewellyn, S. & Kennedy, P. (eds) (2003). *Handbook of Clinical Health Psychology*. Chichester: John Wiley & Sons.

Mostofysky, D.I. & Barlow, D.H. (2000). *The Management of Stress and Anxiety in Medical Disorders* (1st edn). Pearson Allyn & Bacon.

Oldenburg, B. (2002). Preventing chronic disease and improving health: broadening the scope of behavioral medicine research and practice. *International Journal of Behavioral Medicine* 9(1), 1–16.

Petrie, K.J., Cameron, L.D., Ellis, C.J., Buick, D. & Weinman, J. (2002). Changing illness perceptions after myocardial infarction: an early intervention randomized controlled trial. *Psychosomatic Medicine* 64(4), 580–6.

Quine, L. (1998). Effects of stress in an NHS Trust: a study. *Nursing Standard* 13(3), 36–41.

Salmon, P. (2000). *Psychology of Medicine and Surgery. A Guide for Psychologists, Counsellors, Nurses and Doctors*. Chichester: John Wiley & Sons.

Schwartz, M.S. & Andrasik, F. (eds) (2003). *Biofeedback: A Practitioner's Guide* (3rd edn). New York: Guilford Press.

Smith, J.C. (1999). *ABC Relaxation Training: A Practical Guide for Health Professionals*. New York: Springer Publishing Company.

Smith, J.C. (2002). *Stress Management: A Comprehensive Handbook of Techniques and Strategies*. New York: Springer Publishing Company.

Swann, C. (2001). Health psychologists in practice: A view from public health. *Health Psychology Update* 10(3), 23–6.

Tonks, S. (2001). Working towards chartered status: The experiences of a trainee health psychologist in the NHS. *Health Psychology Update* 10(3), 12–13.

White, C.A. (2001). *Cognitive Behavioural Therapy for Chronic Medical Problems: A Guide to Assessment and Treatment in Practice*. Chichester: John Wiley & Sons.

Wray, J. (2001). Health psychologists in paediatric cardiology – is anybody (else) out there? *Health Psychology Update* 10(3), 4–8.

Wren, B. & Michie, S. (2003). Staff experience of the healthcare system. In S. Llewelyn & P. Kennedy (eds), *Handbook of Clinical Psychology*. West Sussex: Wiley.

USEFUL WEBSITES

Action on Smoking and Health UK: http://www.ash.org.uk/
Commission for Health Improvement: www.chi.nhs.uk
Department of Health: www.doh.gov.uk
Department of Health's information on clinical governance: www.doh.gov.uk/clinicalgovernance
Department of Health's information on research: www.doh.gov.uk/research

Health Development Agency: www.hda-online.org.uk
Health Education Board Scotland: www.hebs.scot.nhs.uk
Health Professions Council: http://www.hpc-uk.org/
Health Protection Agency: www.hpa.org.uk
Health Service Journal: www.hsj.co.uk
Institute of Healthcare Improvement: www.ihi.org/
National Co-ordinating Centre for NHS Service Delivery and Organization,
    Research & Development (NCCSDO): www.sdo.lshtm.ac.uk/
National Electronic Library for Health: www.nelh.nhs.uk
National Health Service Modernization Agenda: www.modernnhs.uk
National Health Service UK: http://www.nhs.uk/
National Institute for Clinical Excellence (NICE): www.nice.org.uk
National Service Frameworks: www.doh.gov.uk/nsf.index/
Royal Institute for Public Health: www.riph.org.uk
Royal Society of Medicine: http://www.rsm.ac.uk/
The Health Foundation: http://www.health.org.uk/

Chapter 19

A FRAMEWORK FOR
PROFESSIONAL PRACTICE

Susan Michie

This chapter deals with the development of health psychology as a profession and some of the issues facing applied psychologists working within healthcare. It considers the differing roles that health psychologists can play, the competences necessary to perform these roles and the training required to achieve them. It discusses a range of generic competences in detail, emphasizes the importance of working with other disciplines within and outside psychology, and highlights the particular contributions that health psychology can make.

19.1 ORIGINS AND DEFINITIONS

Health psychology is a rapidly growing sub-discipline of psychology that emerged some three decades ago from several sources. These included social psychologists' increasing interest in health-related issues, a developing awareness among the medical profession that psychological expertise could contribute significantly to understanding and managing disease, and the increasing evidence that lifestyles were major causes of disease, disability and death in the developed world. An international review of the emergence of health psychology (Stone, 1990) concluded that the development of health psychology was facilitated by two main factors: (1) a strong and independent discipline and profession of psychology within countries; and (2) relatedly, access to health research and services that are not dominated by medicine or psychiatry. As health psychology developed, so behaviour change techniques used in clinical, occupational and educational psychology began to be applied in physical healthcare settings such as the treatment of hypertension, obesity, pain and addictions. This, in turn, created a demand for new professional practice and training.

Health psychology can be succinctly defined as the scientific study of the psychological processes involved in health, illness and healthcare. Research findings have been applied to:

- promotion and maintenance of health;
- prevention of illness and enhancement of outcomes of those who are ill;
- analysis and improvement of the healthcare system and health policy.

Health psychology research has been applied to the development and evaluation of interventions designed to change:

- behaviours influencing health (e.g., smoking, diet and physical activity);
- symptom management and illness behaviour (e.g., self-care in chronic illness and prompt and appropriate seeking of medical help);
- the behaviour of healthcare professionals and patients (e.g., in relation to doctor–patient communication);
- treatment behaviour (i.e., adherence).

Such interventions may be conducted at individual, group, organizational, community or population level.

19.2 Health Psychology as a Profession

As the role of health psychology has extended beyond generating knowledge to applying that knowledge, so the professional roles of health psychologists have also developed. While professional skills vary according to type of practice, there are many generic issues and competences that apply across roles, whether it is conducting laboratory research, teaching undergraduates, acting as an organizational consultant, evaluating and developing services, running smoking cessation clinics or helping individuals to manage pain or stress.

The key role of the professional psychologist has been defined as being able 'to develop and apply psychological principles, knowledge, models and methods in an ethical and scientific way in order to promote the development, well-being and effectiveness of individuals, groups, organisations and society' (European Federation of Professional Psychologists' Associations (EFPPA), 2001).

Professional psychologists apply psychology to everyday problems and questions in order to enhance the wellbeing of individuals, groups and systems. Health psychologists are informed by many other fields, such as social psychology, clinical psychology, public health, epidemiology, medicine and sociology. This varies in different countries, as does the route developed to achieve professional competence. Becoming a profession ensures minimum standards of competence in relation to academic and research expertise as well as in relation to practical skills. Professional bodies also ensure accountability in practice. This benefits not just applied psychologists but also the recipients of psychological services, employers, policy developers, other professions and the public. Health psychologists are represented within national professional associations of psychology worldwide and the great majority of these represent both the scientific and professional interests.

In the United States, health psychology was recognized as a separate professional specialty and proficiency by the American Psychological Association in 1997 (www.apa.org). However, this profession is 'clinical health psychology', which focuses on physical health problems and defines their 'client populations' by the physical symptoms or physical illness they experience. This is a narrower conceptualization of health psychology than in other parts of the world, such as Australia and Europe. The Australian College of Health Psychologists, established in 1996 (www.psychsociety.com.au), identifies two areas of practice: health promotion and clinical health. In their definition of health psychology, the first application listed is to 'the promotion and maintenance of health-related behaviour and healthy outcomes'. Professional training involves covering both areas, with the option of specializing in one.

In Europe, countries vary in their emphasis on public health and health promotion activities within health psychology (www.ehps.net). Countries also reflect different stages of professional development, as documented in a report of health psychology in 19 European countries (European Health Psychology Society (EHPS), 2000). This reports that 11 countries had independent postgraduate training in health psychology, seven had systems of professional regulation and three had the profession regulated in law.

In developing countries, the picture is even more diverse. Health psychology developed earliest and most rapidly in those countries with strong commitments to community development and centralized planning of healthcare. A successful example of this is Cuba, where health psychology started in 1969 and enjoys a prominent role within healthcare and community life (Garcia-Averasturi 1980, 1985). A preventative and community-based psychology in primary healthcare is seen as the most effective approach to reduce poverty-related and lifestyle-related ill health and to improve child and family health. Psychologists are central to the multi-disciplinary 'polyclinics' which form the backbone of the Cuban healthcare system. Most professional psychologists are generalists, educating other professionals; contributing to health promotion programmes in communities, schools and workplaces; working to improve communication within families, reduce unwanted pregnancies and foster healthy child development (Kristiansen and Søderstrøm, 1990).

19.3 THE DEVELOPMENT OF PROFESSIONAL HEALTH PSYCHOLOGY IN EUROPE

In 1981, the European Federation of Professional Psychologists' Associations (EFPPA, www.efppa.org) was founded to organize national professional associations of psychology across Europe (worldwide, the International Association of Applied Psychology serves the same purpose: IAAP, www.iaapsy.org). European, applied psychologists work as independent professionals as part of the healthcare services. Health psychologists constitute one of the disciplines of applied psychologists in health and social care: others are clinical psychologists, counselling/psychotherapy psychologists, educational psychologists and occupational psychologists. Overlapping areas between these disciplines have been identified by an EFPPA task force (Marks et al., 1998, p. 153):

Health, clinical and psychotherapy psychologists work with:
(a) individuals, couples, families, groups and communities
(b) people of all ages
(c) in institutions, organizations and companies
(d) in the public, private and voluntary sectors.

They undertake:
(a) assessment and diagnosis
(b) intervention and treatment
(c) teaching and training
(d) supervision, counselling and consultancy
(e) evaluation, research and development

in various areas of application:
(a) promotion of well-being
(b) prevention of deterioration of health
(c) intervention in psychological aspects of physical health
(d) intervention in psychological aspects of mental health
(e) promotion of optimum development and ageing.

They are responsible for:

(a) the delivery of good services with respect to standards of quality and control
(b) planning of new services
(c) informing and influencing the health care system and policy.

These activities require psychologists to have a good grasp of the evidence that informs these activities and to have the professional skills required to translate this evidence into practice.

19.4 PROFESSIONAL ISSUES

Professional health psychologists require an understanding of the place and status of *health psychology in society*, including the health and psychological needs of individuals in their society and their own obligations, rights and restrictions. This involves being well informed of the political, social and legislative context of their work including national and regional health policies, relevant legislation and the codes of ethics and conduct (especially those of their own professional and/or licensing body). The best way of keeping up to date with changing legislation and government policies and strategies is to regularly consult the key websites (such as those of national government departments of health).

Professional practice also requires a knowledge of the variety of *values and codes of behaviour* held within society, including those held by minority ethnic and disadvantaged groups. This is especially important, since health psychologists rarely represent the socio-economic and ethnic mix of their clients. Health psychologists should aim for equality of opportunity in all their work, such that no colleague, research participant or user of psychological services receives less favourable treatment on the grounds of, for example, gender, colour, ethnic origin, nationality, religion, disability or age. They must not condone values or behaviours that are illegal, immoral or harmful to others and must act to protect those at risk of harm.

Many health psychologists work in multidisciplinary settings and teams, whether conducting research, providing services or offering consultancy. This requires awareness of other disciplines' theories, practice and ethical principles, and finding ways of respecting others' views while not always agreeing with them.

All professionals have an obligation to the public and to the profession *to continue their professional development* throughout their working lives. Health psychology is evidence based and theory based: competence includes updating knowledge of both and updating skills of their application (see

Chapter 2). Health psychologists who read current research literature are able to challenge unsubstantiated beliefs about evidence-based practice and keep abreast of the theories for which there is accumulating evidence of their validity. For example, they have pointed out that the popular stages of change, or 'transtheoretical' model is not supported by evidence (Littrell and Girvin, 2002; Sutton, 2000). This requires time: time to read and attend seminars and conferences. Without this investment, professional skills may become outdated and they may not be able to offer the best advice to their clients. For example, in relation to the generation and evaluation of evidence, the ability to perform power calculations to estimate necessary sample sizes in research is fundamental to quality research. Similarly, the competence to plan, conduct and evaluate systematic literature reviews is now expected within health psychology (see Chapter 8): ten years ago, both these skills were regarded as esoteric, now they are part of everyday practice.

There is an expectation that health psychologists will be involved in *training and supervising* psychologists and members of other professions. Psychologists are responsible for monitoring the performance of others in their application of psychological principles and ensuring that they demonstrate competence in their practice. This applies not only to doctoral students and psychology trainees but to nurses, doctors and other professions that psychologists may train. Such training may involve acquisition of the implications of psychological research for practice (e.g., through lectures and seminars in medical and nursing degrees) as well as the development and implementation of skills such as breaking bad news to patients or designing and evaluating behaviour change interventions. The ultimate objective of training should be professional *autonomy and independence*. This requires mutual respect across healthcare professions, and may be helped by legislation and regulations, such as the demand for statutory registration.

Quality control mechanisms help to maintain high standards of practice in line with advances in their field, as does supervision of staff at all levels of experience. For senior staff, this may be most appropriately organized outside their professional specialty. Appraisals, whether formal or informal, are most effective when they are regular and linked to goal setting and continuing professional development. Worthwhile appraisals are geared to future development as well as current practice, addressing the question 'where does the person want/need to get to, and what is required to make that happen?'. Appraisal provides an opportunity for the psychologist to reflect on their recent past achievements, to assess the reasons for strengths and weaknesses, to analyse the potential for progress and to develop strategies to make the most of current opportunities and to create new ones.

Health psychologists cannot always do all the things that others expect of them. Competent practice involves assessing work demands and ensuring that one works *within the limits of one's own competence*. Psychologists must, therefore, be clear about the nature of their qualifications and the limits of their skills, techniques and understanding. When they assess demands to be beyond their levels of competence, they have a responsibility to refer the person or issue on to an appropriately qualified professional, either within or across disciplines. For example, psychologists should not provide counselling or implement behaviour change interventions unless they have been specifically trained and qualified in these techniques. One advantage of a competence-based qualification is that it is precise about the competences that an individual has attained in training. Of course individual health psychologists augment their qualifications and competence and so may, or may not, have the ability to advise on policy development. Psychologists have the responsibility to maintain and develop their professional competence, to recognize and work within their limits and to identify and remedy factors which restrict their competence.

Personal conduct is a professional issue. As a professional, whether one is working within a research, teaching, consultancy or behaviour change setting, there are questions of power boundaries and respect for people's rights and dignity. Awareness of differences across culture, ethnic groups, class and gender is key to sensitive communication and challenging prejudice and discrimination. Professional relationships with colleagues, students and clients requires awareness of power differentials and monitoring any aspects of these relationships which may involve misuse of that power.

They also require clearly established interpersonal boundaries, for example in degree of familiarity and self-disclosure. It is essential that psychologists be familiar with the codes of conduct and ethics of the professional organizations to which they belong. *Conflicts of interest* should always be declared to appropriate managers, colleagues or clients, immediately. Such conflicts may be academic, for example reviewing a journal article reporting work one has been involved with, or professional, for example being asked to provide advice or evaluate a proposal when one has a vested interest in implied resource allocation or personal, for example when one has a pre-existing relationship with a potential client.

'Psychologists . . . strive to help the public in developing informed judgements and choices regarding human behaviour, and to improve the condition of both the individual and society' (EFPPA, 1995). More specifically, an individual or organization has the right to choose whether to receive psychological assessment or intervention and to make the choice on the basis of the best information available. Thus psychologists have an obligation to facilitate and ensure *informed consent in health psychology applications*. Consent should be formal, recorded and reviewed, rather than assumed. This is as true for research and teaching as it is for organizational and individual services.

Research is crucial to the advancement of knowledge and its application and most health psychologists are involved in research. With increasing attention being paid to research governance, there are increasing demands for all research activity to be approved by local or national research ethics committees. A general rule of thumb is that any data collection that may lead to publication or to findings generalizable across settings requires ethical approval. No longer can ethical approval for research be avoided under the guise of audit or service evaluation.

Potential research participants must be informed of all aspects of the research that might influence their willingness to participate, including the aims of the research and any anticipated risks of distress. No pressure for participation should be exerted and patients should be informed that neither consent nor refusal will influence the nature of their care, and that they will be free to withdraw from the research at any time, without giving a reason. This, in turn, has resource implications that need to be taken into account in planning research projects. Informed consent is needed both for research procedures and the publication of results.

The legal duty to ensure *confidentiality* refers to identifiable personal health information. When such information is identifiable, it should be treated with respect and shared only when necessary. The only circumstances in which confidentiality may be broken, without consent, is when the health or safety of others or the public is at risk.

Following informed consent for client material to be published, care needs to be taken to ensure its complete anonymity. This includes clinical audit. When working with other disciplines, psychologists must inform themselves of new confidentiality practices. Psychologists are responsible for ensuring the security of records they keep or contribute to, which includes being aware of the range of access to any such records and knowing when such data should be destroyed. The storage of data on computer is covered by data protection legislation which psychologists must be familiar with.

The ethics of publication also involves appropriate acknowledgement of the contributions that others have made to the work. This implies that authorship rights should be discussed with co-workers at the beginning of the research and as research proceeds towards publication. Different authors may make different contributions, both practical and intellectual (Game & West, 2002) and some journals (e.g., the *British Medical Journal*) now require authors to declare their particular contributions.

Using *the media* to disseminate psychological expertise can be extremely effective. However, psychologists must guard against misrepresentation and sensationalism. Employers may have their own guidelines for dealing with the media, and the public and media training and support from a media officer at work can be invaluable. It is desirable, though not always possible, to see and agree the edited version of what has been said and agreed before transmission. It is also helpful to base one's statements on evidence and clarify their status, for example whether they are the results of research and how extensive that research was, or personal views or views representing the profession or an employer. Psychologists should not comment on areas beyond their competence as this may bring the profession into disrepute. It is also wise to be aware of reporters' motivation to heighten the impact of their stories.

Psychologists may want to express concerns publicly about their employers, practices or legislation. In such instances, consulting relevant individuals or organizations (e.g., line manager, trade union, professional body) can ensure that their comments do not breach guidelines and risk disciplinary action.

Psychologists should ensure that they *safeguard their physical and psychological wellbeing* so that they maintain their *fitness to practise*. In the event that a colleague has become unfit to practise, psychologists have a responsibility to take action on their behalf. Making judgements about one's own and others' fitness to practise involves balancing personal and professional priorities and loyalties with potential costs to clients, colleagues and oneself. Practising while unwell may put others' safety at risk.

19.5 PROFESSIONAL COMPETENCES IN HEALTH PSYCHOLOGY

Professional organizations have an absolute responsibility to ensure that training programmes match the demands of psychologists' employment. Professional qualifications (and their assessments) as well as opportunities for continuing professional development must allow psychologists to competently perform their work roles. The emergence of health psychology as a profession has involved identification of:

- required work competences;
- appropriate methods of teaching and training;
- types of supervised experience necessary to develop skills and confidence; and

- the time needed for people to consolidate their knowledge and skills to the point where they are competent to practise on their own, without supervision (see Chapter 2).

For example, a consultation-based study of professional psychological practice by the British Psychological Society produced a specification of occupational standards in terms of six key roles.

1 Develop, implement and maintain personal and professional standards and ethical practice.
2 Apply psychological and related methods, concepts, models, theories and knowledge derived from reproducible research findings.
3 Research and develop new and existing psychological methods, concepts, models, theories and instruments in psychology.
4 Communicate psychological knowledge, principles, methods, needs and policy requirements.
5 Develop and train the application of psychological skills, knowledge, practices and procedures.
6 Manage the provision of psychological systems, services and resources.

Of these, the first four were considered to apply to all professional psychologists, while the latter two were more specialized roles and more likely to apply once individuals have become independent practitioners rather than being a requirement for practice.

19.6 A Competence-based Qualification in Health Psychology

A competence-based qualification in professional development has been developed in the UK, under the auspices of the British Psychological Society (http://www.health-psychology.org.uk). It is the first competence-based psychology qualification in the UK. In specifying the detailed competences required, the qualification achieves two main purposes:

1 It communicates to the public, employers and service users exactly what health psychologists in general (and individual health psychologists with optional competences) can and cannot do.
2 It allows those who already possess some of the competences to receive accreditation for their prior experience and/or training. One of the advantages of this is to facilitate lateral transfer between different branches of applied psychology.

This qualification requires a first stage of training involving acquisition of a knowledge base (e.g., through an accredited Master's programme) and a second stage to acquire and demonstrate a range of 19 core and two out of eight optional competences. Core competences lie in four areas: generic professional competence, research, teaching and training, and consultancy.

- *Generic professional competence* comprises the competences to implement and maintain systems for legal, ethical and professional standards in applied psychology; contribute to the continuing development of one-self as a professional applied psychologist; provide psychological advice and guidance to others; and provide feedback to clients.
- *Research competence* involves skills in a variety of research types, for example, randomized controlled trials, health service evaluation and clinical audit studies, qualitative studies, analogue or vignette studies as well as systematic reviews of evidence and meta-analyses of quant-itative data. Welcome trends in health psychology research include a shift from understanding causal processes in behavioural regulation, to evaluation of interventions to change health behaviours in practice, and the study of observed, rather than self-reported, behaviour.
- *Teaching and training competence* involves the ability to plan, design, deliver and evaluate training programmes to teach psychological know-ledge, skills and practices. This may be to individuals, communities or the general population.
- *Consultancy* is the process by which one party (individual or organiza-tion) formally seeks and receives the advice of another. The consultee poses the initial questions and the consultant shapes them, proposes a method to address them, implements the process and reports back. The consultant does this on the basis of available relevant evidence and theory and uses research skills to inform and evaluate the con-sultancy. Communication and negotiation skills are crucial to suc-cessful consultancy. Health psychology consultancy is the use of these skills to facilitate, develop or enhance the effectiveness of others in the maintenance and improvement of health. More details of the con-sultancy role and examples of consultancy work can be found in Michie (1998).

The four main units of generic professional competence outlined above each include three to five components which, in turn, are made up of two to eight specific guidelines on how to acquire and assess the competence described by each component. There are 75 core components of com-petence and these are used as the unit of assessment. Candidates are also examined on the components of two further optional units. These are outlined in Appendix 19.1.

19.7 A EUROPEAN FRAMEWORK FOR THE TRAINING OF PSYCHOLOGISTS

In 1990, optimal standards for training required for autonomous professional practice in Europe were agreed (EFPPA, 1990). These were of a general nature and have been used by countries to develop their own qualifications. Although the education and training of professional psychologists vary between European countries, particularly in its structure and in the name of the final title, there is considerable overlap in content and required competences.

In order to ensure uniform minimum standards within Europe, to simplify the recognition of qualifications and to facilitate the mobility of psychologists between countries, a 'European Framework for Psychologists' Training' has been developed (see EFPPA website). This project, funded by the EU under its Leonardo da Vinci programme, and involving 12 countries and EFPPA, is developing a 'European Diploma'. The project team has considered both 'input' (curriculum) and 'output' (competence) approaches to the development of this framework. There is broad agreement that six years' training is required to prepare for independent professional practice, including five years of academic study (providing the basic knowledge base and theoretical foundation and a substantial grounding in research and applications of psychology), and at least one year of supervised practice.

The aim of supervised practice is to enable students to:

- integrate theoretical and practical knowledge;
- apply procedures related to psychological knowledge;
- practise under supervision;
- reflect upon and discuss own and other people's activities;
- work in a setting with professional colleagues.

Supervised practice may be in the following areas: clinical psychology, community psychology, counselling psychology, school and educational psychology, organizational and work psychology, economic psychology, psychological assessment and evaluation, environmental psychology, applied gerontology, forensic psychology, neuropsychology, sport psychology, health psychology, applied cognitive psychology, traffic and transportation psychology, political psychology. In addition, psychologists may be involved in other areas such as disaster, crisis and trauma, consumer behaviour, and issues of cultural and ethnic diversity.

19.8 PROFESSIONAL HEALTH PSYCHOLOGY IN PRACTICE

19.8.1 Healthcare services

Health psychologists have become vital members of multidisciplinary clinical and research teams in a wide variety of medical fields, including rehabilitation, cardiology, paediatrics, oncology, anaesthesiology, family practice and dentistry. They operate at many levels, assessing and advising on individual behaviour of both patients and health professionals and of systems within which they function. Coping with threat, communication and behaviour change are just three issues relevant to both patients and health professionals. Evaluating the effectiveness of services and making recommendations on their development is another area in which health psychologists can make a valuable contribution.

19.8.2 Health promotion and public health

Leading causes of mortality have substantial behavioural components (e.g. drug and alcohol use, unsafe sexual behaviour, smoking and sedentary lifestyle). Thus modifying these behaviours is the main focus of health promotion and disease prevention. While this is most commonly considered in relation to lifestyles and diseases of affluence, it is also true of lifestyles and diseases of poverty, where hygienic behaviours are essential to survival (Aboud, 1998). With increasing appreciation of the economic and social benefits achievable through evidence-based prevention, demand is growing for psychologists to be involved in the design, co-ordination and evaluation of health promotion programmes. For example, health psychologists can identify beliefs, cognitions and regulatory processes that maintain or promote adoption of health-risk behaviours and then design health promotion materials that directs target the psychological antecedents of these behaviours (Abraham et al., 2002).

Although it is generally accepted that health education and promotion programmes are more powerful if they are theory based and evidence based, they have often been only loosely associated with theory and evidence (Michie and Abraham, 2004). Methods for designing interventions so that they are well grounded in theory and evidence have been developed by health and social psychologists (Kok and Schaalma, 1998). Steps include:

- defining performance objectives;
- selecting theory-based methods on the basis of specified criteria for choosing a theory and evaluating evidence;
- translating theoretical methods into practical strategies, for example by identifying determinants of the component behaviours and tailoring the intervention for sub-populations;
- deciding on scope, sequence, materials, pretesting and production;
- setting up mechanisms to facilitate awareness, adoption and implementation;
- anticipating evaluation by carefully stating the expected effects and processes in advance.

Health psychologists are also increasingly to be found in Departments of Epidemiology, Public Health or Population Sciences. 'Public health psychology' has been described as the fusion of three elements (Wardle, 2001a).

1 Consideration of the relevance of psychological processes to public health issues. The shift from individual-level to population-level explanations has meant that factors such as ethnicity and socio-economic status are the subjects of interest rather than potential confounds to be partialled out of statistical analyses. There is a growing interest in understanding how social influences on health get 'under the skin' (Taylor et al., 1997).
2 Use of some of the methodological strengths of epidemiology, with its emphasis on rigorous sampling, studies powered to detect small effects and sophisticated statistical multi-level modelling.
3 The extension of psychology's strong empirical tradition to providing convincing evidence for the effectiveness of psychological interventions on a public health scale.

Following initial results of effectiveness, research can refine and improve the interventions to analyse effects on different sectors of the population and to advise on dissemination and implementation. This is the basis from which to persuade social and health policy-makers to use psychological research findings.

19.8.3 Beyond healthcare systems

Workplace and school-based interventions also have the potential to alter health behaviour patterns because people spend a substantial part of their lives in these contexts, and because the earlier that healthy behaviours are established, the more likely they are to persist. Work site interventions include those aimed at changing individual behaviour and those aimed at organizational change. An example of the former is a trial of a worksite intervention to reduce cardiovascular disease factors, comparing assessment of health risk, education about risk factors and behaviour change counselling (Oldenburg et al., 1995). Behaviour change counselling was both effective at reducing risk after 12 months and cost-effective. An example of the latter is the Brabantia project in the Netherlands which intervened to change both lifestyle and working conditions and found reduced health risks one year later compared to a control group (Maes et al., 1998).

School based interventions focus on establishing health-related behaviours at an early age. This may include promotion of competent problem solving, coping and seeking social support. In such work, educational and health psychologists may benefit from collaboration. Health psychologists have typically been involved in interventions designed to reduce health risk behaviours, such as smoking, drug use or unprotected sex or to increase health-related behaviours such as exercise and eating fruit and vegetables. An example is the development of theory-driven, research-based school sex education programmes (Kirby et al., 1994; Schaalma et al., 1996). Programmes applying psychological principles to school sex education have also been developed and tested in the UK (e.g., Mellanby et al., 1995; Wight & Abraham, 2000). Wight et al. (1988) describe how psychological and sociological theory were combined to develop a framework for the development of intervention materials used in the SHARE ('Sexual Health and Relationships – Safe, Happy and Responsible') sex education programme and Wight and Abraham (2000) discuss the practical difficulties of translating theory and research based interventions into sustainable classroom practice.

19.8.4 Working with other professions

Health psychologists work closely with professionals in other fields, such as medicine, nursing, social work and general management. Within multidisciplinary teams, the psychologist adds a distinct perspective, asks particular types of questions that complement those of other professionals, and uses empirically validated interventions and measures. Psychologists also work with other professionals to help change their behaviour to provide more effective treatment and advice.

While developing multidisciplinary work, health psychologists will strengthen their contribution by working with other psychology disciplines (e.g., clinical and occupational) and with other applied psychologists internationally. Increasing collaboration across and between disciplines and across countries will help to gain more resources for research and its application and to maximize the effective output of those resources.

19.8.5 Disseminating psychological output

Making a difference in practice requires effectively disseminating research findings to those who can make a difference, and helping them find ways of implementing recommendations and maintaining changes (Oldenburg, 2001). While considerable effort and resources have been devoted to developing effective interventions, relatively little attention has been given to developing and researching effective methods for promoting use.

> It's no longer enough to end our papers by saying that our findings have great potential for health gain. We have to prove it. We have to show that our interventions work in the initial test populations, then we have to prove that they work when applied in the real world when administered by individuals not pursuing research, and delivered to individuals who are not subjects in research. We have to assess the potential reach, and therefore the impact of our interventions, and we have to look to developing them into disseminable forms and creating the conditions in which they can readily be adopted. Only by taking this route will we produce evidence that will convince policy makers to take our findings seriously ... We also need to think how to formulate our work so that we can present it to policy makers (Wardle, 2001b: 46).

19.9 FUTURE DEVELOPMENTS

A central principle of the vision for professional health psychology is the WHO goal that all people have a right to health and healthcare (WHO, 1995). Despite this, there are glaring inequalities in health throughout the world and within relatively affluent parts of the world, such as Europe. Health inequalities reflect social inequalities, for example, in wealth, educational opportunities, employment security and experience of discrimination and persecution. The content and form of our professional activity should be shaped by awareness of these variations and by a commitment to work to try to reduce them. There are also inequalities in access to health education and services. The principle of equity requires psychologists to provide their services 'to all people regardless of gender, age, religion, ethnic grouping, social class, material circumstances, political affiliation or sexual orientation. When access is low, or when there is evidence of greater needs, special efforts should be made to target service on those with the poorest access or greatest need, for example, refugees, the homeless, lower income groups' (Marks et al., 2003, pp. 19–20).

A call has been made for health psychologists to move away from individualistic models of health behaviour to:

- work with more collective and population-based models, interventions and outcomes;
- engage in public policy and debates about resource allocation;
- address causes of ill health, such as social inequalities and poverty (e.g., Kaplan, 1994; Oldenburg, 2001; Wardle, 200la).

This will involve a more political role for psychologists:

> For this change to occur, psychologists must assume a more visible profile in lobbying at local, state and national tiers to ensure that behavioral issues are included in policy formation, research agenda, and the allocation of services. This change also dictates an increased involvement of psychologists in public and private efforts and activities that influence health policy. If professional psychology fails to assume this responsibility and meet this challenge, the profession risks being marginalized as a stake holder in the health care system (Johnstone et al., 1995: 346–7).

19.10 Competences Covered

The scientific study of the psychological processes of health, illness and healthcare has generated potentially useful evidence. Such evidence can be used to promote and maintain health; analyse and improve healthcare systems and health policy formation; and prevent illness and disability and enhance outcomes of those who are ill or disabled. To achieve such aims, it is necessary for health psychologists to develop professional skills in research, consultancy and teaching/training. Knowledge of relevant evidence and the skills to apply it equip health psychologists to work effectively in many settings, ranging from working with individuals to prevent or manage health problems to intervening in organizational systems such as health service providers to providing advice at a public health policy level.

The four core units of generic professional competence should not be seen as 'stand alone' but as a dimension of good practice running throughout all the other competences. A key part of professional practice is to ensure legal and ethical standards, which requires a good working knowledge of relevant legislation and professional and institutional policies (unit 1.1). This will include understanding the importance of confidentiality of information and knowing how to manage this (1.1a), ensuring that there are systems in place to monitor and maintain good professional practice (1.1b) and working within the limits of one's competence (1.1c). With increasing detailed and rigorous approaches to research and clinical governance, continuing professional development should be central (unit 1.2.). The competences covered in unit 1.3, 'Providing psychological advice and guidance to others' and unit 1.4. 'Providing feedback to clients' are invaluable for consultancy (units 3.1–3.6) and all the optional units:

5.1 Implement interventions to change health-related behaviour

5.2 Direct the implementation of interventions

5.3 Communicate the processes and outcomes of psychological interventions and consultancies

5.4 Provide psychological advice to aid policy decision making for the implementation of psychological services

5.5 Promote psychological principles, practices, services and benefits

5.6 Provide expert opinion and advice, including the preparation and presentation of evidence in formal settings

5.7 Contribute to the evolution of legal, ethical and professional standards in health and applied psychology

5.8 Disseminate psychological knowledge to address current issues in society.

ACKNOWLEDGEMENTS

This chapter has been informed by the Stage 2 Qualification in Health Psychology developed by the Division of Health Psychology of the British Psychological Society (BPS) and by the Professional Practice Guidelines of the Division of Clinical Psychology, BPS, 1995 and comments on an earlier draft by Professor Suzanne Skevington, University of Bath and Professor Charles Abraham, University of Sussex.

REFERENCES

Aboud, F.E. (1998). *Health Psychology in Global Perspective*. London: Sage.

Abraham, C., Krahé, B., Dominic, R., & Fritsche, I. (2002). Does research into the social cognitive antecedents of action contribute to health promotion? A content analysis of safer-sex promotion leaflets. *British Journal of Health Psychology* 7, 227–46.

EFPPA (1990). *Optimal Standards for Training of Professional Psychologists*. Brussels: European Federation of Professional Psychologists' Associations.

EFPPA (1995). *European Federation of Professional Psychologists' Associations' Metacode of Ethics*. Stockholm: European Federation of Professional Psychologists' Associations.

EFPPA (2001). *A European Framework for Psychologists' Training*. Brussels: European Federation of Professional Psychologists' Associations.

EHPS (2000). *Post-graduate Programs in Health Psychology in Europe: A Reference Guide*. Leiden, The Netherlands: European Health Psychology Society.

Game, A. & West, M.A. (2002). Principles of publishing. *The Psychologist* 15, 126–9.

Garcia-Averasturi, L. (1980). Psychology and health care in Cuba. *American Psychologist* 35, 1090–5.

Garcia-Averasturi, L. (1985). Community health psychology in Cuba. *Journal of Community Psychology* 13, 117–23.

Johnstone, B., Frank, R.G., Belar, C. et al. (1995). Psychology in health care: Future directions. *Professional Psychology: Research and Practice* 26, 341–65.

Kaplan, R.M. (1994). The Ziggy theorem: Toward an outcomes-focused health psychology. *Health Psychology*, 13, 451–60.

Kirby, D., Short, L., Collins, J., et al. (1994). School-based programs to reduce sexual risk behaviours: A review of effectiveness. *Public Health Reports* 10, 339–60.

Kok, G. & Schaalma, H. (1998). Theory-based and evidence-based health education intervention programmes. *Psychology and Health* 13, 747–51.

Kristiansen, S. & Soderstrom, K. (1990). Cuban health psychology: A priority is the primary health care system. *Psychology and Health* 4, 65–72.

Littrell, J.H. & Girvin, H. (2002). Stages of change: A critique. *Behavior Modification* 26, 223–73.

Maes, S., Verhoeven, C., Kittell, F. & Scholten, H. (1998). Effects of a Dutch work-site wellness-health program: The Brabantia project. *American Journal of Public Health* 88, 1037–41.

Marks, D. (1996). Health psychology in context. *Journal of Health Psychology* 1, 7–21.

Marks, D.F., Brucher-Albers, C., Konker, F.J.S. et al. (1998). Health psychology 2000: The development of professional health psychology. *Journal of Health Psychology* 3, 149–60.

Marks, D.F., Sykes, C.M. & McKinley, J.M. (2003). Health psychology: Overview and professional issues'. In A.M. Nezu, C.M. Nezu & P.A. Geller (eds), *Handbook of Psychology*. Vol. 9. *Health Psychology*, 5–23. Hoboken, NJ: John Wiley.

Mellanby, A.R., Phelps, F.A., Crichton, N.J. and Tripp, J.H. (1995). School sex education: An experimental programme with educational and medical benefit. *British Medical Journal* 311, 414–17.

Michie, S. (1998). Consultancy. In D.W. Johnston and M. Johnston (eds), *Health Psychology*, Vol. 8, *Comprehensive Clinical Psychology*, 153–69. Amsterdam: Elsevier Science.

Michie, S. and Abraham, C. (2004). Identifying techniques that promote health behaviour change: Evidence based or evidence inspired? *Psychology and Health* 19, 29–49.

Oldenburg, B. (2001). Public health as social sciences. In N.J. Smelser and P.B. Battes (eds), *The International Encyclopaedia of the Social and Behavioural Sciences*. Oxford: Elsevier.

Oldenburg, B., Owen, N., Parle, M. and Gomel, M. (1995). An economic evaluation of four work site based cardiovascular risk factor interventions. *Health Education Quarterly* 22, 9–19.

Schaalma, H.P., Kok, G., Bosker, R.J., Parcel, G.S., Peters, L., Poelman, J., and Reinders, J. (1996). Planned development and evaluation of AIDS/STD education for secondary-school students in the Netherlands: Short-term effects. *Health Education Quarterly* 23, 469–87.

Stone, G.C. (1990). An international review of the emergence and development of health psychology. *Psychology and Health* 4, 3–17.

Sutton, S. (2000). A critical review of the transtheoretical model applied to smoking cessation. In P. Norman, C. Abraham & M. Conner (eds), *Understanding and Changing Health Behaviour: From Health Beliefs to Self-regulation*, 207–25. Amsterdam: Harwood Academic.

Taylor, S.E., Repetti, R.L. & Seeman, T.E. (1997). Health psychology: What is an unhealthy environment and how does it get under the skin? *Annual Review of Psychology*, 48, 411–47.

Wardle, J. (2001a). Public health psychology: Expanding the horizons of health psychology. *British Journal of Health Psychology* 5, 329–36.

Wardle, J. (2001b). Health psychology in Britain: Past, present and future. *Health Psychology Update*, 10, Division of Health Psychology, British Psychological Society. Leicester: BPS.

Wight, D. & Abraham C. (2000). From psycho-social theory to sustainable classroom practice: Developing a research-based teacher-delivered sex education programme. *Health Education Research*, 15, 25–38.

Wight, D., Abraham, C. & Scott, S. (1998). Towards a psycho-social theoretical framework for sexual health promotion. *Health Education Research* 13, 317–30.

World Health Organization (1995). *Renewing the Health-for-all Strategy: Elaboration of a Policy for Equity Solidarity and Health*. Geneva: WHO.

AUTHOR INDEX

Note: Contributors to multi-authored works, who are not named in the text, are listed with the name of the first author in brackets.

SUBJECT INDEX

Health
PSYCHOLOGY

Edited by Ad Kaptein and John Weinman

Leiden University Medical Centre; University of London

Written by some of the world's leading health psychologists, this textbook is a critical, thought-provoking introduction to a rapidly expanding discipline. The editors provide an in-depth introduction to the field of health psychology and to the volume as a whole, which outlines the major areas of theory and research within the fields of health, illness, and healthcare.

JUNE 2004 / 0-631-21441-0 HB / 0-631-21442-9 PB / 416 PAGES

www.blackwellpublishing.com